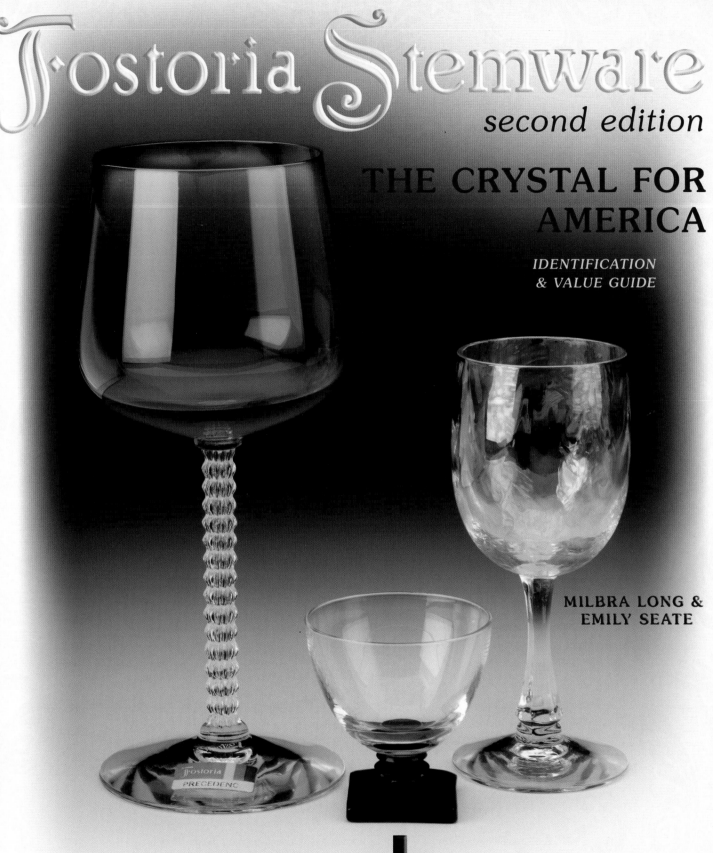

# Fostoria Stemware

## second edition

# THE CRYSTAL FOR AMERICA

*IDENTIFICATION*
*& VALUE GUIDE*

**MILBRA LONG &**
**EMILY SEATE**

## COLLECTOR BOOKS

*A Division of Schroeder Publishing Co., Inc.*

ON THE FRONT COVER
*Yellow Serenity Ice Tea, $35.00; Cobalt Argus Juice Tumbler, $30.00; Blue Navarre Claret, $125.00.*

ON THE BACK COVER
*Gray Mist Precedence Goblet, $45.00; 4020 Ebony Footed Whiskey, $22.00; Firelight Claret, $35.00.*

COVER DESIGN: BETH SUMMERS
—•—•—•—•—•—•—•—•—•—•—•
BOOK LAYOUT: LISA HENDERSON
—•—•—•—•—•—•—•—•—•—•—•
COVER PHOTOGRAPHY: CHARLES R. LYNCH
—•—•—•—•—•—•—•—•—•—•—•
ILLUSTRATION: SHERE CHAMNESS

# COLLECTOR BOOKS

*P.O. Box 3009*
*Paducah, Kentucky 42002-3009*
www.collectorbooks.com

Milbra Long and Emily Seate
P.O. Box 784
Cleburne, TX 76033-0784
www.fostoriacrystal.com
email: longseat@sbcglobal.net

*Copyright © 2008 Milbra Long and Emily Seate*

The current values in this book should be used only as a guide. They are not intended to set prices, which vary from one section of the country to another. Auction prices as well as dealer prices vary greatly and are affected by condition as well as demand. Neither the authors nor the publisher assumes responsibility for any losses that might be incurred as a result of consulting this guide.

## Searching for a Publisher?

We are always looking for people knowledgeable within their fields. If you feel that there is a real need for a book on your collectible subject and have a large comprehensive collection, contact Collector Books.

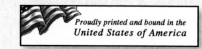
Proudly printed and bound in the
**United States of America**

# Contents

# Quadricentennial Celebration

In 1607, a hearty group of brave souls founded the first successful English settlement in America. In 1608, they built the first glassmaking facility in this country. In the four hundred years since then, glass companies have come and gone, replaced by other glass companies making everything from tableware and windows to fiberoptics and the optics for telescopes that look into the far reaches of space. Glass products influenced the lifestyles and economics of our country as it evolved from those early settlements to 13 colonies to a world superpower.

In the quadricentennial year of glassmaking in America, we dedicate this second edition of *Fostoria Stemware* to all those who have created or continue to create designs in glass and make them into useful products or feasts for the eyes. We salute you all!

# Acknowledgments

We are grateful to the Lancaster Colony Corporation, Inc., of Columbus, Ohio, for permission to use the materials and logo of the Fostoria Glass Company, Inc.

We sincerely appreciate the loan of cherished pieces for photographing by Jim and Sherry Davis and Mike and Gina Lodes.

Our thanks to Billy Schroeder and Collector Books for the opportunity to bring this new version of *Fostoria Stemware* to collectors. Gail Ashburn, Charley Lynch, Beth Summers, Amy Sullivan, Beth Ray, and Lisa Henderson made this second edition even more beautiful.

# Introduction

As one of the first glass companies to recognize the value of advertising and the first to introduce a complete dinner service in crystal, the Fostoria Glass Company, Inc., of Moundsville, West Virginia, was unique. The company took its name from Fostoria, Ohio, its home from 1887 to 1891. Throughout its 99-year history, Fostoria concentrated on making quality, affordable crystal, and eventually advertised Fostoria crystal as "the Crystal for America."

Each piece of Fostoria crystal required the efforts of many people. Blank stemware was blown and hand molded, and even pressed blanks were hand finished. Designs and decorations were applied by hand as well. Working by sight and touch, a craftsman cut patterns onto stemware with a revolving stone wheel. The initial, unpolished cutting was called a "gray" cutting. Fostoria used both "rock crystal" and "polished" at different times in the history of the company to describe a polished cutting.

Carvings required a skilled worker to use heavy tape to mask out all parts of the glass except the areas that were to receive the design. The worker used compressed air to blow an abrasive against the uncovered glass until it gradually eroded the design in a smooth, frosted finish. Etchings, such as Etching 278, Versailles, required 15 separate hand operations to create. Gold and platinum decorations were applied by hand. The creation of each piece of elegant glass demanded craftsmen, grinders, glazers, inspectors, and many other workers. Not surprisingly, during its peak production (around 1950), Fostoria employed more than a thousand people.

Until about 1924, the Fostoria Glass Company created designs which were used on many different blanks. (For the purposes of this book, the word *blank* describes the particular group of undecorated stemware shapes within a pattern.) Hence, one can find Cutting 4 on Blank 766, Blank 863, and Blank 5061. Blank 766, Blank 863, and Blank 880 all featured Plate Etching 237, Garland. After 1924, the company used one stemware blank for several different designs with few exceptions.

As many as 25 different stemware shapes and sizes composed the early blanks, such as Blank 858 and Blank 880. Patterns in the 1930s and 1940s offered from 13 to 16 different stemware shapes and sizes. By the 1960s, that number had been reduced to from six to eight shapes, and by the 1980s, most blanks included only four stemware shapes.

By 1928 the focus turned to the stem shape itself, as well as the total design of the blank. In some cases stems received special treatment; i.e., they were frosted, cut, decorated, or sculpted. Often only the crystal bowl was decorated, and many blanks were offered completely unadorned in an array of colors. Cutting 184, Arbor, and Cutting 188, Berry, were offered on colored bowls. Only the paler colors, with the exception of Amber, Blue, and Green in the 1920s and 1930s, were etched. Stemware with bowls in Ruby, Empire Green, Burgundy, Wisteria, and Regal Blue were not etched, cut, or decorated. Except for a few stems in the Repeal Line, Fostoria only made Blank 877 in solid Regal Blue and Empire Green, and Blank 890 in solid Burgundy.

The years from 1925 to 1943 are the authors' favorites. Many of the more popular Fostoria patterns are from this era and include Plate Etching 278, Versailles, and Plate Etching 279, June. The extraordinary Wisteria color is also from this period. After 1943, both color and etchings were largely abandoned in favor of crystal and cuttings until around 1950.

From time to time we are asked about pieces that are not in our books but are definitely Fostoria patterns. The stem in the photograph shows Rosemary, Plate Etching 339, on the 6025 Cabot blank. In the catalogs and price guides, Rosemary is only offered on Nordic, Blank 892. The following few paragraphs from the 1926 price guide may offer a possible explanation for our odd goblet shown on the next page:

> Special items not listed in Cut or Engraved Patterns cannot be furnished unless ordered in large quantities. We urge that all orders be confined to listed items whenever possible.
>
> In cutting or engraving special items, not carried in stock, it is necessary to cut an excess amount of order to allow for breakage and all finished pieces will be shipped whether in excess or under amount ordered.
>
> All special orders for unlisted items require individual shop attention and are subject to delay in shipment. Special items are not subject to cancellation.

In other words, our Rosemary goblet may have been part of a special order from long ago.

ROSEMARY ETCHING
339 ON 6025 CABOT.

Our series of Fostoria books has come to be called *Fostoria, The Crystal for America*. We thought it appropriate to share this company comment from a 1981 brochure:

### The Crystal for America

Old-world grandeur and contemporary thought are blended in time-honored Fostoria stemware. Because of enduring excellence, we have been commissioned by the White House to manufacture special stemware with the Presidential seal. And our Presidential giftware has been gratefully received by dignitaries around the world.

What's more, Fostoria's reputation for craft and quality has resulted in commissions to produce special crystal giftware for numerous members of Congress over the years.

The care and quality which go into such pieces are reflected in the crystal and glassware we make for every American. Your tastes can be fulfilled in this same spirit of artistry. Whether you're buying that first set of wedding crystal, or choosing something to cherish for another chapter in your life.

Fostoria has an old-fashioned way of doing things. And the result is old-fashioned quality.

©1981 Fostoria Glass Company

On the cover of this second edition we show stems from the last half of Fostoria's 99-year history. After World War II, patterns that were introduced right before the war continued to be offered. In 1949 Bouquet, Etching 342, on Blank 6033, Mademoiselle, and Heather, Etching 343, on Blank 6037, Silver Flutes, were the first new stemware lines since the war. In 1950 Fostoria offered six more cuttings. From this time on, cuttings, crystal prints, and decorations dominated stemware lines.

In 1948, American Lady 5056 was reintroduced in crystal and with Amethyst bowl, originally called Burgundy in the 1930s. The 5412 Colonial Dame pattern was simultaneously made in Empire Green. These two patterns became the first to be offered in color after the war. Other colors made later, reflected the color trends of a particular period. From 1949 until the Fostoria factory closed in 1986, only eleven new plate etchings were offered.

Beginning with the January 1, 1955, price list, the Fostoria Company offered matchings for discontinued patterns and continued this service through 1982. Matchings were for stemware and plates as a rule.

New to this edition are color photographs throughout the stemware section to illustrate the design on the bowl. Color photographs of jugs, barware, and tumblers, as well as original catalog pictures of tumblers, have been added to the appendices.

The section on the American pattern now includes original catalog pictures as well as photographs showing size and shape comparisons. We have included a statement from the 1915 supplement introducing the American pattern, as well as a 1933 statement to retail salespeople concerning this famous pattern's success.

## PRICING

Updated prices in this second edition of *Fostoria Stemware* reflect retail prices from shows, upscale malls, replacement services, and the internet, although the internet is not as reliable a source as the others when arriving at a consistent, stable price. Flea markets, garage sales, and estate sales were not considered. The price range shown for each piece in the first edition has been reduced to one price. Prices reflect retail or replacement values and assume mint condition.

This does not mean that all prices have changed. Many patterns remain about the same, but some have increased in value and some have lost value. It is not always possible to determine the reasons for these changes.

Crystal blank patterns from the 1930s and 1940s have pretty much held their value. The crystal blank with an etching will bring more, depending on the pattern and the piece. Crystal June stems remain about the same except for the claret, wine, and cordial, which have increased in value. In Navarre, the rare continental, or flute champagne, the clarets, and the wine, sherry, brandy, cordial, and magnum wine still command high dollar, while the goblet, champagne, ice tea, etc., remain about the same. The Blue Navarre stems have become increasingly hard to find and may yet see an increase in price. Pink Navarre in good color is not as much in demand as Blue but will usually bring about the same price; the goblet and clarets will bring more. Topaz June has experienced a general increase in price.

Though Fostoria offered a host of beautiful rock crystal or polished cuttings during the 1930s, we seldom see these in the marketplace. There is no noticeable increase in demand or value. Many of these cuttings simply do not sell. However, if a customer does need a pattern that is not popular with collectors, often they will pay a price in line with other cut patterns because of its intrinsic value. Thus, the fact that few people want a cutting doesn't necessarily make it less valuable. The few cuttings on colored blanks are gaining interest. Etched patterns on color are holding, and some have increased in value. Often the goblet, claret-wine, and cordial have increased in value more than other pieces.

## HOW TO USE THIS BOOK

*Fostoria Stemware* has five major sections: one showing the many colors offered; one illustrating each blank stemware pattern and all the etchings, cuttings, and decorations put on that blank; four appendices; a complete listing of prices for each pattern; and two indices.

To identify a piece when you know the name of the pattern, find the name in the alphabetical index at the end of the book and refer back to the pages listed.

To identify a piece when you know nothing about it, turn to the picture index near the end of the book. Match the shape of your piece as closely as you can to a shape in this index. Beneath each pictured shape is a number. That number refers to a blank pattern in the second section in the book. Blank numbers are listed at the top of

each page unless more than one blank pattern is shown on that page. Blanks are in numerical order, lowest to highest. Once the shape is matched and the blank pattern is found, any etching, cutting, or decoration will show on the same page or pages as the blank. If you cannot find the etching, cutting, or decoration, it is possible you have the wrong shape. Many Fostoria shapes are quite similar and easily confused, so don't give up. Most likely you will be near the shape you seek and turning a few pages back or forward will reveal it.

To find the suggested current retail value of your piece, turn to the value guide portion of the book. It, too, is in numerical order by blank patterns. Etchings, cuttings, and decorations placed on the blank patterns are listed with that blank pattern, just as they are in the illustrated section.

When you have found your pattern, identified your pieces, and determined their current suggested values, you may want to see what other pieces were offered in the pattern. By checking the numbers listed in the pattern information for tumblers, jugs, grapefruits, etc., you can look in Appendix A under Tumblers or in Appendix C under Other Pieces to see what these pieces look like. Appendix B is for those who would like to know if their pattern was ever reintroduced by Fostoria. Some of the more popular patterns were, briefly, in 1980. Appendix D shows stemware offered after 1982, when blown ware stopped being made.

Logos — Fostoria marked products with paper stickers that were glued to the pieces. Often the stickers were lost or discarded. An older piece with sticker intact is a real prize for a collector.

1924 – 1957.

THE EARLIEST LOGO,
USED UNTIL 1924.

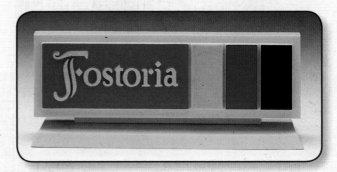

1957 – 1986.

# Color Identification

Fostoria diligently kept abreast of fashion, both in design and color, and its stemware reflected trends of the times. Often color names changed even when no difference could be seen in the color itself. American Lady with a Burgundy bowl and American Lady with an Amethyst bowl appear identical to all but the most discerning eye. The Regal Blue of the 1930s and the Cobalt of 1973 – 1974 as seen in the Distinction pattern are identical in color. However, the Cobalt used to name a color in the Argus pattern bears little resemblance to either Regal Blue or the Distinction Cobalt. Oddly, Colonial Dame, introduced after World War II, kept the prewar Empire Green designation for its dark green color.

Silver Mist, an allover etching that creates a satinlike finish, used primarily before World War II, came back briefly in the early 1980s in patterns like Icicle and Lotus. However, the colors Gray Mist and Green Mist have nothing to do with etchings, but describe a lighter color.

Fostoria often combined crystal and color, but seldom combined two colors. Two examples of the latter are Contrast, with its blown White bowl and Onyx base, and Princess, which was offered with Gray Mist bowl and Onyx base.

It would be good to remember that thicker glass tends to make the color more vivid. The Amber base of the Queen Ann footed tumbler has a depth of color not evident in the thinner bowl of the Seville piece.

DELPHIAN
BLANK 5082
BLUE BASE

VESPER
BLANK 5093
BLUE

VICTORIAN
BLANK 4024
REGAL BLUE

KENMORE
BLANK 5082
BLUE BASE

BRUNSWICK
BLANK 870
BLUE

AMERICAN
LADY
BLANK 5056
REGAL BLUE

BLANK 887
REGAL BLUE

NAVARRE
BLANK 6016
BLUE BOWL

GRAND
MAJESTY
BLANK 6009
BLUE BOWL

DISTINCTION
BLANK 6125
COBALT

JUNE
BLANK 5098
AZURE BOWL

SILHOUETTE
BLANK 6102
BLUE

BLANK 5093
AZURE BOWL

EILENE
BLANK 5082
AZURE BOWL

DISTINCTION
BLANK 6125
BLUE

MEADOW
ROSE
BLANK 6016
AZURE BOWL

LIDO
BLANK 6017
AZURE BOWL

INTIMATE
BLANK 6123
BLUE

BAROQUE
BLANK 2496
AZURE

MESA
BLANK 4186
BLUE

BLUE MEADOW
BLANK 4180
SKY BLUE

FAIRMONT
BLANK 2718
BLUE

SPLENDOR
BLANK 6131
BLUE

NEEDLEPOINT
BLANK 4184
TEAL BLUE

ARGUS
BLANK 2770
COBALT

ICICLE
BLANK 6147
BLUE/BLUE
MIST

BLANK 5083
GREEN
GREEN BASE

MYSTIC
BLANK 5082
GREEN

SPARTAN
BLANK 5097
GREEN BOWL

GLAMOUR
BLANK 6103
GREEN MIST
BOWL

BLANK 5000
GREEN

COLONIAL DAME
BLANK 5412
EMPIRE GREEN
BOWL

SPHERE
BLANK 6121
GREEN MIST
BOWL

SEVILLE
BLANK 870
GREEN

MINUET
BLANK 4020
GREEN BASE

MOONSTONE
BLANK 2882
APPLE GREEN

ACANTHUS
BLANK 5098
GREEN BOWL

CONGO
BLANK 4162
MARINE

CAPRI
BLANK 6045
BITTER GREEN/CINNAMON

11

VERSAILLES
BLANK 5099
TOPAZ BOWL

NEW GARLAND
BLANK 4020
TOPAZ BOWL

SERENITY
BLANK 6127
YELLOW BOWL

TROJAN
BLANK 5099
TOPAZ BOWL

SCEPTRE
BLANK 6017
GOLD TINT BOWL

MISTY
BLANK 6129
YELLOW

FLORENTINE
BLANK 6005
TOPAZ BASE

MINUET
BLANK 6002
TOPAZ BOWL

BEVERLY
BLANK 5097
AMBER BOWL

BLANK 5093
AMBER BASE/
MOTHER OF
PEARL BOWL

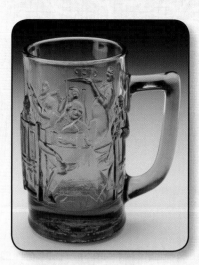

TAVERN MUG
BLANK 2493
AMBER

VERSAILLES
BLANK 5098
ROSE BOWL

ROYAL
BLANK 869
AMBER

HARVEST
BLANK 6097
RUST BOWL

GREEK
BLANK 5097
ROSE BOWL

SEVILLE
BLANK 5084
AMBER

HORIZON
BLANK 5650
CINNAMON

WILMA
BLANK 6016
PINK BOWL

QUEEN ANN
BLANK 4020
AMBER BASE

RING O' ROSES
BLANK 4180
FAWN

SILHOUETTE
BLANK 6102
PINK

13

CONTOUR
BLANK 6060
PINK BOWL

MAYPOLE
BLANK 6149
PEACH

HERMITAGE
BLANK 2449
WISTERIA

JAMESTOWN
BLANK 2719
PINK

LOTUS
BLANK 6144
PEACH MIST BASE

BLANK 6008
WISTERIA
BOWL

LYRIC
BLANK 6061
PINK BASE

MANOR
BLANK 6003
WISTERIA BASE

FUCHSIA
BLANK 6004
WISTERIA BASE

14

NeoClassic
Blank 6011
Burgundy
Bowl

Corsage
Plum
Blank 6126
Plum Base

Westchester
Blank 6012
Ruby Bowl

Blank 890
Burgundy

Distinction
Blank 6125
Plum Bowl

Coin
Blank 1372
Ruby

American
Lady
Blank 5056
Burgundy
Bowl

Fascination
Blank 6080
Ruby Bowl
Lilac Bowl

Pebble
Beach
Blank 2806
Flaming
Orange

Victorian
Blank 4024
Burgundy
Bowl

Blank 6013
Ruby Bowl

Biscayne
Blank 6122
Snow

WINBURN
BLANK 1704
MILK GLASS

CONTRAST
BLANK 6120
WHITE/ONYX

PRECEDENCE
BLANK 6108
GRAY MIST BOWL

VINTAGE
BLANK 2713
MILK GLASS

ELOQUENCE
BLANK 6120
ONYX BASE

CHALICE
BLANK 6059
EBONY BASE

JENNY LIND
BLANK 835
AQUA MILK GLASS
PEACH MILK GLASS

PRECEDENCE
BLANK 6108
ONYX BOWL

PRINCESS
BLANK 6123
GRAY MIST BOWL
ONYX BASE

16

GAZEBO
BLANK 6126
EBONY BASE

BLANK 879
MOTHER OF
PEARL

DECORATION 615
BLANK 6012
CRYSTAL

VENTURE
BLANK 6114
GRAY MIST
BASE

BLANK 858½
MOTHER OF
PEARL

RICHELIEU
BLANK 6016
CRYSTAL

PAVILION
BLANK 6143
GRAY BOWL

CLUB DESIGN A
BLANK 4020
CRYSTAL

SIMPLICITY
BLANK 6017
CRYSTAL

BLACK AND
GOLD
BLANK 660
CRYSTAL

GRAPE STEM
BLANK 870
GREEN/GOLD
STEM

VICTORIAN
BLANK 4024
SILVER MIST

# Fostoria Stemware

BLANK 114
THROUGH BLANK 7780

ETCHINGS, CUTTINGS, AND
DECORATIONS

# BLANK 114 FIFTH AVENUE
No Optic
*Pre1900 – 1920 Crystal*

**Needle Etching 32**
*Pre1900 – 1929 Crystal*

**Needle Etching 46**
*Pre1900 – 1920 Crystal*

**Needle Etching 47**
**LARGE CLOVERLEAF**
*Pre1900 – 1920 Crystal*
Also on Blanks 858 and 5001

# BLANK 660
Regular Optic
*1922 – 1943 Crystal*
*1927 – 1929 Orchid*

**Needle Etching 90 PAGODA**
*1935 – 1943 Crystal*
  (No Parfait)
Additional Pieces:
6", 7", 8" Plates (2337)
4095 Oyster Cocktail
4095 Tumblers

**Plate Etching 264 WOODLAND**
*1922 – 1928 Crystal*
  (No Claret)
Additional Pieces:
8¼", 11" Plates (2283)
837 Oyster Cocktail
945½ Grapefruit and Liner
4011, 4095 Tumblers
300, 303, 1743 Jugs

**Plate Etching 266 WASHINGTON**
*1923 – 1928 Crystal*
Additional Pieces:
5", 6", 7", 8", 9", 11" Plates (2283)
837 Oyster Cocktail
945½ Grapefruit and Liner
869, 887, 889, 4095 Tumblers
300, 303, 318, 2270 Jugs

**Plate Etching 270 MYSTIC**
*1924 – 1928 Crystal*
Additional Pieces:
837 Oyster Cocktail
4095 Tumblers
4095 Jug

114 GOBLET,
LARGE CLOVERLEAF
NEEDLE ETCHING

Blank 114
FIFTH AVENUE

11½ oz. Goblet
11 oz. Goblet
10 oz. Goblet
6 oz. Champagne
3¾ oz. Claret
3 oz. Wine
1¼ oz. Cordial

660 WINE,
WOODLAND
ETCHING

Blank 660

9 oz. Goblet

5 oz. Saucer Champagne

4 oz. Claret

660 WINE,
WASHINGTON
ETCHING

19

Blank 660

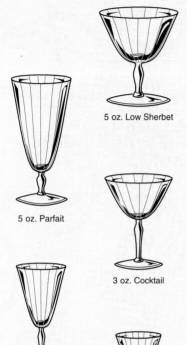

5 oz. Low Sherbet

5 oz. Parfait

2¾ oz. Wine

3 oz. Cocktail

¾ oz. Cordial

660 Wine,
Black and Gold
Decoration

Blank 661

9 oz., 7" Goblet

Blank 660, continued

*Cutting 169 TRELLIS*
*1924 – 1928 Crystal*
   (No Claret)
Additional Pieces:
5", 6", 7", 8" Plates (2283)
837 Oyster Cocktail
945½ Grapefruit and Liner
4011 Handled Tumbler
887, 889, 4076, 4095 Tumblers
303, 724, 2270 Jugs

*Rock Crystal Cutting 753 PINNACLE*
*1935 – 1937 Crystal*
   (No Parfait)
Additional Pieces:
6", 7", 8" Plates (2337)
4095 Tumblers

*Coin Gold Band Decoration 1*
Wide Coin Gold Band bordered by two
   narrow Bands on Bowl
*1906 – 1929 Crystal*

*Decoration 23 BLACK AND GOLD*
Gold Band on Rim and Foot with vertical
   Black enamel and Gold
*1923 – 1924 Crystal*
Additional Pieces:
945 Grapefruit and Liner
889 Tumblers
300 Tankard

*Decoration 50 GOLDWOOD*
Coin Gold Band on Rim and Foot,
   Plate Etching 264, Woodland
*1922 – 1928 Crystal*

## BLANK 661
Regular Optic
*1922 – 1943 Crystal*

*Needle Etching 91 BALLET*
*1935 – 1944 Crystal*
   (No Parfait;
   5½ oz. Saucer Champagne,
   5½ oz. Fruit /Low Sherbet, 4 oz. Claret;
   2¾ oz. Wine)
Additional Pieces:
6", 7", 8" Plates (2337)
4095 Oyster Cocktail
4095 Tumblers

*Plate Etching 265 ORIENT*
*1922 – 1928 Crystal*
   (No Cordial)
Additional Pieces:
8¼", 11" Plates (2283)
837 Oyster Cocktail
945½ Grapefruit and Liner
889, 4085 Tumblers
317, 318 Jugs

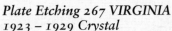

## Plate Etching 267 VIRGINIA
### *1923 – 1929 Crystal*
Additional Pieces:
5", 6", 7", 8", 9", 11" Plates (2283)
837 Oyster Cocktail
945½ Grapefruit and Liner
869, 4085, 4095 Tumblers
303, 318, 2270, 4095 Jugs

## Plate Etching 268 MELROSE
### *1924 – 1929 Crystal*
Additional Pieces:
7", 8", 11" Plates (2283)
837 Oyster Cocktail
945½ Grapefruit and Liner
4085, 4095 Tumblers
303, 4095 Jugs

## Cutting 168 LOUISA
### *1922 – 1928 Crystal*
  (No Claret or Cordial)
Additional Pieces:
8¼", 11" Plates (2283)
945½ Grapefruit and Liner
4011, 4085 Tumblers
303, 317 1/2 Jugs

## Cutting 170 CYNTHIA
### *1924 – 1928 Crystal*
  (No Claret)
Additional Pieces:
6" Plate (2283), 7", 8" Plates (2337)
837 Oyster Cocktail
945½ Grapefruit and Liner
4011, 4085, 4095 Tumblers
724 Tankard
2270 Jug

## Encrusted Gold Decoration 29 EMPRESS
Encrusted Gold Band on Bowl, Gold Band
  on Foot
### *1924 – 1929 Crystal*
Additional Pieces:
945½ Grapefruit and Liner
701, 4085 Tumblers

## Coin Gold Decoration 40 NOME
Coin Gold Band on Bowl, Gold Band on Foot
### *1924 – 1929 Crystal*
Additional Pieces:
945½ Grapefruit and Liner
701, 4085 Tumblers

## Coin Gold Band Decoration 42 MIAMI
Coin Gold Band and Cutting on Bowl,
  Gold Band on Foot
### *1924 – 1929 Crystal*

Blank 661

661 Parfait,
Virginia Etching

6 oz., 4⁷⁄₈"
Saucer Champagne

5½ oz. Claret

6 oz., 3½"
Fruit/Low Sherbet

3 oz. Cocktail

5½ oz., 6" Parfait

2 oz., 4¾" Wine

¾ oz. Cordial

Blank 766

9 oz. Goblet
(Shown with
narrow optic)

7 oz. Goblet
(Shown with
regular optic)

4 oz. Rhine Wine

2 oz. Creme de Menthe

3 oz. Cocktail

4¹/₄ oz. 5⁵/₈" Claret

2 oz., 4⁵/₈" Burgundy

766 GOBLET,
ORIENTAL ETCHING

4011 TUMBLER,
MODERN VINTAGE
ETCHING

## BLANK 766

Regular Optic, Narrow Optic, No Optic
*1898 – 1928 Crystal* (7 oz. Goblet, Rhine Wine, Sorbet, Handled
  Custard, Grapefruit, Whiskey Tumbler, 1898 – 1925)
*1916 – ? Amber Iridescent,* Regular Optic
(Parfait, Saucer Champagne, Fruit, Sherbet only)
*1931 – 1943 Mother of Pearl Iridescent,* Regular Optic
(Goblet, Saucer Champagne, Low Sherbet, Parfait, Cocktail, Wine only)

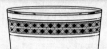

### Needle Etching 36 IRISH LACE
Narrow Optic
*1898 – 1928 Crystal*
Additional Pieces:
837 Oyster Cocktail
820, 833, 858, 4011, 4077 Tumblers
300, 303, 318, 724 Jugs
Also on Blanks 879 and 880

### Needle Etching 42 CHAIN
No Optic
*1898 – 1927 Crystal*

Additional Pieces:
701, 820, 833, 858, 887, 889, 4011
  Tumblers
300, 303, 318 Jugs
Also on Blank 863

### Plate Etching 232 LOTUS
Regular Optic
*1913 – 1927 Crystal*
Additional Pieces:
837 Oyster Cocktail
945½ Grapefruit and Liner
820, 858, 887, 889, 4011 Tumblers
303 Jug
Also on Blank 5070

### Plate Etching 237 GARLAND
No Optic
*1915 – 1928 Crystal*
Additional Pieces:
899 Parfait
701, 820, 833, 887, 889, 4011 Tumblers
4061 Handled Tumbler
300, 724 Tankards
303, 318, 1236 Jugs
Also on Blanks 863 and 880

### Plate Etching 250 ORIENTAL
No Optic

*1918 – 1928 Crystal*
Additional Pieces:
837 Oyster Cocktail
945½ Grapefruit and Liner
701, 820, 887, 889, 4011 Tumblers
300, 303, 724 Jugs

### Plate Etching 255 MODERN VINTAGE
No Optic

*1920 – 1928 Crystal*
Additional Pieces:
837 Oyster Cocktail
945½ Grapefruit and Liner
701, 820, 4011 Tumblers
300, 303, 318 Jugs

### Plate Etching 257 VICTORY
Narrow Optic
*1922 – 1928 Crystal*
Additional Pieces
8¼", 11" Plates (2283)
837 Oyster Cocktail
945½ Grapefruit, 4057 Liner
701, 820, 4011 Tumblers
300, 303, 318, 2100 Jugs

### Rock Crystal Cutting 4
*1903 – 1916 Crystal,* No Optic
*1916 – ? Amber Iridescence,*
  Regular Optic
  (Parfait, Saucer Champagne, Fruit and
  Sherbet only)
Additional Pieces:
945 Grapefruit
300 Tankard
303, 1236 Jugs

### Cutting 125
No Optic
*1915 – 1917 Crystal*
Additional Pieces:
945½ Grapefruit and Liner
701, 820, 833, 887, 889, 4077 Tumblers
300 Tankard
303 Jug
Also on Blank 863

### Cutting 130 PRISCILLA
Narrow Optic
*1918 – 1927 Crystal*
Additional Pieces:
8¼" Plates (2283)
820, 833, 4011 Tumblers
303 Jug

### Rock Crystal Cutting 142 ARROW
No Optic
*1919 – 1924 Crystal*
Additional Pieces:
701, 820, 4011 Tumblers
300, 303, 1734, 2100 Jugs

### Coin Gold Band Decoration 8 CASCADE
Coin Gold Band, Gold Encrusted Etching
36½ on Bowl, Gold Band on Foot
Narrow Optic
*1920s Crystal*
Additional Pieces:
4011 Tumblers
303 Jug

### Coin Gold Band Decoration 9 NEWPORT
Engraved design bordered by two Gold
  Bands on Bowl, Gold Band on Foot
No Optic
*1920s Crystal*
Additional Pieces:
4011 Tumblers
300½ Jug

Blank 766

2³/₄ oz., 5" Wine

³/₄ oz., 3³/₄" Brandy
(Pousse Cafe)

³/₄ oz., 3⁷/₁₆" Cordial

5 oz. Saucer Champagne

4¹/₄ oz., 3¹/₄" Fruit

2⁵/₈" Sherbet

23

## Blank 766

2¹/₁₆" Sorbet

4 oz., 2³/₄"
Handled Custard

Not Shown:
5½ oz., 7¹/₈" Parfait
2 oz., 2³/₈" Sherry
12 oz. Footed, Handled Ice Tea
Grapefruit and Liner
3½ oz. Whiskey Tumbler

## Blank 858

11 oz. Goblet
10 oz. Goblet
9 oz. Goblet
8 oz. Goblet
1 oz. Cordial

4 oz. Hot Whiskey

Blank 766, continued

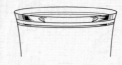

### Coin Gold Band Decoration 15
Wide and Narrow Gold Band on Bowl
  and Foot
Narrow Optic
*1920s Crystal*
Additional Pieces:
4011 Tumblers
303 Jug

### Encrusted Gold Decoration 31
### LAUREL
Encrusted Gold Decoration on Bowl, Gold
  Band on Foot
No Optic
*1920s Crystal*
Additional Pieces:
4011 Tumblers
2100-7 Jug

### Encrusted Gold Decoration 32
### REGENT
Encrusted Gold Decoration on Bowl, Gold
  Band on Foot
No Optic
*1920s Crystal*
Additional Pieces:
4011 Tumblers
2100-7 Jug

---

# BLANK 858
No Optic
*1904 – 1927 Crystal*
*1916 – ? Mother of Pearl Iridescence* on Bowl
  (9, 10 oz. Goblets, 5½ oz. Saucer Champagne, Sherbet,
Cocktail,
  4½ oz. Claret, both Wines, Sherry, Creme de Menthe,
Brandy, Cordial, Oyster Cocktail, Fruit, Hollow Stem
Champagne, Tall Champagne, Hot Whiskey, and Custard only)
Additional Pieces:
858 Tumblers

---

### Needle Etching 47
### LARGE CLOVERLEAF
*Early 1900s Crystal*
Additional Pieces:
701, 858 Tumblers
724 Tankard
300, 303, 316, 317 1/2, 318, 1227, 1236,
2018 Jugs
Also on Blanks 114 and 5001.

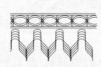

### Needle Etching 73 LENORE
Regular Optic
*1923 – 1930 Crystal*
Additional Pieces:
945½ Grapefruit and Liner
858 Tumblers
300 Tankard
303, 318 Jugs
2270 Jug and Cover

### Plate Etching 204 VINTAGE
Regular Optic, No Optic
*1904 – 1928 Crystal*
Additional Pieces:
837 Oyster Cocktail
822, 863, 5054 Parfaits
945½ Grapefruit and Liner
701, 833, 858, 887, 889 Tumblers
300, 303, 318, 724, 1236, 1851, 1852
    Jugs
Also on Blank 863

### Plate Etching 205 BLACKBERRY
*1908 – 1909 Crystal*
Additional Pieces:
820, 858 Tumblers
300, 303, 318, 1236 Jugs

### Plate Etching 215
*1910 – 1927 Crystal*
Additional Pieces:
701, 820, 833, 858 Tumblers
5036, 5054 Parfaits
300, 724 Tankards
303 Jug

### Plate Etching 227 NEW VINTAGE
*1913 – 1927 Crystal*
Additonal Pieces:
945½ Grapefruit and Liner
766 Footed Handled Ice Tea
4061 Handled Lemonade
822, 5054 Parfaits
701, 858, 887, 889, 4011 Tumblers
1743 Tankard
300, 303, 318, 724, 1236, 1852 Jugs
317½ Jug and Cover
Also on Blanks 863 and 880

### Plate Etching 238 EMPIRE
Regular Optic
*1915 – 1927 Crystal*
Additional Pieces:
822 Parfait
4061 Handled Lemonade
945½ Grapefruit and Liner
833, 858, 887, 889, 4077 Tumblers
300, 724 Tankards
303, 318 Jugs

### Plate Etching 241
### LILY OF THE VALLEY
Narrow Optic
*1915 – 1927 Crystal*
Additional Pieces:
822 Parfait
945½ Grapefruit and Liner
701, 833, 858, 4011, 4077 Tumblers
300, 724 Tankards
303, 318, 2018 Jugs

Blank 858

858 GOBLET,
ETCHING 215

7 oz. Saucer
Champagne

6½ oz. Claret

4 oz. Sherbet

Fruit

Oyster Cocktail

25

## Blank 858

2½ oz. Creme de Menthe

3½ oz. Cocktail

5½ oz. Saucer Champagne

2¾ oz. Wine

2 oz. Sherry

1 oz. Brandy

Blank 858, continued

### Plate Etching 252 NEW ADAM
*1918 – 1927 Crystal*
Additional Pieces:
822 Parfait
837 Oyster Cocktail
4061 Handled Lemonade
766 Footed Handled Ice Tea
945½ Grapefruit and Liner
701, 858 Tumblers
300, 303, 318, 724 Jugs

### Plate Etching 256 FLORID
Regular Optic
*1920 – 1927 Crystal*
Additional Pieces:
805 Parfait
766 Footed Handled Ice Tea
945½ Grapefruit and Liner
833, 858, 4011 Tumblers
300, 303, 318 Jugs
317½ Jug and Cover

### Cutting 77
*1904 – 1913 Crystal*
Additional Pieces:
833, 887, 889 Tumblers
300, 303, 724, 1236 Tankards
1743 Tankard and Cover

### Rock Crystal Cutting 81 LARGE SUNBURST STAR
*1904 – 1927 Crystal*
Additional Pieces:
766 Parfait
945½ Grapefruit and Liner
858, 4011 Tumblers
300, 724 Tankards
303, 1227 Jugs
Also on Blanks 863 and 880

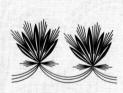

### Cutting 104
*1908 – 1920 Crystal*
Additional Pieces:
945½ Grapefruit and Liner
858 Tumblers
300, 724 Tankards
300, 303, 318, 1227 Jugs

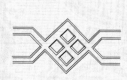

### Cutting 116 MISSION
*1913 – 1928 Crystal*
Additional Pieces:
945½ Grapefruit and Liner
4061 Handled Lemonade
701, 858 Tumblers
300, 724, 1761, 1787, 1852 Tankards
1743 Tankard and Cover
300, 303, 724, 1851 Jugs
Also on Blank 863

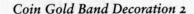

### Cutting 118 BILLOW
#### 1913 – 1917 Crystal
Additional Pieces:
945½ Grapefruit and Liner
1389 Oyster Cocktail
4061 Handled Lemonade
701, 858 Tumblers
300, 724, 1761, 1787, 1852 Tankards
1743 Tankard and Cover
300, 303, 724, 1851 Jugs
Also on Blank 863

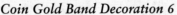

### Coin Gold Band Decoration 2
Etching 71 bordered by two Gold Bands
   on Bowl
#### 1906 – 1914 Crystal
Additional Pieces:
863 Rhine Wine
858 Table Tumbler
303 Jug

### Coin Gold Band Decoration 6
Coin Gold Band on Bowl and Foot
#### 1906 – 1929 Crystal
Additional Pieces:
766 Grapefruit and Liner
766 Footed Handled Ice Tea
858 Tumblers
300 Tankard
303 Jug

### Coin Gold Band Decoration 7
Wide Gold Band on Rim, Gold Band
   on Foot
Regular Optic
#### 1906 – 1928 Crystal
Additional Pieces:
766 Parfait
945½ Grapefruit and Liner
858 Tumblers
1236 Jug

### Enamel and Gold Decoration 12 DRESDEN
Floral Cutting on Black Enamel and Gold
   Leaf on Bowl, Gold Band on Rim
   and Foot
#### 1920s Crystal
Additional Pieces:
127, 4061 Handled Tumblers
701, 820 Tumblers
724 Jug
1743 Jug and Cover

### Enamel Decoration 17 DAISY
White Enamel and Cut Daisies with Gold
   Band on Rim and Foot
#### 1920s Crystal
Additional Pieces:
701, 820 Tumblers
724, 2104 Jugs

Blank 858

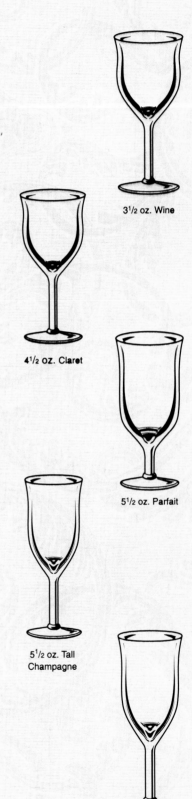

3½ oz. Wine

4½ OZ. Claret

5½ oz. Parfait

5½ oz. Tall
Champagne

7 oz. Bass Ale

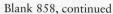

## Blank 858

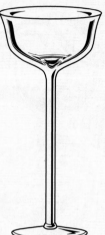

7¹/₂ oz. Long Stem
Champagne

Long Stem
Champagne,
Cut Rim

6 oz. Hollow Stem
Champagne

## Blank 863

10¹/₂ oz. Goblet

9 oz. Goblet,
Short Stem

Blank 858, continued

### Enamel Decoration 19
### BLUE BORDER
Enameled flowers bordered by Blue Bands
*1920s Crystal*
Additional Pieces:
766 Footed Handled Ice Tea
127 Handled Mug
701, 820 Tumblers
2104 Jug
1743 Jug and Cover

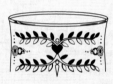

### Enamel Decoration 20
### BLACK BORDER
Enameled flowers on Black, Gold
    bordered Band, Gold Band on Rim
    and Foot
*1920s Crystal*
Additional Pieces:
766 Footed Handled Ice Tea
127 Handled Mug
701, 820 Tumblers
2104 Jug
1743 Jug and Cover

### Enamel and Gold Decoration 21
Floral design with Enamel and Gold, Gold
  Band on Rim and Foot
*1920s Crystal*
Additional Pieces:
701, 820 Tumblers

## BLANK 863
Narrow Optic, No Optic
*1898 – 1927 Crystal*

### Needle Etching 38½ BLOCK
Narrow Optic
*1915 – 1927 Crystal*
Additional Pieces:
945½ Grapefruit and Liner
899 Parfait
701, 820, 833, 858 Tumblers
300, 724, 1787 Tankards
303, 1236 Jugs
Also on Blank 879

### Needle Etching 42 CHAIN
No Optic
*1898 – 1927 Crystal*
Additional Pieces:
5054 Parfait
701, 820, 833, 887, 889, 4011 Tumblers
300, 303, 318, 1236 Jugs
Also on Blank 766

*Needle Etching 67*
**SMALL CLOVERLEAF**
No Optic
*1898 – 1927 Crystal*
Additional Pieces:
810 Tumblers

*Plate Etching 204 VINTAGE*
No Optic
*1904 – 1928 Crystal*
Additional Pieces:
822 Cafe Parfait
5039 Oyster Cocktail and Liner
945½ Grapefruit and Liner
701, 820, 833, 858, 887, 889 Tumblers
300, 724, 1761 Tankards
300, 303, 318, 1236 Jugs
Also on Blank 858

*Plate Etching 210*
No Optic
*1910 – 1927 Crystal*
Additional Pieces:
5039 Oyster Cocktail
945½ Grapefruit
858 Tumblers
300, 724 Tankards
303, 317, 1227 Jugs

*Plate Etching 212*
No Optic
*1910 – 1928 Crystal*
Additional Pieces:
5054 Parfait
945½ Grapefruit and Liner
701, 820, 833, 858, 887, 889 Tumblers
300, 724 Tankards
303, 318, 1236 Jugs

*Plate Etching 214*
No Optic
*1910 – 1927 Crystal*
Additional Pieces:
945½ Grapefruit and Liner
833, 858 Tumblers
300, 300½, 724 Tankards
1236 Jug

*Plate Etching 227 NEW VINTAGE*
No Optic
*1913 – 1927 Crystal*
Additional Pieces:
880, 880½, 945, 945½ Grapefruit and Liner
5036 Parfait
701, 820, 833, 858 Tumblers
300, 724 Tankards
303 Jug
Also on Blanks 858 and 880

Blank 863

7 oz. Goblet,
Long Stem

5½ oz. Goblet

863 CHAMPAGNE,
ETCHING 212

5½ oz. Tall
Champagne

4 oz. Rhine Wine

29

## Blank 863

Fruit

3 oz. Cocktail

3½ oz. Cocktail

5½ oz.
Saucer Champagne

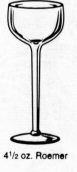
4½ oz. Roemer

5½ oz. Roemer

**FOOTED ALMOND, MISSION CUTTING**

Blank 863, continued

### Plate Etching 237 GARLAND
No Optic
*1915 – 1928 Crystal*
Additional Pieces:
899 Parfait
880, 880½ Grapefruit and Liner
701, 833, 887, 889, 4077 Tumblers
300, 724, 1787 Tankards
303, 1236 Jugs
Also on Blanks 766 and 880

### Plate Etching 253 PERSIAN
No Optic
*1920 – 1927 Crystal*
Additional Pieces:
899 Parfait
945½ Grapefruit and Liner
4061 Handled Lemonade
701, 820, 869 Tumblers
303 Jug

### Cutting 4
No Optic
*1903 – 1916 Crystal*
Additional Pieces:
822 Parfait
945 Grapefruit and Liner
300 Tankard
303 Jug
Also on Blanks 766 and 5061

### Rock Crystal Cutting 81 LARGE SUNBURST STAR
No Optic
*1904 – 1928 Crystal*
Additional Pieces
766½ Parfait
945½ Grapefruit and Liner
858 Tumblers
300, 724 Tankards
303, 1227 Jugs
Also on Blanks 858 and 880

### Cutting 110
No Optic
*1913 – 1924 Crystal*
Additional Pieces:
945½ Grapefruit and Liner
701, 820, 833, 858, 887, 889 Tumblers
300, 300½, 724 Tankards
303, 317, 1227, 1236 Jugs

### Cutting 116 MISSION
No Optic
*1913 – 1928 Crystal*
Additional Pieces:
945, 945½ Grapefruit and Liner
822 Parfait
701, 820, 858, 887, 889 Tumblers
300, 724, 1761, 1787, 1852 Tankards
303, 724 Jugs
Also on Blank 858

## Cutting 118 BILLOW
No Optic
*1913 – 1917 Crystal*
Additional Pieces:
945, 945½ Grapefruit and Liner
701, 820, 833, 858, 887, 889 Tumblers
300, 724, 1761, 1852 Tankards
303, 724 Jugs
Also on Blank 858

## Cutting 125
No Optic
*1915 – 1917 Crystal*
Additional Pieces:
945½ Grapefruit and Liner
899 Parfait
701, 820, 833, 877, 889, 4070 Tumblers
300 Tankard
303 Jug
Also on Blank 766

## Cutting 129
No Optic
*1918 – 1928 Crystal*
Additional Pieces:
822, 805, 766½ Parfaits
837 Oyster Cocktail
945½ Grapefruit and Liner
4061 Handled Lemonade
701, 820, 833, 4011 Tumblers
300, 303, 1124, 1236, 1743, 2100 Jugs

## Cutting 132 CLOVER
No Optic
*1918 – 1928 Crystal*
Additional Pieces:
805 Parfait
837 Oyster Cocktail
701, 820, 833, 889, 4011 Tumblers
303, 1124, 1236, 1793, 2104 Jugs

## Cutting 133 CHRYSANTHEMUM
No Optic
*1918 – 1928 Crystal*
Additional Pieces:
4061 Handled Lemonade
701, 820, 833, 889 Tumblers

## Cutting 135 GENEVA
No Optic
*1918 – 1926 Crystal*
Additional Pieces:
822 Parfait
4061 Handled Lemonade
701, 820, 833, 4011 Tumblers
303, 724 Jugs
Also on Blank 880

Blank 863

3 oz. Wine

4½ oz. Claret

2 oz. Sherry

2½ oz. Creme de Menthe

1 oz. Cordial

1 oz. Brandy (Pousse Cafe)

Not Shown:
Cafe Parfait

## Blank 863

Hollow Stem Champagne,
Cut Flutes

## Blanks 867 and 867 ½

10 oz. Goblet
9 oz. Goblet

5 oz. Claret

5½ oz. Fruit

2¾ oz. Wine

2 oz. Sherry
1 oz. Cordial

6 oz., 4¼"
Saucer Champagne
3 oz. Cocktail
5 oz., 2½" Sherbet

Blank 863, continued

### Cutting 138 APPLE BLOSSOM
No Optic
*1918 – 1928 Crystal*
Additional Pieces:
805 Parfait
945½ Grapefruit and Liner
127 Handled Tumbler
766 Footed Ice Tea
820, 833, 858, 889, 4011 Tumblers
300, 303, 1236, 2100, 2104 Jugs
1743 Jug and Cover

### Cutting 167 FAIRFAX
No Optic
*1922 – 1928 Crystal*
Additional Pieces:
837 Oyster Cocktail
701, 820, 4011 Tumblers
303, 2082 Jugs
2230 Jug and Cover

## BLANK 867, 867½
Regular Optic, No Optic
*1925 – 1930 Crystal*

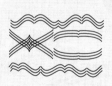

### Needle Etching 78 FRESNO
No Optic
*1925 – 1930 Crystal*
Additional Pieces:
766 Footed Ice Tea
822 Parfait
701, 820, 4095 Tumblers
316 Jug

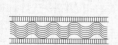

### Needle Etching 53 PARISIAN
Regular Optic
*1904 – 1927 Crystal*
Additional Pieces:
822 Parfait
701, 820, 833, 858, 887, 889, 4011
Tumblers
300, 303, 318 Jugs

# BLANK 869

Regular Optic
*1925 – 1939 Crystal (Parfait, 1925 – 1934)*
*1925 – 1939 Amber (Cordial, 1925 – 1937)*
*1925 – 1939 Green (Claret, 1925 – 1934)*
*1925 – 1927 Blue*
Additional Pieces:
5000 Footed Tumblers
869 Tumblers (5, 8, 12 oz. made in Orchid, 1927 – 1929;
 12 oz. handled made in Green, 1925 – 1934, Amber,
 1925 – 1930)
4095 Tumblers
4095 Jug
Blank 869 continued in production after all decorations were
 discontinued.

### Needle Etching 77 SHERMAN
*1925 – 1930 Crystal*
Additional Pieces:
6", 7", 8" Plates (2283)
945½ Grapefruit and Liner
5000 Footed Tumblers
869, 4095 Tumblers
4095 Jug; 2270 Jug and Cover

### Plate Etching 273 ROYAL
*1925 – 1938 Crystal*
*1925 – 1933 Amber, Green*
*1925 – 1927 Blue*
Additional Pieces:
945½ Grapefruit and Liner
869, 5000 Tumblers
2350 (Pioneer) Dinner Service
5000 Jug

### Cutting 184 ARBOR
*1926 – 1927 Amber, Green, Blue*
First of two cuttings found on color.
Additional Pieces:
6", 7", 8" Plates (2283)
5000 Tumblers, Jug

### Decoration 54 ALASKA
White Gold on Needle Etching 77,
 Sherman
*1925 – 1930 Crystal*
Additional Pieces:
6", 7", 8" Plates (2283)
869, 4095 Tumblers
2270, 4095 Jugs

9 oz., 7" Goblet

5½ oz., 4⅞"
Saucer Champagne

3 oz., 4½" Cocktail

5½ oz. High Sherbet

869 AMBER PARFAIT,
ROYAL ETCHING

2¾ oz., 4¾" Wine
4½ oz., 5⅝" Claret
¾ oz., 3½" Cordial

5½ oz., 3¾"
Low Sherbet
5½ oz. Fruit

6 oz. Parfait

4¾ oz., 3½"
Oyster Cocktail

869 GOBLET,
ALASKA DECORATION

## Blank 870

9 oz., 7" Goblet

870 Blue Parfait,
Brunswick
Needle Etching

4½ oz. Claret

3 oz., 4½" Cocktail

6 oz., 3⅞"
Low Sherbet

6 oz., 5⅛"
High Sherbet

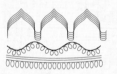

870 Green
Goblet, Seville
Etching

6 oz. Parfait

4¾ oz., 3⅜"
Oyster Cocktail

¾ oz. Cordial

2¾ oz. Wine

870 Green High
Sherbet, Grape Stem
Decoration 63

---

## Blank 870

Regular Optic
*1926 – 1942 Crystal*
*1928 – 1940 Rose*
 (Parfait, 1928 – 1934; Claret, 1935 – 1940;
 Wine and Cocktail, 1928 – 1935)
*1926 – 1940 Green*
 (Cordial and Oyster Cocktail, 1928 – 1935)
*1926 – 1940 Amber*
 (Wine and Oyster Cocktail, 1928 – 1935)
*1926 – 1927 Blue*
*Early 1930's Mother of Pearl Iridescence* on Goblet, High
Sherbet, Cocktail, 5084 Tumblers, 5084 Jug only
870 Oyster Cocktail replaced by 5084 Oyster Cocktail in 1931.

### Needle Etching 79 BRUNSWICK
*1926 – 1932 Crystal, Green, Amber*
*1926 – 1927 Blue*
Additional Pieces:
6", 7", 8" Plates (2283)
869, 5084 Tumblers
5084 Jug (1926 – 1930)

### Needle Etching 92 BARONET
*1926 – 1943 Crystal*
Additional Pieces:
6", 7", 8" Plates (2337)
5084 Oyster Cocktail
5084 Tumblers

### Plate Etching 274 SEVILLE
*1926 – 1933 Crystal, Green, Amber*
Additional Pieces:
2350 (Pioneer) Dinner Service
5084 Jug

### Decoration 60 MONARCH
Etching 79, Brunswick, trimmed with
Gold on Bowl
*1926 – 1928 Crystal*
Additional Pieces:
6", 7", 8" Plates (2283)
945½ Grapefruit and Liner
5084 Tumblers, Jug

### Decoration 61 GRAPE STEM
White Gold on stem
*1926 Crystal*

### Decoration 62 GRAPE STEM
White and Yellow Gold on stem
*1926 Crystal*

### Decoration 63 GRAPE STEM
Gold on Stem
*1926 Green*

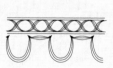

# BLANK 877

Regular Optic, No Optic

***1927 – 1942 Crystal***
(Claret and Cordial, 1927 – 1939; Grapefruit, 1927 – 1936)

***1928 – 1939 Azure***
(Goblet, Low Sherbet, Parfait, Cordial, 1928; Cocktail, 1928 – 1932; Footed Juice, 1928 – 1934; Grapefruit, 1928 – 1936; Claret, 1928 – 1938)

***1927 – 1939 Green***
(Claret, 1927 – 1932; Grapefruit and Cordial, 1927 – 1936; Oyster Cocktail, 1927 – 1937; 9 oz. Footed Tumbler, 1927 – 1930)

***1927 – 1938 Amber***
(Claret, 1927 –1934; Grapefruit and Cordial, 1927 – 1936)

***1927 – 1928 Orchid***

***1934 – 1937 Empire Green*** (Low Sherbet, Cocktail, 1934 – 1936; no Parfait, Wine, Grapefruit or Footed Whiskey)

***1934 – 1937 Regal Blue***
(Claret, 1934 – 1936; no Parfait, Wine, Grapefruit or Footed Whiskey)

***1934 – 1940 Mother of Pearl Iridescent*** available on Blown Repeal
Line 10 oz. Goblet, 6 oz. Saucer Champagne (High Sherbet)
Additional Pieces:
877 Tumblers

Blank 877

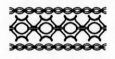

### Needle Etching 82 CORDELIA
Regular Optic
***1927 – 1928 Orchid***
***1927 – 1930 Green***
Additional Pieces:
7", 8" Plates (2283)
5000 Jug

10 oz. 7⁷⁄₈" Goblet
4 oz. Claret
2³⁄₄ oz. Wine

### Plate Etching 277 VERNON
Regular Optic
***1927 – 1933 Crystal***
***1927 – 1928 Orchid***
***1927 – 1933 Green, Amber***
***1928 – 1933 Azure***
Additional Pieces:
2375 (Fairfax) Dinner Service
5000 Jug

877 GREEN GOBLET, VERNON ETCHING

6 oz., 6¹⁄₈"
High Sherbet
3½ oz. Cocktail

6 oz., 4" Low Sherbet

### Brocade Etching 290 OAK LEAF
Regular Optic
***1928 – 1930 Crystal, Green***
Additional Pieces:
6", 7", 8" Plates (2283)
5000 Jug

4½ oz., 3½"
Oyster Cocktail

### Cutting 192 Kingsley
***1929 Crystal***
Additional Pieces:
6", 7", 8" Plates (2283)

12 oz. Footed Ice Tea
9 oz., 5¹⁄₄" Footed Tumbler
5 oz. Footed Juice
2¹⁄₂ oz. Footed Whiskey

### Cutting 196 LATTICE
Regular Optic
***1929 Crystal***
Additional Pieces:
6", 7", 8" Plates (2283)

877 SHERBET,
OAK LEAF
BROCADE ETCHING

³⁄₄ oz. Cordial

Parfait
Grapefruit and Liner
(See Appendix C)

Blank 879

877 Azure Goblet,
Oakwood Decoration

Blank 877, continued

### Rock Crystal Cutting 197
### CHATTERIS
*Regular Optic*
*1929 – 1930 Crystal*
Additional Pieces:
6", 7", 8" Plates (2283)

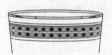

### Decoration 72 OAKWOOD
Brocade Etching 290 with all over
    Iridescence, Gold edge on Bowl and Foot
Regular Optic
*1928 – 1929 Azure*
*1928 Orchid*
Additional Pieces:
6", 7", 8" Plates (2283)
5000 Jug

## BLANK 879
Narrow Optic
*1916 – 1928 Crystal*
*1927 – 1928 Orchid*
*1927 – 1928 Mother of Pearl Iridescence*

9 oz., 6³/₄" Goblet

5 oz., 4¹/₂ " Saucer Champagne
3 oz. Cocktail

5 oz., 2³/₄" Fruit

Not Shown:
4¹/₂ oz. Claret
2³/₄ oz. Wine
2 oz. Sherry
³/₄ oz. Brandy
³/₄ oz. Cordial
2¹/₂ oz. Creme de Menthe

879 Cordial,
Mother of Pearl
Iridescence

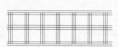

### Needle Etching 36 IRISH LACE
*1916 – 1928 Crystal*
Additional Pieces:
880, 880½ Grapefruit and Liner
5039 Grapefruit and Liner
5054 Parfait
837 Oyster Cocktail
701, 820, 858, 889, 4011, 4077 Tumblers
300, 724 Tankards
303, 318 Jugs
Also on Blanks 766 and 880

### Needle Etching 38½ BLOCK
*1916 – 1927 Crystal*
Additional Pieces:
945, 945½ Grapefruit and Liner
4061 Handled Lemonade
701, 820, 833, 858, 887, 889, 4077
    Tumblers
300, 724 Tankards
303, 1236 Jugs
Also on Blank 863

### Plate Etching 241
### LILY OF THE VALLEY
*1916 – 1927 Crystal*
Additional Pieces:
822 Parfait
4061 Handled Lemonade
945, 945½ Grapefruit and Liner
820, 833, 887, 889, 4077 Tumblers
300, 724 Tankards
303, 318 Jugs
Also on Blank 858

## BLANK 880
Narrow Optic, No Optic
*Pre-1900 – 1926 Crystal*
By 1918 the 880 Line had been cut to 14 stems.

### Needle Etching 36 IRISH LACE
Narrow Optic
*Pre1900 – 1926 Crystal*
Additional Pieces:
767, 5054 Parfaits
837 Oyster Cocktail
880½ Grapefruit and Liner
4061 Handled Lemonade
766 Footed Handled Ice Tea
701, 820, 833, 858, 887, 889, 4011, 4077
  Tumblers
300, 303, 318, 724 Jugs
317½ Jug and Cover
Also on Blanks 766 and 879

### Needle Etching 45 GREEK
Narrow Optic
*Pre1900 – 1926 Crystal*
Additional Pieces:
822 Parfait
945, 945½, Grapefruit and Liner
701, 820, 833, 887, 889, 4011 Tumblers
300, 303, 318, 1227, 1236, 2018 Jugs
300½, 317½ Jug and Cover
724 Tankard
Also on Blank 5097

### Plate Etching 227 NEW VINTAGE
No Optic
*1913 – 1926 Crystal*
Additional Pieces:
822, 5054 Parfait
766 Footed Handled Ice Tea
5039 Oyster Cocktail
701, 820, 887, 889, 4011 Tumblers
300, 724 Tankards
300, 303, 318, 1236 Jugs
Also on Blanks 858 and 863

### Plate Etching 234 KORNFLOWER
No Optic
*1913 – 1917 Crystal*
Additional Pieces:
701, 820, 858 Tumblers
303 Jug

### Plate Etching 237 GARLAND
No Optic
*1915 – 1926 Crystal*
Additional Pieces:
4061 Handled Lemonade
701, 833, 887, 889, 4011, 4077 Tumblers
300, 724 Tankards
300, 318, 724, 1236 Jugs
317½ Jug and Cover
Also on Blanks 766 and 963

**887 TUMBLER, GREEK NEEDLE ETCHING**

11 oz. Goblet
10 oz. Goblet
9 oz. Goblet
8 oz. Goblet

7 oz. Saucer Champagne
5½ oz. Saucer Champagne

5½ oz. Tall Champagne

6½ oz. Claret
4½ oz. Claret

4 oz. Rhine Wine

Grapefruit and Liner
(Appendix C)

Not Shown:
Hollow Stem Champagne   6 oz. Sherbet

## Blank 880

6¹/₂ oz. Tall Ale

4¹/₂ oz., Hot Whiskey
3¹/₂ oz. Wine
2 oz. Sherry

2³/₄ oz. Wine

3¹/₂ oz. Cocktail
3 oz. Cocktail

2¹/₂ oz.
Creme de Menthe

1 oz. Brandy
(Pousse Cafe)
³/₄ oz. Brandy
(Pousse Cafe)

1 oz. Cordial

³/₄ oz. Cordial

Blank 880, Continued

***Plate Etching 249 ROSILYN***
No Optic
***1918 – 1926 Crystal***
Additional Pieces:
837 Oyster Cocktail
822 Parfait
945½ Grapefruit and Liner
701, 820, 833, 4011 Tumblers
300, 303, 318, 724 Jugs

***Cutting 81***
***LARGE SUNBURST STAR***
No Optic
***1904 – 1926 Crystal***
Additional Pieces:
766 Parfait
300, 724 Tankards
303, 1227 Jugs
Also on Blanks 858 and 863

***Cutting 135 GENEVA***
No Optic
***1918 – 1926 Crystal***
Additional Pieces:
822 Parfait
4061 Handled Lemonade
701, 820, 833, 4011 Tumblers
303, 724 Jugs
Also on Blank 863

***Cutting 175 AIRDALE***
No Optic
***1924 – 1927 Crystal***
Additional Pieces:
822 Parfait
837 Oyster Cocktail
945½ Grapefruit and Liner
701, 820, 887, 889, 4011 Tumblers
303, 2082 Jugs

# BLANK 882
Same as Blank 880 with cut stem
No Optic
*1913 – 1924 Crystal*

Blank 882

9 oz. Goblet

**Plate Etching 235 IVY**
*1913 – 1917 Crystal*
Additional Pieces:
701, 858, 887 Tumblers
300 Tankard, Cut Flutes

**Plate Etching 236 GRILLE**
*1913 – 1924 Crystal*
Additional Pieces:
701, 820, 833, 887 Tumblers
300 Tankard, Cut Flutes

6¹/₂ oz. Claret

6¹/₂ oz. Tall Ale

6 oz. Sherbet

4 oz. Rhine Wine

3¹/₂ oz. Cocktail
3 oz. Cocktail

3¹/₂ oz. Wine
2³/₄ oz. Wine
4¹/₂ oz. Hot Whiskey

2¹/₂ oz.
Creme de Menthe

1 oz. Brandy
(Pousse Cafe)
³/₄ oz. Brandy

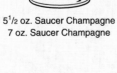

5¹/₂ oz. Saucer Champagne
7 oz. Saucer Champagne

2 oz. Sherry

Hollow Stem
Champagne

³/₄ oz. Cordial
1 oz. Cordial

39

Blank 890

10 oz., 8 1/8" Goblet

890 BURGUNDY
GOBLET

**BLANK 890**
Regular Optic
*1929 – 1932 Crystal, Green, Rose*
*1933 – 1942 Burgundy*
Additional Pieces:
890 Jug

*Plate Etching 281 VERONA*
*1929 – 1931 Crystal, Green, Rose*
(Included a 3 oz. Wine)
Additional Pieces:
877 Grapefruit, 945½ Liner
2375 (Fairfax) Dinner Service
890 Jug

*Rock Crystal Cutting 198*
*WARWICK*
*1929 – 1932 Crystal*
Additional Pieces:
6", 7", 8", 13" Plates (2283)
6", 7", 8" Plates (2419, Mayfair)
890 Jug

4 oz., 6 1/8" Claret-Wine

6 oz. 4 1/8"
Low Sherbet

2 1/2 oz. Footed
Whiskey

3/4 oz. 4" Cordial

6 oz., 6"
Saucer Champagne
3 1/2 oz., 5 1/8" Cocktail

4 1/2 oz., 4"
Oyster Cocktail

Not Shown:
Parfait

5 oz., 4 1/2"
Footed Juice

9 oz., 5 3/8"
Footed Tumbler

12 oz., 6" Footed
Ice Tea

## BLANK 891
Regular Optic (16-Rib)
*1933 – 1939 Crystal*
 (Cordial and Oyster Cocktail, 1933 – 1937)
*1933 – 1939 Topaz/Gold Tint*
 (No Claret, 9 oz. Tumbler, Oyster Cocktail and Cordial)

*Plate Etching 318 SPRINGTIME*
*1933 – 1939 Crystal*
*1933 – 1935 Topaz*
 (Oyster Cocktail and Footed Juice, 1933
 – 1934)
Additional Pieces:
2440 (Lafayette) Dinner Service
6011 Jug
Also on Blank 6012, Westchester

9 oz., 6⁷/₈" Goblet

1 oz., 3⁵/₈"
Cordial

6¹/₂ oz., 4"
Low Sherbet

4 oz., 4¹/₂" Cocktail

5 oz., 3³/₄"
Oyster Cocktail

6¹/₂ oz., 5¹/₈"
High Sherbet

4 oz., 5¹/₂" Claret - Wine

5 oz., 4¹/₂"
Footed Juice

9 oz., 5³/₈"
Footed Tumbler

12 oz., 6" Footed
Ice Tea

## Blank 892
## NORDIC

11 oz., 6½" Goblet

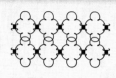
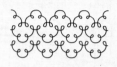

892 CORDIAL,
RINGLET TRACING

4 oz., 4½" Cocktail

1 oz., 3⅜" Cordial

6½ oz., 4" Low Sherbet

892—11 oz. Goblet
Height 6½ in.

CATALOG IMAGE
OF GOBLET
WITH ORCHARD
CARVING

7 oz., 5¼"
Saucer Champaggne

4 oz., 4⅞" Claret
3 oz., 4⅜" Wine

4½ oz. 2⅞"
Oyster Cocktail

5 oz., 3⅞"
Footed Juice

13 oz., 5½"
Footed Ice Tea

42

---

# BLANK 892 NORDIC
No Optic
*1939 – 1943 Crystal*

**Tracing 93 ARIEL**
*1940 – 1943 Crystal*
Additional Pieces:
7" Plate (2337)

**Tracing 95 RINGLET**
*1940 – 1943 Crystal*
Additional Pieces:
7" Plate (2337)

**Plate Etching 339 ROSEMARY**
*1939 – 1943 Crystal*
Additional Pieces:
6", 7", 8" Plates (2337)
6011 Jug

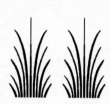

**Carving 48 ORCHID**
*1941 – 1943 Crystal*
Additional Pieces:
7", 8" Plates (2337)

**Cutting 794 INGRID**
Combination Rock Crystal and Gray
  Cutting
Similar to Cutting 836, Ingrid, on Blank
  6052½
*1939 – 1943 Crystal*
Additional Pieces:
6", 7", 8" Plates (2337)
6011 Jug

**Cutting 795 PAPYRUS**
Combination Rock Crystal and Gray
  Cutting
*1939 – 1943 Crystal*
Additional Pieces:
6", 7", 8" Plates (2337)
6011 Jug

**Cutting 796 LYRIC**
Combination Rock Crystal and Gray
  Cutting
*1939 – 1943 Crystal*
Additional Pieces:
6", 7", 8" Plates (2337)
6011 Jug

**Cutting 798 CHRISTINE**
*1939 – 1943 Crystal*
Additional Pieces:
7", 8" Plates (2337)
6011 Jug

Blank 1372
COIN

10½ oz. 6⅝" Goblet

## BLANK 1372 COIN

Pressed

***1958 – 1981 Crystal***
(Water/Scotch and Soda, Ice Tea/Highball, 1958 – 1970;
Goblet, Sherbet, Wine, 1969 – 1970;
Double Old Fashioned, Ice Tea, 1969 – 1981)

***1969 – 1981 Olive Green***
Double Old Fashioned, Ice Tea (Goblet, Sherbet, Wine,
1969 – 1970)

***1969 – 1981 Ruby***
Double Old Fashioned, Ice Tea (Goblet, Sherbet, Wine,
1969 – 1970)

Matchings through 1972 for Goblet, Sherbet, Wine.

9 oz., 4¼" Water/
Scotch and Soda

1372 COIN, RUBY
ICE TEA

5 oz., 5³⁄₁₆" Wine

10 oz., 4" Double
Old Fashioned

9 oz., 3⅝" Juice/
Old Fashioned

14 oz., 5⅝" Ice Tea

12 oz., 5⅛" Ice Tea/
Highball

9 oz., 5⅜" Sherbet

---

Blank 1630
ALEXIS

10 oz. Goblet
3 oz. Wine
2 oz. Wine
¾ oz. Brandy

Low Foot Sherbet
3 oz. Cocktail
6 oz. Tall Champagne

1 oz. Cordial

5 oz. Claret

## BLANK 1630 ALEXIS

Pressed

***1909 – 1925 Crystal***
Additional Pieces:
10 oz., 14 oz. Tumblers
1630½ Jug (½ Gallon)
1630½ Tall Pitcher (½ Gallon)

Not Shown:
High Footed Sherbet
2¼ oz. Creme de Menthe
10 oz. Footed Ice Tea
8 oz. Footed Table Tumbler

9 oz., 5½" Low Goblet
7 oz., 4⅞" Claret

12 oz., 5¾"
Iced Tea, Footed & Flared

7 OZ., 4¾"
CLARET

## BLANK 2056 AMERICAN

Pressed

*1915 – 1982 Crystal*
*1925 Green*
(Regular Ice Tea Tumbler and Regular Table
Tumbler only)
1915 – 1982 Goblet, Hexagon Foot
1932 – 1982 Low Goblet
1933 – 1982 Hexagon Footed Dessert
1924 – 1982 High Sherbet, Flared
1924 – 1982 High Sherbet Regular
1924 – 1982 Low Sherbet, Flared
1924 – 1982 Low Sherbet, Regular
1916 – 1944 Handled Sherbet
1935 – 1970 Footed Cocktail
1934 – 1973 Old Fashioned Cocktail
1976 – 1982 Claret
1915 – 1982 Footed Wine, Hexagon Foot
1932 – 1974 Oyster Cocktail
1916 – 1982 Sundae
1916 – 1923 Footed Handled Lemonade
1932 – 1982 Footed Ice Tea
1939 – 1974 9 oz. Footed Tumbler
1934 – 1982 Footed Juice, 5 oz. Footed Tumbler
1916 – 1982 Ice Tea Tumbler, Flared
1915 – 1974 Table Tumbler, Flared
1915 – 1982 Ice Tea Tumbler, Regular
1915 – 1982 Table Tumbler, Regular
1939 – 1982 5 oz. Tumbler, Regular
1934 – 1975 Whiskey Tumbler
1957 – 1960 Baby Tumbler
1933 – 1943 Beer Mug
1974 – 1982 Beer Mug Reintroduced
1933 – 1944 Tom and Jerry Mug
1980 – 1982 Youth Mug

Fostoria's AMERICAN pattern is the longest running pattern in the history of glassmaking in America. The AMERICAN pattern kept Fostoria alive during the Great Depression, and sold well throughout Fostoria's history.

10 oz., 6⅞" Goblet,
Hexagon Foot

2½ oz., 4⅜" Wine,
Hexagon Foot

9 oz., 4⅜"
Tumbler, Footed

4½ oz., 3½"
Oyster Cocktail

4½ oz., 4½" High
Sherbet, Regular

4½ oz., 4¾"
Dessert, Hexagon Foot

5 oz., 3½" Low Sherbet,
Regular

4½ oz., 3½" Sherbet,
Handled

6 oz., 3⅛" Sundae

4½ oz., 4⅜" High
Sherbet, Flared

5 oz., 3¼" Low Sherbet,
Flared

11 oz., 5¾" Lemonade,
Footed & Handled

5 oz., 4¾"
Tumbler, Footed

2 oz., 2½" Whiskey

3 oz., 2⅞"
Cocktail, Footed

Baby Tumbler

5 oz., 3⅝"
Table Tumbler, Regular

8 oz., 4⅛"
Table Tumbler, Flared

5½ oz., 3¼"
Youth Mug
(also called Tom & Jerry Mug)

8 oz., 3⅞"
Table Tumbler, Regular

12 oz., 5¼"
Ice Tea, Flared

12 oz., 4½" Beer Mug

6 oz., 3⅜"
Old Fashioned Cocktail

12 oz., 5"
Ice Tea, Regular

Ice Tea and 6" Plate

# NO. 2056 AMERICAN PATTERN

The "AMERICAN" Pattern, our latest production, is original and unique, and must be seen to be fully appreciated. It is the most striking design we have ever produced. It is impossible to produce by illustration the real appearance of this design, which is prismatic in effect; by either artificial or sun light it produces all the prismatic "fire" to a greater extent than any table glassware pattern that we have ever produced. We have applied for patent on this pattern. While this pattern looks massive and heavy, at the same time it is the lightest finished table ware line we have ever made. It is as readily kept clean as a colonial design. In the illustrations the "cube" is brought out prominently, but upon examining the glass itself you will see that this cube effect is almost entirely obliterated by the prismatic brilliancy of the pattern. When examined at different angles you see entirely different effects. The novelty of this design will, no doubt, appeal to all up-to-date dealers in high class tableware. We predict it will be a "repeater," not only in the United States but in foreign countries; in fact, foreign dealers have already cabled us for additional samples, and thus give it the stamp of their approval.

Yours truly,
FOSTORIA GLASS CO

January, 1915.

THIS EXTREMELY LONG-LIVED PATTERN (1915 – 1986 IN MOUNDSVILLE) CONTAINS SEVERAL PIECES THAT COULD BE CONFUSED BECAUSE THEY APPEAR QUITE SIMILAR. WE INCLUDE CATALOG PAGES AND PHOTOGRAPHS TO ILLUSTRATE ODDITIES AND PIECES THAT LOOK ALIKE.

THE 1915 CATALOG SHOWED THE SHAPE ON THE LEFT AS THE 6 OZ. SUNDAE. THE SHAPE ON THE RIGHT IS FROM A LATER CATALOG.

THE ONLY DIFFERENCE BETWEEN THE 1915 SHERBET (LATER CALLED THE OYSTER COCKTAIL) AND THE HANDLED SHERBET SEEMS TO BE THE HANDLE.

THE REGULAR LOW SHERBET AND THE SUNDAE DON'T LOOK ALIKE AT ALL, BUT ARE OFTEN CONFUSED.

THESE TWO PIECES ARE BOTH HIGH FLARED SHERBETS, BUT LOOK AT THE DIFFERENCE BETWEEN THEM.

46

THE FOOTED DESSERT IS THE ONLY ONE OF THE "SHERBETS" WITH A HEXAGON FOOT. IN FACT, BESIDES THE DESSERT, ONLY THE GOBLET AND THE WINE ALSO HAVE THE HEXAGON FOOT. KNOWING THAT SHOULD HELP YOU DISTINGUISH THE DESSERT FROM THE REGULAR HIGH SHERBET.

THE CLARET AND THE LOW GOBLET ARE THE MOST OFTEN CONFUSED PAIR OF PIECES. WHEN SET SIDE BY SIDE, THE DIFFERENCES ARE OBVIOUS. THE LOW GOBLET IS LARGER, FOR EXAMPLE. HOWEVER, WHEN SEEN SEPARATELY, KNOWING THE HEIGHT OF EACH IS ABOUT THE ONLY WAY TO BE CERTAIN.

SEEING IS BELIEVING, AND THIS PHOTOGRAPH OF THE REGULAR LOW SHERBET, THE FLARED HIGH SHERBET, AND THE REGULAR HIGH SHERBET WILL KEEP YOU FROM MAKING ANY MISTAKES ABOUT WHICH IS WHICH. (*REGULAR* SIMPLY MEANS "NOT FLARED.")

LOOK CAREFULLY AT THESE TWO PIECES. ONE IS THE JAM POT WITHOUT ITS LID. THE OTHER IS THE OLD FASHIONED. CAN YOU TELL WHICH IS WHICH? (HINT: THE OLD FASHIONED HAS A WIDER BAND AT THE TOP.)

A QUESTION WE ARE OFTEN ASKED IS, "HOW CAN YOU TELL IF A PIECE IS OLDER?" THE ANSWER IS THAT YOU PROBABLY CAN'T. LOOK AT THESE TWO REGULAR ICE TEA TUMBLERS. ONE SEEMS A LITTLE WIDER, ONE SEEMS TALLER, ONE SEEMS TO HAVE A WIDER BAND AT THE TOP. WHICH WOULD YOU THINK IS OLDER? WE DON'T HAVE A CLUE.

# THE "AMERICAN" PATTERN

You as buyer are interested in the salability of every item and line that goes on your shelves and counters.

Salability by the store is measured by serviceability to the customer.

The serviceability of the Fostoria American pattern is attested by its truly phenomenal acceptance in every center of good taste.

It is a matter of record that no pressed ware line has ever approached the sales performance of "American"—in total volume, in sustained demand, and in gains from year to year. There is apparently no end to the popularity of this wonderful pattern.

The fascination of the pattern derives, apparently, from two characteristics: the restful repetition of straight lines in simple geometric forms; and its jewel-like capacity for reflecting light and color.

This famous Fostoria design has been adapted to over one hundred and fifty separate pieces for the home and table.

Blank 2106
VOGUE

## BLANK 2106 VOGUE

Pressed

*1916 – 1928 Crystal*

Additional Pieces:

2106 Flat Tumblers

2106 Serving Pieces

3 -Quart Jug

½ Gallon Jug

3 -Quart Jug and Cover

½ Gallon Jug and Cover

4 oz., 6¼" Parfait

4 oz., 3¼" Sundae

3 oz., 2½" Sherbet

12 oz., 5¾"
Footed Handled
Lemonade

12 oz., Footed Soda
10 oz., Footed Soda
8 oz., Footed Soda
6 oz., Footed Soda
4 oz., Footed Soda

6 oz., 4³⁄₈" Parfait

5 oz., 3" Sherbet

Not Shown:
Goblet
2 oz. Wine
Coca Cola

---

Blank 2183
COLONIAL PRISM

4½ oz., 2¾"
Sherbet, Flared

5½ oz., 3"
Sherbet,
Regular

11 oz., 5"
Handled Tumbler

12½ oz., 5" Ice
Tea Tumbler

9 oz., 4¹⁄₈" Table
Tumbler

## BLANK 2183 COLONIAL PRISM

Pressed

*1918 – 1927 Crystal*

Additional Pieces:

9¼", 4½" Plates (2183)

2183 Footed Tankard

½ Gallon Ice Jug

½ Gallon Jug

3-Quart Ice Jug

5" Grapefruit and Liner

## BLANK 2222 COLONIAL

Pressed

*1920 – 1928 Crystal*

*1928 – 1932*

Tea Room Service (All pieces in Amber and
Green with Mother of Pearl Iridescence except
12 oz. Ice Tea, Wine, Flared Table Tumbler.
A Parfait was added.)

Additional Pieces:

7", 8" Plates (2222)

2222 Serving Pieces

3-Quart Ice Jug

½ Gallon Jug

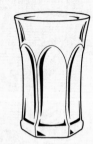

Goblet
5 oz. Wine

3 oz. Fruit Cocktail

8 oz. Regular Tumbler

12 oz., 4¹/₂" Flared Tumbler
8 oz., 4" Flared Tumbler
4¹/₂ oz., 3³/₄ oz. Wine Tumbler

4¹/₂ oz. Low Sherbet
4¹/₂ oz. High Sherbet

Not Shown:
Parfait
Footed Oyster Cocktail

3 oz. Low Sherbet

14 oz. Regular Tumbler

---

Footed Handled Tumbler

9 oz. Goblet
7 oz. Goblet

Footed Tumbler

Footed Handled Custard

Saucer Champagne
Sherbet

2321 BLUE
PRISCILLA, FOOTED,
HANDLED TUMBLER

## BLANK 2321 PRISCILLA

Pressed

*1925 – 1930 Crystal, Green, Amber*

*1925 – 1927 Blue*

Additional Pieces:

8" Plates (2321)

Three Pint Jug

Cup and Saucer

Cream Soup

Boullion

Cream and Sugar

9 oz., 5¹/₈" Goblet

3¹/₂ oz., 4" Cocktail

# Blank 2412 COLONY

Pressed

*1940 – 1973 Crystal*
   (Cocktail, Oyster Cocktail, 12 oz., 9 oz.,
      5 oz. Tumblers, 1940 – 1970)
Matchings through 1978 for Goblet, Sherbet,
   Wine, Footed Ice Tea, Footed Juice; through 1975 for 12 oz.
      Tumbler.
Additional Pieces:
Full Dinner Service

4 oz., 3⁵/₈"
Flat Tumbler

9 oz., 3⁷/₈"
Flat Tumbler

3¹/₄ oz., 4¹/₈" Wine

4 oz., 3³/₈" Oyster
Cocktail

5 oz., 3⁵/₈"
Sherbet

5 oz., 4¹/₂"
Footed Juice

12 oz., 5⁵/₈"
Footed Ice Tea

12 oz., 4⁷/₈"
Flat Tumbler

---

Blank 2449
HERMITAGE

9 oz., 5¹/₄" Goblet

4 oz., 4⁵/₈" Claret

2 oz., 2¹/₂" Footed
Whiskey
5 oz., 4" Footed
Juice

7 oz., 3" Low Sherbet
5 oz., 2³/₈"
Fruit Cocktail

5¹/₂ oz., 3¹/₄"
High Sherbet

4 oz., 3"
Oyster Cocktail

9 oz., 4¹/₈" Footed
Table Tumbler

9 oz., 4¹/₄" Handled
Beer Mug
12 oz., 5¹/₄" Handled
Beer Mug

12 oz., 5¹/₄" Footed
Ice Tea

# Blank 2449 HERMITAGE

Pressed

*1932 – 1944 Crystal*
*1932 – 1942 Azure*
*1932 – 1941 Green*
*1932 – 1941 Amber*
*1932 – 1936 Topaz*
*1937 – 1943 Gold Tint*
*1932 – 1938 Wisteria*

6 oz., 3¹/₄"
Old Fashioned Cocktail
2 oz., 2¹/₂" Tumbler

5 oz., 3⁷/₈"
Tumbler
9 oz., 4³/₄"
Tumbler

Not Shown:
4 oz., 3"
Oyster Cocktail

13 oz., 5⁷/₈"
Tumbler

Hermitage, continued

Exceptions: The 12 oz. Beer Mug (1933 – 1936) and the 9 oz. Beer Mug (1933 – 1938) were made in Crystal only. The Claret and Footed Whiskey were not made in Azure or Wisteria. The Old Fashioned Cocktail and the 2 oz. Tumbler were discontinued after 1940. The Footed Whiskey was discontinued in Amber and Gold Tint after 1938, Crystal after 1942. The Fruit Cocktail was discontinued in Green after 1937, Crystal after 1943. The Claret was discontinued after 1943.

Additional Pieces:
Full Dinner Service

2449 WISTERIA
HERMITAGE FRUIT
COCKTAIL

2496 AZURE
BAROQUE GOBLET

# BLANK 2496 BAROQUE

Pressed

*1937 – 1958 Crystal*
  (Footed Cocktail, Old Fashioned Cocktail,
   12 oz. and 9 oz. Footed Tumblers, and 5 oz.
   Tumbler, 1937 – 1939)

*1937 – 1943 Azure*
  (5 oz. Tumbler, 1937 – 1939)

*1937 – 1943 Gold Tint*

Additional Pieces:
Full Dinner Service

Blank 2496
BAROQUE

9 oz., 6³/₄" Goblet

3¹/₂ oz., 3"
Footed Cocktail

5 oz., 3⁷/₈" Sherbet

12 oz., 6" Footed Ice Tea
9 oz., 5¹/₂" Footed Tumbler

14 oz., 5⁷/₈ oz.
Flat Ice Tea
9 oz., 4¹/₄"
Flat Tumbler
5 oz., 3⁷/₈"
Flat Tumbler

6¹/₂ oz., 3³/₈"
Old Fashioned Cocktail

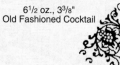

## BLANK 2510 SUNRAY, GLACIER

Pressed

*1935 – 1943 Crystal*
(Goblet, Sherbet, 9 oz. Footed Tumbler,
1935 – 1940; Old Fashioned, 1935 – 1939)

*1935 – 1938 Azure*
*1935 – 1940 Green*
*1935 – 1938 Amber*
*1935 – 1936 Topaz*
*1937 – 1940 Gold Tint*
Only the Goblet, Sherbet and 9 oz. Footed
Tumbler were made in color.

*1935 – 1943 Silver Mist* decoration on rays only
(called GLACIER)

Additional Pieces:
Full Dinner Service in both SUNRAY and GLACIER

Blank 2510
SUNRAY
GLACIER

9 oz., 5³/₄" Goblet

5 oz., 4⁵/₈ "
Footed Juice

5¹/₂ oz., 3¹/₂ " Sherbet
3¹/₂ oz., 3¹/₄"
Fruit Cocktail

13 oz., 5¹/₄" Footed Ice Tea
9 oz., 4³/₄" Footed Tumbler

4 oz., 3"
Footed Cocktail

6 oz., 3¹/₂"
Old Fashioned Cocktail
2 oz., 2¹/₄" Whiskey

4¹/₂ oz., 4⁷/₈" Claret

13 oz., 5¹/₈" Flat Ice Tea
9 oz., 4¹/₈" Flat Tumbler
5 oz., 3¹/₂" Flat Tumbler

53

Blank 2620
WISTAR
BETSY ROSS

9 oz., 5⅞" Goblet

# BLANK 2620
# WISTAR, BETSY ROSS

Pressed

*1941 – 1943 Crystal*
*1958 – 1965 White Milkglass*
  (Called BETSY ROSS, 5 oz. Tumbler,
  1958 – 1959)
Additional Pieces:
7" Plates (2620)
2620 Serving Pieces

6 oz., 4⅛" High Sherbet

5 oz., 3¾" Tumbler

12 oz., 5½" Tumbler

2620 BETSY ROSS
WHITE MILKGLASS
GOBLET

---

Blank 2630
CENTURY

10½ oz., 5¾" Goblet

3½ oz., 4½" Wine

5½ oz., 4¼" Sherbet

3½ oz., 4⅛" Cocktail

4½ oz., 3¾" Oyster Cocktail

# BLANK 2630 CENTURY

Pressed

*1950 – 1982 Crystal*
  (Oyster Cocktail, 1950 – 1972; Cocktail, Footed
  Juice, 1950 – 1974)
Additional Pieces:
Full Dinner Service
Several decorations were done on tableware; none on stemware.
Tableware was introduced in 1949; stemware in 1950.

12 oz., 5⅞" Footed Ice Tea
5 oz., 4¾" Footed Juice

## Blank 2700 RADIANCE

Blank 2700
RADIANCE

Pressed
*1956 – 1957 Crystal*
Additional Pieces:
Full Dinner Service

10 oz., 5³/₄" Beverage

6 oz., 3" Sherbet

5¹/₂ oz., 4¹/₂" Footed Juice

## Blank 2713 VINTAGE

Blank 2713
VINTAGE

Pressed
*1958 – 1965 White Milkglass*
Additional Pieces:
8" Plate (2713)

11 oz., 6¹/₄" Goblet

7¹/₂ oz., 4³/₄" Sherbet

13 oz., 6¹/₄" Footed Ice Tea

2713 VINTAGE
WHITE MILKGLASS
GOBLET

Blank 2718
FAIRMONT

10¹/₂ oz., 5⁷/₈" Goblet

6 oz., 4³/₈" Sherbet

5 oz., 5¹/₈" Footed Juice

## Blank 2718 FAIRMONT

Pressed
*1958 – 1965 Crystal*
*1958 – 1965 Blue*
*1958 – 1965 Green*
*1958 – 1965 Amber*
Additional Pieces:
8" Plate

13 oz., 6³/₈" Footed Ice Tea

2718 FAIRMONT
BLUE GOBLET

## Blank 2719 Jamestown

Blank 2719
JAMESTOWN

9½ oz., 5¾" Goblet
4 oz., 4⁵/₁₆" Wine

# Blank 2719 Jamestown

Pressed

*1958 – 1970 Crystal*
*1958 – 1982 Amber*
*1961 – 1982 Brown*
*1958 – 1982 Blue*
*1958 – 1974 Green*
*1959 – 1982 Pink*
*1960 – 1970 Amethyst*
*1964 – 1982 Ruby*

 (9 oz. Tumbler, 1958 – 1970; 12 oz. Tumbler,
  1958 – 1973)
Matchings through 1978 for Goblet, Sherbet, Wine and Footed
 Juice in Crystal and Green.
Additional Pieces:
8" Plate
Serving Pieces
Pitcher made in all colors except Ruby.

11 oz., 6" Footed Ice Tea
5 oz., 4¾" Footed Juice

2719 Jamestown
Pink Footed Juice

6½ oz., 4¼" Sherbet

9 oz., 4¼" Flat Tumbler

12 oz., 5⅛" Flat Tumbler

---

Blank 2770
ARGUS

10½ oz., 6⁷/₁₆" Goblet

4 oz., 4¾" Wine

8 oz., 5" Sherbet

4½ oz., 2⅞"
Juice

10 oz., 3⅞"
Old Fashioned

## Blank 2770 Argus

# Blank 2770 Argus

Pressed Flint Glass
Made by special arrangement with the Henry Ford Museum

*1963 – 1982 Crystal*
*1963 – 1982 Olive Green*
*1963 – 1980 Cobalt*
*1964 – 1982 Ruby*
*1972 – 1980 Gray*

Matchings through 1982 for Cobalt and Gray.
Additional Pieces:
8" Plate
5" Fruit Bowl
Compote and Cover
Sugar with Cover
Creamer

13 oz., 6¾" Footed Ice Tea

12 oz., 5¼" Highball

2770 Argus
Cobalt Wine

56

Blank 2806
PEBBLE BEACH

10 oz., 6" Goblet

## BLANK 2806 PEBBLE BEACH

Pressed
*1968 – 1970 Crystal Ice*
*1968 – 1970 Pink Lady*
*1969 – 1970 Mocha*
*1968 – 1973 Black Pearl*
*1968 – 1973 Lemon Twist*
*1968 – 1973 Flaming Orange*
Matchings through 1971 for Crystal Ice, Pink Lady; through
  1974 for Black Pearl, Lemon Twist, Flaming Orange.
Additional Pieces:
8" Plate
Quart Pitcher (No Flaming Orange)

14 oz., 5³/₄"
Ice Tea

2806 PEBBLE
BEACH FLAMING
ORANGE GOBLET

8 oz., 4¹/₈" On the Rocks/Wine

7 oz., 4⁵/₈" Juice

7 oz., 2³/₄"
Sherbet

---

Blank 2832
SORRENTO

9 oz. Goblet
6¹/₂ oz. Wine

13 oz. Footed Ice Tea

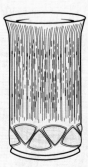

10 oz. Double
Old Fashioned

6¹/₂ oz. Sherbet

## BLANK 2832 SORRENTO

Pressed
*1971 – 1974 Blue, Green, Brown*
*1972 – 1974 Plum*
*1973 – 1974 Pink*
Matchings through 1976 for Goblet, Sherbet, Wine and Footed
  Ice Tea.
Additional Pieces:
8" Plate

11 oz. Tumbler

Blank 2860
PANELLED
DIAMOND POINT

## BLANK 2860 PANELLED DIAMOND POINT

Pressed Lead Crystal
Made by special arrangement with the Henry Ford Museum.
*1973 – 1974 Crystal*
Matchings through 1976.
Additional Pieces:
8" Plate

10½ oz., 6½"
Goblet

6½ oz., 5½" Wine

7 oz., 4⅝"
Dessert/Champagne

13 oz., 6⁵⁄₁₆"
Footed Ice Tea

---

Blank 2882
MOONSTONE

10 oz., 6½"
Goblet

7 oz., 5½"
Sherbet

5 oz., 5⅛"
Wine

13 oz., 6½"
Footed Ice Tea

12 oz., 4" Double
Old Fashioned

15 oz., 5½"
Highball

## BLANK 2882 MOONSTONE

Pressed
*1974 – 1982 Apple Green, Pink, Blue, Yellow*
*1978 – 1980 Crystal*
*1978 – 1982 Dark Blue, Taupe (Brown)*

2882 MOONSTONE
APPLE GREEN
GOBLET

## Blank 2885
### STRATTON

10 oz., 3" Double
Old Fashioned

7 oz., 5¼"
Sherbet

10 oz., 6½"
Goblet

5 oz., 5½" Wine

12 oz., 6⅝"
Footed Ice Tea

12 oz., 5½"
Highball

## Blank 2887
### HERITAGE

10½ oz., 7¼"
Goblet

8 oz., 4⅞"
Sherbet

10 oz., 4" Double
Old Fashioned

12 oz., 7⅛"
Footed Ice Tea

6½ oz., 6" Wine

## Blank 2887 (HE03)
### HERITAGE
Pressed Lead Crystal
*1979 – 1986 Crystal*
*1979 – 1982 Sherbet*
Additional Pieces:
8" Plate

12 oz., 5¼"
Highball

59

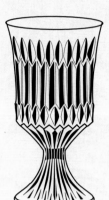

## BLANK 2903 (M011)
# MONARCH
Pressed Lead Crystal
*1979 – 1982 Crystal*
*1979 – 1986 Double Old Fashioned and Highball*
Additional Pieces:
Dessert/Salad

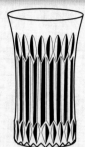

6½ oz., 5½"  Wine

11 oz., 6½"
Goblet

10 oz., 3½" Double
Old Fashioned

12 oz., 5³/₈"
Highball

14 oz., 6½"
Footed Ice Tea

---

Blank 2916
FAIRLANE

9 oz., 5¹¹/₁₆"
Champagne

2 oz., 3³/₈"
Cordial

11 oz., 3½" Double
Old Fashioned

14 oz., 5½"
Highball

11 oz., 7⁵/₁₆"
Goblet

6½ oz., 6³/₁₆"  Wine

## BLANK 2916 (FA03) FAIRLANE
Pressed Lead Crystal
*1976 – 1982 Crystal*

14 oz., 6⁵/₈"
Footed Ice Tea

*Cutting 935 GREENFIELD*
*1976 – 1982 Crystal*
   (No Double Old Fashioned or Highball)

*Decoration 694 BRACELET*
Platinum Band on Rim
*1976 – 1982 Crystal*
   (No Double Old Fashioned or Highball)

Blank 2921
WOODLAND

# BLANK 2921 WOODLAND

Pressed
*1975 – 1980 Crystal*
*1976 – 1981 Blue, Brown, Green*
Matchings through 1982 in Crystal.

9¹/₂ oz., 6¹³/₁₆" Goblet

8 oz., 5¹/₄" Sherbet

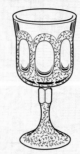

6¹/₂ oz., 5³/₁₆" Wine

14¹/₂ oz., 6¹¹/₁₆"
Footed Ice Tea

Blank 2936
TRANSITION

# BLANK 2936 (TR05) TRANSITION

Pressed Lead Crystal
*1978 – 1986 Crystal*

10 oz., 4¹/₈"
Double Old Fashioned

7 oz., 5"
Wine/Juice

12 oz., 5⁵/₈"
Highball

Blank 2977
VIRGINIA

7 oz., 5¹/₈" Sherbet

6 oz., 6¹/₁₆" Wine

10 oz., 7¹/₄"
Goblet

13 oz., 6⁷/₈"
Footed Ice Tea

# BLANK 2977 (VI04) VIRGINIA

Pressed
*1978 – 1986 Green, Brown*
*1980 – 1986 Dark Blue, Light Blue*
*1983 – 1986 Peach*
*1985 – 1986 Crystal*
*1985 – 1986 Sun Gold*
 (No Sherbet)
Additional Pieces:
8", 10" Plates in 1984.
Lancaster Colony Corporation continued to make Blank 2977
 after purchasing the Fostoria Company in 1983.

Blank 2990
KIMBERLY

10 oz., 7½" Goblet
7 oz., 6½" Wine

## BLANK 2990 (KI01)
## KIMBERLY
Pressed Lead Crystal
*1979 – 1982 Crystal*
*1983 – 1986 Kimberly Gold*
  (Gold Band on Bowl)
*1983 – 1986 Kimberly Platinum*
  (Platinum Band on Bowl)
Additional Pieces:
Bell
Bell with Gold Handle
2903 (Monarch) Barware (Double Old
  Fashioned and Highball)

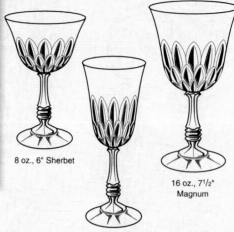

8 oz., 6" Sherbet

8 oz., 7½" Flute
Champagne/Parfait

16 oz., 7½"
Magnum

---

Blank 3008
VISION

## BLANK 3008 VISION
An Old Morgantown Glass Company pattern
*1971 – 1973 Crystal, Ebony, Nutmeg*
*1971 – 1972 Midnight Blue, White*
Matchings through 1973 for Midnight Blue
  and White

7 oz., 6⅜" Tulip Wine

12 oz., 7⅛" Goblet

11 oz., 5¾" Sherbet

2 oz., 3⅝"
Cordial

8 oz., 6" Claret

13 oz., 6⅝"
Footed Ice Tea

---

Blank 3113
RADIANCE

10 oz., 7⁵⁄₁₆" Goblet

8 oz., 5¹³⁄₁₆" Champagne

6½ oz., 6⁵⁄₁₆"
Wine

14 oz., 6⁵⁄₁₆"
Footed Ice Tea

## BLANK 3113 (RA02)
## RADIANCE
Pressed Lead Crystal
*1981 – 1982 Crystal*
Additional Pieces:
2887 (Heritage) Barware (Highball and Double Old Fashioned)

# BLANK 4020

No Optic

*1929 – 1943 Crystal*
*1929 – 1940 Green Base*
*1929 – 1940 Amber Base* (Wine, Claret, 1934 only; High Sherbet, Whiskey, 1929 – 1935; Cocktail, 10 oz. Tumbler, 1929 – 1939)
*1929 – 1940 Ebony Base* (Cocktail, Footed Juice, 1929 – 1939)
*1929 – 1940 Rose Bowl* (Wine, Claret, 1934 only; Footed Juice, 1929 – 1937; Footed Ice Tea, 10 oz. Footed Tumbler, 1929 – 1939)
*1929 – 1936 Topaz Bowl*
*1937 – 1943 Gold Tint Bowl* (Cocktail, Claret, 13 oz. and 10 oz. Tumblers, 1937 – 1940)
*1931 – 1938 Wisteria Bowl* (Wine, Claret, 1934 only; Whiskey, 1931 – 1934)

Additional Pieces:
Claret and Wine added to Blank 4020 in 1934.
4020½ Cocktail, 4 oz.
4020 Footed Jug (Crystal, 1929 – 1940; Green Base, Amber Base, 1929 – 1936; Topaz/Gold Tint Bowl, Rose Bowl, Wisteria Bowl; 1931 – 1937; Wisteria Base, 1931 – 1934; Ebony Base, 1929 – 1939)
4020 Footed Decanter (1929 – 1932), not made in Wisteria.

### Plate Etching 283 KASHMIR
*1930 – 1933 Green Base*
Additional Pieces:
4020 Jug
2419 (Mayfair) Dinner Service
Also on Blank 5099

### Plate Etching 284 NEW GARLAND
*1930 – 1933 Amber Base, Rose Bowl, Topaz Bowl*
Additional Pieces:
4020 Jug
2419 (Mayfair) Dinner Service
Also on Blank 6002

### Plate Etching 285 MINUET
*1930 – 1933 Green Base*
Additional Pieces:
4020 Jug, Decanter, Shaker, Sugar, Creamer
5000 Jug
2419 (Mayfair) Dinner Service
Also on Blank 6002

### Plate Etching 305 FERN
*1929 – 1933 Crystal*
*1929 – 1933 Ebony Base*
Additional Pieces:
4020 Jug, Sugar, Creamer (Crystal and Ebony Base)
2419 (Mayfair) Dinner Service in Crystal and Rose only
Also on Blank 5098

### Plate Etching 306 QUEEN ANN
*1929 – 1933 Crystal*
*1929 – 1933 Amber Base*
Additional Pieces:
4020 Jug, Sugar, Creamer (Crystal and Amber Base)
2419 (Mayfair) Dinner Service

Blank 4020

4020 FOOTED TUMBLER, NEW GARLAND ETCHING

11 oz., 5¾" Goblet

4020 GREEN ICE TEA, MINUET ETCHING

7 oz., 4⅜" High Sherbet

4020 JUICE, FERN ETCHING

7 oz., 3" Low Sherbet

5 oz., 2⅞" Low Sherbet

4020 AMBER BASE ICE TEA, QUEEN ANN ETCHING

## Blank 4020

5 oz., 4¹/₈"
Footed Juice

10 oz., 5"
Footed Tumbler

13 oz., 5¹/₄"
Footed Tumbler

16 oz., 6"
Footed Ice Tea

Blank 4020, continued

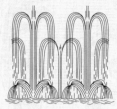

### Plate Etching 307 FOUNTAIN
*1929 – 1930 Crystal*
*1929 – 1930 Green Base*
Additional Pieces:
4020 Jug, Sugar, Creamer
2419 (Mayfair) Dinner Service

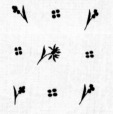

### Cutting 195 MILLEFLEUR
*1929 – 1939 Crystal* (Wine, 1934 –
     1935; Claret, 1934 – 1936; Whiskey,
     1929 – 1936)
*1929 – 1934 Ebony Base*
Additional Pieces:
4020 Jug, Sugar, Creamer (1929 – 1934)
2419 (Mayfair) and 2350 (Pioneer)
     combined Dinner Service

### Cutting 700 FORMAL GARDEN
*1930 only Crystal*
*1930 only Ebony Base*
Additional Pieces:
6", 7", 8" Plates (2419, Mayfair

### Cutting 701 TAPESTRY
1930 only Crystal
Additional Pieces:
6", 7", 8" Plates (2419, Mayfair)

### Cutting 702 COMET
*1930 – 1942 Crystal*
*1930 – 1932 Ebony Base* (No Wine or
     Claret)
*1934 only Green Base*
Additional Pieces:
6", 7", 8" Plates (2419 Mayfair)
4020 Jug (1930 – 1934), Sugar and
Creamer (1930 – 1932), After Dinner Cup
     and Saucer (1930 – 1932), Footed Cup
     and Saucer

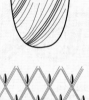

### Cutting 703 NEW YORKER
*1930 – 1943 Crystal* (Footed Whiskey,
     1930 – 1940)
*1930 – 1932 Green Base*
*1934 only Ebony Base*
Additional Pieces:
6", 7", 8" Plates (2419, Mayfair) in
     Crystal only
4020 Jug (1930 – 1934), Decanter (1930
     – 1932), Sugar and Creamer (1930
     – 1933)

### Rock Crystal Cutting 773 RHYTHM
*1938 – 1942 Crystal* (No Footed Ice
     Tea)
Additional Pieces:
7", 8" Plates (2419, Mayfair)
4020 Jug

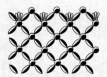

### Rock Crystal Cutting 783 CHELSEA
*1938 – 1943 Crystal* (No Footed Ice Tea)
Additional Pieces:
7", 8" Plates (2419, Mayfair)
4020 Jug

### Decoration 603 CLUB DESIGN A
Alternating Single and Double Black
  Enamel Lines
*1929 – 1930 Crystal*

### Decoration 604 CLUB DESIGN B
Ebony Base, Gold Lines on Crystal Bowl
*1931 – 1932 Ebony Base*
Additional Pieces:
2419 (Mayfair), 2350 (Pioneer), 2375
(Fairfax) combined Dinner Service, All
Ebony with Gold Lines.

4020 FOOTED TUMBLER,
CLUB DESIGN, GOLD LINES,
NOT LISTED IN CATALOGS

4 oz. Claret

### Decoration 605 SATURN
Ebony Base, Black Enamel Lines on
  Crystal Bowl
*1931 – 1932 Ebony Base*
Additional Pieces:
6", 7", 8" Plates (2419 Mayfair), Crystal
4020 Jug, Sugar, and Creamer (Ebony
  Base)

3 oz. Wine

### Decoration 607 POLKA DOT
Ebony Base, Black Enamel Dots on
  Crystal Bowl
*1931 – 1932 Ebony Base*
Additional Pieces:
4020 Jug, Sugar, Creamer

4 oz., 3⁵/₈"
Cocktail

### Decoration 611 CLUB DESIGN C
Solid Crystal with Green Enamel Lines on
  Bowl
*1931 – 1932 Crystal* (No Goblet, High
  Sherbet, 5 oz. Sherbet, or Cocktail)
Additional Pieces:
7" Plates (2419, Mayfair)
4020 Jug, Decanter

3¹/₂ oz., 2¹/₂"
Cocktail

### Decoration 612 CLUB DESIGN D
Solid Crystal with Orange Enamel Lines
  on Bowl
*1931 – 1932 Crystal* (No Goblet, High
  Sherbet, 5 oz. Sherbet, or Cocktail)
Additional Pieces:
7" Plate (2419, Mayfair)
4020 Jug, Decanter

2 oz., 2¹/₈"
Whiskey

## Blank 4024 VICTORIA

10 oz., 5⅝" Goblet

11 oz., 6⅛" Goblet

6½ oz., 4½" Saucer Champagne

5½ oz., 3⅞" Sherbet
4 oz., 3⅝" Cocktail

1 oz., 3⅛" Cordial

3½ oz., 5⅞" Rhine Wine

1½ oz., 2½" Footed Whiskey

3½ oz., 4½" Claret - Wine
2 oz., 3⅞" Sherry

12 oz., 5½" Footed Ice Tea
8 oz., 4¾" Footed Tumbler
5 oz., 4¼" Footed Juice
4 oz., 3⅜" Oyster Cocktail

66

4024 FOOTED ICE TEA, MANHATTAN CUTTING

4024 BURGUNDY COCKTAIL

4024 SILVER MIST WINE

### BLANK 4024 VICTORIAN
No Optic

*1933 – 1943 Crystal* (11 oz. Goblet, 1933 – 1942)
*1933 – 1943 Burgundy Bowl* ( 8 oz. Tumbler, 1933 – 1939; Sherry, Cordial, 1933 – 1941; Footed Whiskey, 1933 – 1942)
*1935 – 1937 Ruby Bowl* (Only Rhine Wine, Sherry, Cordial)
*1933 – 1942 Empire Green Bowl* (Oyster Cocktail, 8 oz. Tumbler, 1933 – 1939; Sherry, Cordial, 1933 – 1941)
*1933 – 1942 Regal Blue Bowl* (Footed Whiskey, 1933 – 1935; Sherry, Oyster Cocktail, 8 oz. Tumbler, 1933 – 1939; Claret – Wine, Footed Juice, 1933 – 1941)
*1934 – 1938 Silver Mist Bowl and Stem* (No 8 oz. Footed Tumbler; included 701, 1184 Tumblers)
*1933 – 1938 Silver Mist Base* (No Rhine Wine)
*1934 Mother of Pearl Iridescence on Bowl* (Sherry and Cordial only)

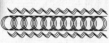

### Double Needle Etching 89 ELSINORE
*1934 – 1943 Crystal* (No 11 oz. Goblet, Cocktail, Claret – Wine, Rhine Wine, Sherry, Footed Whiskey)
Additional Pieces:
701, 887, 1184 Tumblers

### Rock Crystal Cutting 725 MANHATTAN
*1933 – 1938 Crystal* (Rhine Wine, Sherry, Footed Whiskey, 1933 – 1935)
Additional Pieces:
6", 7", 8" Plates (2337)
701, 887, 1184 Tumblers

### Cutting 726 METEOR
*1933 – 1939 Crystal* (Rhine Wine, Footed Whiskey, 1933 – 1935)
Additional Pieces:
6", 7", 8" Plates (2337)
701, 887, 1184 Tumblers
6011 Jug, Decanter

### Cutting 727 NATIONAL
*1933 –1943 Crystal*
Additional Pieces:
6", 7", 8" Plates (2337)
701, 887, 1184 Tumblers
6011 Jug, Decanter

### Cutting 728 EMBASSY
*1933 – 1937 Crystal* (11 oz. Goblet, Footed Whiskey, 1933 – 1934)
Additional Pieces:
6", 7", 8", 11" Plates (2337)
701, 887, 1184 Tumblers
6011 Jug, Decanter

### Cutting 732 SEAWEED
1934 – 1935 Crystal
Additional Pieces:
6", 7", 8" Plates (2337)
795 Hollow Stem Champagne
906 Brandy Inhaler
701, 887, 1184 Tumblers
6011 Jug, Decanter

Blank 4024, continued

***Rock Crystal Cutting 733***
**MARQUETTE**
*1934 – 1935 Crystal*
Additional Pieces:
6", 7", 8" Plates (2337)
701, 1184 Tumblers
6011 Jug, Decanter

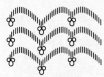

4024 REGAL BLUE
WINE

Blank 4186
MESA

13 oz. Goblet

## BLANK 4186 MESA

*1967 – 1974 Crystal*
*1967 – 1974 Olive Green*
*1967 – 1974 Brown*
*1967 – 1974 Amber*
*1967 – 1974 Blue*
*1968 – 1970 Ruby*
Additional Pieces:
8" Plate
Dessert
2-Quart Pitcher

8 oz. Sherbet

9 oz. Wine/
On the Rocks

12 oz. Double
Old Fashioned
7 oz. Juice

15 oz. Ice Tea

4186 BLUE MESA
GOBLET

Blank 5001

11 oz. Goblet
8³⁄₄ oz. Goblet
7¹⁄₂ oz. Goblet
1 oz. Cordial
³⁄₄ oz. Cordial
5³⁄₄ oz. Tall
Champagne
3¹⁄₂ oz. Wine
2 oz. Wine

4 oz. Cocktail
3 oz. Cocktail
2¹⁄₂ oz. Cocktail
5¹⁄₂ oz. Claret
4³⁄₄ oz. Claret

4 oz. Rhine Wine
2¹⁄₂ oz. Rhine Wine

5 oz. Saucer Champagne

## BLANK 5001

Regular Optic, No Optic
*c. 1906 – 1927 Crystal*

***Needle Etching 47 LARGE***
***CLOVERLEAF***
Regular Optic, No Optic
*c.1906 – 1927 Crystal*
Also on Blanks 114 and 858

5 oz. Hot Whiskey

2¹⁄₂ oz. Sherry
2 oz. Sherry
1¹⁄₂ oz. Sherry
³⁄₄ oz. Brandy

Blank 5056
AMERICAN LADY

## AMERICAN LADY

No Optic
*1934 – 1971 Crystal* (Matchings through 1973)
*1934 – 1943 Empire Green Bowl*
*1934 – 1943 Regal Blue Bowl*
*1934 – 1943 Burgundy Bowl*
*1948 – 1964 Amethyst Bowl*
Additional Pieces:
7", 8" Plates (2337), Crystal
7" Plates (2337), Amethyst, 1950 – 1958

10 oz., 6¹/₈" Goblet

5056 AMERICAN
LADY WINE,
BURGUNDY BOWL

5056 AMERICAN
LADY GOBLET,
REGAL BLUE BOWL

3¹/₂ oz., 4⁵/₈" Claret

2¹/₂ oz., 4¹/₈" Wine
3¹/₂ oz., 4⁵/₈" Claret

1 oz., 3¹/₈" Cordial

5¹/₂ oz., 4¹/₈" Sherbet

3¹/₂ oz., 4" Cocktail

4 oz., 3¹/₂" Oyster Cocktail

5 oz., 4¹/₈" Footed Juice

12 oz., 5¹/₂" Footed Ice Tea

68

# BLANK 5061
Regular Optic
*1903 – 1914 Crystal*

### Rock Crystal Cutting 4
*1903 – 1914 Crystal*
Additional Pieces:
858 Tumblers
303 Jug
Also on Blanks 766 and 863.

4¹/₂ oz. Rhine Wine

3³/₄ oz. Hollow
Stem Champagne

6 oz. Saucer
Champagne

11 oz. Goblet
10 oz. Goblet
9 oz. Goblet
8 oz. Goblet

6¹/₂ oz. Claret
4¹/₂ oz. Claret
3¹/₂ oz. Wine
2 oz. Sherry
³/₄ oz. Cordial

Not Shown:
3¹/₂ oz. Cocktail
2¹/₂ oz. Creme de Menthe
5 oz. Tall Champagne
4 oz. Hot Whiskey

³/₄ oz. Brandy
(Pousse Cafe)

# BLANK 5070
Regular Optic, No Optic
*1906 – 1927 Crystal*

### Plate Etching 231 POUPEE
(Pronounced "Poppy")
Regular Optic
*1913 – 1927 Crystal*
Additional Pieces:
300, 724 Tankards
303 Jug

### Plate Etching 232 LOTUS
Regular Optic
*1913 – 1927 Crystal*
Additional Pieces:
300, 318 Tankards
303 Jug
Also on Blank 766

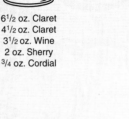

5070 CORDIAL,
POUPEE ETCHING

10 oz. Goblet
9 oz. Goblet
8 oz. Goblet
6 oz. Claret
4¹/₂ oz. Claret
4¹/₂ oz. Rhine Wine
3 oz. Wine
4 oz. Hot Whiskey
5¹/₂ oz.
Tall Champagne
2 oz. Sherry
1 oz. Cordial
³/₄ oz. Cordial

1 oz. Brandy
(Pousse Cafe)
³/₄ oz. Brandy
(Pousse Cafe)

5¹/₂ oz. Saucer
Champagne
3¹/₂ oz. Cocktail
3 oz. Cocktail
2¹/₂ oz. Creme
de Menthe
6 oz. Sherbet

4¹/₂ oz. Hollow
Stem Champagne

69

### Blank 5082

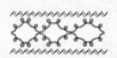

5082 GOBLET,
RICHMOND ETCHING

9 oz., 7⅝" Goblet

4½ oz., 5¾"
Claret

¾ oz., 3¾"
Cordial

2¾ oz., 5⅛" Wine

5082 AZURE WINE,
EILENE NEEDLE
ETCHING

2½ oz., 4½"
Cocktail

5 oz., 3¾"
Low Sherbet

837 OYSTER
COCKTAIL, ROGENE
ETCHING

5 oz., 5¼" Saucer
Champagne

## BLANK 5082

Regular Optic (12-Rib), Spiral Optic, Loop Optic
Made with Mother of Pearl Iridescence
*1924 – 1943 Crystal,* Regular Optic
*1924 – 1943 Green,* Spiral Optic (No Claret; Wine, 1924 – 1935)
*1924 – 1943 Green Base,* Spiral Optic (Cocktail, Cordial, 1926 – 1939)
*1924 – 1943 Amber Base,* Loop Optic (Parfait, Grapefruit, 1927 – 1934; Low Sherbet, Cocktail, Wine, Cordial, 1927 – 1939)
*1928 – 1943 Rose Bowl,* Regular Optic (Parfait, 1928 – 1934; Low Sherbet, 1928 – 1939)
*1928 – 1943 Azure Bowl,* Regular Optic (Parfait, 1928 – 1935)
*1928 – 1943 Green Bowl,* Regular Optic (Low Sherbet, 1928 – 1935)
*1925 – 1927 Blue Base,* Regular Optic
Six stems introduced in 1924; Claret and Cordial, 1926; Grapefruit, 1927.
Additional Pieces:
4095 Tumblers
4095 Jug

### Needle Etching 74 RICHMOND
Regular Optic
*1924 – 1943 Crystal*
Additional Pieces:
6", 7" Plates (2283)
945½ Grapefruit and Liner
701, 869, 887, 889, 4095 Tumblers
303, 318, 2270 Jugs

### Needle Etching 83 EILEEN
Regular Optic
*1928 – 1932 Crystal* (Claret, 1928 – 1930)
*1928 – 1932 Green* Bowl
*1928 – 1932 Rose* Bowl
*1928 – 1932 Azure* Bowl (Cordial, 1928 – 1931)
Additional Pieces:
6", 7", 8" Plates (2283)
4095 Tumblers, Jug (Solid Color)
837, 4095 Oyster Cocktail

### Plate Etching 269 ROGENE
Regular Optic
*1924 – 1929 Crystal*
Additional Pieces:
5", 6", 7", 8", 11" Plates (2283)
837 Oyster Cocktail
945½ Grapefruit and Liner
889, 4095 Tumblers
318, 4095 Jugs
2270 Jug, Jug and Cover

### Plate Etching 270 1/2 MYSTIC
Spiral Optic
*1924 – 1928 Green*
Additional Pieces:
6", 7", 8", 13" Plates (2283)
4095 Tumblers, Jug
Also on Blank 660

Blank 5082, continued

### Plate Etching 272 DELPHIAN
Regular Optic
*1925 – 1927 Blue Base*
Additional Pieces:
6", 7", 8" Plates (2283)
4095 Tumblers, Jug

### Cutting 176 KENMORE
Regular Optic
*1925 – 1927 Blue Base*
Additional Pieces:
6", 8", 13" Plates (2283)
7", 8" Plates (2337)
701, 887, 889, 4011, 4095 Tumblers
303, 2082, 4095 Jugs

### Coin Gold Band 43 PRINCESS
Needle Etching 74, Richmond, Coin Gold
    Band on Bowl and Foot
Regular Optic
*1925 – 1928 Crystal*
Additional Pieces:
6", 7" Plates (2883)
945½ Grapefruit and Liner
4095 Tumblers
2270 Jug

### Coin Gold Band 51 DUCHESS
Plate Etching 272, Delphian, Coin Gold
    Band on Bowl
Regular Optic
*1925 – 1927 Blue Base*
Additional Pieces:
6", 7", 8" Plates (2283)
4095 Tumblers, Jug

5082 GREEN
GOBLET, MYSTIC
ETCHING

5082 CORDIAL,
BLUE BASE,
DELPHIAN ETCHING

Blank 5082

6 oz., 5⅞"
Parfait

Spiral Optic

Grapefruit and Liner
(See Appendix C)

Loop Optic

5082 PARFAIT,
KENMORE CUTTING

---

## BLANK 5083
Regular Optic, Spiral Optic, Loop Optic, No Optic
*1925 – 1932 Crystal,* No Optic
*1925 – 1932 Green,* Spiral Optic
*1925 – 1932 Green Base,* Spiral Optic
*1925 – 1932 Amber Base,* Loop Optic
*1925 – 1926 Blue Base,* Regular Optic
Additional Pieces:
4095 Tumblers

Blank 5083

### Cutting 180 LYNN
No Optic
*1925 – 1926 Crystal*
Additional Pieces:
7", 8", 10" Plates (2222,
    Colonial)
701, 820, 889, 4011
    Tumblers
2082 Jug

Regular Optic

Loop Optic

No Optic

9 oz. Goblet

5083 GREEN GOBLET, 5083
GREEN BASE COCKTAIL

Not Shown:
6 oz. Parfait

2¾ oz. Wine
(Shown with
Spiral Optic)

5½ oz. Low Sherbet

5½ oz. High Sherbet
3 oz. Cocktail

71

Blank 5093

9 oz., 7¹/₈" Goblet

5093 BLUE PARFAIT GOBLET, VESPER ETCHING

## BLANK 5093

Regular Optic (12-Rib), Spiral Optic, Loop Optic

*1926 – 1940 Green,* Regular Optic (Claret, Cordial, 1926 – 1936)

*1926 – 1940 Amber,* Regular Optic

*1926 – 1940 Green Base,* Spiral Optic (Wine, 1926 – 1938; Champagne, 1926 – 1939)

*1926 – 1940 Amber Base,* Loop Optic (Wine, Claret, 1926 – 1938)

*1926 – 1927 Blue,* Regular Optic

*1926 – 1927 Blue Base,* Regular Optic

*1929 – 1940 Rose Bowl,* Regular Optic (Goblet, Low Sherbet, 1929 – 1939)

*1929 – 1940 Azure Bowl,* Regular Optic (Claret, Cordial, 1929 – 1939)

*1931 – 1937 Mother of Pearl Iridescence,* Amber Base, Loop Optic

Additional Pieces:

5000 Tumblers: 12 oz., 9 oz., 5 oz., 2½ oz.

5000 Jug

5082½ Grapefruit, 945½ Liner

Loop Optic

Spiral Optic

### Needle Etching 85 AVALON
Regular Optic

*1929 – 1930 Rose Bowl*
*1929 – 1930 Azure Bowl*

Additional Pieces (Rose, Azure):
6", 7", 8" Plates (2283)
5000 Tumblers
5082½ Grapefruit, 945½ Liner
5000 Jug

5093 CORDIAL, LOOP OPTIC, AMBER BASE

### Plate Etching 275 VESPER
Regular Optic

*1926 – 1927 Blue*
*1926 – 1933 Amber, Green*

Additional Pieces (Blue, Green, Amber):
5082½ Grapefruit, 945½ Liner
5000 Tumblers
5000 Jug
2350 (Pioneer) Dinner Service

4¹/₂ oz., 5⁵/₈" Claret

5093 CORDIAL, AZURE BOWL

6 oz., 4" Low Sherbet

3 oz., 4¹/₂" Cocktail

6 oz., 5" High Sherbet

2³/₄ oz., 4³/₄" Wine

³/₄ oz., 3³/₈" Cordial

# BLANK 5097

Regular Optic (12-Rib), Spiral Optic, Loop Optic

*1927 – 1943 Crystal,* Regular Optic

*1927 – 1929 Orchid Bowl,* Regular Optic

*1928 – 1940 Rose Bowl,* Regular Optic (Cordial, 1928 – 1938; Claret, 1928–1939)

*1927 – 1940 Green Bowl,* Regular Optic

*1927 – 1940 Amber Bowl,* Regular Optic (Cordial, 1927 – 1938)

*1931 – 1938 Mother of Pearl Iridescence* on Bowl, Green Base, Amber Base

*1931 – 1940 Green Base,* Spiral Optic

*1931 – 1940 Amber Base,* Loop Optic

Additional Pieces:

7", 8" Plates (2283)

5097½ Grapefruit, all colors except Amber Base (1927 – 1936); Amber Bowl (1927 – 1937); 945½ Liner

5000 Tumblers: 12 oz., 9 oz., 5 oz., 2½ oz.

5000 Jug in Crystal, Amber Base, Amber Bowl, Green Bowl (1927 – 1936); Rose Bowl (1928 – 1937); Mother of Pearl Iridescence (1931 – 1938)

### Needle Etching 45 GREEK

Regular Optic

*1930 – 1932 Green Bowl*

*1930 – 1932 Amber Bowl* (No Parfait)

*1930 – 1932 Rose Bowl*

Additional Pieces:

6", 7", 8" Plates (2283)

5097½ Grapefruit, 945½ Liner

5000 Tumblers

5000 Jug

Also on Blank 880

### Needle Etching 80 SPARTAN

Regular Optic

*1927 – 1943 Crystal*

*1927 – 1940 Green Bowl* (Claret, 1927 – 1936)

*1927 – 1940 Amber Bowl* (Parfait, 1927 – 1935; Wine, Cordial, 1927 – 1938; Cocktail, 1927 – 1939)

*1927 – 1929 Orchid Bowl*

Additional Pieces:

7", 8" Plates (2283)

5097½ Grapefruit, 945½ Liner

869 Tumblers (Crystal only after 1934)

5000 Tumblers

5000 Jug

Blank 5097

5097 HIGH SHERBET, ROSE BOWL, GREEK NEEDLE ETCHING

9 oz., 7 1/8" Goblet

4 oz., 5 1/2" Claret

2 1/2 oz., 4 7/8" Wine

3/4 oz., 3 1/2" Cordial

5097 PARFAIT, GREEN BOWL, SPARTAN NEEDLE ETCHING

5 1/2 oz., 5" High Sherbet

3 oz., 4 5/8" Cocktail

Loop Optic

Spiral Optic

5 1/2 oz., 4" Low Sherbet

5 1/2 oz., 6" Parfait

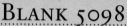

### Plate Etching 276 BEVERLY
Regular Optic
*1927 – 1933* **Crystal**
*1927 – 1933* **Green Bowl**
*1927 – 1933* **Amber Bowl**
Additional Pieces:
5097½ Grapefruit, 945½ Liner
5000 Tumblers
2350 (Pioneer) Dinner Service
5000 Jug

Blank 5098

5097 WINE, AMBER
BOWL, BEVERLY
ETCHING

9 oz., 8¼" Goblet

4 oz., 6" Claret

2½ oz., 5⅜" Wine

¾ oz., 3⅞" Cordial

3 oz., 5⅛" Cocktail

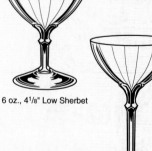

6 oz., 4⅛" Low Sherbet

6 oz., 6" High Sherbet

5098 WINE, ROSE
BOWL, VERSAILLES
ETCHING

## BLANK 5098
Regular Optic (12-Rib)
*1928 – 1943* **Crystal** (Footed Whiskey, 1928 – 1939)
*1928 – 1943* **Azure Bowl** (Cordial, 1928 – 1936; Parfait, 1928 – 1940)
*1928 – 1940* **Rose Bowl** (Cordial, 1928 – 1938; Claret, 1928 – 1939)
*1928 – 1940* **Green Bowl** (Cordial, 1928 – 1936)
*1928 – 1940* **Amber Bowl** (Claret, 1928 – 1936; Cocktail, 1928 – 1938)
*1928 – 1935* **Mother of Pearl Iridescence** on Azure Bowl
*1929 – 1936* **Topaz Bowl**
*1937 – 1943* **Gold Tint Bowl** (Claret, 1937 – 1942; No Oyster Cocktail)
*1931 – 1938* **Wisteria Bowl** (No Parfait; Oyster Cocktail, 1931 – 1934; Wine, Cocktail, 1931 – 1935)
Additional Pieces:
5082½ Grapefruit, 945½ Liner (Azure, 1928 – 1936; Amber, 1928 – 1937; not made in Wisteria)
5000 Jug (Not made in Wisteria)

### Needle Etching 84 CAMDEN
*1928 – 1930* **Green Bowl**
*1928 – 1930* **Amber Bowl**
Additional Pieces:
6", 7", 8" Plates (2283)
5082½ Grapefruit, 945½ Liner
5000 Jug (Green, Amber)

### Plate Etching 278 VERSAILLES
*1928 – 1936* **Green Bowl** (Footed Whiskey, 1928 – 1934)
*1928 – 1940* **Rose Bowl** (Parfait, 1928 – 1936; Claret, 1928 – 1939)
*1928 – 1943* **Azure Bowl** (Parfait, 1928 – 1936; Cordial, Footed Whiskey, 1928 – 1940)
Additional Pieces:
5082½ Grapefruit, 945½ Liner
2375 (Fairfax) Dinner Service (Green, Rose, Azure, Topaz)
5000 Jug (Green, 1928 – 1934; Rose, Azure, Topaz)
Also on Blank 5099

### Plate Etching 279 JUNE
*1928 – 1951 Crystal* (Matchings through 1958)
*1928 – 1940 Rose Bowl* (Parfait, Cordial, 1928 – 1938)
*1928 – 1943 Azure Bowl* (Parfait, 1928 – 1938; Cordial, 1928 – 1939)
*1929 – 1936 Topaz Bowl*
*1937 – 1943 Gold Tint Bowl* (Parfait, 1937 – 1938; Claret, 1937 – 1942)
Reintroduced in 1980 as part of the Nostalgia Line (see Appendix B for more information).
Additional Pieces:
5082½ Grapefruit, 945½ Liner (Crystal only after 1934)
2375 (Fairfax) Dinner Service (Crystal, Rose, Azure, Topaz/Gold Tint)
5000 Jug in Crystal, Rose, 1928 – 1940; Azure,1928 – 1939; Topaz/Gold Tint, 1929 – 1940.

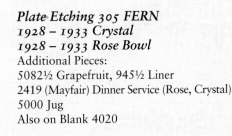

### Plate Etching 282 ACANTHUS
*1930 – 1932 Green Bowl*
*1930 – 1932 Amber Bowl*
Additional Pieces:
5082½ Grapefruit, 945½ Liner
2375 (Fairfax) Dinner Service
5000 Jug

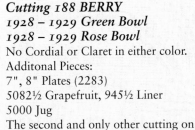

### Plate Etching 305 FERN
*1928 – 1933 Crystal*
*1928 – 1933 Rose Bowl*
Additional Pieces:
5082½ Grapefruit, 945½ Liner
2419 (Mayfair) Dinner Service (Rose, Crystal)
5000 Jug
Also on Blank 4020

### Cutting 188 BERRY
*1928 – 1929 Green Bowl*
*1928 – 1929 Rose Bowl*
No Cordial or Claret in either color.
Additonal Pieces:
7", 8" Plates (2283)
5082½ Grapefruit, 945½ Liner
5000 Jug
The second and only other cutting on colored stemware.

### Cutting 199 DELPHINE
*1931 only Crystal*
This Pattern was found listed in the July, 1931 Supplementary Price List only. It may never have been made.
Additional Pieces:
8" Plates (2283)

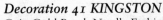

### Decoration 41 KINGSTON
Coin Gold Band, Needle Etching 84, Camden, on Bowl
*1928 – 1929 Green Bowl*
Additional Pieces:
6", 7", 8" Plates (2283)
5082½ Grapefruit, 945½ Liner
5000 Jug

Blank 5098

5098 GOBLET, AZURE BOWL, JUNE ETCHING

5098 JUICE, GREEN BOWL, ACANTHUS ETCHING

5098 PARFAIT, FERN ETCHING

2½ oz., 2⅞"
Footed Whiskey

5 oz., 3¾"
Oyster Cocktail

6 oz., 5¼" Parfait

5 oz., 4⅜"
Footed Juice

9 oz., 5¼"
Footed Tumbler

12 oz., 6"
Footed Ice Tea

Blank 5099

9 oz., 8¼" Goblet

5099 WINE, TOPAZ BOWL, VERSAILLES ETCHING

4 oz., 6" Claret

2½ oz., 5½" Wine

5099 WINE, TOPAZ BOWL, TROJAN ETCHING

¾ oz., 3⅞" Cordial

3 oz., 5⅛" Cocktail

6 oz., 4¼" Low Sherbet

## BLANK 5099

Regular Optic
*1928 – 1940* *Green Bowl* (Oyster Cocktail, 1928 – 1939)
*1928 – 1940* *Rose Bowl*
*1928 – 1943* *Azure Bowl* (Footed Tumblers, 1928 – 1934; Cordial, 1928 – 1939; Parfait, 1928 – 1942)
*1929 – 1936* *Topaz Bowl*
*1937 – 1943* *Gold Tint Bowl* (Parfait, 1937 – 1939; Cordial, 1937 – 1940)
*1931 – 1938* *Wisteria Bowl* (No Parfait; Cordial, 1931 – 1937)
Additional Pieces:
5082½ Grapefruit (No Wisteria or Azure after 1936; no Gold Tint after 1939), 945½ Liner
5000 Jug

*Plare Etching 278 VERSAILLES*
*1929 – 1936* *Topaz Bowl*
*1937 – 1943* *Gold Tint Bowl* (Parfait, 1937 – 1940; Cordial, 1937 – 1942)
Additional Pieces:
2375 (Fairfax) Dinner Service
5000 Jug
Also on Blank 5098

*Plate Etching 280 TROJAN*
1929 – 1934 Rose Bowl
1929 – 1936 Topaz Bowl
1937 – 1943 Gold Tint Bowl (Parfait, 1937 – 1939; Footed Whiskey, 1937 – 1942)
Additional Pieces:
5082½ Grapefruit, 945½ Liner
2375 (Fairfax) Dinner Service
5000 Jug

*Plate Etching 283 KASHMIR*
*1930 – 1933* *Azure Bowl*
*1930 – 1933* *Topaz Bowl*
Additional Pieces:
5082½ Grapefruit, 945½ Liner
2375 (Fairfax) Dinner Service
4020, 5000 Jugs
Also on Blank 4020

6 oz., 6⅛" High Sherbet

12 oz., 5⅞" Footed Ice Tea
9 oz., 5⅜" Footed Tumbler
5 oz., 4½" Footed Juice
4½ oz., 3½" Oyster Cocktail
2½ oz., 3" Footed Whiskey

## BLANK 5412 COLONIAL DAME

No Optic
*1948 – 1964 Empire Green Bowl*
*1950 – 1965 Crystal*
Additional Pieces:
7" Plates (2337) in Empire Green (1953 – 1964)

11 oz., 6³/₈" Goblet

1 oz., 3¹/₄" Cordial

4¹/₂ oz., 3⁷/₈"
Oyster Cocktail

3³/₄ oz., 4⁵/₈"
Claret - Wine

3¹/₂ oz., 4" Cocktail

5 oz., 4⁵/₈"
Footed Juice

6¹/₂ oz., 4⁵/₈" Sherbet

5412 COLONIAL
DAME GOBLET,
EMPIRE GREEN
BOWL

12 oz., 6" Footed Ice Tea

Blank 6000

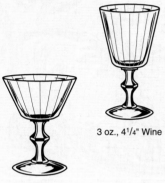

10 oz., 6¼" Goblet

3 oz., 4¼" Wine

3½ oz., 3¾"
Cocktail

6 oz., 3⅞"
Low Sherbet

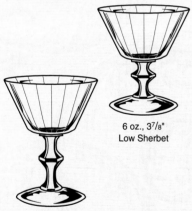

6 oz., 4¾"
High Sherbet

13 oz., 5¼" Footed Ice Tea
5 oz., 3⅝" Footed Juice
4 oz., 2⅞" Oyster Cocktail

Regular Optic (16-Rib)
*1933 – 1943 Crystal* (Footed Juice, 1933 – 1942)
*1931 – 1937 Green* (Low Sherbet, Cocktail, Footed Ice Tea, 1931 – 1934)
*1931 – 1940 Amber* (High Sherbet, Low Sherbet, 1931 – 1939)
*1931 – 1936 Topaz*
*1937 – 1940 Gold Tint* (Cocktail, 1937 – 1939; No Footed Ice Tea)

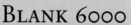

**Needle Etching 86 MONROE**
*1933 – 1939 Crystal*
Additional Pieces:
7" Plate (2283)

**Plate Etching 309 LEGION**
*1933 – 1939 Crystal*
Additional Pieces:
887, 889, 4076 Tumblers
2375 (Fairfax) Plates, Cup, Saucer, Sugar, Creamer

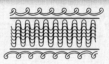

**Rock Crystal Cutting 712 WATERBURY**
*1933 – 1943 Crystal*
Additional Pieces:
7", 8" Plates (2283)

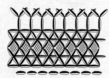

**Rock Crystal Cutting 749 CELEBRITY**
*1935 – 1943 Crystal*
Additional Pieces:
6", 7", 8" Plates (2337)
5000 Jug

**Rock Crystal Cutting 750 MEMORIES**
*1935 only Crystal* (No Oyster Cocktail, Footed Ice Tea, Footed Juice)
Additional Pieces:
7", 11" Plates (2337)

10 oz. Goblet

6002 OYSTER
COCKTAIL, TOPAZ
BOWL, MINUET
ETCHING

## BLANK 6002
Regular Optic
*1931 – 1933 Rose Bowl*
*1931 – 1933 Topaz Bowl*
*1931 – 1933 Green Base*
*1931 – 1933 Ebony Base*
Additional Pieces:
5000 Jug

### Plate Etching 284 NEW GARLAND
*1931 – 1933 Rose Bowl*
Additional Pieces:
2419 (Mayfair) Dinner Service in Rose,
    Amber, Topaz
4020, 5000 Jugs
Also on Blank 4020

### Plate Etching 285 MINUET
*1930 – 1933 Topaz Bowl*
Additional Pieces:
2419 (Mayfair) Dinner Service in Green
    and Topaz
4020, 5000 Jugs
Also on Blank 4020

4¹/2 oz. Claret

2¹/2 oz. Wine

1 oz. Cordial

6 oz. High Sherbet

6 oz. Low Sherbet

4¹/2 oz. Oyster Cocktail

5 oz. Footed Juice
2 oz. Footed Whiskey

10 oz. Footed Tumbler

13 oz. Footed Ice Tea

Blank 6003

10 oz., 6¼" Goblet

6003 GOBLET,
WISTERIA BASE,
MANOR ETCHING

3½ oz., 4³/₈"
Cocktail

1¼ oz., 3³/₈"
Cordial

13 oz., 5½"
Footed Ice Tea

4½ oz., 3¼"
Oyster Cocktail

2½ oz., 2⁷/₈"
Footed Whiskey

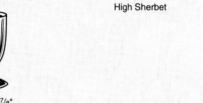

6 oz., 4⁵/₈"
High Sherbet

10 oz., 5¹/₈"
Footed Tumbler

6 oz., 3¹/₈"
Low Sherbet

5 oz., 4³/₈"
Footed Juice

## BLANK 6003

No Optic
*1931 – 1938 Crystal*
*1931 – 1938 Green Bowl*
*1931 – 1936 Topaz Bowl* (Cocktail, 1931 – 1935)
*1937 – 1938 Gold Tint Bowl*
*1931 – 1938 Wisteria Base* (Cordial, 1931 – 1935)

*Plate Etching 286 MANOR*
*1931 – 1943 Crystal* (Cocktail, Oyster
    Cocktail, Footed Tumblers, 1931
    – 1940)
*1931 – 1934 Green Bowl*
*1931 – 1936 Topaz Bowl* (Cordial,
    Footed Whiskey, 1931 – 1934)
*1931 – 1936 Wisteria Base* (Footed
    Whiskey, 1931 – 1935)
Additional Pieces:
2419 (Mayfair) Dinner Service
4020 Jug, Wisteria Base (1931 – 1934),
    Topaz Bowl (1931 – 1935), Green Bowl
Also on Blank 6007

# BLANK 6004

Regular Optic (16-Rib), Loop Optic
*1933 – 1943 Crystal,* Regular Optic
 (Cordial, 1933 – 1939; Parfait, 1933 – 1940)
*1933 – 1940 Green Base,* Loop Optic
 (Parfait, 1933 – 1934; Wine, 1933 – 1935; High Sherbet,
Oyster Cocktail, 1933 – 1939)
*1933 – 1938 Wisteria Base,* Regular Optic
 (9 oz. Footed Tumbler, 1933 – 1936)

### Plate Etching 310 FUCHSIA
Regular Optic
*1933 – 1943 Crystal* (Footed Whiskey,
 1933 – 1936; Parfait, 1933 – 1940)
*1933 – 1935 Wisteria Base*
Additional Pieces:
2440 (Lafayette) Dinner Service (Crystal)
833 Tumblers (Crystal)

### Rock Crystal Cutting 707 STAUNTON
Regular Optic
*1933 – 1943 Crystal* (No Parfait,
 Cordial)
Additional Pieces:
7", 8" Plates (2283)

### Rock Crystal Cutting 708 NAIRN
Regular Optic
*1933 – 1943 Crystal* (No Parfait,
 Cordial)
Additional Pieces:
7", 8" Plates (2283)

Blank 6004

6004 GOBLET,
WISTERIA BASE,
FUCHSIA ETCHING

9 oz., 7³/₈" Goblet

Loop Optic

5¹/₂ oz., 4¹/₈" Low Sherbet

2¹/₂ oz., 5" Wine

³/₄ oz., 3⁵/₈" Cordial

4 oz., 5⁵/₈" Claret

5¹/₂ oz., 5³/₈" High Sherbet

3 oz., 4³/₄" Cocktail

5¹/₂ oz., 6" Parfait

12 oz., 6" Footed Ice Tea
9 oz., 5¹/₄" Footed Tumbler
5 oz., 4¹/₄" Footed Juice
4¹/₂ oz., 3¹/₂" Oyster Cocktail
2¹/₂ oz., 2³/₄" Footed Whiskey

## Blank 6005

9 oz., 7³/₈" Goblet

6005 Goblet, Topaz
Base, Florentine
Etching

# Blank 6005

Regular Optic (16-Rib)
*1933 – 1943 Crystal*
*1933 – 1936 Topaz Base*
*1937 – 1941 Gold Tint Base*
*1933 – 1937 Green Base* (No Parfait)
*1933 – 1937 Mother of Pearl Iridescence* on Bowl,
 Topaz Base
Additional Pieces:
4005 Tumblers, Crystal only, 1933 – 1936

### Plate Etching 311 FLORENTINE
*1933 – 1943 Crystal*
*1933 – 1936 Topaz Base*
*1937 – 1942 Gold Tint Base*
Additional Pieces:
2440 (Layayette) Dinner Service
4005 Tumblers, Crystal only, 1933 – 1936

### Plate Etching 312 MAYDAY
*1931 only Green Base*
This pattern was found only in July 1931
 Supplementary Price List.
Additional Pieces:
2440 (Lafayette) Dinner Service

5 oz., 5⁷/₈" Claret

3 oz., 5" Wine

1 oz., 3³/₄" Cordial

7 oz., 4³/₄" Low Sherbet

5¹/₂ oz., 5⁵/₈" High Sherbet

12 oz., 5¹/₂" Footed Ice Tea
9 oz., 5¹/₈" Footed Tumbler
5 oz., 4¹/₈" Footed Juice
6 oz., 3¹/₂" Oyster Cocktail
2¹/₂ oz., 3¹/₈" Footed Whiskey

6 oz., 6" Parfait

4 oz., 4⁷/₈" Cocktail

## BLANK 6007

Regular Optic (16 – Rib), Loop Optic
*1933 – 1943 Crystal,* Regular Optic
(Footed Whiskey, 1933 – 1940)
*1933 – 1936 Amber Base,* Regular Optic
(Oyster Cocktail, 1933 – 1934)
*1933 – 1940 Green Bowl,* Loop Optic (Footed Juice, Footed Whiskey, 1933 – 1934 Low Sherbet, Cordial, 1933 – 1938)
*1933 – 1936 Topaz Bowl,* Loop Optic
*1937 – 1943 Gold Tint Bowl,* Loop Optic (Cocktail, Wine, Footed Ice Tea, 9oz. Footed Tumbler, Footed Whiskey, 1937 – 1940)
*1933 – 1938 Wisteria Bowl,* Loop Optic (Footed Juice, 1933 – 1934)

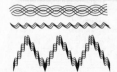

### Needle Etching 87 CASTLE
Regular Optic
*1933 – 1943 Crystal*
Additional Pieces:
6", 7", 8" Plates (2283)

### Plate Etching 286 MANOR
Regular Optic
*1933 – 1943 Crystal* (Footed Whiskey, 1933 – 1940)
Additional Pieces:
2419 (Mayfair) Dinner Service
4020 Jug, Decanter
Also on Blank 6003

### Plate Etching 313 MORNING GLORY
Regular Optic
*1933 – 1943 Crystal*
*1933 – 1934 Amber Base*
Additional Pieces:
2440 (Lafayette) Dinner Service
2270 Jug in Crystal

### Rock Crystal Cutting 709 YORK
Regular Optic
*1933 – 1943 Crystal* (Footed Whiskey, 1933 – 1934)
Additional Pieces:
7", 8" Plates (2283)

### Rock Crystal Cutting 710 BRISTOL
Regular Optic
*1933 – 1938 Crystal* (Footed Whiskey, 1933 – 1934)
Additional Pieces:
7", 8" Plates (2283)

### Rock Crystal Cutting 711 INVERNESS
Regular Optic
*1933 – 1935 Crystal*
Additional Pieces:
7", 8" Plates (2283)

### Rock Crystal Cutting 713 EATON
Regular Optic
*1933 – 1938 Crystal*
Additional Pieces:
6", 7", 8" Plates (2283)

6007 CORDIAL, CASTLE NEEDLE ETCHING

Blank 6007

10 oz., 7½" Goblet

Loop Optic

4 oz., 5⅜" Claret
3 oz., 5" Wine
1 oz., 3⅝" Cordial

5½ oz., 4" Low Sherbet

6007 FOOTED GOBLET, MORNING GLORY ETCHING

5½ oz., 5⅜" High Sherbet
3½ oz., 4⅝" Cocktail

12 oz., 5⅝" Footed Ice Tea
9 oz., 5⅛" Footed Tumbler
5 oz., 4¼" Footed Juice
4½ oz., 3⅛" Oyster Cocktail
2 oz., 2¾" Footed Whiskey

## Blank 6008

10 oz., 6⅝" Goblet

Dimple Optic

*Rock Crystal Cutting 714 OXFORD*
Regular Optic
*1933 – 1943 Crystal* (Footed Whiskey,
   1933 – 1935)
Additional Pieces:
7", 8" Plates (2283)

5½ oz., 5⅜"
High Sherbet
3¼ oz., 4¼"
Cocktail

4 oz., 5" Wine
1 oz., 3⅜" Cordial

5½ oz., 4⅛"
Low Sherbet

6008 GOBLET,
WISTERIA BOWL,
DIMPLE OPTIC

**BLANK 6008**
Regular Optic (16-Rib), Dimple Optic
*1933 – 1943 Crystal,* Regular Optic, Dimple Optic
*1933 – 1936 Wisteria Bowl,* Dimple Optic
*1933 – 1936 Topaz Bowl,* Dimple Optic
*1937 – 1938 Gold Tint Bowl,* Dimple Optic
(No Cordial, Footed Juice)

*Plate Etching 315 CHATEAU*
Regular Optic
*1933 – 1939 Crystal*
Additional Pieces:
2440 (Lafayette) Dinner Service

12 oz., 5¾" Footed Ice Tea
9 oz., 5¼" Footed Tumbler
5 oz., 4½" Footed Juice
5 oz., 3½" Oyster Cocktail

6008 CORDIAL,
CHATEAU ETCHING

*Rock Crystal Cutting 715
CARLISLE*
Regular Optic
*1933 – 1935 Crystal*
Additional Pieces:
7", 8" Plates (2283)

*Rock Crystal Cutting 716
CANTERBURY*
Regular Optic
*1933 – 1935 Crystal*
Additional Pieces:
7", 8" Plates (2283)

*Rock Crystal Cutting 717
MARLBORO*
Regular Optic
*1933 – 1938 Crystal*
Additional Pieces:
7", 8" Plates (2283)

# BLANK 6009/CA13/CA14 CAMELOT

*Regular Optic (12-Rib)*
*1933 – 1957 Crystal*
*1933 – 1940 Amber (All Footed Tumblers, 1933 – 1938)*
*1933 – 1940 Rose Bowl*
*1979 – 1980 Crystal (Matchings through 1982)*
*1979 – 1980 Blue Bowl (Matchings through1982)*

The 1979 reintroduction of Blank 6009 was called CAMELOT and included a Goblet, Dessert/Champagne, Wine, Magnum, and 16 oz. Footed Ice Tea.

***Double Needle Etching 88 CAMEO***
*1934 – 1940 Crystal*
Additional Pieces:
701, 887, 1184, 4122 Tumblers

***Plate Etching GRO3/GRO4 GRAND MAJESTY***
*1979 – 1980 Crystal*
*1979 – 1980 Blue Bowl*
Matchings through 1982 for both. Pattern included Goblet, Dessert/Champagne, Wine, Magnum and 16 oz. Footed Ice Tea.

***Plate Etching 316 MIDNIGHT ROSE***
*1933 – 1957 Crystal*
Additional Pieces:
795 Hollow Stem Champagne
846 Sherry
2464 11 oz. Tumbler
887 Whiskey Sham
1934 – 1936 906 Brandy Inhaler
1184 7 oz. Old Fashioned Cocktail, 1934 – 1943
2440 (Lafayette) Dinner Service
2464 Ice Jug

***Rock Crystal Cutting 718 DONCASTER***
*1933 – 1943 Crystal*
Additional Pieces:
6", 7", 8" Plates (2337)

***Rock Crystal Cutting 719 LANCASTER***
1933 – 1935 Crystal
Additional Pieces:
6", 7", 8" Plates (2337)

Blank 6009/CA13/CA14
CAMELOT

6009 GOBLET,
BLUE BOWL, GRAND
MAJESTY ETCHING

9 oz., 7⅝" Goblet
3¾ oz., 5⅜" Claret-Wine
1 oz., 3¾" Cordial
•13 oz., 8³⁄₁₆" Goblet
•9 oz., 7⅜" Wine

5½ oz., 4⅜" Low Sherbet

5½ oz., 5⅝" High Sherbet
3¾ oz., 4¾" Cocktail
•9 oz., 6⅜" Dessert/ Champagne

6009 CORDIAL,
MIDNIGHT ROSE
ETCHING

•16 oz., 7¾" Magnum

12 oz., 5⅞" Footed Ice Tea
9 oz., 5¼" Footed Tumbler
5 oz., 4⅜" Footed Juice
4¾ oz., 3¾" Oyster Cocktail
•16 oz., 6¾" Footed Ice Tea

•1979 Reintroductions

Blank 6009, continued

### Rock Crystal Cutting 720 NOTTINGHAM
*1933 – 1934 Crystal*
Additional Pieces:
7", 8" Plates (2337)

### Rock Crystal Cutting 721 BUCKINGHAM
*1933 – 1934 Crystal*
Additional Pieces:
7", 8" Plates

## BLANK 6010
Regular Optic (12-Rib)
*1933 – 1939 Crystal*

Blank 6010

9 oz., 7½" Goblet
4½ oz., 5⅝" Claret-Wine
1 oz., 3¾" Cordial

### Plate Etching 317 SHERATON
*1933 – 1938 Crystal*
Additional Pieces:
5" Plate (2283)
7", 8" Plates (2337)
869 Finger Bowl

5½ oz., 4⅛" Low Sherbet

### Rock Crystal Cutting 722 WELLINGTON
Cut Bowl and Stem
*1933 – 1942 Crystal*
Additional Pieces:
7", 8" Plates (2337)

5½ oz., 5½" High Sherbet
4 oz., 4⅝" Cocktail

5½ oz., 3½"
Oyster Cocktail

### Rock Crystal Cutting 722½ LEICESTER
Same as 722, Wellington, except uncut
   stem
*1933 – 1934 Crystal*
Additional Pieces:
6", 7", 8" Plates (2337)

### Rock Crystal Cutting 723 WESTMINSTER
Cut Bowl and Stem
*1933 – 1938 Crystal*
Additional Pieces:
6", 7", 8" Plates (2337)

12 oz., 5⅞" Footed Ice Tea
9 oz., 5½" Footed Tumbler
5 oz., 4½" Footed Juice

# BLANK 6011 NEO CLASSIC

No Optic
*1934 – 1943 Crystal*
*1949 – 1965 Crystal*
*1934 – 1942 Regal Blue Bowl* (Rhine Wine, 1934 – 1937; Cordial, 1934 – 1938; Sherry, 10 oz. Footed Tumbler, 1934 – 1939; Champagne, 1934 – 1941)
*1934 – 1943 Burgundy Bowl* (Rhine Wine, Sherry, 1934 – 1936; Cocktail, Wine, 1934 – 1939; Claret, Creme de Menthe, Brandy, 1934 – 1941; in 1943, only Goblet, Champagne, Footed Ice Tea made)
*1934 – 1940 Amber Base* (Claret, 1934 – 1937)
*1934 – 1940 Ruby Bowl* (Footed Juice, 1934 – 1937; Claret, 1934 – 1938)
*1936 – 1940 Empire Green Bowl* (Rhine Wine, Brandy 1936; Cordial, 1936 – 1937; Cocktail, 10 oz. Footed Tumbler, 1936 – 1938; Champagne, Footed Ice Tea, 1936 – 1939)
*1935 – 1943 Mother of Pearl Iridescent Bowl*
*1934 – 1938 Silver Mist Stem*
*1949 – 1958 Empire Green Bowl*
*1949 – 1964 Amethyst Bowl*
The 1949 reintroduction included Goblet, Champagne, Cocktail, Wine, Brandy, Footed Ice Tea, and in 1950, Footed Juice.
Additional Pieces:
6011 Jug (all colors except Silver Mist, Ruby, 1934 – 1942)
6011 Decanter (Crystal, Regal Blue Bowl, Burgundy Bowl, Empire Green Bowl, Amber Base)

**Plate Etching 322 NECTAR**
*1936 – 1942 Crystal*
Additional Pieces:
6", 7", 8" Plates (2337)
701, 1184, 4122 Tumblers
6011 Jug

**Cutting 729 ROCKET**
*1934 – 1943 Crystal*
Matchings from 1955 through 1965
Additional Pieces:
6", 7", 8" Plates (2337)
6011 Jug, Decanter

**Cutting 730 WHIRLPOOL**
*1934 – 1939 Crystal*
Additional Pieces:
6", 7", 8" Plates (2337)
795, 863 Hollow Stem Champagne
906 Brandy Inhaler
701, 887, 1184, 4122 Tumblers
6011 Jug, Decanter

**Cutting 731 CELESTIAL**
*1934 – 1937 Crystal*
Additional Pieces:
6", 7", 8" Plates (2337)
6011 Jug, Decanter

**Cutting 734 PLANET**
*1934 – 1935 Crystal*
Additional Pieces:
6", 7", 8" Plates (2337)
6011 Jug

Blank 6011
NEO CLASSIC

6011 CHAMPAGNE,
NECTAR ETCHING

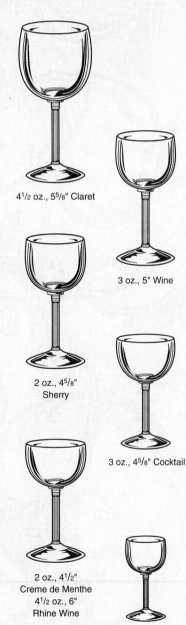

10 oz., 6³/₈" Goblet

4¹/₂ oz., 5⁵/₈" Claret

3 oz., 5" Wine

2 oz., 4⁵/₈" Sherry

3 oz., 4⁵/₈" Cocktail

2 oz., 4¹/₂" Creme de Menthe

4¹/₂ oz., 6" Rhine Wine

1 oz., 3¹/₄" Cordial

87

6011 CORDIAL,
SHOOTING STARS
CUTTING

1 oz., 4" Brandy

5½ oz., 4¾"
Saucer Champagne

5½ oz., 3¼"
Low Sherbet

2 oz., 2¾"
Footed Whiskey

4 oz., 3¼"
Oyster Cocktail

5 oz., 3⅞"
Footed Juice

10 oz., 4½"
Footed Tumbler

6011 COCKTAIL,
ATHENIAN CUTTING

6011 AMBER BASE
CORDIAL; 6011 BRANDY,
REGAL BLUE BOWL

13 oz., 5⅜"
Footed Ice Tea

6011 WINE,
BURGUNDY BOWL

## Cutting 735 SHOOTING STARS
*1934 – 1943 Crystal*
Matchings from 1955 through 1965.
Additional Pieces:
6", 7", 8" Plates (2337)

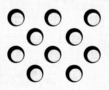

## Cutting 736 DIRECTOIRE
*1935 – 1939 Crystal*
Matchings from 1955 through 1965.
Additional Pieces:
6", 7", 8", 11" Plates (2337)
6011 Decanter

## Cutting 737 QUINFOIL
*1935 – 1937 Crystal*
Additional Pieces:
6", 7", 8" Plates (2337)
6011 Jug, Decanter

## Cutting 765 MARDI GRAS
*1937 – 1943 Crystal* (No Rhine Wine,
Sherry, Creme de Menthe, Brandy or
Footed Whiskey)
Matchings from 1955 through 1965.
Additional Pieces:
6", 7", 8" Plates (2337)
6011 Jug

## Cutting 770 ATHENIAN
*1938 – 1943 Crystal* (No Rhine Wine,
Sherry, Creme de Menthe or Footed
Whiskey)
Matchings from 1955 through 1965.
Additional Pieces:
7" Plates (2337)

## Decoration 614 GOLDEN SWIRL
Cutting 730, Whirlpool, with Gold on
Bowl
*1935 – 1937 Crystal* (No Sherry,
Oyster Cocktail, Footed Juice)
Additional Pieces:
6", 7", 11" Plates (2337)
6011 Decanter

# BLANK 6012 WESTCHESTER

No Optic

*1934 – 1970 Crystal* (Rhine Wine, Sherry, Brandy, Creme de Menthe, 1934 – 1943; Oyster Cocktail, 1934 – 1967)

*1935 – 1940 Empire Green Bowl* (Rhine Wine, 1935; Claret, Cordial, Oyster Cocktail, 10 oz. Footed Tumbler, Footed Juice, 1935 – 1938)

*1935 – 1942 Regal Blue Bowl* (Rhine Wine, Oyster Cocktail, 10 oz. Footed Tumbler, Footed Juice 1935 – 1938; Low Sherbet, Wine, Cocktail, 1935 – 1940)

*1935 – 1942 Ruby Bowl* (Rhine Wine, 1935 – 1939; Cordial, Footed Juice, 1935 – 1940; Oyster Cocktail – 1935 – 1941)

*1935 – 1943 Burgundy Bowl* (Claret, Oyster Cocktail, Footed Juice, 1935 – 1938; Sherry, Creme de Menthe, Cordial, 10 oz. Footed Tumbler, 1935 – 1940)

*1935 – 1949 Mother of Pearl Iridescence* on Bowl (Sherry, 1935 – 1939; Rhine Wine, Creme de Menthe, 1935 – 1942; Brandy, Cordial, 1933 – 1943)

### Plate Etching 318 SPRINGTIME
*1935 – 1943 Crystal*
Additional Pieces:
2440 (Lafayette) Dinner Service, some pieces in Topaz
6011 Jug
Also on Blank 891

### Plate Etching 323 RAMBLER
*1935 – 1957 Crystal*
Additional Pieces:
6", 7", 8" Plates (2337)
795 Hollow Stem Champagne
701, 1184, 4122 Tumblers

### Cutting 738 FESTOON
*1934 – 1939 Crystal*
Additional Pieces:
6", 7", 8" Plates (2337)
863 Hollow Stem Champagne
701, 1185, 4122 Tumblers
6011 Jug, Decanter

### Cutting 739 ROCK GARDEN
*1934 – 1943 Crystal*
Additional Pieces:
6", 7", 8" Plates (2337)
863 Hollow Stem Champagne
701, 1185, 4122 Tumblers
6011 Jug, Decanter

### Cutting 740 RONDEAU
*1934 – 1935 Crystal* (No 10 oz. Footed Tumbler, Footed Juice)
Additional Pieces:
7" Plates (2337)
863 Hollow Stem Champagne
701, 4122 Tumblers
6011 Jug, Decanter

### Cutting 741 WATERCRESS
*1934 – 1943 Crystal*
Additional Pieces:
6", 7", 8" Plates (2337)
863 Hollow Stem Champagne
701, 1185, 4122 Tumblers
6011 Jug, Decanter

Blank 6012
WESTCHESTER

6012 WESTCHESTER CORDIAL, RUBY BOWL

10 oz., 6⅞" Goblet

4½ oz., 5¾" Claret
3 oz., 5¼" Wine
2 oz., 4½" Sherry

3 oz., 4⅝" Cocktail
1 oz., 3½" Cordial

2 oz., 4½"
Creme de Menthe

6012 HIGH SHERBET, WATERCRESS CUTTING

1 oz., 4"
Brandy

Not Shown:
Rhine Wine

# Blank 6012
# WESTCHESTER

5½ oz., 4"
Low Sherbet

5½ oz., 5"
High Sherbet

13 oz., 5¾"
Footed Ice Tea

10 oz., 5⅜"
Footed Tumbler

5 oz., 4¼"
Footed Juice

4 oz., 3½"
Oyster Cocktail

6012 CORDIAL,
HERALDRY CUTTING

6012 BRANDY,
REGENCY CUTTING

6012 HIGH SHERBET,
DECORATION 615

Blank 6012, continued

### Cutting 742 ORBIT
*1934 – 1936 Crystal* (No 10 oz. Footed Tumbler, Footed Juice)
Additional Pieces:
6", 7", 8" Plates (2337)
863 Hollow Stem Champagne
701, 1185, 4122 Tumblers
6011 Jug, Decanter

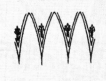

### Cutting 743 HERALDRY
*1935 – 1969 Crystal*
Matchings through 1970
Additional Pieces:
6", 7", 8" Plates (2337)
701, 1185 Tumblers
6011 Jug, Decanter

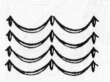

### Cutting 744 REGENCY
*1935 – 1943 Crystal*
Additional Pieces:
6", 7", 8" Plates (2337)
701, 1185 Tumblers
6011 Jug

### Rock Crystal Cutting 745 IVY
*1935 – 1943 Crystal*
Additional Pieces:
6", 7", 8" Plates (2337)
701, 1185 Tumblers
6011 Jug

### Cutting 746 GOSSAMER
*1935 – 1939 Crystal* (No Rhine Wine, Sherry, Creme de Menthe or Brandy)
Additional Pieces:
6", 7" Plates (2337)
6011 Jug

### Cutting 763 CYRENE
*1937 – 1943 Crystal* (No Rhine Wine, Sherry, Creme de Menthe or Brandy)
Additional Pieces:
6", 7", 8" Plates (2337)
6011 Jug

### Rock Crystal Cutting 764 PIERETTE
*1937 – 1939 Crystal* (No Rhine Wine, Sherry, Creme de Menthe or Brandy)
Additional Pieces:
6", 7", 8" Plates (2337)
6011 Jug

### Decoration 615
Plate Etching 323, Rambler, with Gold on Bowl
*1935 – 1949 Crystal*
Additional Pieces:
6", 7", 8" Plates (2337)
701, 1184, 4122 Tumblers
6011 Jug

### Decoration 616 ST. REGIS
Cut and Gold Encrusted Edge on Bowl
*1939 – 1943 Crystal* (No Rhine Wine, Sherry, Creme de Menthe or Brandy)
Additional Pieces:
6", 7", 8" Plates (2337)
4132 Tumblers
6011 Jug

# BLANK 6013

Narrow Optic (Crystal only), No Optic (Colors)
*1935 – 1943 Crystal*
*1935 – 1942 Regal Blue Bowl* (Wine, 1935 – 1938)
*1935 – 1942 Ruby Bowl* (Wine, 1935 – 1938)
*1935 – 1943 Burgundy Bowl* (Wine, 1935 – 1938; Cocktail,
Footed Ice Tea, 1935 – 1942)
The Low Goblet, Low Sherbet, Claret, Cordial, Oyster Cocktail,
and Footed Juice were made in Crystal only.

Blank 6013

### Plate Etching 324 DAISY
*1935 – 1943 Crystal*
Additional Pieces:
6", 7", 8" Plates (2337)
701 Tumblers
5000 Jug

### Rock Crystal Cutting 747 FANTASY
*1935 – 1936 Crystal*
Additional Pieces:
6", 7", 8" Plates (2337)
1184 Old Fashioned Tumbler
5000 Jug (1935 only)

### Rock Crystal Cutting 748 ALLEGRO
*1935 – 1943 Crystal*
Additional Pieces:
6", 7", 8" Plates
701, 1184 Tumblers
5000 Jug

### Rock Crystal Cutting 756 BOUQUET
*1935 – 1938 Crystal* (Footed Juice, 1935)
Additional Pieces:
6", 7", 8" Plates (2337)
5000 Jug

### Rock Crystal Cutting 757 SOCIETY
*1935 – 1937 Crystal*
Additional Pieces:
6", 7", 8" Plates (2337)
5000 Jug (1935 only)

6013 CHAMPAGNE,
RUBY BOWL

10 oz., 7³/₄" Goblet

9 oz., 5³/₄" Low Goblet

4 oz., 6¹/₄" Claret
3 oz., 5¹/₂" Wine

1 oz., 4" Cordial

6013 CHAMPAGNE,
ALLEGRO CUTTING

3¹/₂ oz., 5¹/₂" Cocktail

5 oz., 4¹/₈" Low Sherbet

6 oz., 5¹/₂" Saucer Champagne

13 oz., 5¹/₂" Footed Ice Tea
5 oz., 4¹/₂" Footed Juice
4 oz., 3¹/₂" Oyster Cocktail

91

## Blank 6014

9 oz., 7³/₈" Goblet
4 oz., 5⁷/₈" Claret
3 oz., 5¹/₄" Wine
1 oz., 3³/₄" Cordial

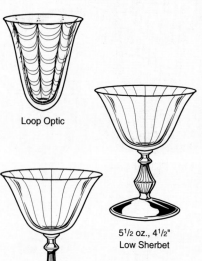

Loop Optic

5¹/₂ oz., 4¹/₂"
Low Sherbet

5¹/₂ oz., 5³/₈"
Saucer Champagne

3¹/₂ oz., 5"
Cocktail

12 oz., 6" Footed Ice Tea
9 oz., 5¹/₂" Footed Tumbler
5 oz., 4³/₄" Footed Juice
4 oz., 3³/₄" Oyster Cocktail

6014 WINE,
CORSAGE ETCHING

6014 GOBLET,
ARCADY ETCHING

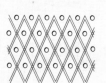

6014 CORDIAL,
PALMETTO ETCHING

---

# BLANK 6014, 6014½

Regular Optic (16 – Rib), Loop Optic
*1935 – 1958 Crystal,* Regular Optic
*1935 – 1943 Crystal,* Loop Optic (Called WAVECREST in 1936)
*1936 – 1943 Azure Bowl,* Loop Optic (Footed Juice, 1936 – 1939; Claret, 1936 – 1942)
*1937 – 1943 Gold Tint Bowl,* Loop Optic (Cordial, 1937 – 1938; Wine, Oyster Cocktail, 1937 – 1941; 9 oz. Footed Tumbler, Footed Juice, 1937 – 1942)

### Plate Etching 325 CORSAGE
Regular Optic
*1935 – 1959 Crystal*
Additional Pieces:
6", 7", 8" Plates (2337)
2440 (Lafayette) Dinner Service
2496 (Baroque) Serving Pieces
5000 Jug
Part of the Nostalgia Line (See Appendix B)

### Plate Etching 326 ARCADY
Regular Optic
*1936 – 1954 Crystal*
Additional Pieces:
2440 (Lafayette), 2375 (Fairfax), 2496 ( Baroque) combined for Dinner Service
5000 Jug

### Rock Crystal Cutting 754 CAVENDISH
Regular Optic
*1935 – 1939 Crystal*
Additional Pieces:
6", 7", 8" Plates (2337)
5000 Jug

### Rock Crystal Cutting 755 PALMETTO
Regular Optic
*1935 – 1939 Crystal*
Additional Pieces:
6", 7", 8" Plates (2337)
5000 Jug

### Cutting 758 BORDEAUX
Regular Optic
*1936 – 1943 Crystal*
Additional Pieces:
6", 7", 8" Plates (2337)
5000 Jug

### Cutting 759 WEYLIN
Regular Optic
*1936 – 1938 Crystal*
Additional Pieces:
7" Plate (2337)
5000 Jug

# BLANK 6016 WILMA

Regular Optic (16 – Rib)
*1936 – 1982 Crystal*
*1936 – 1944 Azure Bowl*
*1974 – 1982 Blue Bowl*
*1974 – 1978 Pink Bowl* (Matchings through 1982)
The Goblet, Saucer Champagne, Low Sherbet, Claret Cordial, Footed Ice Tea and Footed Juice were made from 1936 – 1982; Cocktail, Wine , Oyster Cocktail, 10 oz. Footed Tumbler, 1936 – 1973; Large Claret, 1973 – 1982; Continental Champagne, 1975 – 1982.
The Magnum (1973 – 1982), Brandy Inhaler (1976 – 1982), Cocktail/Sherry, Double Old Fashioned, Highball (1980 – 1982) were only made with Etching 327, NAVARRE.

### Plate Etching 327 NAVARRE
*1936 – 1982 Crystal* (Cocktail, Wine, Oyster Cocktail, 8 oz. Footed Tumbler, 1936 – 1973; Large Claret, Magnum, 1973 – 1982; Continental Champagne, 1975 – 1982; Brandy Inhaler, 1976 – 1982; Cocktail/Sherry, Double Old Fashioned, Highball, 1980 – 1982)
*1973 – 1978 Pink Bowl* (Goblet, Saucer Champagne, Claret, Large Claret and Footed Ice Tea only) Matchings through 1982.
*1973 – 1982 Blue Bowl* (Goblet, Saucer Champagne, Claret, Large Claret, Footed Ice Tea, 1973 – 1982; Magnum, 1978 – 1982. These were the only stems made in Blue.)
Additional Pieces:
2496 (Baroque) and 2440 (Lafayette) combined Dinner Service in Crystal only
5000 Jug

The Lenox Company bought the Navarre pattern in 1982 from the Fostoria Company. At that time Navarre was estimated to be the most successful handblown pattern Fostoria had created, accounting for nearly 9% of the bridal stemware business. Lenox continued to make the later stems in Crystal, Pink and Blue.

No difference exists between Lenox Navarre and Fostoria Navarre except that the Fostoria Pink color is similar to Fostoria's Wisteria color, and the Lenox Pink is a true pink.

### Plate Etching 328 MEADOW ROSE
*1936 – 1975 Crystal* (Cocktail, Wine, Oyster Cocktail, 10 oz. Footed Tumbler, 1936 – 1973) Matchings available through 1982.
Part of the Nostalgia Line (see Appendix B)
*1936 – 1943 Azure Bowl*
Additional Pieces:
2496 (Baroque) Dinner Service in Crystal, 1936 – 1970; Azure, 1936 – 1943
5000 Jug

### Rock Crystal Cutting 761 MELBA
*1936 – 1943 Crystal*
Additional Pieces:
6", 7", 8" Plates (2337)
5000 Jug

Blank 6016
WILMA

6016 WILMA
GOBLET, PINK BOWL

6½ oz., 6¼"
Large Claret

•6 oz., 6³/₁₆"
Cocktail/Sherry

•15 oz., 5½"
Brandy Inhaler

6016 CLARET,
AZURE BOWL,
NAVARRE ETCHING

•16 oz., 7¼" Magnum

•13 oz., 3⅝"
Double Old Fashioned

•12 oz., 4⅞" Highball

6016 WINE, AZURE
BOWL, MEADOW ROSE
ETCHING

•Produced only with
Plate Etching 327 Navarre

93

## Blank 6016
## WILMA

10 oz., 7⁵/₈" Goblet

6016 GOBLET,
RICHELIEU DECORATION

4¹/₂ oz., 6" Claret

3¹/₄ oz., 5¹/₄" Wine

³/₄ oz., 3⁷/₈"
Cordial

6 oz., 5⁵/₈"
Saucer Champagne

3¹/₂ oz., 5¹/₄" Cocktail

6 oz., 4³/₈" Low Sherbet

5 oz., 8¹/₈"
Continental
Champagne

4 oz., 3⁵/₈"
Oyster Cocktail

5 oz., 4⁵/₈"
Footed Juice

10 oz., 5³/₈"
Footed Tumbler

13 oz., 5⁷/₈"
Footed Ice Tea

---

Blank 6016, continued

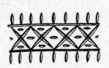

### *Rock Crystal Cutting 762*
### CUMBERLAND
### *1936 – 1939 Crystal*
Additional Pieces:
6", 7" Plates (2337)

### *Decoration 515 RICHELIEU*
Etched and Gold Filled Bowl
### *1938 – 1939 Crystal*
Additional Pieces:
7", 8" Plates (2337)
2560 (Coronet) Serving Pieces
5000 Jug

### *Decoration 696 VICTORIA*
Platinum Band on Bowl
1980 – 1982 Crystal
Only Goblet, Saucer Champagne,
Large Claret and Footed Ice Tea were
made.

### *Decoration 697 REGIS*
Gold Band on Bowl
### *1980 – 1982 Crystal*
Only Goblet, Saucer Champagne, Large
Claret and Footed Ice Tea were made.

# BLANK 6017 SCEPTRE

No Optic
*1937 – 1971 Crystal* (Matchings through 1977)
*1937 – 1943 Azure Bowl* (No 14 oz. Tumbler)
*1937 – 1943 Gold Tint Bowl* (No 14 oz. Tumbler)
Additional Pieces:
4132 Tumblers
6011 Jug

### Plate Etching 329 LIDO
*1937 – 1954 Crystal*
*1937 – 1943 Azure Bowl*
Additional Pieces:
7" Plate (2337), Crystal only
4132 Tumblers, Crystal only
2496 (Baroque) Dinner Service in Crystal, Azure
6011 Jug

### Plate Etching 330 LENOX
*1937 – 1943 Crystal*
Additional Pieces:
6", 7", 8" Plates (2337)
4132 Tumblers
6011 Jug

### Plate Etching 331 SHIRLEY
*1938 – 1956 Crystal*
Matchings through 1969 for stemware
   and plates.
Additional Pieces:
6", 7", 8", 9" Plates (2337)
2496 (Baroque) Dinner Service, 2350
(Pioneer) Cup and Saucer
6011 Jug

### Plate Etching 341 ROMANCE
*1942 – 1971 Crystal* (No 14 oz.
   Tumbler) Matchings through 1977 for
   stemware and plates.
Additional Pieces:
6", 7", 8", 9" Plates (2337)
2364 (Sonata), 2350 (Pioneer) combined
   for Dinner Service
6011 Jug
Reintroduced in Nostalgia Line
   (See Appendix B)

### Cutting 766 RIPPLE
*1937 – 1943 Crystal*
Matchings through 1969.
Additional Pieces:
6", 7", 8" Plates (2337)
4132 Tumblers
6011 Jug

### Rock Crystal Cutting 767 BEACON
*1937 – 1954 Crystal*
Matchings through 1971 for stemware.
Additional Pieces:
6", 7", 8' Plates (2337)
4132 Tumblers
2496 (Baroque) Serving Pieces
6011 Jug

### Cutting 768 BRIDAL SHOWER
*1937 – 1938 Crystal*
Additional Pieces:
6", 7", 8" Plates (2337)
4132 Tumblers
6011 Jug

6017 Goblet,
Blue Bowl, Lido
Etching

9 oz. 7³/₈ oz. Goblet

6017 High Sherbet,
Shirley Etching

3¹/₂ oz., 4⁷/₈" Cocktail

4 oz., 5⁷/₈" Claret

6017 Cordial,
Romance Etching

3 oz., 5¹/₂" Wine

6017 Low Sherbet,
Beacon Cutting

³/₄ oz., 3⁷/₈" Cordial

95

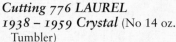

## Blank 6017
## SCEPTRE

6017 COCKTAIL,
CYNTHIA CUTTING

6 oz., 4½"
Low Sherbet

6 oz., 5½"
High Sherbet

4 oz., 3⅝"
Oyster Cocktail

5 oz., 4¾"
Footed Juice

6017 CORDIAL,
SIMPLICITY
DECORATION

9 oz., 5½"
Footed Tumbler

14 oz., 6½"
Footed Tumbler

12 oz., 6"
Footed Ice Tea

6017 JUICE, TOPAZ
BOWL

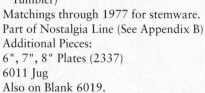

### Cutting 776 LAUREL
*1938 – 1959 Crystal* (No 14 oz.
Tumbler)
Matchings through 1977 for stemware.
Part of Nostalgia Line (See Appendix B)
Additional Pieces:
6", 7", 8" Plates (2337)
6011 Jug
Also on Blank 6019.

### Rock Crystal Cutting 777 RAYNEL
*1938 – 1939 Crystal* (No 14 oz.
Tumbler)
Matchings through 1969 for stemware
and plates.
Additional Pieces:
6", 7", 8" Plates (2337)
4132 Tumblers, Decanter
6011 Jug

### Rock Crystal Cutting 778 LUCERNE
*1938 – 1939 Crystal* (No 14 oz.
Tumbler)
Additional Pieces:
6", 7", 8" Plates (2337)
4132 Tumblers, Decanter
6011 Jug

### Rock Crystal Cutting 784 DRAPE
*1938 – 1943 Crystal* (No 14 oz.
Tumbler)
Matchings through 1969 for stemware.
Additional Pieces:
6011 Jug

### Cutting 785 CYNTHIA
*1938 – 1965 Crystal* (No 14 oz.
Tumbler)
Matchings through 1977 for stemware.
Additional Pieces:
2560 (Coronet) Serving Pieces
6011 Jug
Part of Nostalgia Line (See Appendix B)

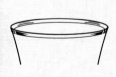

### Decoration 618 SIMPLICITY
Gold Band on Bowl and Foot
*1938 – 1967 Crystal* (No 14 oz.
Tumbler)
Matchings through 1975 for stemware
and plates.
Additional Pieces:
6", 7", 8" Plates (2337)
2350 (Pioneer) Dinner Service
6011 Jug

# BLANK 6019 RONDEL

No Optic
*1937 – 1943 Crystal*
*1937 – 1943 Azure Bowl* (No Parfait)
*1937 – 1940 Gold Tint Bowl* (No Parfait)
Additional Pieces:
6011 Jug

**Cutting 771 FEDERAL**
*1937 – 1943 Crystal* (Parfait, Footed
Juice, 1937 – 1940)
Additional Pieces:
6", 7", 8" Plates (2337)
4132 Tumblers, Decanter (1937 – 1940)

***Rock Crystal Cutting 772 TULIP***
*1937 – 1943 Crystal* (Parfait, Claret,
1937 – 1940)
Additional Pieces:
6", 7", 8" Plates (2337)
4132 Tumblers, Decanter (1937 – 1940)

**Cutting 776 LAUREL**
*1939 – 1943 Crystal*
Additional Pieces:
6", 7", 8" Plates (2337)
2574 (Raleigh) Serving Pieces
6011 Jug
Also on Blank 6017

10 oz., 5 1/8" Goblet

6 1/2 oz., 4 1/8" Sherbet

4 1/2 oz., 4 3/8" Claret

3 1/2 oz., 4" Cocktail

3 1/2 oz., 4" Wine

6 oz., 4 1/4" Parfait

5 oz., 3 7/8" Footed Juice

12 oz., 5 3/8" Footed Ice Tea

4 3/4 oz., 3 1/2" Oyster Cocktail

97

## Blank 6020 MELODY

9 oz., 7¼" Goblet

6020 CORDIAL,
MAYFLOWER
ETCHING

3½ oz., 5⅜" Wine

4½ oz., 5¾" Claret

Not shown:
Parfait

3½ oz., 4⅞" Cocktail

1 oz., 3¾" Cordial

6 oz., 4⅝" Low Sherbet

6 oz., 5½" Saucer Champagne

12 oz., 6⅜" Footed Ice Tea

9 oz., 5¾" Footed Tumbler

5 oz., 4⅞" Footed Juice

4 oz., 3¾" Oyster Cocktail

---

## BLANK 6020 MELODY
Regular Optic (12-Rib)
*1938 – 1957 Crystal*

*Plate Etching 332 MAYFLOWER*
*1938 – 1954 Crystal* (Parfait, 1938
– 1942)
Matchings through 1957.
Additional Pieces:
2560 (Coronet) Dinner Service
4140 Jug

*Rock Crystal Cutting 774 GOTHIC*
*1938 – 1943 Crystal* (Parfait, 1938
– 1942)
Additional Pieces:
6", 7", 8" Plates (2337)
5000 Jug

*Rock Crystal Cutting 775*
*KIMBERLEY*
*1938 – 1943 Crystal* (Parfait, 1938
– 1942)
Additional Pieces:
6", 7", 8" Plates (2337)
5000 Jug

98

# BLANK 6023 COLFAX

No Optic
*1940 – 1973 Crystal* (Cocktail, Oyster Cocktail, 9 oz. Footed
Tumbler, 1940 – 1972)
Matchings through 1977.

6023 GOBLET,
COLONIAL MIRROR
ETCHING

9 oz., 6³/₈" Goblet

### Tracing 94 SPENCERIAN
*1940 – 1943 Crystal*
Additional Pieces:
7" Plates (2337)

### Plate Etching 334 COLONIAL MIRROR
*1939 – 1944 Crystal*
Matchings from 1955 through 1969
Additional Pieces:
2574 (Raleigh) Dinner Service
6011 Jug

4 oz., 4³/₄" Claret-Wine

### Plate Etching 335 WILLOW
*1939 – 1944 Crystal*
Additional Pieces:
2574 (Raleigh) Dinner Service
6011 Jug

### Rock Crystal Cutting 786 DOLLY MADISON
Cut Flutes at Bottom of Bowl
*1939 – 1973 Crystal* (Matchings through
1977)
Additional Pieces:
6", 7", 8" Plates (2337), not cut
846 Sherry
833½ Tumblers
4132 Decanter
6011 Jug
Part of the Nostalgia Line
(See Appendix B)

6023 WINE,
WILLOW ETCHING

3³/₄ oz., 4³/₈" Cocktail

### Rock Crystal Cutting 787 PILGRIM
*1939 – 1951 Crystal*
Additional Pieces:
2574 (Raleigh) Dinner Service
6011 Jug

### Rock Crystal Cutting 788 CHIPPENDALE
*1939 – 1943 Crystal*
Additional Pieces:
6", 7", 8" Plates (2337)
6011 Jug

6 oz., 4⁷/₈"
Saucer Champagne

### Rock Crystal Cutting 792 CATHEDRAL
*1939 – 1943 Crystal*
Additional Pieces:
6", 7", 8" Plates (2337)
6011 Jug

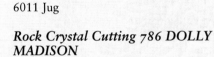

1 oz., 3³/₈" Cordial

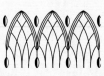

99

## Blank 6023
## COLFAX

6 oz., 4¹/₈" Low Sherbet

4 oz., 3⁵/₈" Oyster Cocktail

5 oz., 4¹/₂" Footed Juice

9 oz., 5¹/₈" Footed Tumbler

12 oz., 5³/₄" Footed Ice Tea

6023 CORDIAL,
WAKEFIELD CUTTING

Blank 6023, continued

*Rock Crystal Cutting 793 SPIRE*
*1939 – 1943 Crystal*
Additional Pieces:
6", 7", 8" Plates (2337)
6011 Jug

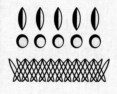

*Rock Crystal Cutting 801*
*BRIGHTON*
*1940 – 1954 Crystal*
Additional Pieces:
7", 8" Plates (2337)
6011 Jug

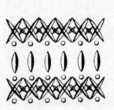

*Rock Crystal Cutting 802*
*WENTWORTH*
*1940 – 1943 Crystal*
Additional Pieces:
7", 8" Plates (2337)
6011 Jug

*Rock Crystal Cutting 820*
*WAKEFIELD*
*1942 – 1972 Crystal* (Matchings
  through 1977)
Additional Pieces:
6", 7", 8" Plates (2337)
6011 Jug

*Rock Crystal Cutting 825 REVERE*
*1950 – 1960 Crystal* (No 9 oz.
  Tumbler)
Matchings through 1971.
Additional Pieces:
7", 8" Plates (2337)

# BLANK 6024 CELLINI

Regular Optic (12 – Rib), Loop Optic
*1938 – 1970 Crystal* (Claret, Cordial, Footed Juice,
 1938 – 1943)
Matchings through 1975.

### Plate Etching 333 WILLOWMERE
Regular Optic
*1938 – 1970 Crystal*
Matchings through 1975.
Additional Pieces:
2560 (Coronet) Dinner Service
5000 Jug (Optic)
Part of the Nostalgia Line (See Appendix B)

### Rock Crystal Cutting 782 REGAL
Regular Optic
*1939 – 1942 Crystal*
Matchings from 1955 through 1957.
Additional Pieces:
6", 7", 8" Plates (2337), Optic
5000 Jug (Optic)

### Decoration 623 CORAL PEARL
All over Mother of Pearl Iridescence
 Loop Optic
*1940 – 1960 Crystal*
Matchings through 1965.
Additional Pieces:
6", 7", 8" Plates (2337), Loop Optic

6024 ICE TEA,
WILLOWMERE ETCHING

Blank 6024
CELLINI

10 oz., 7<sup>1</sup>/8" Goblet

4 oz., 5<sup>3</sup>/4" Claret

3<sup>1</sup>/2 oz., 5<sup>3</sup>/8" Wine

1 oz., 3<sup>3</sup>/4" Cordial

6 oz., 5<sup>5</sup>/8" Saucer Champagne

3<sup>1</sup>/2 oz., 4<sup>3</sup>/4" Cocktail

6 oz., 4<sup>1</sup>/4" Low Sherbet

4<sup>1</sup>/2 oz., 3<sup>1</sup>/2" Oyster Cocktail

12 oz., 5<sup>3</sup>/4" Footed Ice Tea

9 oz., 5<sup>1</sup>/4" Footed Tumbler

5 oz., 4<sup>5</sup>/8" Footed Juice

## Blank 6025
## CABOT

10 oz., 5¹/₂" Goblet

6025 GOBLET,
PLYMOUTH ETCHING

Dimple Optic

4 oz., 4" Claret-Wine
1 oz., 2⁷/₈" Cordial

3¹/₂ oz., 3¹/₂" Cocktail

6 oz., 3³/₄" Sherbet

4 oz., 3¹/₂" Oyster Cocktail

12 oz., 5⁵/₈" Footed Ice Tea
5 oz., 4¹/₄" Footed Juice

6025 OYSTER COCKTAIL,
MINUET CUTTING

---

## BLANK 6025, 6025/1 CABOT
No Optic, Dimple Optic
*1939 – 1957 Crystal,* No Optic
*1940 – 1943 Crystal,* Dimple Optic
Additional Pieces:
7" Plates (2337/1), Dimple Optic

### Plate Etching 336 PLYMOUTH
No Optic
*1939 – 1944 Crystal*
Additional Pieces:
2574 (Raleigh) Dinner Service
6011 Jug

### Plate Etching 337 SAMPLER
No Optic
*1939 – 1943 Crystal*
Additional Pieces:
2574 (Raleigh) Dinner Service
6011 Jug

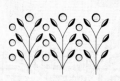

### Rock Crystal Cutting 789 SUFFOLK
No Optic
*1939 – 1959 Crystal*
Additional Pieces:
6", 7", 8" Plates (2337)
6011 Jug

### Rock Crystal Cutting 790 HAWTHORN
No Optic
*1939 – 1943 Crystal*
Additional Pieces:
6", 7", 8" Plates (2337)
6011 Jug

### Rock Crystal Cutting 791 GEORGIAN
Cut Flutes at Bottom of Bowl
No Optic
*1939 – 1943 Crystal*
Additional Pieces:
6", 7", 8" Plates (2337), not cut
6011 Jug

### Cutting 826 MINUET
Combination Rock Crystal and Gray
  Cutting
No Optic
*1950 – 1959 Crystal*
Additional Pieces:
7", 8" Plates (2574, Raleigh)
2574 (Raleigh) Serving Pieces

## BLANK 6026, 6026/2
# GREENBRIAR

Regular Optic (16-Rib), Niagara Optic
*1940 – 1973 Crystal*, Regular Optic
 (Cocktail, Cordial, Oyster Cocktail, Footed Juice, 1940
 – 1972)
Matchings through 1977.
*1940 – 1965 Crystal*, Niagara Optic (called NIAGARA)
Additional Pieces:
7" Plates (2337/2), Niagara Optic

### Plate Etching 338 CHINTZ
Regular Optic
*1940 – 1973 Crystal*
Matchings through 1977 for stemware
 except Cocktail, Cordial and Footed Juice.
Additional Pieces:
2496 (Baroque) Dinner Service
5000 Jug
Part of the Nostalgia Line (See Appendix B)

### Rock Crystal Cutting 799 MULBERRY
Regular Optic
*1940 – 1959 Crystal*
Additional Pieces:
7", 8" Plates (2337), Optic
5000 Jug
Part of the Nostalgia Line (See Appendix B)

### Rock Crystal Cutting 800 SELMA
Regular Optic
*1940 – 1943 Crystal*
Additional Pieces:
7", 8" Plates (2337), Optic
5000 Jug

### Rock Crystal Cutting 803 RHEIMS
Regular Optic
*1940 – 1943 Crystal*
Additional Pieces:
7", 8" Plates (2337), Optic
5000 Jug

Blanks 6026, 6026/2
GREENBRIAR

6062 CORDIAL,
CHINTZ ETCHING

6062 CORDIAL,
MULBERRY CUTTING

6062 GOBLET,
RHEIMS CUTTING

9 oz., 6 1/8" Low Goblet

Niagara Optic

9 oz., 7 5/8" Goblet

4 1/2 oz., 5 3/8" Claret-Wine

1 oz., 3 7/8" Cordial

6 oz., 5 1/2"
Saucer Champagne

5 oz., 4 3/4" Footed Juice

13 oz., 6" Footed Ice Tea

4 oz., 3 5/8" Oyster Cocktail

4 oz., 5" Cocktail

6 oz., 4 3/8"
Low Sherbet

103

## Blank 6027
## ENVOY

10 oz., 5¹/₄" Goblet

4 oz., 4³/₈" Wine

1 oz., 2³/₄" Cordial

5¹/₂ oz., 4¹/₄"
Saucer Champagne

5¹/₂ oz., 3¹/₄"
Low Sherbet

3¹/₂ oz., 3⁷/₈" Cocktail

4 oz., 3" Oyster Cocktail

5 oz., 4"
Footed Juice

12 oz., 5¹/₂"
Footed Ice Tea

---

## BLANK 6027 ENVOY
No Optic
*1940 – 1957 Crystal*

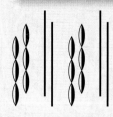

### *Cutting 804 SALON*
1940 – 1943 Crystal
Matchings from 1955 through 1957 for
stemware.
Additional Pieces:
6011 Jug

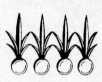

### *Cutting 805 ALOHA*
1940 – 1953 Crystal
Matchings from 1955 through 1957 for
stemware.
Additional Pieces:
6011 Jug

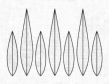

### *Rock Crystal Cutting 806*
### CADENCE
1940 – 1943 Crystal
Additional Pieces:
6011 Jug

### *Rock Crystal Cutting 824*
### PRINCESS
1950 – 1951 Crystal (No Saucer
Champagne)
Matchings from 1955 through 1957.
Additional Pieces:
7", 8" Plates (2337)

### *Decoration 619 FLORIN*
¾" Gold Band on Bowl
1940 – 1943 Crystal
Additional Pieces:
6", 7", 8" Plates (2337)
6011 Jug

# BLANK 6029 CHALICE
Not made without Cutting 812, full cut and polished stem
No Optic
*1941 – 1943 Crystal*
Additional Pieces:
863 Hollow Stem Champagne, C.F.
833½ Tumblers

*Rock Crystal Cutting 813*
*SAYBROOKE*
Full cut and polished stem
*1941 – 1943 Crystal*
Additional Pieces:
6", 7", 8" Plates (2337)
6011 Jug

9 oz., 8¼" Goblet

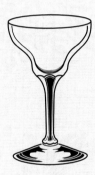

3½ oz., 5" Cocktail

6½ oz., 5⅜" Saucer Champagne

4½ oz., 3⅞" Oyster Cocktail

3 oz., 5⅞" Wine

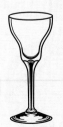

1 oz., 3⅞" Cordial

4 oz., 6¼" Claret

105

## Blank 6030, 6030/3
## ASTRID

10 oz., 7⁷/₈" Goblet

10 oz., 6³/₈" Low Goblet

3¹/₂ oz., 6" Claret-Wine
1 oz., 3⁷/₈" Cordial

6 oz., 5⁵/₈"
Saucer Champagne

3¹/₂ oz., 5¹/₄" Cocktail

Sculpted Stem
No Optic, Loop Optic
*1942 – 1974 Crystal,* No Optic
 (Oyster Cocktail, 1942 – 1972; Cocktail, Cordial, Footed Juice, 1942 – 1973)
Matchings through 1980.
*1942 – 1943 Crystal,* Loop Optic

### Plate Etching 340 BUTTERCUP
No Optic
*1942 – 1959 Crystal*
Additional Pieces:
2364 (Sonata) Dinner Service, 2350
 (Pioneer) Cup and Saucer
6011 Jug
Part of the Nostalgia Line (See Appendix B)

### Rock Crystal Cutting 814 CHRISTIANA
*1942 – 1969 Crystal,* No Optic
Matchings through 1977.
Additional Pieces:
7", 8" Plates (2337)
6011 Jug
Part of the Nostalgia Line (See Appendix B)

### Cutting 815 HOLLY
Combination Rock Crystal and Gray
 Cutting
No Optic
*1942 – 1980 Crystal*
Matchings through 1982.
Additional Pieces:
6", 7", 8" Plates (2337)
2364 (Sonata) Serving Pieces
6011 Jug
Part of the Nostalgia Line (See Appendix B)

6030 CORDIAL,
BUTTERCUP ETCHING

6030 CORDIAL,
CHRISTIANA CUTTING

6030 CORDIAL,
HOLLY CUTTING

106

### Cutting 816 GADROON
Combination Rock Crystal and Gray
  Cutting
No Optic
*1942 – 1956 Crystal*
Matchings through 1971.
Additional Pieces:
6", 7", 8" Plates (2337)
6011 Jug

### Cutting 822 TRELLIS
Combination Rock Crystal and Gray
  Cutting
No Optic
*1950 – 1954 Crystal*
Matchings through 1971.
Additional Pieces:
7", 8" Plates (2337)

6030 JUICE,
TRELLIS CUTTING

Blank 6030, 6030/3
ASTRID

6030 JUICE,
GADROON CUTTING

12 oz., 6" Footed Ice Tea

5 oz., 4⁵⁄₈" Footed Juice

4 oz., 3³⁄₄" Oyster Cocktail

6 oz., 4³⁄₈" Low Sherbet

Wavemere pattern

## BLANK 6031
Sculpted Stem
No Optic
*1942 – 1957 Crystal*

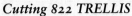

### Cutting 817 MOUNT VERNON
*1942 – 1955 Crystal*
Additional Pieces:
6", 7", 8" Plates (2337)
6011 Jug

Blank 6031

10 oz., 7⁷⁄₈" Goblet
3¹⁄₂ oz., 6" Claret-Wine
1 oz., 3³⁄₄" Cordial

10 oz., 6¹⁄₄" Low Goblet

12 oz., 5⁷⁄₈" Footed Ice Tea
5 oz., 4¹⁄₂" Footed Juice
4 oz., 3⁵⁄₈" Oyster Cocktail

6 oz., 5⁵⁄₈" Saucer Champagne
3¹⁄₂ oz., 5¹⁄₄" Cocktail
6 oz., 4¹⁄₄" Low Sherbet

Blank 6032
TEMPO

6 oz., 5³⁄₄" Saucer Champagne
6 oz., 4¹⁄₂" Low Sherbet
3¹⁄₂ oz., 5¹⁄₈" Cocktail

9 oz., 7¹⁄₂" Goblet
4¹⁄₂ oz., 5⁵⁄₈" Claret
3¹⁄₂ oz., 5¹⁄₈" Wine
1 oz., 3⁵⁄₈" Cordial

13 oz., 5⁷⁄₈" Footed Ice Tea
5 oz., 4⁵⁄₈" Footed Juice
4 oz., 3¹⁄₂" Oyster Cocktail

6032 Ice Tea, Greek
Key Cutting

# Blank 6032 TEMPO

Sculpted Stem
No Optic
*1942 – 1943 Crystal*

### Rock Crystal Cutting 818
### FORMALITY
*1942 – 1951 Crystal*
Additional Pieces:
6", 7", 8" Plates (2337)
6011 Jug

### Rock Crystal Cutting 819
### GREEK KEY
*1942 – 1943 Crystal*
Additional Pieces:
6", 7", 8" Plates (2337)
6011 Jug

Blank 6033
MADEMOISELLE

10 oz., 6¹⁄₄" Goblet

6033 Ice Tea,
Bouquet Etching

4 oz., 4³⁄₄" Claret-Wine

1 oz., 3⁵⁄₈" Cordial

4 oz., 4¹⁄₄" Cocktail

6 oz., 4³⁄₄" High Sherbet

108

6033 Parfait,
Sprite Cutting

# Blank 6033 MADEMOISELLE

No Optic
*1949 – 1971 Crystal* (Parfait, 1949 – 1966)
Matchings through 1975.

### Plate Etching 342 BOUQUET
*1949 – 1960 Crystal*
Matchings through 1975 for stemware
  and plates.
Additional Pieces:
2630 (Century) Dinner Service
2630 Jug

### Rock Crystal Cutting 821 SPINET
*1950 – 1960 Crystal*
Matchings through 1975.
Additional Pieces:
7", 8" Plates (2337)

### Cutting 823 SPRITE
Combination Rock Crystal and Gray
  Cutting
*1950 – 1968 Crystal*
Matchings through 1975 for stemware
  and plates.
Additional Pieces:
7", 8" Plates (2337)
2630 (Century) Serving Pieces
6011 Jug

Blank 6033, continued

### Decoration 625 REFLECTION
Platinum Band on Bowl
*1952 – 1971 Crystal*
Matchings through 1975.
Additional Pieces:
7", 8" Plates (2337)

6 oz., 5⅝" Parfait

5 oz., 4½" Footed Juice

6 oz., 4" Low Sherbet

4 oz., 3¾" Oyster Cocktail

13 oz., 5⅞" Footed Ice Tea

# BLANK 6036 RUTLEDGE
No Optic
*1951 – 1973 Crystal* (Parfait, 1951 – 1969)
Matchings through 1974.

### Plate Etching 344 CAMELIA
*1952 – 1965 Crystal*
Matchings through 1976 for stemware
and plates.
Additional Pieces:
2630 (Century) Dinner Service
2630 Jug

Blank 6036
RUTLEDGE

9½ oz., 6⅞" Goblet

6036 WINE,
CAMELIA ETCHING

### Cutting 827 ROSE
Combination Rock Crystal and Gray
Cutting
*1951 – 1973 Crystal*
Matchings through 1977 for stemware
and plates.
Additional Pieces:
7", 8" Plates (2337)
2666 (Contour) Serving Pieces
6011 Jug
Part of the Nostalgia Line (See Appendix B)

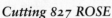

3¼ oz., 4¾" Claret-Wine

1 oz., 3¼" Cordial

3½ oz., 4⅛" Cocktail

6 oz., 4¾" High Sherbet

6036 WINE, ROSE
CUTTING

109

12 oz., 6¹/₈" Footed Ice Tea

5 oz., 4⁵/₈" Footed Juice

4 oz., 3³/₄" Oyster Cocktail

5¹/₂ oz., 5⁷/₈" Parfait

6 oz., 4¹/₈" Low Sherbet

6036 ICE TEA,
BALLET CUTTING

*Rock Crystal Cutting 828 BALLET*
*1952 – 1965 Crystal*
Additional Pieces:
7", 8" Plates (2337)

*Rock Crystal Cutting 829*
*CHATHAM*
*1952 – 1960 Crystal*
Additional Pieces:
7", 8" Plates (2337)

---

Blank 6037
SILVER FLUTES

6037 WINE,
HEATHER ETCHING

## BLANK 6037 SILVER FLUTES

Regular Optic
*1949 – 1971 Crystal*
Matchings through 1976 for Goblet, Low Goblet, High Sherbet,
Low Sherbet, Claret-Wine, and Footed Ice Tea.

*Plate Etching 343 HEATHER*
*1949 – 1971 Crystal*
Matchings through 1976 for stemware
and plates.
Additional Pieces:
2630 (Century) Dinner Service
2630 Jug
Part of the Nostalgia Line (See Appendix B)

9 oz., 7⁷/₈" Goblet
4 oz., 6" Wine
1 oz., 4" Cordial

4 oz., 5" Cocktail

9 oz., 6³/₈" Low Goblet

7 oz., 4³/₄" Low Sherbet

7 oz., 6" High Sherbet

6 oz., 6¹/₈" Parfait

12 oz., 6¹/₈" Footed Ice Tea
5 oz., 4⁷/₈" Footed Juice
4¹/₂ oz., 4" Oyster Cocktail

# BLANK 6045 CAPRI

No Optic
*1952 – 1965 Crystal*
*1952 – 1958 Bitter Green Base*
*1952 – 1958 Cinnamon Base*
Additional Pieces:
7", 8" Plates (2665)

Blank 6045
CAPRI

### *Rock Crystal Cutting 830 RONDO*
*1952 – 1954 Crystal*
Matchings through 1961.
Additional Pieces:
8" Plate (2665)

15¾ oz., 5⅞" Goblet
4¾ oz. 4" Claret - Wine
1½ oz., 2⅝" Cordial

16 oz., 6⅛" Footed Ice Tea
7¼ oz., 4⅝" Footed Juice

### *Rock Crystal Cutting 831 MARQUISE*
*1952 – 1954 Crystal*
Matchings through 1961.
Additional Pieces:
8" Plate (2665)

9 oz., 3¾" Sherbet
4¾ oz., 3" Cocktail

6045 Cordials, Bitter Green and Cinnamon Bases

---

# BLANK 6049 WINDSOR

No Optic
*1952 – 1965 Crystal*

Blank 6049
WINDSOR

### *Plate Etching 345 STARFLOWER*
1952 – 1957 Crystal
Additional Pieces:
2630 (Century) Dinner Service
2630 Jug

11¼ oz., 7" Goblet

### *Rock Crystal Cutting 832 AVALON*
*1952 – 1954 Crystal*
Matchings through 1961.
Additional Pieces:
7", 8" Plates (2337)

5 oz., 5⅝" Claret

4 oz., 5⅛" Wine

1¼ oz., 3½"
Cordial

7¼ oz., 5¼"
High Sherbet

7¼ oz., 4⅜"
Low Sherbet

4 oz., 4⅞" Cocktail

6¾ oz., 6" Parfait

4½ oz., 4"
Oyster Cocktail

5¾ oz., 4⅞"
Footed Juice

15¼ oz., 6¼"
Footed Ice Tea

## Blanks 6051, 6051½
### RINGLET, COURTSHIP

**Horizontal Optic**

10½ oz., 6³/₁₆" Goblet

4 oz., 4½"
Claret-Wine

6½ oz., 4⅜" Sherbet

3¼ oz., 3⅞"
Cocktail

1¼ oz., 3⅛"
Cordial

12¼ oz., 6⅛"
Footed Ice Tea

5 oz., 4" Footed Juice

4¼ oz., 3¾"
Oyster Cocktail

6051½ CORDIAL,
BRIDAL WREATH
CUTTING

6051½ CORDIAL,
NOSEGAY CUTTING

6051½ CORDIAL,
WHEAT CUTTING

6051½ SHERBET,
PLUME CUTTING

---

## BLANK 6051, 6051½ RINGLET, COURTSHIP

Horizontal Optic, No Optic
*1953 – 1965 Crystal*, Horizontal Optic
*1953 – 1976 Crystal*, No Optic
Matchings through 1978 for Goblet, Sherbet, Wine, Footed Ice Tea, No Optic.

### Cutting 833 BRIDAL WREATH
Combination Rock Crystal and Gray Cutting
*1952 – 1965 Crystal*
Additional Pieces:
2630 (Century) Dinner Service
6011 Jug

### Rock Crystal Cutting 834 NOSEGAY
No Optic
*1953 – 1972 Crystal*
Matchings through 1976.
Additional Pieces:
7", 8" Plates (2337)
2666 (Contour) Serving Pieces
Part of the Nostalgia Line (See Appendix B)

### Cutting 837 FOSTORIA WHEAT
Combination Rock Crystal and Gray Cutting
No Optic
*1953 – 1973 Crystal*
Matchings through 1977.
Additional Pieces:
7", 8" Plates (2337)
2666 (Contour) Dinner Service
Part of the Nostalgia Line (See Appendix B)

### Rock Crystal Cutting 838 BRACELET
No Optic
*1953 – 1956 Crystal*
Matchings through 1971.
Additional Pieces:
7", 8" Plates (2337)

### Cutting 839 PLUME
Combination Rock Crystal and Gray Cutting
No Optic
*1954 – 1960 Crystal*
Matchings through 1971.
Additional Pieces:
7", 8" Plates (2337)
2666 (Contour) Serving Pieces

### Decoration 626 WEDDING RING
Platinum Band on Bowl
No Optic
*1953 – 1975 Crystal*
Matchings through 1982.
Additional Pieces:
7", 8" Plates (2337)
2666 (Contour) Serving Pieces
Part of the Nostalgia Line (See Appendix B)

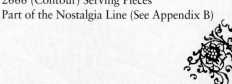

# BLANK 6052, 6052½ MOON RING, CONTINENTAL

Horizontal Optic, No Optic
*1953 – 1965 Crystal,* Horizontal Optic
*1953 – 1971 Crystal,* No Optic
Matchings through 1975, No Optic
Additional Pieces:
4132 (Standish) Tumblers, Horizontal Optic, No Optic

Blanks 6052, 6052½
MOON RING,
CONTINENTAL

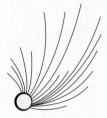

### Plate Etching 346 THISTLE
No Optic
*1953 – 1970 Crystal*
Matchings through 1971 for stemware
   and 7" plate
Additional Pieces:
2666 (Contour) Dinner Service
2666 Pitcher

### Gray Cutting 835 PINE
No Optic
*1953 – 1972 Crystal*
Matchings through 1974.
Additional Pieces:
7", 8" Plates (2337)
2666 (Contour) Dinner Service

### Cutting 836 INGRID
Combination Rock Crystal and Gray
   Cutting
No Optic
*1953 – 1970 Crystal*
Matchings through 1971.
Additional Pieces:
7", 8" Plates (2337)
2666 (Contour) Service Pieces
Cutting 836, Ingrid, resembles Cutting
   794, Ingrid.

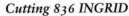

6052½ SHERBET,
PINE CUTTING

9³/₄ oz., 5⁷/₈" Goblet

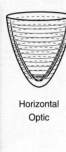

Horizontal
Optic

6052½ GOBLET,
INGRID

4¹/₄ oz., 4³/₈"
Claret-Wine

1¹/₄ oz., 3¹/₈"
Cordial

6¹/₂ oz., 4³/₈" Sherbet

3³/₄ oz., 3⁷/₈" Cocktail

5¹/₂ oz., 4⁷/₈" Footed Juice

4¹/₂ oz., 3⁷/₈" Oyster Cocktail

13 oz., 6¹/₈" Footed Ice Tea

113

10 oz., 6⅛" Goblet

Loop Optic

6055½ CORDIAL,
SPRAY CUTTING

4½ oz., 4⅝"
Claret-Wine

6 oz., 4½" Sherbet

3½ oz., 3⅞" Cocktail

12¼ oz., 6⅛" Footed Ice Tea

5½ oz., 4⅞" Footed Juice

4¾ oz., 4" Oyster Cocktail

1¼ oz., 3⁵⁄₁₆" Cordial

# BLANK 6055, 6055½
# MARILYN, RHAPSODY

Loop Optic, No Optic
*1954 – 1974 Crystal*, Loop Optic
 (Cocktail, Cordial, Oyster Cocktail, Footed Juice, 1954 – 1971)
Matchings through 1977 for Goblet, Sherbet, Claret-Wine,
 Footed Ice Tea.
*1954 – 1971 Crystal*, No Optic
*1955 – 1965 Turquoise Bowl*, No Optic
Additional Pieces:
7" Plates (2337), Loop Optic

### Rock Crystal Cutting 840 CIRCLET
No Optic
*1954 – 1969 Crystal*
Matchings through 1974.
Additional Pieces:
7", 8" Plates (2337)
2664 (Sonata) and 2666 (Contour)
 Serving Pieces

### Cutting 841 SPRAY
Combination Rock Crystal and Gray Cutting
No Optic
*1954 – 1972 Crystal*
Matchings through 1975.
Additional Pieces:
7", 8" Plates (2337)
2666 (Contour) Dinner Service

### Decoration 633 SHELL PEARL
Mother of Pearl Iridescence on Bowl
Loop Optic
*1954 – 1974 Crystal* (Cocktail, Cordial,
 Oyster Cocktail, Footed Juice, 1954
 – 1971)
Matchings through 1977 for Goblet,
 Sherbet, Claret-Wine, Footed Ice Tea.
Additional Pieces:
7" Plate (2337), Loop Optic
 2666 (Contour) Serving Pieces

### Decoration 634 ANNIVERSARY
Gold Band on Bowl
No Optic
*1954 – 1970 Crystal*
Matchings through 1975.
Additional Pieces:
7", 8" Plates (2337)

Blank 6056
DIADEM

# BLANK 6056 DIADEM
Bubble Stem, No Optic
*1954 – 1965 Crystal*

1¼ oz., 3" Cordial

5¼ oz., 4⅞" Juice

10 oz., 5⅝" Goblet

6½ oz., 4" Sherbet

3 oz., 3⅜" Cocktail

4¾ oz., 4¹/₁₆"
Oyster Cocktail

4 oz., 4¼" Claret-Wine

13 oz., 6⅜" Footed Ice Tea

---

Blank 6059
CHALICE

4½ oz., 3¾"
Wine-Cocktail

5½ oz., 4½"
Footed Juice

11 oz., 5⅜" Goblet

7 oz., 3½" Sherbet

1 oz., 2½" Cordial

6059 CHALICE
CORDIAL, EBONY
BASE

Ebony Stem

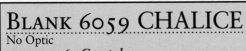

# BLANK 6059 CHALICE
No Optic
*1955 – 1965 Crystal*
*1955 – 1959 Ebony Stem*

14 oz., 5⅞"
Footed Ice Tea

## Blank 6060 CONTOUR

10½ oz., 5⅞" Goblet
5 oz., 4½" Wine-Cocktail
1 oz., 2⅞" Cordial

14 oz., 6¼"
Footed Ice Tea
5½ oz., 4½"
Footed Juice

6½ oz., 4½" Sherbet

6060 CONTOUR
CORDIAL, PINK BOWL

6060 CORDIAL,
WINDFALL CUTTING

## BLANK 6060 CONTOUR

S-shaped Stem, No Optic
*1955 – 1971 Crystal* (Matchings through 1976)
*1955 – 1965 Pink Bowl*
Additional Pieces:
2666 (Contour) Dinner Service

*Crystal Print 1 SYLVAN*
*1955 – 1965 Crystal*
Matchings through 1971 for stemware,
7" plate.
Additional Pieces:
2666 (Contour) Dinner Service

*Gray Cutting 844 SPRING*
*1955 – 1958 Crystal*
Matchings through 1971.
Additional Pieces:
7", 8" Plates (2337)

*Rock Crystal Cutting 870*
*WINDFALL*
*1958 – 1962 Crystal*
Matchings through 1971.
Additional Pieces:
7", 8" Plates (2337)

---

## Blank 6061 LYRIC

11 oz., 5⅛" Goblet
4 oz., 3⅞" Wine-Cocktail
1 oz., 2½" Cordial

12 oz., 5" Footed Ice Tea
6 oz., 4¾" Footed Juice

7½ oz., 4" Sherbet

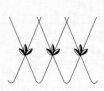

6061 LYRIC
SHERBET, PINK BASE

## BLANK 6061 LYRIC

No Optic
*1955 – 1965 Crystal*
*1955 – 1958 Pink Base*

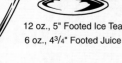

*Crystal Print 2 SKYFLOWER*
*1955 – 1958 Crystal*
Matchings through 1965.
Additional Pieces:
2666 (Contour) Dinner Service

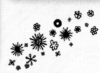

*Gray Cutting 842 REGAL*
*1955 – 1958 Crystal*
Matchings through 1965.
Additional Pieces:
7", 8" Plates (2337)

*Gray Cutting 843 CREST*
*1955 – 1962 Crystal*
Matchings through 1965
Additional Pieces:
7", 8" Plates (2337)

# BLANK 6064, 6064½
# PATRICIAN, ELEGANCE

No Optic, Narrow Optic
*1956 – 1970 Crystal,* No Optic
*1956 – 1970 Crystal,* Narrow Optic
Additional Pieces:
7" plates (2337), Narrow Optic

Blanks 6064, 6064 ¹/₂
PATRICIAN, ELEGANCE

### Crystal Print 3 ROSETTE
No Optic
*1956 only Crystal*
Matchings through 1970.
Additional Pieces:
7", 8" Plates (2337)

### Cutting 845 MAYTIME
No Optic
*1956 – 1958 Crystal*
Matchings through 1970.
Additional Pieces:
7", 8" Plates (2337)

### Cutting 846 SKYLARK
No Optic
*1956 – 1958 Crystal*
Matchings through 1970.
Additional Pieces:
7", 8" Plates (2337)

### Decoration 636 CASCADE
Mother of Pearl Iridescence on Bowl
Narrow Optic
*1956 – 1965 Crystal*
Matchings through 1970.
Additional Pieces:
7" Plates (2337), Narrow Optic

9³/₄ oz., 7" Goblet

Narrow Optic

5³/₄ oz., 5³/₄" Claret

3¹/₄ oz., 5¹/₈" Wine

4 oz., 4¹/₂" Cocktail

1 oz., 3⁵/₈" Cordial

5¹/₂ oz., 4⁷/₈" Footed Juice

7 oz., 4⁵/₈" Low Sherbet

7³/₄ oz., 3⁵/₈" Seafood Cocktail

8 oz., 5³/₄" High Sherbet

13¹/₂ oz., 6⁷/₁₆" Footed Ice Tea

## Blank 6065
## SYMPHONY

11 oz., 6⅛" Goblet

6065 CORDIAL,
SWIRL CUTTING

4 oz., 4⅝"
Wine-Cocktail

7½ oz., 4¾" Sherbet

1 oz., 3⅛" Cordial

6 oz., 4⅞"
Footed Juice

12 oz., 6⅜"
Footed Ice Tea

# BLANK 6065 SYMPHONY
No Optic, Open Stem
*1956 – 1970 Crystal*

### Crystal Print 4 LYNWOOD
*1956 – 1965 Crystal*
Matchings through 1971.
Additional Pieces:
7", 8" Plates (2337)

### Crystal Print 5 LIVING ROSE
*1956 – 1958 Crystal*
Matchings through 1971.
Additional Pieces:
7", 8" Plates (2337)

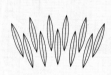

### Rock Crystal Cutting 847 BARONET
*1956 – 1965 Crystal*
Matchings through 1971.
Additional Pieces:
7", 8" Plates (2337)

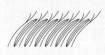

### Rock Crystal Cutting 848 SWIRL
*1956 – 1965 Crystal*
Matchings through 1971.
Additional Pieces:
7", 8" Plates (2337)

### Rock Crystal Cutting 849 HERITAGE
*1956 – 1957 Crystal*
Matchings through 1971.
Additional Pieces:
7", 8" Plates (2337)

### Decoration 635 LEGACY
Platinum Band on Bowl
*1956 – 1967 Crystal*
Matchings through 1971.
Additional Pieces:
7", 8" Plates (2337)

### Decoration 637 AMBASSADOR
Gold Band on Bowl and Foot
*1956 – 1970 Crystal*
Matchings through 1971.
Additional Pieces:
7", 8" Plates (2337)

# BLANK 6068, 6068½ PURITAN, VICTORIA

No Optic, Narrow Optic
*1957 – 1971 Crystal,* No Optic
*1957 – 1964 Crystal,* Narrow Optic (Matchings through 1969)
Additional Pieces:
7" Plate (2337), Narrow Optic

### Rock Crystal Cutting 850 AUTUMN
No Optic
*1957 – 1958 Crystal*
Matchings through 1971.
Additional Pieces:
7", 8" Plates (2337)

### Rock Crystal Cutting 851 STARDUST
No Optic
*1957 – 1970 Crystal*
Matchings through 1971.
Additional Pieces:
7", 8" Plates (2337)

### Cutting 852 GOSSAMER
No Optic
*1957 – 1962 Crystal*
Matchings through 1971.
Additional Pieces:
7", 8" Plates (2337)

### Rock Crystal Cutting 853 DUCHESS
No Optic
*1957 – 1958 Crystal*
Matchings through 1971.
Additional Pieces:
7", 8" Plates (2337)

### Rock Crystal Cutting 866 APRIL LOVE
No Optic
*1958 – 1959 Crystal*
Matchings through 1972.
Additional Pieces:
7", 8" Plates (2337)

### Decoration 638 RAINBOW
Mother of Pearl Iridescence on Bowl
Narrow Optic
*1957 – 1963 Crystal*
Matchings through 1969.
Additional Pieces:
7" Plates (2337), Narrow Optic

6068 CORDIAL, APRIL
LOVE CUTTING

10 oz., 5¾" Goblet

Narrow Optic

4¼ oz., 4½"
Wine-Cocktail

1¼ oz., 3"
Cordial

6½ oz., 4⅝" Sherbet

5 oz., 4½"
Footed Juice

13 oz., 5⅞"
Footed Ice Tea

## Blank 6071 PRELUDE

11½ oz., 6⅜" Goblet
4½ oz., 5" Wine-Cocktail
1¼ oz., 3¼" Cordial

13 oz., 6"
Footed Ice Tea

5¼ oz., 4½"
Footed Juice

7 oz., 4¾" Sherbet

6071 FOOTED ICE TEA,
KIMBERLY CUTTING

## BLANK 6071 PRELUDE

No Optic
*1957 – 1969 Crystal*

### *Rock Crystal Cutting 854* WILDWOOD
*1957 only Crystal*
Matchings through 1969.
Additional Pieces:
7", 8" Plates (2574, Raleigh)

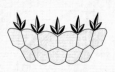

### *Rock Crystal Cutting 855* KIMBERLY
*1957 – 1965 Crystal*
Matchings through 1969.
Additional Pieces:
7", 8" Plates (2574, Raleigh)

---

## Blank 6072 CELESTE

10 oz., 6⅜" Goblet
4½ oz., 4⅞"
Wine-Cocktail
1 oz., 3⅛" Cordial

13 oz., 6⅜"
Footed Ice Tea
5¼ oz., 4⅞"
Footed Juice

7¼ oz., 5" Sherbet

## BLANK 6072 CELESTE

No Optic
*1957 – 1973 Crystal*
Matchings through 1975.

### *Rock Crystal Cutting 856* MOONBEAM
*1957 – 1965 Crystal*
Matchings through 1969.
Additional Pieces:
7", 8" Plates (2337)

### *Rock Crystal Cutting 868* SERENITY
*1958 – 1965 Crystal*
Matchings through 1971.
Additional Pieces:
7", 8" Plates (2337)

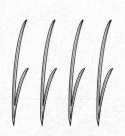

### *Cutting 881 MELODY*
*1960 – 1965 Crystal*
Matchings through 1971.
Additional Pieces:
7", 8" Plates (2337)

### *Decoration 639 BRIDAL BELLE*
Platinum Band with Polished Cutting
*1957 – 1973 Crystal*
Matchings through 1975.
Additional Pieces:
7", 8" Plates (2337)

# BLANK 6074 ENCHANTMENT
No Optic
*1958 – 1965 Crystal*

### Rock Crystal Cutting 857 SWEETBRIAR
*1958 – 1959 Crystal*
Matchings through 1968.
Additional Pieces:
7", 8" Plates (2337)

### Decoration 640 GOLDEN LOVE
Gold Band and Rock Crystal Cutting on
  Bowl
*1958 – 1965 Crystal*
Matchings through 1968.
Additional Pieces:
7", 8" Plates (2337)

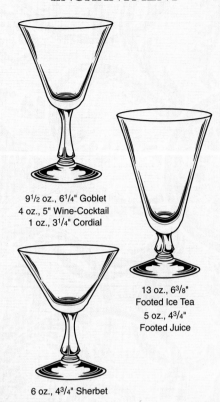

9½ oz., 6¼" Goblet
4 oz., 5" Wine-Cocktail
1 oz., 3¼" Cordial

13 oz., 6³/₈"
Footed Ice Tea
5 oz., 4³/₄"
Footed Juice

6 oz., 4³/₄" Sherbet

# BLANK 6077 NORDIC
No Optic
*1958 – 1965 Crystal*

### Gray Cutting 858 AMERICAN BEAUTY
*1958 – 1962 Crystal*
Matchings through 1965.
Additional Pieces:
7", 8" Plates (2337)

### Cutting 859 GARLAND
Combination Rock Crystal and Gray
  Cutting
*1958 – 1959 Crystal*
Matchings through 1965.
Additional Pieces:
7", 8" Plates (2337)

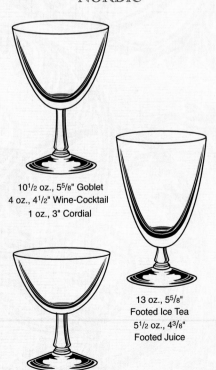

10½ oz., 5⁵/₈" Goblet
4 oz., 4½" Wine-Cocktail
1 oz., 3" Cordial

13 oz., 5⁵/₈"
Footed Ice Tea
5½ oz., 4³/₈"
Footed Juice

7 oz., 4¼" Sherbet

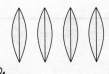

### Rock Crystal Cutting 860 ENCORE
*1958 – 1959 Crystal*
Matchings through 1965.
Additional Pieces:
7", 8" Plates (2337)

121

## Blank 6079
### KENT

11 oz., 6½" Goblet
6½ oz., 5" Sherbet
3½ oz., 3⅞" Cocktail
4 oz., 4⅞" Claret-Wine
1 oz., 3⅜" Cordial

13½ oz., 6¼"
Footed Ice Tea
5½ oz., 4¾"
Footed Juice

## Blanks 6080, 6080½
### FASCINATION

10 oz., 6¾" Goblet
8 oz., 5¾" Large Claret
6 oz., 5¾" Claret

4 oz., 5⅛"
Claret-Wine
1 oz., 3½" Cordial

4 oz., 4⅜" Cocktail

13½ oz., 5½"
Footed Ice Tea
5 oz., 4¼"
Footed Juice

7 oz., 4¾" Sherbet

6080 FASCINATION
WINE, RUBY BOWL;
CORDIAL, LILAC BOWL

6080 JUICE,
CAROUSEL CUTTING

---

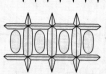

# BLANK 6079 KENT
No Optic
*1958 – 1970 Crystal*

**Polished Cutting 861 EMPRESS**
*1958 – 1970 Crystal*
Additional Pieces:
7", 8" Plates (2337)

**Polished Cutting 874 WILLIAMSBURG**
*1960 – 1969 Crystal*
Matchings through 1970.
Additional Pieces:
7", 8" Plates (2337)

# BLANK 6080, 6080½
# FASCINATION
No Optic, Loop Optic
*1958 – 1982 Crystal,* No Optic (Cocktail, Footed Juice, 1958 – 1974; 8 oz. Large Claret, 1973 – 1982)
*1958 – 1974 Lilac Bowl,* No Optic (8 oz. Large Claret, 1970 – 1972; 6 oz. Large Claret, 1973 – 1974; Matchings through 1976)
*1958 – 1965 Ruby Bowl,* No Optic (No 6 oz. or 8 oz. Large Claret)
Additional Pieces:
7" Plates, Crystal and Lilac; 8" Plates, Crystal (2337)

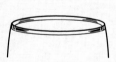

**Gray Cutting 862 TRUE LOVE**
No Optic
*1958 – 1967 Crystal*
Matchings through 1975.
Additional Pieces:
7", 8" Plates (2337)

**Gray Cutting 863 CAROUSEL**
No Optic
*1958 – 1975 Crystal*
Matchings through 1982.
Additional Pieces:
7", 8" Plates (2337)

**Decoration 641 CLASSIC GOLD**
Gold Band on Bowl
No Optic
*1958 – 1982 Crystal*
Additional Pieces:
7", 8" Plates (2337)

**Decoration 642 TROUSSEAU**
Platinum Band on Bowl
No Optic
*1958 – 1982 Crystal*
Additional Pieces:
7", 8" Plates (2337)

**Decoration 657 FIRELIGHT**
Mother of Pearl Iridescence on Bowl
Loop Optic (Blank 6080½)
*1962 – 1981 Crystal* (No Large Claret; Cocktail, Footed Juice, 1962 – 1974)
Matchings through 1982.
Additional Pieces:
7" Plates (2337), Loop Optic

# BLANK 6083 EMBASSY

No Optic
*1959 – 1971 Crystal*
Matchings through 1975 for stemware.
Additional Pieces:
7", 8" Plates (2337)

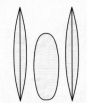

### Rock Crystal Cutting 872 WESTMINISTER
*1959 – 1972 Crystal*
Matchings through 1975.
Additional Pieces:
7", 8" Plates (2337)

### Rock Crystal Cutting 873 ST. REGIS
*1959 – 1960 Crystal*
Matchings through 1971.
Additional Pieces:
7", 8" Plates (2337)

### Decoration 644 GOLDEN GRAIL
Encrusted Gold Band on Bowl
*1959 – 1970 Crystal*
Matchings through 1975.
Additional Pieces:
7", 8" Plates (2337)

11½ oz., 6¼" Goblet
4 oz., 4⁹⁄₁₆" Wine-Cocktail
1¼ oz., 3⁵⁄₁₆" Cordial

14 oz., 6¼"
Footed Ice Tea

5½ oz., 4¾"
Footed Juice

7¾ oz., 4¾" Sherbet

# BLANK 6085 PETITE

No Optic
*1959 – 1975 Crystal* (Cordial, Footed Juice, 1959 – 1974)
Matchings through 1978 for Goblet, Sherbet, Wine, Footed Ice Tea.
Additional Pieces:
7", 8" Plates (2337)

### Gray Cutting 865 JULIET
*1959 – 1969 Crystal*
Matchings through 1973.
Additional Pieces:
7", 8" Plates (2337)

### Decoration 645 GOLDEN LACE
Crystal Print with Gold Band on Bowl
*1959 – 1975 Crystal*
Matchings through 1978 for all except
Cordial and Footed Juice.
Additional Pieces:
7", 8" Plates (2337)

### Decoration 649 MOONGLOW
Platinum Band with Gray Cutting on Bowl
*1960 – 1967 Crystal*
Matchings through 1973.
Additional Pieces:
7", 8" Plates (2337)

### Decoration 650 SUNGLOW
Gold Band with Gray Cutting on Bowl
*1960 – 1967 Crystal*
Matchings through 1971.
Additional Pieces:
7", 8" Plates (2337)

8¾ oz., 6½" Goblet
4 oz., 5" Wine-Cocktail
1¼ oz., 3½" Cordial

11¾ oz., 6³⁄₁₆"
Footed Ice Tea

5½ oz., 4⁹⁄₁₆"
Footed Juice

6 oz., 5³⁄₁₆" Sherbet

11³/₄ oz., 6³/₈" Goblet
5¹/₂ oz., 4⁷/₁₆" Wine-Cocktail
1¹/₄ oz., 3³/₁₆" Cordial

13 oz., 6³/₁₆"
Footed Ice Tea
5¹/₂ oz., 4¹/₂"
Footed Juice

7¹/₂ oz., 4⁷/₈" Sherbet

## BLANK 6086 VESPER
No Optic
*1959 – 1965 Crystal*
Matchings through 1969.

**Crystal Print 17 FANTASY**
*1959 – 1965 Crystal*
Matchings through 1969.
Additional Pieces:
7", 8" Plates (2337)

**Polished Cutting 864 SERENADE**
*1959 – 1965 Crystal*
Matchings through 1969.
Additional Pieces:
7", 8" Plates (2337)

**Rock Crystal Cutting 867
OVERTURE**
*1959 – 1960 Crystal*
Matchings through 1969.
Additional Pieces:
7", 8" Plates (2337)

**Rock Crystal Cutting 871 STAR
SONG**
*1959 – 1965 Crystal*
Matchings through 1969.
Additional Pieces:
7", 8" Plates (2337)

8¹/₄ oz., 7" Goblet
6¹/₂ oz., 5⁷/₁₆" Sherbet
3¹/₄ oz., 5¹/₄"
Wine-Cocktail
1¹/₄ oz., 3¹/₂" Cordial

11 oz., 6³/₈"
Footed Ice Tea
5 oz., 5"
Footed Juice

## BLANK 6087 CHATEAU
No Optic
*1959 – 1969 Crystal*

**Gray Cutting 869 EVENING STAR**
*1959 – 1965 Crystal*
Matchings through 1969.
Additional Pieces:
7", 8" Plates (2337)

**Decoration 643 GOLDEN FLAIR**
Gold Band on Bowl
*1959 – 1967 Crystal*
Matchings through 1969.
Additional Pieces:
7", 8" Plates (2337)

## BLANK 6089 ORLEANS

No Optic
*1960 – 1974 Crystal*
Matchings through 1977 for all except Brandy, Footed Juice.

### Rock Crystal Cutting 875 WHISPER
*1960 – 1970 Crystal*
Matchings through 1973.
Additional Pieces:
7", 8" Plates (2337)

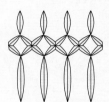

### Rock Crystal Cutting 876 DEVON
*1960 – 1962 Crystal*
Matchings through 1971.
Additional Pieces:
7", 8" Plates (2337)

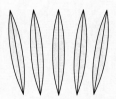

### Rock Crystal Cutting 882 BRIDAL CROWN
*1961 – 1965 Crystal*
Matchings through 1972.
Additional Pieces:
7", 8" Plates (2337)

### Decoration 647 BELOVED
Platinum Band on Bowl
*1960 – 1973 Crystal*
Matchings through 1977.
Additional Pieces:
7", 8" Plates (2337)

11$^1$/$_2$ oz., 6$^3$/$_{16}$" Goblet

4$^1$/$_2$ oz., 5$^1$/$_4$"
Wine-Cocktail

1$^1$/$_2$ oz., 4$^1$/$_{16}$"
Brandy

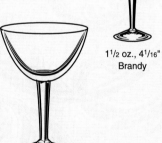

7 oz., 5$^5$/$_{16}$" Sherbet

5 oz., 4$^3$/$_4$"
Footed Juice

13 oz., 6$^3$/$_{16}$"
Footed Ice Tea

## Blank 6092
## PRISCILLA

10½ oz., 7¹/₁₆" Goblet

6092 GOBLET,
SWEETHEART ROSE
CUTTING

4 oz., 5¼"
Wine-Cocktail

1½ oz., 3½"
Cordial

7 oz., 5⁷/₁₆" Sherbet

5½ oz., 4¾"
Footed Juice

6092 SHERBET,
BURGUNDY
CUTTING

14 oz., 6³/₈"
Footed Ice Tea

126

## BLANK 6092 PRISCILLA
No Optic
*1960 – 1982 Crystal* (Footed Juice, 1960 – 1977)

### Cutting 877 SWEETHEART ROSE
Combination Rock Crystal and Gray
   Cutting
*1960 – 1974 Crystal*
Matchings through 1982.
Additional Pieces:
7", 8" Plates (2337)

### Cutting 879 BURGUNDY
Combination Cutting and Crystal Print
*1960 – 1968 Crystal*
Matchings through 1973.
Additional Pieces:
7", 8" Plates (2337)

### Rock Crystal Cutting 883 TWILIGHT
*1961 – 1962 Crystal*
Matchings through 1971.
Additional Pieces:
7", 8" Plates (2337)

### Rock Crystal Cutting 884 SPRING SONG
*1961 – 1962 Crystal*
Matchings through 1971.
Additional Pieces:
7", 8" Plates (2337)

### Decoration 648 ENGAGEMENT
Platinum Band on Bowl
*1960 – 1982 Crystal*
Additional Pieces:
7", 8" Plates (2337)

### Decoration 651 AURORA
Gold Band on Bowl
*1960 – 1974 Crystal*
Matchings through 1978.
Additional Pieces:
7", 8" Plates (2337)

### Decoration 693 REGAL
Stainless Steel on Crystal
*1972 – 1973 Crystal with Stainless
   Steel Overlay*
Only Goblet, Sherbet, Wine-Cocktail,
   Footed Ice Tea made.

# BLANK 6093 AND CUTTING 879
# STOCKHOLM

Polished and Cut Stem, No Optic
(Blank 6093 not made without Cutting 879)
*1960 – 1968 Crystal*
Matchings through 1969.
Additional Pieces:
833½ Highball, Double Old Fashioned Cocktail (Cut Base)

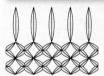

*Rock Crystal Cutting 880 BRISTOL*
*1960 – 1962 Crystal*
Matchings through 1969.
Additional Pieces:
7", 8" Plates (2337)

Blank 6093
STOCKHOLM

10¼ oz., 7³/₁₆" Goblet

4 oz., 4³/₈" Cocktail

1¼ oz., 3⁵/₈"
Cocktail

4½ oz., 5⁵/₁₆" Wine

12 oz., 6⁷/₈"
Footed Ice Tea

5 oz., 5¹/₁₆"
Footed Juice

7 oz., 5½" Sherbet

127

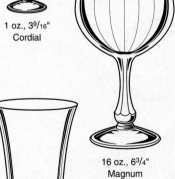

10 oz., 6³/₈" Goblet
7 oz., 6" Claret

Regular Optic

3½ oz., 5"
Wine-Cocktail

7 oz., 5³/₁₆" Sherbet

1 oz., 3⁹/₁₆"
Cordial

16 oz., 6³/₄"
Magnum

12 oz., 6⁷/₁₆" Footed Ice Tea
5 oz., 4¹¹/₁₆" Footed Juice

6096 HARVEST
RUST WINE

## BLANK 6097, HA01
## SHERATON, HARVEST

No Optic, Regular Optic
*1961 – 1982 Crystal,* No Optic
 (Claret, 1968 – 1982)
*1979 – 1982 Rust Bowl,* Regular Optic
 (Goblet, Sherbet, Claret, 16 oz. Magnum, Footed Ice Tea only;
  called HARVEST)
Additional Pieces:
833½ Highball, Double Old Fashioned, Crystal only, 1968 – 1982.

*Crystal Print 25 SENTIMENTAL*
No Optic
*1971 – 1975 Crystal* (No Wine-Cocktail, Cordial, Footed Juice)
Matchings through 1976.
Additional Pieces:
7" Plates (2337)

*Rock Crystal Cutting 885 GEORGIAN*
Hand Cut Flutes at Bottom of Bowl
No Optic
*1961 – 1982 Crystal*
Additional Pieces:
833½ Highball, Double Old Fashioned Cocktail

*Rock Crystal Cutting 886 MONTICELLO*
No Optic
*1961 – 1970 Crystal* (No Claret)
Matchings through 1971.

*Rock Crystal Cutting 898 GLOUCESTER*
No Optic
*1963 – 1969 Crystal* (No Claret)
Matchings through 1971.
Additional Pieces:
7", 8" Plates (2337)

*Decoration 653 SHEFFIELD*
Platinum Band on Bowl
No Optic
*1961 – 1982 Crystal*
Additional Pieces:
7", 8" Plates (2337)
2666 (Contour) Serving Pieces

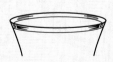

*Decoration 654 RICHMOND*
Gold Band on Bowl
No Optic
*1961 – 1982 Crystal*
Additional Pieces:
7", 8" Plates (2337)
2785 (Gourmet) Serving Pieces

*Decoration 665 ANDOVER*
Encrusted Gold Band on Bowl
No Optic
*1964 – 1974 Crystal*
Matchings through 1975.
Additional Pieces:
7", 8" Plates (2337)

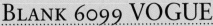

## BLANK 6099 VOGUE

No Optic
*1961 – 1974 Crystal* (Cordial, Footed Juice, 1961 –1973)
Matchings through 1978.
*1961 – 1971 Gold Tint Bowl*
Additional Pieces:
7" Plates (2337), Gold Tint

### Rock Crystal Cutting 887 EMBRACE
*1961 – 1965 Crystal*
Matchings through 1971.
Additional Pieces:
7", 8" Plates (2337)

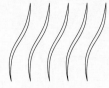

### Rock Crystal Cutting 888 CHAPEL BELLS
*1961 – 1974 Crystal*
Matchings through 1982.
Additional Pieces:
7", 8" Plates (2337)

### Decoration 652 CANDLELIGHT
Platinum Band on Bowl
*1961 – 1971 Crystal*
Matchings through 1973.
Additional Pieces:
7", 8" Plates (2337)

### Decoration 655 LOVE SONG
Platinum Band with Rock Crystal Cutting
   on Bowl
*1961 – 1973 Crystal*
Matchings through 1982.
Additional Pieces:
7", 8" Plates (2337)

### Decoration 662 GOLDEN SONG
Gold Band with Rock Crystal Cutting on
   Bowl
*1964 – 1968 Crystal*
Matchings through 1971.
Additional Pieces:
7", 8" Plates (2337)

6099 GOBLET, CHAPEL
BELLS CUTTING

11 oz., 6⁷/₈" Goblet

4¹/₂ oz., 5⁵/₁₆"
Wine-Cocktail

6¹/₂ oz., 5¹/₁₆" Sherbet

1 oz., 3⁹/₁₆"
Cordial

5¹/₂ oz., 4⁷/₈"
Footed Juice

14 oz., 6⁵/₈"
Footed Ice Tea

129

## Blank 6100
## DEBUTANTE

11 oz., 6⁵/₈" Goblet

1¹/₂ oz., 2¹³/₁₆"
Brandy

5¹/₂ oz., 5⁹/₁₆"
Tulip Wine

7¹/₂ oz., 5⁵/₁₆"
Claret

7¹/₂ oz., 4¹/₈"
Sherbet

14¹/₂ oz., 6⁵/₈"
Footed Ice Tea

---

## BLANK 6100 DEBUTANTE

No Optic
*1962 – 1973 Crystal*
*1962 – 1982 Gray Mist Bowl* (Brandy, 1962 – 1975)
Additional Pieces:
7" Plates (2337), Gray Mist

### Rock Crystal Cutting 891 EVENING BREEZE
*1962 – 1965 Crystal*
Matchings through 1971.
Additional Pieces:
7", 8" Plates (2337)

### Rock Crystal Cutting 892 COTILLION
*1962 – 1970 Crystal*
Matchings through 1973.
Additional Pieces:
7", 8" Plates (2337)

### Rock Crystal Cutting 893 PRINCESS ANN
*1962 – 1967 Crystal*
Matchings through 1971.
Additional Pieces:
7", 8" Plates (2337)

### Decoration 658 BRIDESMAID
Platinum Band with Rock Crystal Cutting on Bowl
*1962 – 1970 Crystal*
Matchings through 1971.
Additional Pieces:
7", 8" Plates (2337)

### Decoration 659 FLOWER GIRL
Gold Band with Rock Crystal Cutting on Bowl
*1962 – 1967 Crystal*
Matchings through 1971.
Additional Pieces:
7", 8" Plates (2337)

# BLANK 6101 CRYSTAL TWIST
No Optic
*1962 – 1970 Crystal*

### Rock Crystal Cutting 894 FLOWER SONG
*1962 – 1966 Crystal*
Matchings through 1970.
Additional Pieces:
7", 8" Plates (2337)

### Decoration 656 CORONET
Platinum Band with Polished Cutting on
  Bowl
*1962 – 1970 Crystal*
Additional Pieces:
7", 8" Plates (2337)

10 oz., 6 1/8" Goblet

5 oz., 4 7/8"
Wine-Cocktail

1 1/2 oz., 3 1/8" Cordial

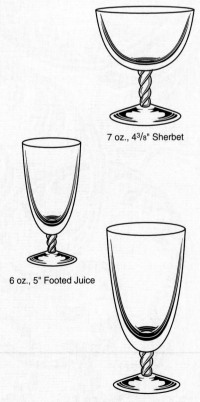

7 oz., 4 3/8" Sherbet

6 oz., 5" Footed Juice

14 oz., 6 1/8" Footed Ice Tea

131

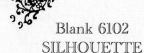

Blank 6102
SILHOUETTE

11 oz., 8" Goblet

10 oz., 7" Goblet

10 oz., 6³/₄" Large Claret

4 oz., 3³/₈" Brandy

6102 SHERBET,
BIANCA CRYSTAL
PRINT

6102 SILHOUETTE
PINK TULIP WINE

6102 SILHOUETTE
CLASSICS BLUE
GOBLET

## BLANK 6102 SILHOUETTE

No Optic
*1963 – 1982 Crystal*
*1963 – 1975 Pink* (Matchings through 1977)
The 11 oz. Goblet, 10 oz. Large Claret, Sherry, and Flute
 Champagne were added in 1980.
*1980 – 1982 Blue* (SILHOUETTE CLASSICS)
*1980 – 1982 Ebony* (SILHOUETTE CLASSICS)
Only 11 oz. Goblet, Sherbet, 10 oz. Large Claret, and Footed Ice
 Tea made.
Additional Pieces:
7" Plates (2337), Pink

### Crystal Print 19 ROSALIE
*1963 – 1975 Crystal*
Matchings through 1978.
Additional Pieces:
7", 8" Plates (2337)

### Crystal Print 22 BIANCA
*1969 – 1970 Crystal*
Matchings through 1974.
Additional Pieces:
7", 8" Plates (2337)

### Crystal Print 26 FLEURETTE
*1972 – 1974 Crystal* (Goblet, Sherbet,
 Tulip Wine, Footed Ice Tea only)
Matchings through 1977.
Additional Pieces:
7" Plates (2337)

### Rock Crystal Cutting 895 MILADY
*1963 – 1965 Crystal*
Matchings through 1971.
Additional Pieces:
7", 8" Plates (2337)

### Rock Crystal Cutting 896 VENUS
*1963 – 1974 Crystal*
Matchings through 1976.
Additional Pieces:
7", 8" Plates (2337)

### Rock Crystal Cutting 897 BRIDAL SHOWER
*1963 – 1970 Crystal*
Matchings through 1973.
Additional Pieces:
7", 8" Plates (2337)

Blank 6102, continued

### Gray Cutting 899 LINEAL
*1963 – 1965 Crystal*
Matchings through 1971.
Additional Pieces:
7", 8" Plates (2337)

### Cutting 920 WEDDING FLOWER
Combination Silver Mist and Gray
  Cutting on Bowl
*1969 – 1970 Crystal*
Matchings through 1971.
Additional Pieces:
7", 8" Plates (2337)

### Decoration 660 INVITATION
Platinum Band on Bowl
*1963 – 1982 Crystal*
Additional Pieces:
7", 8" Plates (2337)
2785 (Gourmet) Serving Pieces

### Decoration 661 VERMEIL
Gold Band on Bowl
*1963 – 1974 Crystal*
Matchings through 1978.
Additional Pieces:
7", 8" Plates (2337)
2785 (Gourmet) Serving Pieces

### Decoration 663 PLATINA ROSE
Platinum Band with Crystal Print on Bowl
*1964 – 1974 Crystal*
Matchings through 1982.
Additional Pieces:
7", 8" Plates (2337)

### Decoration 664 GOLDEN GARLAND
Gold Band with Crystal Print on Bowl
*1964 – 1967 Crystal*
Matchings through 1971.
Additional Pieces:
7", 8" Plates (2337)

## Blank 6102
## SILHOUETTE

6102 GOBLET,
WEDDING FLOWER
CUTTING

5$^{1/2}$ oz., 5$^{7/8}$" Tulip Wine

7$^{1/2}$ oz., 5$^{3/4}$" Claret

8 oz., 5$^{1/8}$" Sherbet

14 oz., 6$^{5/8}$" Footed Ice Tea

Not Shown:
7 oz., 7$^{9/16}$" Flute Champagne
4 oz., 5$^{1/2}$" Cocktail-Sherry

## Blank 6103 GLAMOUR

12 oz., 7¼" Goblet

6103 GLAMOUR
GREEN MIST CLARET

7 oz., 6³⁄₈" Tulip Wine

7½ oz., 5¾" Claret

8 oz., 5⅛" Sherbet

3½ oz., 3⅞"
Brandy

14 oz., 6⁵⁄₈"
Footed Ice Tea

6103 TULIP WINE,
BARCELONA CRYSTAL
PRINT

---

## BLANK 6103 GLAMOUR

No Optic
1964 – 1982 Crystal
1968 – 1982 Green Mist Bowl
1969 – 1982 Gray Mist Bowl
1970 – 1982 Blue Bowl
1969 – 1975 Onyx Base

### Crystal Print 21 NUPTIAL
*1969 – 1974 Crystal*
Matchings through 1976.
Additional Pieces:
7", 8" Plates (2337)

### Crystal Print 27 BARCELONA
*1971 – 1973 Crystal*
Matchings through 1977.
Additional Pieces:
7" Plates (2337)

### Gray Cutting 900 BALLERINA
*1964 – 1967 Crystal*
Matchings through 1971.
Additional Pieces:
7", 8" Plates (2337)

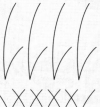

### Gray Cutting 901 FOUNTAIN
*1964 – 1965 Crystal*
Matchings through 1971.
Additional Pieces:
7", 8" Plates (2337)

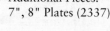

### Gray Cutting 904 FOREVER
*1964 – 1965 Crystal*
Matchings through 1971.
Additional Pieces:
7", 8" Plates (2337

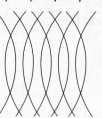

### Decoration 666 ANNOUNCEMENT
Platinum Band on Bowl
*1964 – 1982 Crystal*
Additional Pieces:
7", 8" Plates (2337)
2785 (Gourmet) Serving Pieces

### Decoration 667 REHEARSAL
Gold Band on Bowl
*1964 – 1974 Crystal*
Matchings through 1976.
Additional Pieces:
7", 8" Plates (2337)
2785 (Gourmet) Serving Pieces

### Decoration 681 CHERISH
Platinum Band on Bowl
*1969 – 1982 Gray Mist Bowl*
Additional Pieces:
7" Plates (2337), Gray Mist

### Decoration 685 SOMETHING BLUE
Platinum Band on Bowl
*1970 – 1975 Blue Bowl*
Matchings through 1982.

# BLANK 6104, 6104½
# JEFFERSON

Blank 6104½ has polished, cut stem.
No Optic
*1964 – 1972 Crystal*
Matchings through 1973.

## Rock Crystal Cutting 902 SAVANNAH
*1964 – 1968 Crystal*
Matchings through 1971.
Additional Pieces:
7", 8" Plates (2337)

## Rock Crystal Cutting 903 TIARA
*1964 – 1970 Crystal*
Matchings through 1972.
Additional Pieces:
7", 8" Plates (2337)

## Rock Crystal Cutting 905 QUEEN ANNE
*1965 – 1970 Crystal*
Matchings through 1972.
Additional Pieces:
7", 8" Plates (2337)

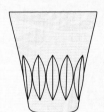

## Rock Crystal Cutting 912 MONTE CARLO
*1967 – 1970 Crystal*
Matchings through 1972.
Additional Pieces:
7", 8" Plates (2337)

## Rock Crystal Cutting 915 CARILLON
*1967 – 1968 Crystal*
Matchings through 1971.
Additional Pieces:
7", 8" Plates (2337)

## Rock Crystal Cutting 917 BEACON HILL
Polished Cut Stem (Blank 6104½)
*1968 – 1970 Crystal*
Matchings through 1971.
Additional Pieces:
7", 8" Plates (2574, Raleigh)

6104 WINE, SAVANNAH CUTTING

11 oz., 6 7/8" Goblet

7 oz., 5" Claret

6 oz., 5 5/8" Wine

9 oz., 5" Sherbet

1 1/2 oz., 3 1/2" Cordial

13 1/2 oz., 6 1/2" Footed Ice Tea

135

## Blank 6105
## BERKSHIRE

11 oz., 7 1/8" Goblet

9 oz., 5 3/4" Sherbet

13 1/2 oz., 6 7/8" Footed Ice Tea

# BLANK 6105 BERKSHIRE
No Optic
*1965 – 1974 Crystal*
Matchings through 1975.

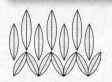

### Rock Crystal Cutting 906 GEORGETOWN
*1965 – 1973 Crystal*
Matchings through 1975.
Additional Pieces:
7", 8" Plates (2337)

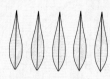

### Rock Crystal Cutting 907 CANTATA
*1965 – 1970 Crystal*
Matchings through 1971.
Additional Pieces:
7", 8" Plates (2337)

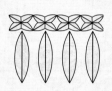

### Rock Crystal Cutting 914 STRATFORD
*1967 – 1968 Crystal*
Matchings through 1971.
Additional Pieces:
7", 8" Plates (2337)

7 oz., 6 1/2" Claret

1 1/2 oz., 3 7/8" Cordial

6 oz., 5 3/4" Wine

## BLANK 6106 CELEBRITY
No Optic
*1966 – 1971 Crystal*

**Rock Crystal Cutting 908 EMPIRE**
*1966 – 1969 Crystal*
Matchings through 1970.
Additional Pieces:
7", 8" Plates (2574, Raleigh)

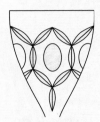

**Rock Crystal Cutting 909 BERKELEY**
*1966 –1967 Crystal*
Matchings through 1970.
Additional Pieces:
7", 8" Plates (2337)

**Decoration 674 BROCADE**
Gold Encrusted Band on Bowl
*1966 – 1970 Crystal*
Additional Pieces:
7", 8" Plates (2337)

**Decoration 675 MANTILLA**
Platinum Encrusted Band on Bowl
*1966 – 1970 Crystal*
Additional Pieces:
7", 8" Plates (2337)

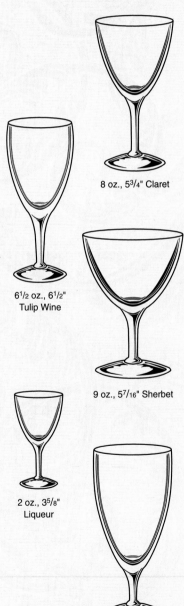

12 oz., 7" Goblet

8 oz., 5³/4" Claret

6¹/2 oz., 6¹/2"
Tulip Wine

9 oz., 5⁷/16" Sherbet

2 oz., 3⁵/8"
Liqueur

14 oz., 6³/4" Footed Ice Tea

## Blank 6107
## INSPIRATION

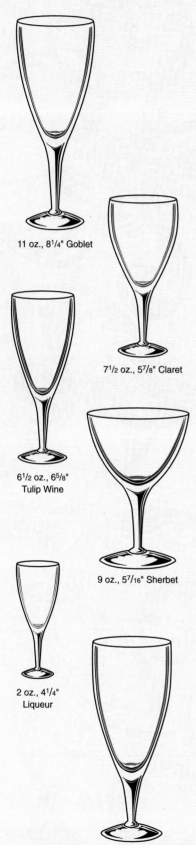

11 oz., 8¹/₄" Goblet

7¹/₂ oz., 5⁷/₈" Claret

6¹/₂ oz., 6⁵/₈"
Tulip Wine

9 oz., 5⁷/₁₆" Sherbet

2 oz., 4¹/₄"
Liqueur

14 oz., 7¹/₄" Footed Ice Tea

*Rock Crystal Cutting 910*
*MATRIMONY*
No Optic
*1966 – 1969 Crystal*
Matchings through 1972.
Additional Pieces:
7", 8" Plates (2337)

***Rock Crystal Cutting 911 ORANGE
BLOSSOM***
No Optic
*1966 – 1967 Crystal*
Matchings through 1971.
Additional Pieces:
7", 8" Plates (2337)

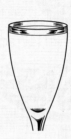

***Decoration 670 REMEMBRANCE***
Gold Band on Bowl
No Optic
*1966 – 1968 Crystal*
Matchings through 1971.
Additional Pieces:
7", 8" Plates (2337)

***Decoration 671 LOVELIGHT***
Platinum Band on Bowl
No Optic
*1966 – 1970 Crystal*
Matchings through 1971.
Additional Pieces:
7", 8" Plates (2337)

***Decoration 672 ALLEGRO***
Gold Band on Bowl
Narrow Optic
*1966 – 1970 Crystal*
Matchings through 1971.
Additional Pieces:
7" Plates (2337), Narrow Optic

***Decoration 673 BETROTHAL***
Platinum Band on Bowl
Narrow Optic
*1966 – 1970 Crystal*
Matchings through 1972.
Additional Pieces:
7" Plates (2337), Narrow Optic

# BLANK 6108 PRECEDENCE

No Optic
*1967 – 1973 Crystal*
*1967 – 1973 Gray Mist Bowl*
Matchings through 1974 for all except Liqueur.
*1967 – 1974 Onyx Bowl*
Additional Pieces:
7" Plates (2337), Crystal and Gray Mist
8" Plates (2337), Crystal only

12 oz., 7¹/₂" Goblet

8 oz., 6¹/₈" Claret

9 oz., 5³/₄" Champagne

7 oz., 5³/₄" Tulip Wine

14 oz., 6¹/₂" Footed Ice Tea

2 oz., 3⁷/₈"
Liqueur

6108 CORDIAL,
GRAY MIST BOWL

6108 GOBLET,
ONYX BOWL

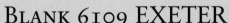

10 oz., 7¹/₂" Goblet

7 oz., 5⁷/₈" Sherbet

6 oz., 5⁵/₈" Wine

3¹/₂ oz., 5³/₈"
Sherry-Liqueur

12 oz., 6³/₄"
Footed Ice Tea

# BLANK 6109 EXETER

Made by special arrangement with the Henry Ford Museum.
No Optic
*1967 – 1971 Crystal*
*1967 – 1971 Amethyst*
Additional Pieces:
7", 8" Plates (2337), Crystal
7" Plates (2337), Amethyst

## Blank 6110
## PROMISE

11 oz., 7³/₄" Goblet

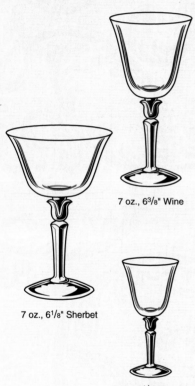

7 oz., 6³/₈" Wine

7 oz., 6¹/₈" Sherbet

2 oz., 4¹/₈" Liqueur

14 oz., 6³/₈" Footed Ice Tea

# BLANK 6110 PROMISE
No Optic
*1967 – 1974 Crystal*
Matchings through 1978 for all except Liqueur.

### Rock Crystal Cutting 916 GREENFIELD
*1967 – 1968 Crystal*
Matchings through 1971.
Additional Pieces:
7", 8" Plates (2337)

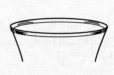

### Rock Crystal Cutting 919 GLENDALE
*1967 – 1972 Crystal*
Matchings through 1974.
Additional Pieces:
7", 8" Plates (2337)

### Decoration 676 RECEPTION
Platinum Band on Bowl
*1967 – 1974 Crystal*
Matchings through 1977.
Additional Pieces:
7", 8" Plates (2337)

### Decoration 677 GOLDEN BELLE
Gold Band on Bowl
*1967 – 1974 Crystal*
Matchings through 1977.
Additional Pieces:
7", 8" Plates (2337)

## BLANK 6111 ILLUSION
No Optic
*1968 – 1982 Crystal*

### Rock Crystal Cutting 918 FIRST LOVE
*1968 – 1970 Crystal*
Matchings through 1971.
Additional Pieces:
7", 8" Plates (2337)

### Decoration 678 RENAISSANCE GOLD
Gold Bands with Crystal Print on Bowl
*1968 – 1982 Crystal*
Additional Pieces:
7", 8" Plates (2337)

### Decoration 679 OLYMPIC PLATINUM
Platinum Band with Gray Cutting on Bowl
*1968 – 1970 Crystal*
Matchings through 1971.
Additional Pieces:
7", 8" Plates (2337)

### Decoration 680 OLYMPIC GOLD
Gold Band with Gray Cutting on Bowl
*1968 – 1970 Crystal*
Matchings through 1971.
Additional Pieces:
7", 8" Plates (2337)

### Decoration 682 RENAISSANCE PLATINUM
Platinum Bands with Crystal Print on Bowl
*1969 – 1982 Crystal*
Additional Pieces:
7", 8" Plates (2337)

6111 CORDIAL,
RENAISSANCE GOLD
DECORATION

Blank 6111
ILLUSION

12 oz., 7¹/₈" Goblet

7¹/₂ oz., 6" Claret

7 oz., 6¹/₈" Wine

9 oz., 5¹/₈" Sherbet

2 oz., 3⁷/₈" Cordial

15 oz., 6⁵/₈"
Footed Ice Tea

Blank 6112
GOLD TRIUMPH
SILVER TRIUMPH

## BLANK 6112 GOLD TRIUMPH, SILVER TRIUMPH

Gold Triumph made with Gold-colored metal base, Silver Triumph made with Silver-colored metal base.
No Optic
*1968 – 1972 Crystal Bowl*
Additional Pieces:
7", 8" Plates (2337)

10 oz., 7" Goblet          14 oz., 7¹/₈" Footed Ice Tea          5¹/₂ oz., 6¹/₂" Tulip Wine          8 oz., 5¹/₈" Sherbet

Blank 6113
VERSAILLES

6113 SHERBET,
VERSAILLES
DECORATION

14 oz., 6⁷/₈" Goblet

9 oz., 6" Claret

10 oz., 5³/₄" Sherbet          2¹/₂ oz., 3⁷/₈" Brandy

## BLANK 6113, DECORATION 683 VERSAILLES OR 684 MOON MIST

Gold Decorated Stem (Versailles) and Silver Mist Decorated Stem (Moon Mist)
Blank 6113 was never offered without either Decoration 683, Versailles, or Decoration 684, Moon Mist.
No Optic
*1969 – 1972 Crystal*

8 oz., 6³/₈" Wine

15 oz., 6¹/₄"
Footed Ice Tea

6113 BRANDY,
MOON MIST
DECORATION

# BLANK 6114 VENTURE
No Optic
*1969 – 1970 Gray Mist Base*

14 oz., 6⁷/₈" Goblet

9 oz., 2⁷/₈" Sherbet

8 oz., 5¹/₂" Wine

3¹/₂ oz., 3¹/₂" Brandy

6114 VENTURE
WINE, GRAY MIST
BASE

### Blanks 6115 through 6119
## SOMMELIER COLLECTION

14 oz., 6³/₄"
6116, Grande

8¹/₂ oz., 7"
6117, Vin Blanc

3¹/₂ oz., 5⁵/₈"
6118, Sherry

9¹/₂ oz., 6"
6115, Continental

9 oz., 8"
6119, Tulip

# BLANKS 6115 THROUGH 6119
## SOMMELIER COLLECTION
Each Stem has a separate number.
No Optic
*1970 – 1973 Crystal*

6115, Continental
6116, Grande
6117, Vin Blanc
6118, Sherry
6119, Tulip

## Blank 6120
## ELOQUENCE

14 oz., 7" Goblet

6120 ELOQUENCE
SHERBET, ONYX BASE

9 oz., 5<sup>15</sup>/16" Claret

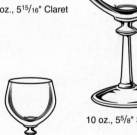

10 oz., 5<sup>5</sup>/8" Sherbet

6120 CORDIAL,
VENISE DECORATION

2 oz., 3<sup>5</sup>/8" Liqueur

15 oz., 6<sup>7</sup>/8" Footed Ice Tea

6120 CONTRAST
CORDIAL

### BLANK 6120 ELOQUENCE
No Optic
*1970 – 1974 Crystal*
*1970 – 1974 Onyx Base*
Matchings through 1978.
*1970 – 1972 White Bowl, Onyx Base*
 (Called CONTRAST)
Matchings through 1973.
Additional Pieces:
7", 8" Plates (2337), Crystal
7" Plates (2337), Onyx

*Decoration 686 ELOQUENCE
GOLD*
Gold Band on Bowl
*1970 – 1974 Crystal*
Additional Pieces:
7", 8" Plates (2337)

*Decoration 687 ELOQUENCE
PLATINUM*
Platinum Band on Bowl
*1970 – 1977 Crystal*
Additional Pieces:
7", 8" Plates (2337)

*Decoration 688 VENISE*
Platinum Bands with Crystal Print on
  Bowl
*1970 – 1974 Crystal*
Matchings through 1978.
Additional Pieces:
7" Plates (2337)

Blank 6121
SPHERE

# BLANK 6121 SPHERE

No Optic
*1971 – 1972 Terra Bowl*
*1971 – 1972 Gray Mist Bowl*
*1971 – 1972 Green Mist Bowl*

14 oz., 5³/₈" Goblet

9 oz., 4¹/₂" Sherbet

7 oz., 4³/₈" Wine

14 oz., 5⁷/₈" Footed Ice Tea

6121 SPHERE WINE,
GREEN MIST BOWL

---

Blank 6122
BISCAYNE

11 oz., 6¹/₈" Goblet

9 oz., 4⁵/₈" Sherbet

6¹/₂ oz., 5¹/₂" Wine

13 oz., 6¹/₄" Footed Ice Tea

6122 BISCAYNE
SNOW HIGHBALL

14 oz., 4³/₄" Highball

10 oz., 3¹/₈" On the Rocks

# BLANK 6122 BISCAYNE

No Optic
*1971 – 1973 Blue*
*1971 – 1973 Nutmeg*
*1971 – 1973 Onyx*
*1971 – 1973 Snow*
*1971 – 1973 Gold*
Additional Pieces:
Highball and On the Rocks, 1971 – 1972

*Decoration 689 HALO*
Platinum Band on Bowl
*1970 – 1971 Onyx*
(No Highball or On the Rocks)

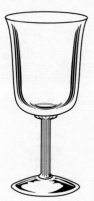

8¹/₂ oz., 6¹/₂" Goblet

7¹/₂ oz., 5¹/₄" Sherbet

5¹/₂ oz., 5³/₄" Wine

11¹/₂ oz., 6" Footed Ice Tea

6123 PRINCESS
GOBLET, GRAY MIST
BOWL, ONYX BASE

6123 WINE,
INTIMATE CRYSTAL
PRINT

## BLANK 6123 PRINCESS

No Optic
*1971 – 1982 Crystal*
*1971 – 1982 Green Mist Bowl*
*1971 – 1980 Blue Bowl*
*1972 – 1980 Gray Mist Bowl, Onyx Base*
Matchings through 1982 for Blue and Gray Mist.
Additional Pieces:
7" Plates (2337), Green Mist, Gray Mist, Onyx, Crystal

**Crystal Print 28 CAMEO**
*1971 – 1982 Green Mist Bowl*
Additional Pieces:
7" Plates (2337), Green Mist

**Crystal Print 31 INTIMATE**
*1971 – 1974 Blue Bowl*
Matchings through 1977.

**Crystal Print 32 POETRY**
*1972 – 1982 Crystal*

**Gray Cutting 922 PETIT FLEUR**
*1971 – 1972 Crystal*
Matchings through 1974.
Additional Pieces:
7" Plates (2337)

**Decoration 690 PRINCESS
PLATINUM**
Platinum Band on Bowl
*1971 – 1982 Crystal*
Additional Pieces:
7" Plates (2337)

**Decoration 691 TENDERNESS**
Platinum Band on Bowl
*1971 – 1974 Green Mist Bowl*
Matchings through 1976.
Additional Pieces:
7" Plates (2337), Green Mist, Decorated

**Decoration 692 MARQUIS**
Platinum Band with Crystal Print on Bowl
*1971 – 1974 Crystal*
Matchings through 1977.
Additional Pieces:
7" Plates (2337)

# BLANK 6124 SPLENDOR

No Optic
*1971 – 1973 Crystal*
Matchings through 1974.

### *Crystal Print 30 BROCADE*
*1971 – 1973 Crystal*
Matchings through 1974.
Additional Pieces:
7" Plates (2337)

### *Gray Cutting 923 GRANADA*
*1971 – 1972 Crystal*
Matchings through 1974.
Additional Pieces:
7" Plates (2337)

10½ oz., 6⅞" Goblet

14 oz., 6⅜" Footed Ice Tea

9 oz., 5⅛" Sherbet

7 oz., 6" Wine

6125 DISTINCTION
CHAMPAGNE, COBALT
BOWL

9 oz., 4½" Champagne

6½ oz., 6¼" Wine

11 oz., 7⅜" Goblet

13 oz., 6¾" Footed Ice Tea

# BLANK 6125 DISTINCTION

No Optic
*1972 – 1973 Crystal*
*1972 – 1982 Blue Bowl*
*1972 – 1975 Plum Bowl* (Matchings through 1976)
*1972 only Ruby Bowl* (Actually made July – December 1972)
*1973 – 1974 Cobalt Bowl* (Matchings through 1976)
Additional Pieces:
7" Plates (2337), Crystal, Blue, Plum

6125 DISTINCTION
ICE TEA, PLUM
BOWL

6125
DISTINCTION
GOBLET, BLUE
BOWL

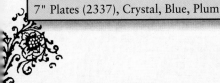

147

Blank 6126
WIMBLEDON

12 oz., 7" Goblet

7 oz., 5³/₄" Wine

6126 WIMBLEDON
WINE, CORSAGE PLUM

## BLANK 6126 WIMBLEDON
Regular Optic
*1974 – 1982* **Crystal**
*1973 – 1974* **Plum Stem** (Matchings through 1975; called CORSAGE PLUM, No Optic)
*1980 – 1982* **Ebony Base** (called GAZEBO)
*1981 – 1982* **Rust Base** (called GAZEBO RUST)
Additional Pieces:
7" Plates (2337), Plum

*Plate Etching 34 TARA*
*1974 – 1982* **Crystal**

9 oz., 5⁵/₈"
Saucer Champagne

13 oz., 6" Footed Ice Tea

6126 WIMBLEDON
WINE, GAZEBO

Blank 6127
FESTIVE

12 oz., 7³/₈" Goblet

9 oz., 5³/₄" Champagne

7 oz., 6¹/₄" Claret

15 oz., 7" Footed Ice Tea

6127 WINE, YELLOW
BOWL, SERENITY
ETCHING

## BLANK 6127 FESTIVE
Loop Optic
*1975 – 1982* **Crystal**
*1975 – 1980* **Yellow Bowl**
*1976 – 1982* **Blue Bowl**

*Plate Etching 35 SERENITY*
*1975 – 1982* **Crystal**
*1975 – 1980* **Yellow Bowl** (Matchings through 1982)
*1976 – 1982* **Blue Bowl**

## BLANK 6128 REGENCY

No Optic
*1976 – 1977 Crystal*
Matchings through 1980.

*Plate Etching 36 HEIRLOOM*
*1976 – 1982 Crystal*

*Gray Cutting 934 NOVA*
*1976 – 1978 Crystal*
Matchings through 1982.

10 oz., 6³/₄" Goblet

7 oz., 5⁷/₁₆" Champagne

7 oz., 6¹/₈" Claret

14 oz., 6¹¹/₁₆" Footed Ice Tea

6129 MISTY
CLARET, YELLOW

7 oz., 4⁹/₁₆" Champagne

7 oz., 5³/₄" Claret

16 oz., 5⁷/₈" Magnum

Blank 6129
MISTY

10 oz., 6³/₄" Goblet

13 oz., 6⁵/₈"
Footed Ice Tea

## BLANK 6129 MISTY

No Optic
*1978 – 1982 Blue*
*1978 – 1982 Yellow*
*1978 – 1982 Brown*

*Decoration 695*
*MISTY PLATINUM*
Platinum Band on Bowl
*1978 – 1980 Crystal*
Matchings through 1982.

149

Blank 6131
SPLENDOR

11 oz., 6½" Goblet

9 oz., 4½" Champagne

7 oz., 5½" Claret

14 oz., 6½" Footed Ice Tea

6131 SPLENDOR
BLUE GOBLET

Blank 6143
PAVILION

6143 PAVILION
WINE, GRAY
BOWL

10 oz., 7⅞" Goblet

7 oz., 6⅛" Cocktail

7½ oz., 7⁷⁄₁₆" Wine

14 oz., 6⁵⁄₁₆" Footed Ice Tea

## BLANK 6143 PAVILION
Spiral Optic
*1980 – 1982 Crystal*
*1980 – 1982 Gray Bowl*

*Plate Etching 42 NOUVEAU*
*1980 – 1982 Crystal*
*1980 – 1981 Gray Bowl*

# BLANK 6144 LOTUS

No Optic

*1980 – 1982 Crystal Mist Base* (Actually July 1980 – June 1982)
*1980 – 1982 Ebony Base* (Actually July 1980 – June 1982)
*1982 only Peach Mist Base* (Actually January 1982 – June 1982)
The Flute Champagne was added in 1981.
Additional Pieces:
Coordinating Giftware including Low Candlestick, High
  Candlestick, Bud Vase in all colors.

Blank 6144
LOTUS

6144 LOTUS FLUTE,
PEACH MIST BASE

10 oz., 7¹/₄" Claret

8 oz., 6¹/₂" Champagne

14 oz., 7¹/₂" Footed Ice Tea

6 oz., 8⁷/₈" Flute

11 oz., 8¹/₄" Goblet

# BLANK 6147 GALA

No Optic

*1981 – 1982 Crystal*

**Plate Etching 45 FESTIVAL**
*1981 – 1982 Crystal*
This Etching is similar to Plate Etching
  341, Romance, or Plate Etching 279,
  June. It has been modified and appears
  on one side of the bowl only.

Blank 6147
GALA

**Carving 59 ICICLE**
Frosted Base
*1982 only Crystal Bowl, Crystal
  Frosted Base*
*1982 only Blue Bowl, Blue Frosted
  Base*
*1982 only Yellow Bowl, Yellow
  Frosted Base*

6147 WINE, ICICLE
CARVING, BLUE BOWL,
BLUE FROSTED BASE

9 oz., 5" Champagne

12 oz., 7³/₈" Goblet

**Decoration 698 CELEBRATION**
Platinum Band on Bowl
*1981 – 1982 Crystal*

9 oz., 6⁵/₈" Wine

**Decoration 699 JUBILEE**
Gold Band on Bowl
*1981 – 1982 Crystal*

14 oz., 7" Footed Ice Tea

Blank 6149
MAYPOLE

12 oz., 7¹/₂" Goblet

15 oz., 7¹/₁₆" Footed Ice Tea

8¹/₂ oz., 6³/₄" Wine

## BLANK 6149 MAYPOLE
Spiral Optic
*1982 only Light Blue*
*1982 only Yellow*
*1982 only Peach*
This pattern is similar to the Blank 2412 (Colony)
  pattern.
Additional Pieces:
Coordinating Giftware including Bowl, Candlesticks,
  Torte Plate, and Bud Vase in all colors.

9 oz., 5³/₈" Champagne

6149 MAYPOLE
PEACH GOBLET

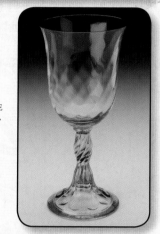

Blank 7780
THE PRESIDENT'S HOUSE

11 oz., 6⁷/₈" Goblet
9¹/₂ oz., 6¹/₄" Burgundy Wine
8 oz., 5³/₄" Wine
5 oz., 5" Wine

6 oz., 6³/₄"
Whiskey Sour

6 oz., 4¹/₂"
Champagne

11 oz., 8" Tulip
Champagne

8 oz., 3¹/₂"
Old Fashioned

6 oz., 3" Low
Champagne

11 oz., 5¹/₈" Highball
5 oz., 3⁷/₈" Juice

12 oz., 5⁷/₈"
Footed Ice Tea

## BLANK 7780
# THE PRESIDENT'S HOUSE
An Old Morgantown Glass Company Pattern
No Optic
*1971 – 1973 Crystal*

# Appendices

APPENDIX A – TUMBLERS
APPENDIX B – THE NOSTALGIA LINE
APPENDIX C – OTHER PIECES
APPENDIX D – AFTER 1982

# APPENDIX A
# TUMBLERS

In its 99-year history, the Fostoria Company produced many tumblers, both flat and footed. Appendix A contains those tumblers which were used with more than one pattern, especially true of the patterns made before 1943. Also included are tumblers which were considered to be independent lines, such as 2670 Dawn, 2671 Dusk, 4183 Homespun, and 4184 Needlepoint.

The 4180 Casual Flair tumblers are of special note since they were designed to coordinate with the Melamine dinnerware produced in a separate factory under Fostoria auspices in the late 1950s. Prices given are for blank tumblers only. Since most tumblers were used with many different patterns, refer to the pattern for price and production dates.

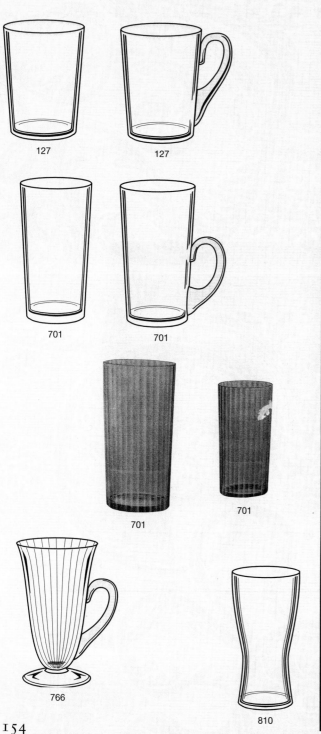

127  127

701  701

701  701

766  810

***Blank 127***
No Optic
9 oz. Flat, $6.00
9 oz. Handled, $10.00

***Blank 701***
Regular Optic, Narrow Optic, Spiral
  Optic, No Optic
Colors: Crystal, Rose, Green, Amber,
  Topaz, Wisteria
Flat: 4 oz., 5 oz., 6 oz., 6½ oz., 7 oz.,
  7½ oz., 8 oz., 9 oz., 10 oz., 11 oz.,
  11½ oz., 12 oz., 13 oz., 14 oz.,
  15 oz., 17 oz., 18 oz., 19 oz., 20 oz.,
  21 oz.
Handled: 8 oz.
Price: $14.00 – 35.00 depending on size
  and color

***Blank 766***
Narrow Optic
12 oz. Footed, Handled, $15.00

***Blank 810***
Regular Optic, No Optic
Flat (Tall): 3 oz., 5 oz., 8 oz., 10 oz.
Flat (Regular Height): 4 oz., 5 oz., 6 oz.,
  8 oz., 9 oz., 11 oz.
Price: $4.00 – 9.00

**Blank 820**
No Optic
Flat Table Tumbler, $5.00

**Blank 820½**
No Optic
Flat Table Tumbler with Cut Flutes, $6.00

**Blank 833**
Narrow Optic, No Optic
Flat: 1 oz., 1½ oz., 2 oz., 3 oz., 4 oz.,
 5 oz., 6 oz., 7 oz., 8 oz., 9 oz.,
 10 oz., 12 oz., 14 oz.
Price: $3.00 – 10.00

**Blank 833½ Heatherbell**
No Optic
Tumbler, sham: 5 oz., 8 oz., 10 oz.,
 12 oz., 14 oz., $4.00 – 10.00
Old Fashioned Cocktail, sham, 7 oz.,
 $5.00
Whiskey, sham, 1½ oz., $7.00

**Blank 835**
**JENNY LIND**
Blown Milk Glass
Colors: White Milkglass, 1955 –
 1965; Peach Milkglass 1957 – 1959;
 Aqua Milkglass, 1957 – 1959
Flat: 13 oz. Tumbler
Price: $65.00 – 85.00

**Blank 837**
Regular Optic, No Optic
Flat: 3 oz., 5 oz., 9 oz., $5.00 – 6.00
Footed, Handles: 12 oz., $10.00
Oyster Cocktail, $10.00
 (see also Appendix C)

**Blank 858**
No Optic
Flat: 3½ oz., 5 oz., $5.00
Table: 6½ oz., 8 oz., 10 oz., 12 oz.,
 14 oz., 16 oz., $5.00 – 6.00

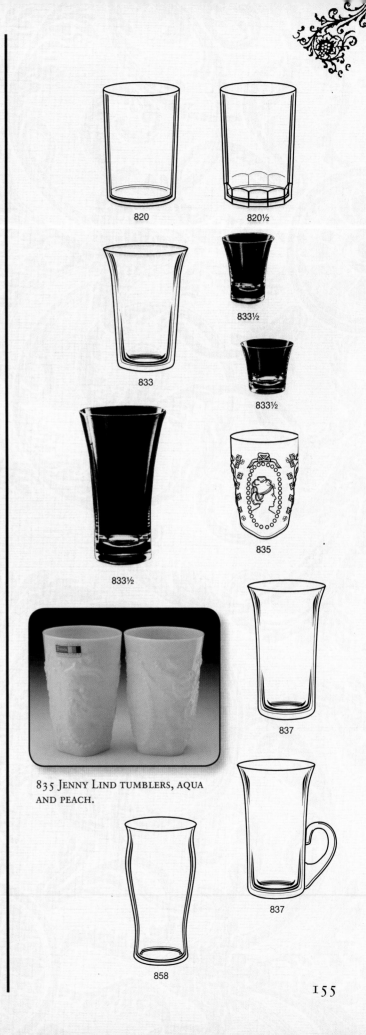

835 JENNY LIND TUMBLERS, AQUA
AND PEACH.

869

869

869 5 oz. Tumbler,
Brunswick Needle
Etching

877 Oakwood
Footed Ice Tea

887

887

889

889

887 Regal Blue
Whiskey

923

1184

1184

**Blank 869**
Regular Optic
Colors: Crystal, Amber, Green, Blue,
    and Orchid 5 oz., 8 oz., 12 oz.
Flat: 2 oz., 5 oz., 8 oz., $10.00 – 20.00
Table: 12 oz., $14.00 – 25.00
Table, Handled: 12 oz., $18.00

**Blank 877**
Regular Optic
Colors: Crystal, Azure, Green, Amber
Footed: 2½ oz., 4½ oz., 5 oz., 9 oz., 12 oz.
Price: $18.00– 60.00 depending on size
    and color.

**Blank 887**
Regular Optic, Narrow Optic, No Optic
Colors:
    1¾ oz. Whiskey, No Optic, Regal
        Blue, Burgundy, Empire Green, Ruby,
        $34.00; Regular Optic, Crystal,
        $7.00, Amber, $22.00
    2½ oz. Tumbler, Narrow Optic, Rose,
        Green, Amber, Topaz, Azure, $22.00;
        Wisteria, $36.00
Flat, Crystal: 1½ oz., 1¾ oz., 2 oz., 2¼ oz.,
    2½ oz., 2¾ oz., 3 oz., 3½ oz., 4 oz.,
    4¼ oz., 4½ oz., 5 oz. $4.00 – 7.00

**Blank 889**
Regular Optic, Narrow Optic, No Optic
Available with Cut Flutes (Cut 8)
Flat: 3 oz., 4 oz., 4½ oz., 5 oz., 5½ oz.,
    6 oz., 7 oz., 8 oz., 9 oz., 10 oz.,
    11 oz., 12 oz., 13 oz., 14 oz., 15 oz.,
    16 oz., 18 oz., 21 oz., $6.00 – 14.00
Handled, Crystal: 8 oz., 14 oz.,
    $14.00 – 16.00
Colors: Amber, 10 oz. Flat Sham, 13 oz.
    Flat Regular Optic, 5 oz. Regular Optic,
    Narrow Optic, $20.00 – 22.00; Rose,
    Green, Empire Green, Ruby, Burgundy,
    Regal Blue, Empire Green, Topaz,
    Wisteria, 5 oz. Flat, $22.00 – 36.00

**Blank 923**
No Optic
Handled: 7 oz., $12.00

**Blank 1184**
Narrow Optic, No Optic
Flat: 7 oz. Old Fashioned Cocktail:
    Crystal, $15.00; Rose, Amber, Green,
    Topaz, $25.00; Azure, $29.00;
    Wisteria, $45.00.
Other Flat: 1¾ oz., 2 oz., 2¼ oz., 2¾ oz.,
    3 oz., 3½ oz., 4 oz., 4¼ oz., 4½ oz.,
    5 oz., 6 oz., $12.00 – 14.00
Handled: 5 oz., $15.00

**Blank 1185**
Flat: 8 oz. Old Fashioned Cocktail, Sham:
   Crystal, $8.00; Regal Blue, Burgundy,
   Empire Green, Ruby, $34.00
Flat: 5 oz. Whiskey Sour, Sham, Crystal,
   $7.00

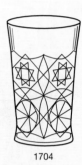

1185

**Blank 1704**
**WINBURN**
Pressed Milkglass
*1958 – 1962*
Flat: 7 oz. Water
Price: $32.00

**Blank 2464** *(see Appendix C)*

1704 WINBURN
TUMBLER

1704

**Blank 2502**
Flat: 2 oz. Whiskey, $18.00

**Blank 2518** *(see Appendix C)*

2502

**Blank 2643**
**HOLIDAY**
Pressed
*1949 – 1958*
Crystal
Flat: 1½ oz. Whiskey, 4 oz. Cocktail,
   6 oz. Old Fashioned, 9 oz. Scotch and
      Soda, 12 oz. Double Old Fashioned,
         12 oz. Highball
Price: $4.00 – 12.00

2643

**Blank 2670**
**DAWN**
Pressed
*1953 – 1965*
Crystal, Lime, Tokay, Honey
Flat: 6 oz. Dessert, 5 oz. Juice, 10½ oz.
   Water, 12½ oz. Ice Tea
Price: $6.00 – 18.00

2670

**Blank 2671**
**DUSK**
Pressed
*1953 – 1965*
Crystal, Lime, Tokay, Honey
Flat: 6 oz. Dessert, 5 oz., Juice, 10 oz.
   Water, 13½ oz. Ice Tea
Price: $6.00 – 18.00

2671

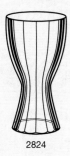
2675

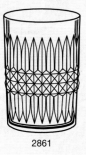
2824

2824

2861

2862

2863
Cutting 924

2863
Cutting 925

*Blank 2675*
**RANDOLPH**
Pressed Milkglass
*1954 – 1965*
Footed: 9 oz.
Price: $22.00

*Blank 2824*
**MODULE**
Regular Optic
*1970 – 1972*
Crystal, Dusk, Sunrise
Flat: 5 oz. Wine/Juice, 9 oz. Goblet,
    13 oz. Ice Tea
Price: $12.00 – 14.00

*Blank 2861*
**ASPEN**
Pressed Lead Crystal
*1974 – 1982*
Flat: 11 oz. Double Old Fashioned,
    13 oz. Highball
Price: $15.00

*Blank 2862*
**STOWE**
Pressed Lead Crystal
*1974 – 1982*
Flat: 11 oz. Double Old Fashioned,
    13 oz. Highball
Price: $20.00

*Blank 2863*
Pressed Lead Crystal
Centennial II Collection
*1974 – 1975*
Flat: 11 oz. Double Old Fashioned,
    13 oz. Highball

Cutting 924
ALTA

Cutting 925
VALE

Price: $15.00

**Blank 2934**
*YORK*
Pressed Lead Crystal
*1979 – 1982*
Flat: 10 oz. Double Old Fashioned,
  13 oz. Highball
Price: $14.00

2934

2934

**Blank 4005**
Regular Optic
Flat: 2½ oz., 5 oz., 9 oz., 12 oz.
Price: $12.00 – 20.00

4011 TUMBLER,
ORIENTAL ETCHING

4005

4011

**Blank 4011**
Regular Optic, Narrow Optic, No Optic
Flat: 6 oz., 8 oz., 11 oz., 12 oz., 15 oz.,
  18 oz.
Handled: 12 oz.
Blank 4011½
Table: 10 oz.
Price: $7.00 – 14.00

4061 HANDLED
LEMONADE AND 6"
PLATE, ORIENTAL
ETCHING

4011

**Blank 4061**
Regular Optic
Footed, Handled Lemonade, $18.00

**Blank 4076**
Regular Optic
Flat: 10 oz., Crystal, $16.00
Flat: 9 oz, Amber, Green, Rose, Topaz,
  $22.00

4061

4076

4077

**Blank 4077**
Regular Optic
Table: 3 oz., 5½ oz., 8 oz., 9 oz., 9½ oz.,
  11 oz., 12½ oz., 15 oz.
Price: $5.00 – 14.00

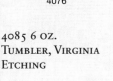

4085

**Blank 4085**
Regular Optic
Flat: 2½ oz., 6 oz., $6.00
Table: 13 oz., $14.00
Handled: 13 oz., $18.00

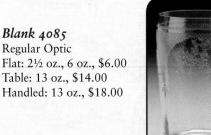

4076

4085 6 OZ.
TUMBLER, VIRGINIA
ETCHING

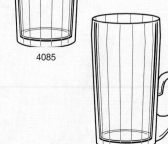

4085

4095

4095
OYSTER
COCKTAIL,
WOODLAND
ETCHING

4115/4115½

4122

4132

4132 7½ OZ.
OLD FASHIONED
COCKTAIL, HOUSE OF
REPRESENTATIVES SEAL

4139

4139

4139

4139

*Blank 4095*
Regular Optic, Spiral Optic, Loop Optic
*1923 – 1929*
Colors: Crystal, Green, Azure Bowl,
   Green Bowl, Rose Bowl, Amber Base,
   Green Base, Blue Base
Footed: 2½ oz., 5 oz., 10 oz., 13 oz.
4 oz. Oyster Cocktail
6 oz. Parfait
Price: $12.00 – 30.00 depending on size
   and color

*Blank 4101 (see Appendix C)*

*Blank 4115/4115½*
Used with Fish Canape
Footed: 3 oz., 4 oz., $4.00 – 5.00

*Blank 4118 (see Appendix C)*

*Blank 4122*
Flat: 1½ oz. Whiskey, Sham, $12.00

*Blank 4132*
*STANDISH*
No Optic, Horizontal Optic
*1937 – 1943 Crystal, Azure, Gold Tint*
*1953 – 1982 Crystal*
Flat: 1½ oz. Whiskey (1937 – 1943;
   1953 – 1972)
5 oz. Whiskey Sour (1953 – 1972)
5 oz. Tumbler, Sham (1937 – 1943)
7½ oz. Old Fashioned Cocktail (1937
   – 1943; 1953 – 1972)
9 oz. Scotch and Soda (1937 – 1943; 1953
   – 1972)
12 oz. Highball (1937 – 1943; 1953
   – 1972)
13 oz. Double Old Fashioned
14 oz. Tumbler, Sham (1937 – 1943)
Price: $8.00 – 20.00

*Blank 4139*
*ESQUIRE*
No Optic
Flat: 1¾ oz. Whiskey, 5 oz., 7 oz.
   Old Fashioned, 9 oz., 10 oz., 12 oz.,
   14 oz., 16 oz.
Price: $6.00 – 10.00

*Blank 4140 (see Appendix C)*

*Blank 4141 (see Appendix C)*

*Blank 4142 (see Appendix C)*

*Blank 4146*
## HUMPTY DUMPTY
No Optic
Used for enamel decorations before
World War II
Flat: 1 oz., 4 oz., 9 oz.
Price (without decoration): $7.00 – 8.00

*Blank 4161*
## KARNAK
*1955 – 1965*
Crystal, Pink, Smoke, Marine, Amber
Flat: 6 oz. Juice, 14 oz. Beverage, 21 oz.
   Cooler
Price: $12.00 – 15.00

*Blank 4162*
## CONGO
*1955 – 1965*
Crystal, Pink, Smoke, Marine, Amber
Flat: 6 oz. Juice, 14 oz. Beverage, 21 oz.
   Cooler
Price: $10.00 – 15.00

*Blank 4163*
## INCA
*1955 – 1965*
Crystal, Pink, Smoke, Marine, Amber
Flat: 6 oz. Juice, 14 oz. Beverage, 21 oz.
   Cooler
Price: $12.00 – 15.00

*Blank 4180*
## CASUAL FLAIR
*1958 – 1962*
Crystal Print decorated tumblers for
   decorated Melamine dinnerware.
Colors: Crystal, Harvest Yellow,
   Sky Blue, Fawn, Mint Green
Flat: 7 oz. Juice, 12 oz. Tumbler
Price: $8.00
Price (All Crystal Prints): $12.00

Crystal Print 8
BLUE MEADOW, Sky Blue

Crystal Print 9
RING O' ROSES, Fawn

Crystal Print 10
KISMET, Sky Blue

Crystal Print 11
PLAIN 'N FANCY, Harvest Yellow

4146

4146

4146

4161

4162

Blue Meadow

4163

4162 CONGO
MARINE JUICE

4180

Ring 'O Roses

Plain 'N Fancy

Kismet

4180 CASUAL FLAIR
TUMBLER, BLUE MEADOW

4180 CASUAL FLAIR
TUMBLER, RING O' ROSES

Golden Twilight

Country Garden

Greenbriar

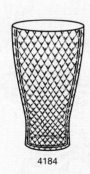

Sun Valley

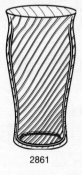

2861

4184

4184
NEEDLEPOINT
OLD FASHIONED,
TEAL BLUE

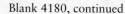

Blank 4180, continued

Crystal Print 12
GOLDEN TWILIGHT, Fawn

Crystal Print 13
COUNTRY GARDEN, Sky Blue

Crystal Print 14
GREENBRIAR, Mint Green

Crystal Print 15
SUN VALLEY, Harvest Yellow

### Blank 4183
### HOMESPUN
### 1959 – 1965
Blown Tumbler
Colors: Gold, Moss Green, Teal Blue
Flat: 9 oz. Juice/Old Fashioned,
    11½ oz. Water/Scotch and Soda,
    15 oz. Ice Tea/Highball
Price: $28.00

### Blank 4184
### NEEDLEPOINT
### 1959 – 1965
Blown Tumbler
Colors: Gold, Moss Green, Teal Blue
Flat: 8 oz. Juice/Old Fashioned, 12¼ oz.
    Water/Scotch and Soda, 16½ oz.
    Ice Tea/ Highball
Price: $30.00

### Blank 5000
Regular Optic
*1927 – 1943*
Colors: Crystal, Amber, Green, Blue, Blue
  Base, Green Base, Amber Base, Amber
  Bowl, Green Bowl, Orchid Bowl,
  Rose Bowl, Azure Bowl, Amber Base
  with Mother Of Pearl Iridescence on
  Bowl, Green Base with Mother of
  Pearl Iridescence on Bowl
Footed: 2½ oz. Whiskey, 4½ oz. Oyster
  Cocktail, 5 oz. Juice, 6 oz. Parfait,
  7 oz., 9 oz., 12 oz. Ice Tea
Price: $12.00 – 38.00 depending on size
  and color

5000

5000 GREEN
12 OZ. ICE
TEA

### Blank 5084
Regular Optic
*1921 – 1942*
Colors: Crystal, Green, Amber, Rose, Blue
Footed: 2½ oz., 5 oz., 9 oz., 12 oz.
Price: $12.00 – 42.00 depending on size
  and color

5084

5084

5084 AMBER 12 OZ.
FOOTED TUMBLER

### Blank 5650
### HORIZON
Blown Tumbler
*1951 – 1958*
Colors: Crystal, Cinnamon Bowl, Spruce
  Bowl
Footed: Juice/Cocktail, Sherbet/
  Old Fashioned, Water/Scotch and
  Soda, Ice Tea/Highball
Price: $10.00 – 15.00

5650 HORIZON
HIGHBALL, CINNAMON

5650

6044

6046

**Blank 6044**
*TIARA*
Blown Tumbler
*1951 – 1958*
Colors: Crystal, Cinnamon Bowl,
   Spruce Bowl
Footed: Juice/Cocktail, Sherbet/Old
   Fashioned, Water/Scotch and Soda,
   Ice Tea/Highball
Price: $14.00

**Blank 6046**
*CATALINA*
Blown Tumbler
*1951 – 1958*
Colors: Cinnamon Bowl, Spruce Bowl,
   Chartreuse Bowl
Footed: Juice/Cocktail, Sherbet/Old
   Fashioned, Water/Scotch and Soda,
   Ice Tea/Highball
Price: $14.00

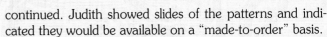

# APPENDIX B
# NOSTALGIA LINE

In 1980, Judith Olert, the Fostoria Company's "Table Top Representative," presented a program on the Nostalgia line to the Fostoria Glass Society of America. The Nostalgia line was part of a special promotional package to reissue several patterns which had been dis-

continued. Judith showed slides of the patterns and indicated they would be available on a "made-to-order" basis.

Although no data was available to the authors regarding production, probably the promotional effort lasted through 1982.

The patterns and the pieces offered in each pattern are included here. Notice that pattern names are the same, but the numbers that have been assigned to each are different. The original pattern number is included in parenthesis after the name.

## BRIDAL BELLE (Decoration 639, Blank 6072)

| | | |
|---|---|---|
| BR02/002 | 10 oz. | Goblet<br>Height 6⅜" |
| BR02/011 | 7¼ oz. | Dessert/Champagne<br>Height 5" |
| BR02/027 | 4½ oz. | Wine/Cocktail<br>Height 4⅞" |
| BR02/063 | 13 oz. | Luncheon Goblet/Ice Tea<br>Height 6⅜" |

## BUTTERCUP (Etching 340, Blank 6030)

| | | |
|---|---|---|
| BU01/002 | 10 oz. | Goblet<br>Height 7⅞" |
| BU01/003 | 10 oz. | Low Goblet<br>Height 6⅜" |
| BU01/008 | 6 oz. | High Dessert/Champagne<br>Height 5⅝" |
| BU01/011 | 6 oz. | Low Dessert/Champagne<br>Height 4⅜" |
| BU01/027 | 3½ oz. | Claret/Wine<br>Height 6" |
| BU01/063 | 12 oz. | Luncheon Goblet/Ice Tea<br>Height 6" |

## CHINTZ (Etching 338, Blank 6026)

| | | |
|---|---|---|
| CH01/002 | 9 oz. | Goblet<br>Height 7⅝" |
| CH01/003 | 9 oz. | Low Goblet<br>Height 6⅛" |
| CH01/008 | 6 oz. | High Dessert/Champagne<br>Height 5½" |
| CH01/011 | 6 oz. | Low Dessert/Champagne<br>Height 4⅜" |
| CH01/027 | 4½ oz. | Claret/Wine<br>Height 5⅜" |
| CH01/060 | 13 oz. | Luncheon Goblet/Ice Tea<br>Height 6" |

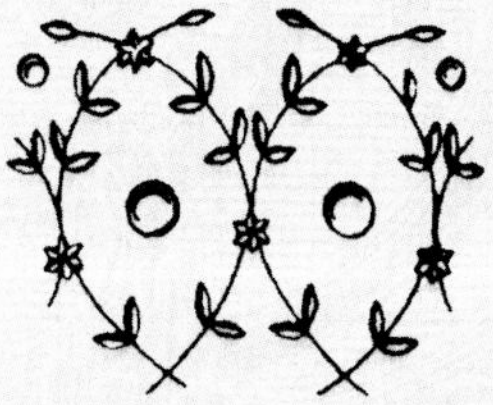

## CHRISTIANA (Cutting 814, Blank 6030)

| | | |
|---|---|---|
| CH02/002 | 10 oz. | Goblet |
| | | Height 7⅞" |
| CH02/003 | 10 oz. | Low Goblet |
| | | Height 6⅜" |
| CH02/008 | 6 oz. | High Dessert/Champagne |
| | | Height 5⅝" |
| CH02/011 | 6 oz. | Low Dessert/Champagne |
| | | Height 4⅜" |
| CH02/027 | 3½ oz. | Claret/Wine |
| | | Height 6" |
| CH02/063 | 12 oz. | Luncheon Goblet/Ice Tea |
| | | Height 6" |

## CORSAGE (Etching 325, Blank 6014)

| | | |
|---|---|---|
| CO12/002 | 9 oz. | Goblet |
| | | Height 7⅜" |
| CO12/011 | 5½ oz. | Dessert/Champagne |
| | | Height 5⅜" |
| CO12/025 | 4 oz. | Claret |
| | | Height 5⅞" |
| CO12/063 | 12 oz. | Luncheon Goblet/Ice Tea |
| | | Height 6" |

## CYNTHIA (Cutting 785, Blank 6017)

| | | |
|---|---|---|
| CY01/002 | 9 oz. | Goblet |
| | | Height 7⅜" |
| CY01/008 | 6 oz. | High Dessert/Champagne |
| | | Height 5½" |
| CY01/011 | 6 oz. | Low Dessert/Champagne |
| | | Height 4½" |
| CY01/025 | 4 oz. | Claret |
| | | Height 5⅞" |
| CY01/026 | 3 oz. | Wine |
| | | Height 5½" |
| CY01/063 | 12 oz. | Luncheon Goblet/Ice Tea |
| | | Height 6" |

## DOLLY MADISON (Cutting 786, Blank 6023)

| | | |
|---|---|---|
| DO01/002 | 9 oz. | Goblet |
| | | Height 6⅜" |
| DO01/008 | 6 oz. | High Dessert/Champagne |
| | | Height 4⅞" |
| DO01/011 | 6 oz. | Low Dessert/Champagne |
| | | Height 4⅛" |
| DO01/027 | 4 oz. | Claret/Wine |
| | | Height 4¾" |
| DO01/063 | 12 oz. | Luncheon Goblet/Ice Tea |
| | | Height 5¾" |

## HEATHER (Etching 343, Blank 6037)

| | | |
|---|---|---|
| HE01/002 | 9 oz. | Goblet |
| | | Height 7⅞" |
| HE01/003 | 9 oz. | Low Goblet |
| | | Height 6⅜" |
| HE01/008 | 7 oz. | High Dessert/Champagne |
| | | Height 6" |
| HE01/011 | 7 oz. | Low Dessert/Champagne |
| | | Height 4¾" |
| HE01/027 | 4 oz. | Claret/Wine |
| | | Height 6" |
| HE01/063 | 12 oz. | Luncheon Goblet/Ice Tea |
| | | Height 6⅛" |

## HOLLY (Cutting 815, Blank 6030)

| | | |
|---|---|---|
| HO01/002 | 10 oz. | Goblet |
| | | Height 7⅞" |
| HO01/003 | 10 oz. | Low Goblet |
| | | Height 6⅜" |
| HO01/008 | 6 oz. | High Dessert/Champagne |
| | | Height 5⅝" |
| HO01/011 | 6 oz. | Low Dessert/Champagne |
| | | Height 4⅜" |
| HO01/027 | 3½ oz. | Claret/Wine |
| | | Height 6" |
| HO01/063 | 12 oz. | Luncheon Goblet/Ice Tea |
| | | Height 6" |

## JUNE (Etching 279, Blank 5098)

Color Key
JU01 – Crystal
JU02 – Blue
JU03 – Yellow

| | | |
|---|---|---|
| 002 | 9 oz. | Goblet |
| | | Height 8¼" |
| 011 | 6 oz. | High Dessert/Champagne |
| | | Height 6" |
| 025 | 4 oz. | Claret |
| | | Height 6" |
| 063 | 12 oz. | Luncheon Goblet/Ice Tea |
| | | Height 6" |

## LAUREL (Cutting 776, Blank 6017)

| | | |
|---|---|---|
| LA01/002 | 9 oz. | Goblet |
| | | Height 7⅜" |
| LA01/008 | 6 oz. | High Dessert/Champagne |
| | | Height 5½" |
| LA01/011 | 6 oz. | Low Dessert/Champagne |
| | | Height 4½" |
| LA01/025 | 4 oz. | Claret |
| | | Height 5⅞" |
| LA01/026 | 3 oz. | Wine |
| | | Height 5½" |
| LA01/063 | 12 oz. | Luncheon Goblet/Ice Tea |
| | | Height 6" |

## MEADOW ROSE (Etching 328, Blank 6016)

| | | |
|---|---|---|
| ME02/002 | 10 oz. | Goblet |
| | | Height 7⅝" |
| ME02/008 | 6 oz. | High Dessert/Champagne |
| | | Height 5⅝" |
| ME02/011 | 6 oz. | Low Dessert/Champagne |
| | | Height 4⅜" |
| ME02/025 | 4½ oz. | Claret |
| | | Height 6" |
| ME02/060 | 13 oz. | Luncheon Goblet/Ice Tea |
| | | Height 5⅞" |

## MULBERRY (Cutting 799, Blank 6026)

| | | |
|---|---|---|
| MU01/002 | 9 oz. | Goblet |
| | | Height 7⅝" |
| MU01/003 | 9 oz. | Low Goblet |
| | | Height 6⅛" |
| MU01/008 | 6 oz. | High Dessert/Champagne |
| | | Height 5½" |
| MU01/011 | 6 oz. | Low Dessert/Champagne |
| | | Height 4⅜" |
| MU01/027 | 4½ oz. | Claret/Wine |
| | | Height 5⅜" |
| MU01/060 | 13 oz. | Luncheon Goblet/Ice Tea |
| | | Height 6" |

## NOSEGAY (Cutting 834, Blank 6051½)

| | | |
|---|---|---|
| N001/002 | 10½ oz. | Goblet |
| | | Height 6¼" |
| N001/007 | 6½ oz. | Dessert/Champagne |
| | | Height 4⅜" |
| N001/027 | 4 oz. | Claret/Wine |
| | | Height 4½" |
| N001/060 | 12¼ oz. | Luncheon Goblet/Ice Tea |
| | | Height 6⅛" |

## ROMANCE (Etching 341, Blank 6017)

| | | |
|---|---|---|
| RO02/002 | 9 oz. | Goblet |
| | | Height 7⅜" |
| RO02/008 | 6 oz. | High Dessert/Champagne |
| | | Height 5½" |
| RO02/011 | 6 oz. | Low Dessert/Champagne |
| | | Height 4½" |
| RO02/025 | 4 oz. | Claret |
| | | Height 5⅞" |
| RO02/026 | 3 oz. | Wine |
| | | Height 5½" |
| RO02/063 | 12 oz. | Luncheon Goblet/Ice Tea |
| | | Height 6" |

## ROSE *(Cutting 827, Blank 6036)*

| | | |
|---|---|---|
| RO04/002 | 9½ oz. | Goblet |
| | | Height 6⅞" |
| RO04/008 | 6 oz. | High Dessert/Champagne |
| | | Height 4¾" |
| RO04/011 | 6 oz. | Low Dessert/Champagne |
| | | Height 4⅛" |
| RO04/027 | 3¼ oz. | Claret/Wine |
| | | Height 4¾" |
| RO04/063 | 12 oz. | Luncheon Goblet/Ice Tea |
| | | Height 6⅛" |

## SPRAY *(Cutting 841, Blank 6055½)*

| | | |
|---|---|---|
| SP03/002 | 10 oz. | Goblet |
| | | Height 6⅛" |
| SP03/007 | 6 oz. | Dessert/Champagne |
| | | Height 4½" |
| SP03/027 | 4¼ oz. | Claret/Wine |
| | | Height 4⅝" |
| SP03/060 | 12¼ oz. | Luncheon Goblet/Ice Tea |
| | | Height 6⅛" |

## SPRITE *(Cutting 823, Blank 6033)*

| | | |
|---|---|---|
| SP02/002 | 10 oz. | Goblet |
| | | Height 6¼" |
| SP02/008 | 6 oz. | High Dessert/Champagne |
| | | Height 4¾" |
| SP02/011 | 6 oz. | Low Dessert/Champagne |
| | | Height 4" |
| SP02/027 | 4 oz. | Claret/Wine |
| | | Height 4¾" |
| SP02/060 | 13 oz. | Luncheon Goblet/Ice Tea |
| | | Height 5⅞" |

## WEDDING RING *(Decoration 626, Blank 6051½)*

| | | |
|---|---|---|
| WE02/002 | 10½ oz. | Goblet |
| | | Height 6¼" |
| WE02/007 | 6½ oz. | Dessert/Champagne |
| | | Height 4⅜" |
| WE02/027 | 4 oz. | Claret/Wine |
| | | Height 4½" |
| WE02/060 | 12¼ oz. | Luncheon Goblet/Ice Tea |
| | | Height 6⅛" |

### FOSTORIA WHEAT (Cutting 837, Blank 6051½)

| FO01/002 | 10½ oz. | Goblet |
| | | Height 6¼" |
| FO01/007 | 6½ oz. | Dessert/Champagne |
| | | Height 4⅜" |
| FO01/027 | 4 oz. | Claret/Wine |
| | | Height 4½" |
| FO01/060 | 12¼ oz. | Luncheon Goblet/Ice Tea |
| | | Height 6⅛" |

### WILLOWMERE (Etching 333, Blank 6024)

| WI05/002 | 10 oz. | Goblet |
| | | Height 7⅛" |
| WI05/008 | 6 oz. | High Dessert/Champagne |
| | | Height 5⅝" |
| WI05/011 | 6 oz. | Low Dessert/Champagne |
| | | Height 4¼" |
| WI05/025 | 4 oz. | Claret |
| | | Height 5¾" |
| WI05/026 | 3½ oz. | Wine |
| | | Height 5⅜" |
| WI05/063 | 12 oz. | Luncheon Goblet/Ice Tea |
| | | Height 5¾" |

## APPENDIX C
## OTHER PIECES

Included here are pieces which were used again and again with patterns and are referred to in the main text in the portion of each entry called "Additional Pieces." Grapefruits, parfaits, oyster cocktails, jugs and tankards, plates, beverage sets and barware, and a complete listing of the Repeal line compose Appendix C.

Full and partial dinner service patterns are presented fully in *Fostoria Tableware: 1924 – 1943, Fostoria Tableware: 1944 –1986,* and *Fostoria, Useful and Ornamental*. To be listed as having a "complete dinner service," the pattern must have included a dinner plate and a cup and saucer.

Refer to the main text for pricing indicators. Length of production, color, and whether the piece was etched, cut, or decorated all figure into the pricing.

## GRAPEFRUITS

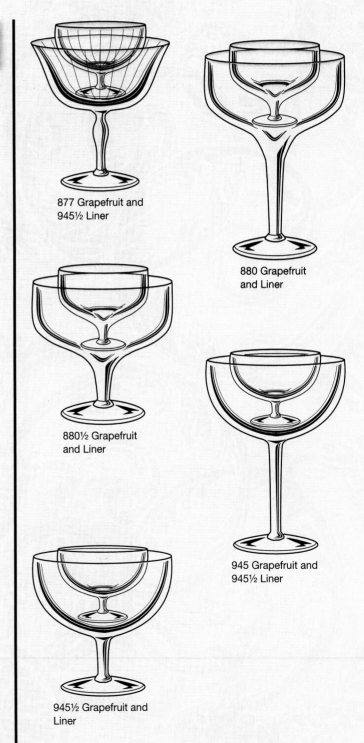

877 Grapefruit and
945½ Liner

880 Grapefruit
and Liner

880½ Grapefruit
and Liner

945 Grapefruit and
945½ Liner

945½ Grapefruit and
Liner

*Blank 877*
Grapefruit, 945½ Liner
Regular Optic
Colors: Crystal, $35.00; Mother of Pearl, $25.00;
   Amber, $45.00; Green, $54.00; Orchid, Azure, $65.00

*Blank 880*
Grapefruit and Liner (Tall)
No Optic
Price: $35.00

*Blank 880½*
Grapefruit and Liner (Short)
No Optic
Price: $30.00

*Blank 945*
Grapefruit, 945½ Liner (Tall)
Regular Optic, No Optic
Price: $35.00

*Blank 945½*
Grapefruit and Liner (Short)
Regular Optic, No Optic
Price: $30.00

5082½ Grapefruit
and 945½ Liner

5297½ Grapefruit
and 945½ Liner

Grapefruits, continued

**Blank 5082½**
Grapefruit and 945½ Liner
Regular Optic
Colors: Rose Bowl, Azure Bowl, Green Bowl, $65.00;
  Amber Base, Green Base, Blue Base, $54.00;
  Solid Green, Spiral Optic, $50.00

**Blank 5097½**
Grapefruit and 945½ Liner
Regular Optic
Colors: Crystal, Mother of Pearl, $30.00; Amber, $50.00;
  Green, Rose, $60.00; Orchid, $65.00

# PARFAITS

766 Parfait

766½ Parfait

766 AND 766½
PARFAITS, ORIENTAL
ETCHING

**Blank 766**
Parfait, 6 oz., 7½" (Tall)
Regular Optic
Price: $20.00

**Blank 766½**
Parfait, 6 oz., 5¼" (Short)
Regular Optic
Price: $20.00

805 Parfait

822 Parfait

**Blank 805**
Parfait, 6 oz. 5 1/16"
Regular Optic
Price: $20.00

**Blank 822**
Parfait, 6 oz., 5⅜"
No Optic
Price: $18.00

858½ Parfait

858½ PARFAIT,
MOTHER OF PEARL
IRIDESCENSE

**Blank 858½**
Parfait, 5½ oz.
Regular Optic
Price: $18.00

Parfaits, continued

### Blank 869
Parfait, 6 oz., 5⅝"
Regular Optic
Colors: Crystal, $22.00; Amber, Green, $25.00; Blue, $30.00

### Blank 877
Parfait, 5½ oz.
Regular Optic
Colors: Crystal, Mother of Pearl, $27.00; Amber, Green, $40.00;
   Orchid, Azure, $50.00

### Blank 899
Parfait, 6 oz., 6¹¹⁄₁₆"
No Optic
Price: $18.00

### Blank 4095
Parfait, 6 oz.
Regular Optic, Spiral Optic, Loop Optic
Colors: Crystal, $20.00; Amber Base, $34.00;
   Green Base, Green, Green Bowl, $40.00;
   Azure Bowl, Rose Bowl, Blue Base, $50.00

### Blank 5054
Parfait, 5½ oz., 5⅝"
Regular Optic
Price: $20.00

869 Parfait

877 Parfait

899 Parfait

4095 Parfait

5054 Parfait

# OYSTER COCKTAILS

### Blank 837
Oyster Cocktail
See also Appendix A, Blank 837
Price: $10.00

### Blank 5039
Oyster Cocktail
Price: $30.00

837 Oyster Cocktail

5039 Oyster Cocktail

173

300 Jug or Tankard

300 Jug, Woodland
Etching

300½ Jug

303 Jug, Grille
Etching

303 Jug

# JUGS AND TANKARDS

See also *Fostoria, Useful and Ornamental*, pages 153 through 158.

***Blank 300***
Jug or Tankard
Size 8, 7, 6, 5, 4, 3, 2, 1
Price: $75.00

***Blank 300½***
Jug
Size 7, 6, 5, 4
Price: $80.00

***Blank 303***
Jug
Size 8, 7, 6, 5, 4
Price: $65.00

Jugs and Tankards, continued

### Blank 316
Jug
Size 7
Regular Optic
Price: $78.00

316 Jug

### Blank 317-7
### Blank 317½-7
Jug, with or without Cover
Size 7
Price: $65.00 – 75.00

317½-7 Jug, Oriental
Etching

317½-7 Jug

### Blank 318
Jug
Size 7, 6, 5, 4
Regular Optic, No Optic
Price: $50.00 – 78.00 depending on size.

318 Jug

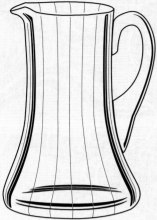

724 Jug or Tankard

890 Footed Jug

890 Rose Jug,
Verona Etching

1227 Jug

Jugs and Tankards, continued

### Blank 724
Jug or Tankard
Size 7, 6
Price: $80.00

### Blank 890
Footed Jug
Size 7
Colors: Crystal, $125.00; Rose, Green, $250.00

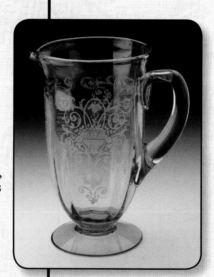

### Blank 1227
Jug
Size 7
Available with Cut Neck
Price: $65.00

Jugs and Tankards, continued

## Blank 1236
Jug
Size 7, 6, 5, 4, 3, 2, 1
Colors: Crystal, $95.00; Amber, $150.00; Green, $175.00;
   Blue, $250.00. Sizes 7, 6. Smaller sizes would sell for less.

1236 Jug

## Blank 1761
Tankard, Claret
Price: $125.00

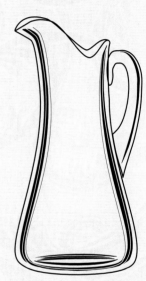

1761 Tankard, Claret

## Blank 1787
Jug or Tankard
Price: $75.00

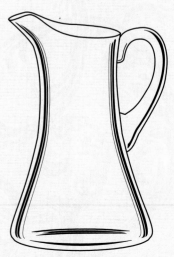

1787 Jug or Tankard

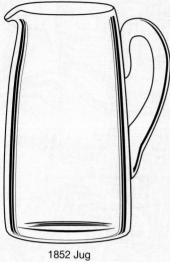

1852 Jug

2040 Jug

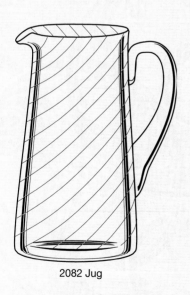

2082 Jug

**Blank 1852**
Jug
Size 7, 6
Price: $75.00

**Blank 2040**
Jug
Size 8, 7
No Optic
Price: $65.00

**Blank 2082**
Jug
Size 37, 47, or 60 oz.
Plain or Spiral Optic
Colors: Crystal, $65.00; Green, SO, $95.00

Jugs and Tankards, continued

### Blank 2100
Tankard
Size 7
Regular Optic
Price: $85.00

2100 Tankard

### Blank 2104
Jug and Tumbler
Price: $125.00

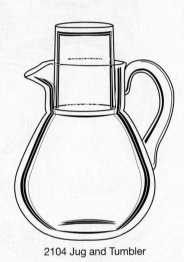

2104 Jug and Tumbler

### Blank 2270
Jug
Size 7
Colors without Cover: Crystal, $75.00; Amber, $90.00;
    Green, $110.00; Blue, $125.00
Colors with Cover: Crystal, $84.00; Amber, $95.00;
    Green, $125.00; Blue, $145.00

2270 Jug

2321 Footed Jug
PRISCILLA

**Blank 2321**

*Priscilla*

Footed Jug

Colors: Crystal, $95.00; Amber, $100.00; Green, $125.00;
Blue, $165.00

2321 BLUE PRISCILLA JUG

2666 Jug
CONTOUR

**Blank 2666**

*Contour*

Jug

Pint, $30.00

3-Pint, $55.00

Quart, $45.00

**Blank 4020**

Footed Jug

½ Gallon

Colors: Crystal, $150.00; Ebony Base, $195.00;
Amber Base, $225.00; Green Base, $250.00;
Wisteria Base, $495.00; Green Bowl, Rose Bowl,
Topaz Bowl, $350.00; Wisteria Bowl, $700.00

4020 Footed Jug

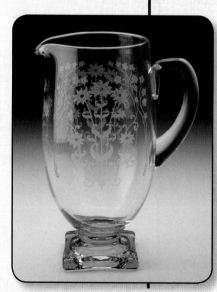

4020 JUG, MANOR
ETCHING, WISTERIA
BASE

Jugs and Tankards, continued

## Blank 4095
Footed Jug
Size 7
½ Gallon
Colors: Crystal, RO, $175.00; Amber Base, LO, $225.00;
Green Base, SO, $250.00; Green, SO, $275.00;
Green Bowl, RO, Rose Bowl, RO, $295.00;
Blue Base, RO, $300.00; Azure Bowl, RO, $325.00

4095 AZURE JUG, EILENE
NEEDLE ETCHING

4095 Footed Jug

## Blank 4140
Jug
60 oz.
Regular Optic
Colors: Crystal, $150.00; Amber, $225.00; Azure, $300.00;
Regal Blue, $500.00

4140 JUG,
MAYFLOWER ETCHING

4140 Jug

## Blank 5000
Footed Jug
Size 7
Regular Optic
Colors: Crystal, $150.00; Green, $250.00;
Green Base, $200.00; Green Bowl, $225.00;
Amber Base, $200.00; Amber, Amber Bowl, $200.00;
Blue Base, $400.00; Blue, $700.00; Orchid, Orchid Bowl,
$600.00; Azure, Azure Bowl, $375.00;
Rose Bowl, Topaz Bowl, $350.00

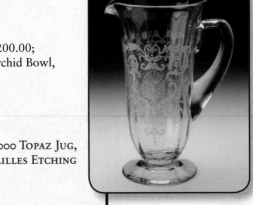

5000 TOPAZ JUG,
VERSAILLES ETCHING

5000 Footed Jug

Green Seville 870 Footed Iced Tea Tumbler and 5084 Jug; Amber Seville 870 Goblet and Amber 5084 Jug.

5084 Footed Jug

6011 Footed Jug

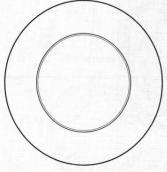

2283,
No Optic

Jugs and Tankards, continued

### Blank 5084
Footed Jug
Size 7
Regular Optic
Colors: Crystal, $145.00; Amber, $250.00; Green, $300.00; Rose, $350.00; Blue, $700.00

### Blank 6011
Footed Jug
63 oz.
Colors: Crystal, $145.00; Amber Base, $195.00; Gold Tint Bowl, $325.00; Azure Bowl, $350.00; Regal Blue Bowl, Burgundy Bowl, Empire Green Bowl, $600.00

6011 Jug, Regal Blue Bowl

# PLATES

See also *Fostoria, Useful and Ornamental*, pages 173 through 177.

### Blank 2283
Regular Optic, Spiral Optic, No Optic
Plate, 5", 7" (Cut 175, 177, or 178, also made in Canary, not made in Blue), 9", 10", 12" (not made in Crystal), 7" RO, 8" RO
Colors: Crystal, $6.00 – 18.00; Amber, $8.00 – 25.00; Green, $9.00 – 32.00; Blue, $12.00 – 48.00, Canary (7" only), $25.00
Plate, 6", 7", 8", 11" (not made in Orchid, Rose, or Azure), 13" (not made in Crystal or Azure), 6" RO (also made in Topaz, not Canary), 6" SO (not made in Canary); 7", SO; 8", SO; 13" SO (not made in Crystal)
Colors: Crystal $7.00 – 12.00; Amber, $9.00 – 47.00; Green, $9.00 – 52.00; Blue, $12.00 – 60.00; Canary, $14.00 – 68.00; Topaz (6" RO only), $10.00; Orchid, $12.00 – 62.00; Rose, $10.00 – 50.00; Azure, $12.00 – 54.00
Plate 9" SO, 10" SO
Colors: Amber, $18.00, $27.00; Green, $20.00, $34.00; Rose, $20.00, $35.00; Azure, $20.00, $40.00

Plates, continued

## Blank 2337

Regular Optic, Narrow Optic, Spiral Optic, Loop Optic, Dimple
 Optic (Not Shown), Niagara Optic, No Optic
Plate, 6", 7", 8", RO, $6.00 – 10.00
Plate 9", 10", No Optic, $12.00, $18.00
Plate, 6", 7", 8", LO, $8.00 – 14.00
Plate, 7", Niagara Optic, $15.00
Plate, 7", Narrow Optic, $15.00
Plate, 7"
Colors: Crystal, $8.00; Onyx, $12.00; Gray Mist, Green Mist,
 $14.00; Amber, Green, Plum, Gold, Lilac, Pink, $16.00; Blue,
 $18.00; Regal Blue, Empire Green, Burgundy, Amethyst,
 $32.00; Ruby, $34.00
Plate, 8"
Colors: Crystal, $10.00; Amber, $18.00; Green, $20.00; Blue,
 $24.00; Regal Blue, Burgundy, Empire Green, $34.00; Ruby,
 $36.00
Plate, 11"
Colors: Crystal, $18.00; Regal Blue, Empire Green, Burgundy,
 $45.00; Ruby, $50.00

## Blank 2574
## Raleigh
Plate, 6", 7", 8", 9", $5.00 – 18.00

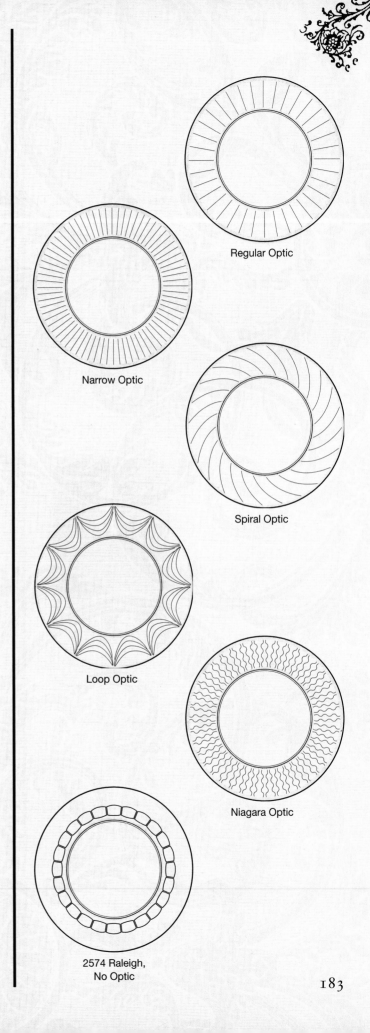

Regular Optic

Narrow Optic

Spiral Optic

Loop Optic

Niagara Optic

2574 Raleigh,
No Optic

808, 810, 811
Beer Goblet

889
Whiskey Sour

1861
Beer Mug

2435
Beer Mug

2460
Goblet

2439 Azure
Versailles Decanter
(courtesy Jim and
Sherry Davis)

2460
Footed Ice Tea

2460
Low Sherbet

# BEVERAGE SETS AND BARWARE

See also *Fostoria, Useful and Ornamental*, pages 20 through 34.

*Blank 808*
Beer Goblet, 8 oz., 4¾", plain or optic, $10.00

*Blank 810*
Beer Goblet, 12 oz., 5½", plain, $9.00

*Blank 811*
Beer Goblet, 14 oz., 5½", plain, $10.00

*Blank 889*
Whiskey Sour, 5 oz., 3½"
See Appendix A, Blank 889 for colors and prices.

*Blank 1861*
Beer Mug, 11 oz., 4½" and 15 oz., 5¼"
Colors: Crystal, $40.00; Amber Handle, $47.00;
    Regal Blue Handle, Empire Green Handle, $60.00

*Blank 2435*
Beer Mug, 9 oz., 4¾"
Colors: Crystal, $40.00; Amber Handle, $47.00;
    Regal Blue Handle, Empire Green Handle, $60.00

*Blank 2439*
Decanter
Colors: Crystal, $300.00/Market; Amber, $400.00/Market;
    Topaz, $475.00/Market; Rose, Azure, Green, $600.00/Market

*Blank 2460*
Goblet, 10 oz., $18.00
Low Sherbet, 6 oz., $15.00
Oyster Cocktail, 4 oz., $15.00
Footed Ice Tea, 13 oz., $18.00
Made in Rose, Green, Amber, Crystal, Topaz

Beverage Sets and Barware, continued

### Blank 2464
Ice Jug, ½ Gallon
Colors: Crystal, $225.00; Amber, $280.00; Green, Rose,
Topaz, $325.00
11 oz. Tumbler
Colors: Crystal, $25.00; Amber, Green, Topaz, $32.00;
Rose, $35.00

### Blank 2487
Beer Mug, 12 oz.
Colors: Crystal, $35.00; Amber, $45.00
Beer Mug, 14 oz., 5⅝"
Colors: Crystal, $44.00; Amber, Topaz, $48.00; Green,
Rose, $50.00; Wisteria, $95.00

### Blank 2493
Beer Mug, 14 oz., 5⅝", Handled (1933 – 1934)
Colors: Crystal, $45.00; Amber, Topaz, $48.00
Tavern Mug, Milkglass (1954 – 1959), $57.00
BiCentennial Tavern Mug (1974 – 1978) dated 1776 – 1976
on bottom
Colors: Crystal, $45.00; Amber, $48.00

2464
Tumbler

2464
Ice Jug

2464 JUG, MIDNIGHT ROSE
ETCHING

2487
Beer Mug

2493 AMBER
TAVERN MUG

2493
Beer Mug

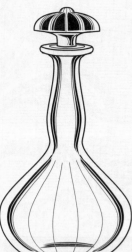

2494 Empire Green
Bitters Bottle

2494
Decanter and Stopper

### Blank 2494

Decanter and Stopper, 26 oz., 9¼"
Colors: Crystal, RO, Mother of Pearl, $150.00; Amber,
RO, $200.00; Regal Blue, Burgundy, Empire Green, $275.00;
Ruby, $300.00
Cordial Bottle, 14 oz., 7½"
Colors: Crystal, Silver Mist, Mother of Pearl, $85.00;
Amber, $95.00; Regal Blue, Empire Green, Burgundy, $150.00;
Ruby, $175.00
Bitters Bottle, 5¾ oz., 5¾"
Colors: Crystal, $67.00; Amber, 75.00; Regal Blue,
Empire Green, Burgundy, Ruby, $95.00

2494 Ruby Decanter
and Stopper

2494 SilverMist Cordial Set:
Silver Mist Cordial Bottle,
Assorted Cordials on 2429
Silver Mist Cordial Tray

2502

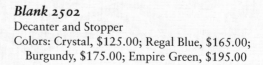

### Blank 2502

Decanter and Stopper
Colors: Crystal, $125.00; Regal Blue, $165.00;
Burgundy, $175.00; Empire Green, $195.00

Beverage Sets and Barware, continued

### Blank 2518

Jug, 44 oz., 9"
Colors: Crystal, $95.00; Burgundy, Crystal Handle,
Empire Green, Crystal Handle, $125.00; Regal Blue,
Crystal Handle, $135.00
Cocktail Shaker, 38 oz.,12¼", Metal Top
Colors: Crystal, $95.00; Regal Blue, Empire Green,
Burgundy, $145.00; Ruby, $175.00
Cocktail Shaker, 28 oz., 7⅜", Gold Top
Colors: Crystal, $95.00; Regal Blue, Empire Green, Burgundy,
Ruby, $145.00
Decanter, 30 oz., 9½"
Colors: Crystal, $95.00; Burgundy, $175.00; Regal Blue,
Empire Green, Ruby, $195.00
Footed Cocktail, 3 oz., 3⅜"
Wine, 5 oz., 3½"
Tumbler, 10 oz., 4⅝"
Whiskey, 2 oz., 2¼"
Colors: Crystal, $15.00; Regal Blue, Empire Green, Burgundy,
Ruby, $30.00

REGAL BLUE 2518 JUG, RUBY 2518 DECANTER,
WHISKEY, WINE, REGAL BLUE 2524 COCKTAIL
MIXER (COURTESY OF MIKE AND GINA LODES)

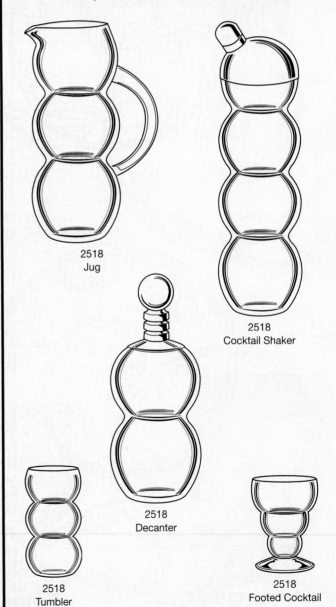

2518
Jug

2518
Cocktail Shaker

2518
Decanter

2518
Tumbler

2518
Footed Cocktail

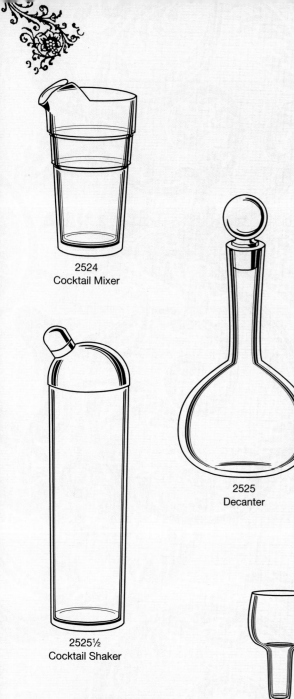

2524
Cocktail Mixer

2525
Decanter

2525½
Cocktail Shaker

4098
Hollow Stem Beer

4098 HOLLOW STEM BEER,
BURGUNDY BASE

Beverage Sets and Barware, continued

### Blank 2524
Cocktail Mixer, 21 oz., 6½"
Colors: Crystal, $35.00; Regal Blue, Empire Green,
   Burgundy, $60.00

### Blank 2525
Cocktail Shaker, 42 oz., 12½", Metal Top
Colors: Crystal, $75.00; Burgundy, $135.00; Regal Blue,
   Ruby, $145.00; Empire Green, $175.00
Decanter and Stopper, 28 oz., 10½"
Colors: Crystal, $125.00; Burgundy, $225.00; Regal Blue,
   Empire Green, $275.00

### Blank 2525½
Cocktail Shaker, 30 oz., 7½", Metal Top
Colors: Crystal, $75.00; Regal Blue, Ruby, $95.00

### Blank 4098
Hollow Stem Beer, 12 oz., 4¾"
Colors: Crystal, $25.00; Amber Base, $35.00; Burgundy Base,
   $37.00; Regal Blue Base, Empire Green Base, $40.00

Beverage Sets and Barware, continued

## Blank 4020
Footed Decanter and Stopper
Colors: Crystal, $395.00; Amber Base, Ebony Base, $565.00;
   Green Base, $600.00; Rose Bowl, Topaz Bowl, $625.00
2 oz. Footed Whiskey
Colors: Crystal, Ebony Base, Amber Base, Green Base,
   Rose Bowl, Topaz Bowl, $30.00; Wisteria Bowl, $45.00

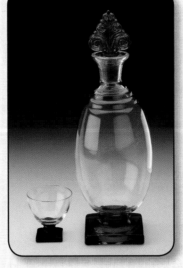

4020 WHISKEY, EBONY BASE;
4020 DECANTER, GREEN BASE

4020
Footed Decanter
and Stopper

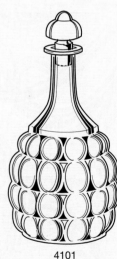

4020
Footed Whiskey

## Blank 4101
Regular Optic, No Optic
Jug, 80 oz.
Colors: Amber, $95.00; Green, Topaz, $125.00; Rose,
   Azure, $150.00
Decanter and Stopper, 38 oz.
Colors: Amber, $125.00; Green, Topaz, $150.00; Rose,
   Azure, $175.00
2½ oz., 3" Tumbler
Colors: Amber, $10.00; Green, Topaz, $12.00; Rose,
   Azure, $14.00
9 oz., 4⅝" Tumbler
Colors: Amber, Green, Topaz, $8.00; Rose, Azure, $10.00
13 oz., 5¼" Tumbler
Colors: Amber, $10.00, Green, Topaz, $12.00; Rose,
   Azure, $14.00

4101 Jug

4101 Tumbler

4101
Decanter and Stopper

4101 GREEN JUG AND TUMBLERS

4118 Jug

4118
Tumbler

4118 Ruby
Jug and
Tumbler

4140 Jug

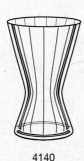

4140
Tumbler

4141 Jug

4141
Tumbler

Beverage Sets and Barware, continued

### Blank 4118

Jug, 60 oz., 8½"
Colors: Crystal, $145.00; Regal Blue, Empire Green, Burgundy,
    Ruby, $300.00
12 oz. Tumbler, 5"
Colors: Crystal, $25.00; Regal Blue, Empire Green,
    Burgundy, $38.00; Ruby, $45.00

### Blank 4140

7-Piece Ice Tea Set
60 oz. Jug, 7½"
Six 12 oz. Tumblers, 5"

### Blank 4140

7-Piece Water Set
60 oz. Jug, 7½"
Six 10 oz. Tumblers, 4½"

Price for Each Set: Crystal, $150.00; Amber, $195.00;
    Azure, $235.00; Regal Blue, $300.00

### Blank 4141

7-Piece Ice Tea Set
59 oz. Jug, 7"
Six 12 oz. Tumblers, 4¾"

### Blank 4141

7-Piece Water Set
59 oz. Jug, 7"
Six 10 oz. Tumblers, 3⅜"

Price for Each Set: Crystal, $150.00; Amber, $195.00;
    Azure, $235.00; Regal Blue, $300.00

Beverage Sets and Barware, continued

*Blank 4142*
7-Piece Ice Tea Set
58 oz. Jug, 7¼"
Six 12 oz. Tumblers, 4⅞"

*Blank 4142*
7-Piece Water Set
58 oz. Jug, 7¼"
Six 10 oz. Tumblers, 4"

Price for Each Set: Crystal, $150.00; Amber, $195.00;
   Azure, $235.00; Regal Blue, $300.00

*Blank 5068*
Cocktail, 3½ oz., Crystal, No Optic, $34.00

*Blank 5069*
Cordial, 1 oz., Crystal, No Optic, $45.00

*Blank 5510*
Pilsener, 12 oz., 8", Crystal, $64.00

*Blank 6011*
Decanter, 26 oz., 11⅜"
Colors: Crystal, $195.00; Amber Base, $250.00;
   Regal Blue Bowl, Burgundy Bowl,
   Empire Green Bowl, $625.00
3 oz. Cocktail, 4⅝"
Colors: Crystal, $15.00; Silver Mist Stem, $25.00;
   Amber Base, $32.00; Burgundy/Amethyst, Empire Green,
   Regal Blue, Ruby Bowl, $45.00

4142
Tumbler

4142 Jug

5068
Cocktail

5069
Cordial

5510
Pilsener

6011
Decanter

6011
Cocktail

6011 REGAL BLUE
DECANTER

Beverage Sets and Barware, continued

## Repeal Blown Stemware
### 1934 – 1942 (Crystal, 1934 – 1943)

**Blank 795**
5½ oz. Hollow Stem Champagne
Colors:  Crystal, Mother of Pearl, $16.00; Amber Base, Regal Blue Base,
    Empire Green Base, Burgundy Base, $58.00

**Blank 846**
2 oz. Sherry
Colors:  Crystal, Mother of Pearl, $14.00; Amber Base, Regal Blue Base,
    Empire Green Base, Burgundy Base, $65.00

**Blank 858**
1 oz. Brandy, 7 oz. Long Stem Champagne, 1 oz. Cordial
Colors:  Crystal, Mother of Pearl, $35.00; Amber Base, $75.00; Burgundy Base,
    Regal Blue Base, Empire Green Base, $125.00

**Blank 863**
5 oz. Hollow Stem Champagne (See Blank 863)
Colors:  Crystal, Mother of Pearl, $12.00; Amber Base, Regal Blue Base,
    Empire Green Base, Burgundy Base, $58.00

**Blank 877**
6 oz. Saucer Champagne
1¾ oz. Whiskey Sham (See Appendix A)
Colors:  Crystal, Mother of Pearl, $22.00; Amber Base, Regal Blue Base,
    Empire Green Base, Burgundy Base, $95.00

**Blank 877½**
10 oz. Goblet
Colors:  Crystal, Mother of Pearl, $25.00; Amber Base, Regal Blue Base,
    Empire Green Base, Burgundy Base, $125.00

**Blank 887**
1¾ oz. Whiskey
Colors:  Crystal, Mother of Pearl, $12.00; Amber, Regal Blue, Burgundy,
    Empire Green, Ruby, $34.00

**Blank 902**
5 oz. Wine
3 oz. Martini Cocktail
Colors:  Crystal, Mother of Pearl, $22.00; Amber Base, Regal Blue Base, Empire Green Base,
    Burgundy Base, $58.00

877½ GOBLET,
EMPIRE GREEN FOOT

**Blank 906**
4¾ oz. Brandy Inhaler
Colors:  Crystal, Mother of Pearl, $26.00; Amber Base, Regal Blue Base,
    Empire Green Base, Burgundy Base, $95.00

**Blank 932**
5½ oz. Saucer Champagne
Colors:  Crystal, $20.00; Regal Blue Base, Burgundy Base, $58.00

**Blank 952**
3 oz. Cocktail
Colors:  Crystal, Mother of Pearl, $20.00; Amber Base, Regal Blue Base,
    Empire Green Base, Burgundy Base, $54.00

**Blank 963**
4½ oz. Rhine Wine, 3½ oz. Cocktail, 2 oz. Creme de Menthe
1 oz. Cordial
Colors:  Crystal, Mother of Pearl, $25.00; Amber Base, Regal Blue Base,
    Empire Green Base, Burgundy Base, $75.00

**Blank 1184**
7 oz. Whiskey Sham (See Appendix A)
Colors:  Crystal, Mother of Pearl, $20.00; Azure, Gold Tint, Wisteria, $35.00

**Blank 1554**
5 oz. Pressed Hollow Stem Champagne (see *Fostoria, Useful and Ornamental*, page 27)
Crystal, $10.00

**Blank 4122**
1½ oz. Whiskey Sham (see Appendix A)
Colors:  Crystal, Mother of Pearl, $18.00

963
4½ oz. Rhine Wine

902
5 oz. Wine

952
3 oz. Cocktail

902
3 oz. Martini Cocktail

963
3½ oz. Cocktail

858
1 oz. Brandy

846
2 oz. Sherry

963
1 oz. Cordial

963
2 oz. Creme de Menthe

932
5½ oz. Saucer Champagne

858
1 oz. Cordial

906
Brandy Inhaler

877½
10 oz. Goblet

877
6 oz. Saucer Champagne

795
5½ oz. Hollow Stem Champagne

858
7 oz. Long Stem Champagne

# Appendix D
# After 1982

Lancaster Colony Corporation, Inc., introduced six patterns at the Fostoria plant in Moundsville from 1983 to the final closing of the plant in 1986. After 1983, it continued to make Virginia, Transition, Heritage, Kimberley, Kimberley Gold, Kimberley Platinum, Monarch, and York.

Goblet

**Blank CH05, CHIPPENDALE**
Lead Crystal
*1983 – 1986 Crystal*
Plate Etching Similar to Etching 327, Navarre

Pieces made:
Goblet, 10 oz., $32.00
Champagne, 8 oz., $25.00
Wine, 7 oz., $35.00
Flute/Parfait, 8 oz., $45.00
Footed Ice Tea, 14 oz., $32.00

Goblet

**Blank SA05, SATIN RIBBONS**
Lead Crystal
*1983 – 1986 Crystal*
Plate Etching similar to Etching 341, Romance

Pieces made:
Goblet, 10 oz., $30.00
Champagne, 8 oz., $28.00
Wine, 7 oz., $32.00
Flute/Parfait, 8 oz., $45.00
Footed Ice Tea, 14 oz., $30.00

Goblet

**Blank JU05 JUNIPER**
Pressed Lead Crystal with Polished Cutting
*1983 – 1986 Crystal*

Pieces made:
Goblet, 10 oz., $20.00
Champagne, 8 oz., $18.00
Wine, 7 oz., $20.00
Flute/Parfait, 8 oz., $26.00
Footed Ice Tea, 14 oz., $20.00
Double Old Fashioned, $16.00
Highball, $16.00

### Blank BE04, BENNINGTON
Pressed Lead Crystal with Polished Cutting
*1983 – 1986 Crystal (Tumblers, 1982 – 1986)*

Pieces made:
Goblet, 10 oz., $20.00
Champagne, 8 oz., $18.00
Wine, 7 oz., $20.00
Flute/Parfait, 8 oz., $26.00
Footed Ice Tea, 14 oz., $20.00
Double Old Fashioned, $16.00
Highball, $16.00

Goblet

### Blank CA16, CAPTIVA
Pressed Lead Crystal
*1983 – 1986 Crystal, Light Blue, Peach*

Pieces made:
Goblet/Ice Tea, 13 oz., $22.00
Wine/Juice, 8 oz., $22.00
Mug/Cup, 9 oz., $22.00

Goblet

### Blank M012, MONET
Pressed Lead Crystal
*1985 – 1986 Crystal Mist (Frosted Stem)*
*Light Blue, Peach, Dark Blue, Lilac, Gray*

Pieces made:
Goblet, $12.00
Wine, $12.00
Footed Ice Tea, $12.00

Goblet

# Value Guide

### FIFTH AVENUE, Blank 114

| | |
|---|---|
| Goblet, 11½ oz. | $4.00 |
| Goblet, 11 oz. | $4.00 |
| Goblet, 10 oz. | $4.00 |
| Champagne | $4.00 |
| Claret | $4.00 |
| Wine | $4.00 |
| Cordial | $4.00 |

### ETCHING 32, Blank 114

| | |
|---|---|
| Goblet, 10 oz. | $5.00 |
| Champagne | $5.00 |
| Claret | $5.00 |
| Wine | $5.00 |
| Cordial | $5.00 |

### ETCHING 46, Blank 114

| | |
|---|---|
| Goblet, 10 oz. | $5.00 |
| Champagne | $5.00 |
| Claret | $5.00 |
| Wine | $5.00 |

### LARGE CLOVERLEAF, Etching 47, Blank 114

| | |
|---|---|
| Goblet, 10 oz. | $5.00 |
| Champagne | $5.00 |
| Claret | $5.00 |
| Wine | $5.00 |
| Cordial | $5.00 |

### Blank 660
#### Crystal

| | |
|---|---|
| Goblet | $6.00 |
| Saucer Champagne | $6.00 |
| Low Sherbet | $6.00 |
| Parfait | $6.00 |
| Cocktail | $6.00 |
| Claret | $6.00 |
| Wine | $6.00 |
| Cordial | $15.00 |

#### Orchid

| | |
|---|---|
| Goblet | $35.00 |
| Saucer Champagne | $30.00 |
| Low Sherbet | $30.00 |
| Parfait | $35.00 |
| Cocktail | $30.00 |
| Claret | $42.00 |
| Wine | $40.00 |
| Cordial | $45.00 |

### PAGODA, Etching 90, Blank 660

| | |
|---|---|
| Goblet | $7.00 |
| Saucer Champagne | $7.00 |
| Low Sherbet | $7.00 |
| Cocktail | $7.00 |
| Claret | $10.00 |

| | |
|---|---|
| Wine | $7.00 |
| Cordial | $14.00 |

### WOODLAND, Etching 264, Blank 660

| | |
|---|---|
| Goblet | $20.00 |
| Saucer Champagne | $12.00 |
| Low Sherbet | $10.00 |
| Parfait | $20.00 |
| Cocktail | $12.00 |
| Wine | $15.00 |
| Cordial | $25.00 |

### WASHINGTON, Etching 266, Blank 660

| | |
|---|---|
| Goblet | $12.00 |
| Saucer Champagne | $8.00 |
| Low Sherbet | $8.00 |
| Parfait | $12.00 |
| Cocktail | $8.00 |
| Claret | $15.00 |
| Wine | $12.00 |
| Cordial | $20.00 |

### MYSTIC, Etching 270, Blank 660

| | |
|---|---|
| Goblet | $25.00 |
| Saucer Champagne | $12.00 |
| Low Sherbet | $12.00 |
| Parfait | $25.00 |
| Cocktail | $12.00 |
| Claret | $25.00 |
| Wine | $18.00 |
| Cordial | $30.00 |

### TRELLIS, Cutting 169, Blank 660

| | |
|---|---|
| Goblet | $10.00 |
| Saucer Champagne | $10.00 |
| Low Sherbet | $10.00 |
| Parfait | $10.00 |
| Cocktail | $10.00 |
| Wine | $12.00 |
| Cordial | $15.00 |

### PINNACLE, Cutting 753, Blank 660

| | |
|---|---|
| Goblet | $9.00 |
| Saucer Champagne | $9.00 |
| Low Sherbet | $6.00 |
| Cocktail | $9.00 |
| Claret | $9.00 |
| Wine | $9.00 |
| Cordial | $12.00 |

### COIN GOLD, Decoration 1, Blank 660

| | |
|---|---|
| Goblet | $8.00 |
| Saucer Champagne | $8.00 |
| Low Sherbet | $7.00 |
| Parfait | $8.00 |

| | |
|---|---|
| Cocktail | $8.00 |
| Claret | $9.00 |
| Wine | $9.00 |
| Cordial | $10.00 |

### BLACK AND GOLD, Decoration 23, Blank 660

| | |
|---|---|
| Goblet | $45.00 |
| Saucer Champagne | $45.00 |
| Low Sherbet | $40.00 |
| Parfait | $45.00 |
| Cocktail | $45.00 |
| Claret | $45.00 |
| Wine | $45.00 |
| Cordial | $54.00 |

### GOLDWOOD, Decoration 50, Blank 660

| | |
|---|---|
| Goblet | $20.00 |
| Saucer Champagne | $18.00 |
| Low Sherbet | $18.00 |
| Parfait | $20.00 |
| Cocktail | $18.00 |
| Claret | $20.00 |
| Wine | $20.00 |
| Cordial | $25.00 |

### Blank 661

| | |
|---|---|
| Goblet | $6.00 |
| Saucer Champagne | $6.00 |
| Fruit/Low Sherbet | $6.00 |
| Parfait | $6.00 |
| Cocktail | $6.00 |
| Claret | $6.00 |
| Wine | $6.00 |
| Cordial | $6.00 |

### BALLET, Etching 91, Blank 661

| | |
|---|---|
| Goblet | $8.00 |
| Saucer Champagne, 5½ oz. | $8.00 |
| Fruit/Low Sherbet, 5½ oz. | $7.00 |
| Cocktail | $7.00 |
| Claret, 4 oz. | $10.00 |
| Wine, 2¾ oz. | $10.00 |
| Cordial | $10.00 |

### ORIENT, Etching 265, Blank 661

| | |
|---|---|
| Goblet | $8.00 |
| Saucer Champagne | $8.00 |
| Fruit/Low Sherbet | $7.00 |
| Parfait | $8.00 |
| Cocktail | $8.00 |
| Claret | $9.00 |
| Wine | $10.00 |

### VIRGINIA, Etching 267, Blank 661

| | |
|---|---|
| Goblet | $15.00 |

Saucer Champagne...................... $12.00
Fruit/Low Sherbet ..................... $12.00
Parfait ........................................ $15.00
Cocktail ...................................... $12.00
Claret.......................................... $20.00
Wine ........................................... $15.00
Cordial........................................ $25.00

### MELROSE, Etching 268, Blank 661

Goblet......................................... $15.00
Saucer Champagne...................... $12.00
Fruit/Low Sherbet ..................... $12.00
Parfait ........................................ $15.00
Cocktail ...................................... $12.00
Claret.......................................... $20.00
Wine ........................................... $15.00
Cordial........................................ $25.00

### LOUISA, Cutting 168, Blank 661

Goblet......................................... $12.00
Saucer Champagne...................... $12.00
Fruit/Low Sherbet ..................... $10.00
Parfait ........................................ $12.00
Cocktail ...................................... $12.00
Wine ........................................... $12.00

### CYNTHIA, Cutting 170, Blank 661

Goblet......................................... $12.00
Saucer Champagne...................... $12.00
Fruit/Low Sherbet ..................... $10.00
Parfait ........................................ $12.00
Cocktail ...................................... $12.00
Wine ........................................... $12.00
Cordial........................................ $15.00

### EMPRESS, Decoration 29, Blank 661

Goblet......................................... $12.00
Saucer Champagne...................... $12.00
Fruit/Low Sherbet ..................... $12.00
Parfait ........................................ $12.00
Cocktail ...................................... $12.00
Claret.......................................... $12.00
Wine ........................................... $12.00
Cordial ....................................... $14.00

### NOME, Decoration 40, Blank 661

Goblet......................................... $10.00
Saucer Champagne...................... $10.00
Fruit/Low Sherbet ...................... $10.00
Parfait ........................................ $10.00
Cocktail ...................................... $10.00
Wine ........................................... $10.00
Cordial ....................................... $18.00

### MIAMI, Decoration 42, Blank 661

Goblet, 9 oz. .............................. $14.00
Saucer Champagne...................... $14.00
Fruit/Low Sherbet ..................... $12.00
Parfait ........................................ $14.00

Cocktail ...................................... $14.00
Claret.......................................... $14.00
Wine ........................................... $14.00
Cordial........................................ $22.00

### Blank 766

Goblet, 9 oz. .............................. $10.00
Goblet, 7 oz. .............................. $10.00
Saucer Champagne...................... $10.00
Sherbet........................................ $7.00
Fruit ........................................... $7.00
Parfait ........................................ $10.00
Cocktail ...................................... $7.00
Claret.......................................... $10.00
Rhine Wine ................................ $12.00
Wine ........................................... $10.00
Burgundy ................................... $12.00
Sherry.......................................... $12.00
Crème de Menthe....................... $12.00
Brandy (Pousse Café) ................. $12.00
Cordial........................................ $12.00
Sorbet......................................... $7.00
Footed Ice Tea, Handled ............. $12.00
Handled Custard......................... $7.00
Grapefruit and Liner ................... $30.00
Whiskey Tumbler......................... $7.00

### IRISH LACE, Etching 36, Blank 766

Goblet......................................... $10.00
Saucer Champagne...................... $10.00
Sherbet........................................ $8.00
Fruit ........................................... $8.00
Parfait ........................................ $15.00
Cocktail ...................................... $10.00
Claret.......................................... $15.00
Rhine Wine ................................ $12.00
Wine ........................................... $12.00
Burgundy ................................... $12.00
Sherry.......................................... $12.00
Crème de Menthe....................... $12.00
Brandy ....................................... $20.00
Cordial........................................ $28.00
Sorbet......................................... $8.00
Footed Ice Tea, Handled ............. $24.00
Handled Custard......................... $8.00
Grapefruit and Liner ................... $30.00

### CHAIN, Etching 42, Blank 766

Goblet......................................... $10.00
Saucer Champagne...................... $10.00
Fruit ........................................... $7.00
Cocktail ...................................... $10.00
Claret.......................................... $10.00
Footed Ice Tea, handled .............. $11.00

### LOTUS, Etching 232, Blank 766

Goblet......................................... $15.00

Saucer Champagne...................... $12.00
Sherbet........................................ $10.00
Fruit ........................................... $10.00
Parfait ........................................ $15.00
Cocktail ...................................... $12.00
Claret.......................................... $18.00
Rhine Wine ................................ $15.00
Wine ........................................... $12.00
Burgundy ................................... $15.00
Sherry.......................................... $12.00
Crème de Menthe....................... $12.00
Brandy ....................................... $18.00
Cordial........................................ $22.00
Sorbet......................................... $10.00
Footed Ice Tea, Handled ............. $20.00
Custard ...................................... $8.00
Grapefruit and Liner ................... $25.00

### GARLAND, Etching 237, Blank 766

Goblet......................................... $18.00
Saucer Champagne...................... $15.00
Sherbet........................................ $14.00
Fruit ........................................... $12.00
Parfait ........................................ $15.00
Cocktail ...................................... $15.00
Claret.......................................... $20.00
Rhine Wine ................................ $20.00
Wine ........................................... $18.00
Burgundy ................................... $15.00
Sherry.......................................... $18.00
Crème de Menthe....................... $18.00
Brandy ....................................... $25.00
Cordial ....................................... $25.00
Sorbet......................................... $8.00
Footed Ice Tea, Handled ............. $22.00
Handled Custard......................... $7.00
Grapefruit and Liner ................... $25.00

### ORIENTAL, Etching 250, Blank 766

Goblet......................................... $22.00
Saucer Champagne...................... $20.00
Sherbet........................................ $15.00
Fruit ........................................... $10.00
Parfait ........................................ $30.00
Cocktail ...................................... $15.00
Claret.......................................... $35.00
Wine ........................................... $30.00
Sherry.......................................... $18.00
Brandy ....................................... $20.00
Cordial........................................ $35.00
Footed Ice Tea, Handled ............. $35.00
Custard ...................................... $12.00

### MODERN VINTAGE, Etching 255, Blank 766

Goblet......................................... $12.00
Saucer Champagne...................... $9.00
Fruit ........................................... $8.00
Parfait ........................................ $18.00
Cocktail ...................................... $9.00

| Wine | $12.00 |
|---|---|
| Cordial | $18.00 |
| Footed Ice Tea, Handled | $20.00 |

### VICTORY, Etching 257, Blank 766

| | |
|---|---|
| Goblet, 9 oz. | $12.00 |
| Goblet, 7 oz. | $10.00 |
| Saucer Champagne | $10.00 |
| Sherbet | $8.00 |
| Fruit | $8.00 |
| Parfait | $15.00 |
| Cocktail | $10.00 |
| Claret | $15.00 |
| Wine | $12.00 |
| Footed Ice Tea, Handled | $18.00 |
| Grapefruit and Liner | $20.00 |

### CUTTING 4, Blank 766

| | |
|---|---|
| Goblet | $10.00 |
| Saucer Champagne | $10.00 |
| Sherbet | $8.00 |
| Fruit | $8.00 |
| Parfait | $8.00 |
| Cocktail | $8.00 |
| Claret | $10.00 |
| Rhine Wine | $10.00 |
| Wine | $10.00 |
| Burgundy | $12.00 |
| Sherry | $10.00 |
| Crème de Menthe | $10.00 |
| Brandy | $12.00 |
| Cordial | $12.00 |
| Sorbet | $7.00 |
| Footed Ice Tea, Handled | $12.00 |
| Handled Custard | $5.00 |

### CUTTING 125, Blank 766

| | |
|---|---|
| Goblet | $12.00 |
| Saucer Champagne | $12.00 |
| Sherbet | $10.00 |
| Fruit | $10.00 |
| Parfait | $12.00 |
| Cocktail | $12.00 |
| Claret | $12.00 |
| Rhine Wine | $12.00 |
| Wine | $12.00 |
| Burgundy | $12.00 |
| Sherry | $12.00 |
| Crème de Menthe | $12.00 |
| Brandy | $15.00 |
| Cordial | $15.00 |
| Sorbet | $8.00 |
| Footed Ice Tea, Handled | $15.00 |
| Handled Custard | $7.00 |
| Grapefruit and Liner | $16.00 |

### PRISCILLA, Cutting 130, Blank 766

| | |
|---|---|
| Goblet | $12.00 |
| Saucer Champagne | $12.00 |

| Sherbet | $9.00 |
|---|---|
| Fruit | $9.00 |
| Parfait | $12.00 |
| Cocktail | $10.00 |
| Claret | $12.00 |
| Rhine Wine | $12.00 |
| Wine | $12.00 |
| Burgundy | $12.00 |
| Sherry | $12.00 |
| Crème de Menthe | $12.00 |
| Brandy (Pousse Café) | $15.00 |
| Cordial | $15.00 |
| Sorbet | $7.00 |
| Footed Ice Tea, Handled | $15.00 |
| Custard | $7.00 |
| Grapefruit and Liner | $15.00 |

### ARROW, Cutting 142, Blank 766

| | |
|---|---|
| Goblet | $12.00 |
| Saucer Champagne | $12.00 |
| Fruit | $8.00 |
| Parfait | $18.00 |
| Cocktail | $9.00 |
| Footed Ice Tea, Handled | $20.00 |

### CASCADE, Decoration 8, Blank 766

| | |
|---|---|
| Goblet | $18.00 |
| Saucer Champagne | $15.00 |
| Sherbet | $10.00 |
| Fruit | $10.00 |
| Parfait | $18.00 |
| Cocktail | $10.00 |
| Claret | $20.00 |
| Wine | $18.00 |
| Cordial | $25.00 |
| Footed Ice Tea, Handled | $20.00 |
| Grapefruit and Liner | $25.00 |

### NEWPORT, Decoration 9, Blank 766

| | |
|---|---|
| Goblet | $12.00 |
| Saucer Champagne | $12.00 |
| Sherbet | $12.00 |
| Fruit | $12.00 |
| Parfait | $20.00 |
| Cocktail | $12.00 |
| Footed Ice Tea, Handled | $20.00 |

### COIN GOLD, Decoration 15, Blank 766

| | |
|---|---|
| Goblet | $10.00 |
| Saucer Champagne | $10.00 |
| Sherbet | $8.00 |
| Fruit | $8.00 |
| Parfait | $10.00 |
| Cocktail | $9.00 |
| Footed Ice Tea, Handled | $12.00 |

### LAUREL, Decoration 31, Blank 766

| | |
|---|---|
| Goblet | $12.00 |

| Saucer Champagne | $12.00 |
|---|---|
| Fruit | $10.00 |
| Parfait | $12.00 |
| Cocktail | $12.00 |
| Wine | $12.00 |
| Cordial | $20.00 |
| Footed Ice Tea, Handled | $18.00 |

### REGENT, Decoration 32, Blank 766

| | |
|---|---|
| Goblet | $12.00 |
| Saucer Champagne | $12.00 |
| Fruit | $10.00 |
| Parfait | $18.00 |
| Cocktail | $12.00 |
| Wine | $12.00 |
| Cordial | $20.00 |
| Footed Ice Tea, Handled | $20.00 |

### Blank 858

| | |
|---|---|
| Goblet, 11 oz. | $7.00 |
| Goblet, 10 oz. | $7.00 |
| Goblet, 9 oz. | $6.00 |
| Goblet, 8 oz. | $5.00 |
| Saucer Champagne, 7 oz. | $5.00 |
| Saucer Champagne, 5½ oz. | $5.00 |
| Sherbet | $5.00 |
| Fruit | $5.00 |
| Parfait | $7.00 |
| Cocktail | $5.00 |
| Claret, 6½ oz. | $10.00 |
| Claret, 4½ oz. | $6.00 |
| Wine, 3½ oz. | $6.00 |
| Wine, 2¾ oz. | $6.00 |
| Sherry | $6.00 |
| Crème de Menthe | $6.00 |
| Brandy | $10.00 |
| Cordial | $10.00 |
| Oyster Cocktail | $4.00 |
| Hollow Stem Champagne | $10.00 |
| Tall Champagne | $6.00 |
| Lone Stem Champagne | $18.00 |
| Long Stem Champagne, Cutting R. | $18.00 |
| Bass Ale | $15.00 |
| Hot Whiskey | $6.00 |

### LARGE CLOVERLEAF, Etching 47, Blank 858

| | |
|---|---|
| Goblet, 9 oz. | $8.00 |
| Saucer Champagne, 5½ oz. | $8.00 |
| Fruit | $8.00 |
| Wine, 2¾ oz. | $8.00 |

### LENORE, Etching 73, Blank 858

| | |
|---|---|
| Goblet, 9 oz. | $8.00 |
| Saucer Champagne, 5½ oz. | $8.00 |
| Sherbet | $6.00 |
| Fruit | $6.00 |

Cocktail ........................................ $8.00
Claret, 4½ oz. ............................. $10.00
Parfait ........................................ $10.00
Wine, 2¾ oz. .............................. $10.00
Cordial ........................................ $10.00

### VINTAGE, Etching 204, Blank 858

Goblet, 11 oz. .............................. $9.00
Goblet, 10 oz. .............................. $9.00
Goblet, 9 oz. ................................ $8.00
Saucer Champagne, 7 oz. .............. $8.00
Saucer Champagne, 5½ oz. ............ $6.00
Sherbet ........................................ $6.00
Fruit ............................................ $6.00
Parfait ........................................ $10.00
Cocktail ...................................... $6.00
Claret, 6½ oz. ............................. $10.00
Claret, 4½ oz. .............................. $8.00
Wine, 3½ oz. ................................ $6.00
Wine, 2¾ oz. ................................ $6.00
Sherry .......................................... $6.00
Crème de Menthe ........................ $6.00
Brandy ........................................ $6.00
Cordial ...................................... $15.00
Oyster Cocktail ............................ $5.00
Hollow Stem Champagne .............. $10.00
Tall Champagne .......................... $10.00
Long Stem Champagne ................ $25.00
Long Stem Champagne,
  Cutting R ................................. $25.00
Hot Whiskey ................................ $7.00

### BLACKBERRY, Etching 205, Blank 858

Goblet, 11 oz. .............................. $6.00
Goblet, 10 oz. .............................. $6.00
Goblet, 9 oz. ................................ $6.00
Goblet, 8 oz. ................................ $6.00
Saucer Champagne, 7 oz. .............. $6.00
Saucer Champagne, 5½ oz. ............ $6.00
Sherbet ........................................ $6.00
Fruit ............................................ $6.00
Parfait .......................................... $6.00
Cocktail ...................................... $6.00
Claret, 6½ oz. ............................. $6.00
Claret, 4½ oz. .............................. $6.00
Wine, 3½ oz. ................................ $6.00
Wine, 2¾ oz. ................................ $6.00
Sherry .......................................... $6.00
Crème de Menthe ........................ $6.00
Brandy ........................................ $8.00
Cordial ........................................ $8.00
Oyster Cocktail ............................ $7.00
Hollow Stem Champagne .............. $10.00
Tall Champagne .......................... $10.00
Long Stem Champagne ................ $25.00
Long Stem Champagne, Cutting R .. $18.00
Bass Ale ...................................... $15.00
Hot Whiskey ................................ $6.00

### ETCHING 215, Blank 858

Goblet, 11 oz. .............................. $6.00
Goblet, 10 oz. .............................. $6.00
Goblet, 9 oz. ................................ $6.00
Saucer Champagne, 7 oz. .............. $6.00
Sherbet ........................................ $6.00
Fruit ............................................ $6.00
Cocktail ...................................... $6.00
Claret, 6½ oz. ............................. $6.00
Claret, 4½ oz. .............................. $6.00
Wine, 3½ oz. ................................ $6.00
Wine, 2¾ oz. ................................ $6.00
Sherry .......................................... $6.00
Crème de Menthe ........................ $6.00
Brandy ........................................ $8.00
Cordial ........................................ $8.00
Hollow Stem Champagne .............. $10.00
Tall Champagne .......................... $10.00
Long Stem Champagne ................ $25.00
Hot Whiskey ................................ $8.00

### NEW VINTAGE, Etching 227, Blank 858

Goblet, 11 oz. ............................ $10.00
Goblet, 10 oz. .............................. $8.00
Goblet, 9 oz. ................................ $8.00
Saucer Champagne, 7 oz. .............. $8.00
Saucer Champagne, 5½ oz. ............ $6.00
Sherbet ........................................ $6.00
Fruit ............................................ $6.00
Parfait ........................................ $14.00
Cocktail ...................................... $6.00
Claret, 6½ oz. ............................. $10.00
Claret, 4½ oz. ............................ $10.00
Wine, 3½ oz. .............................. $10.00
Wine, 2¾ oz. .............................. $10.00
Sherry ........................................ $10.00
Crème de Menthe ........................ $6.00
Brandy ...................................... $12.00
Cordial ...................................... $18.00
Oyster Cocktail ............................ $6.00
Hollow Stem Champagne .............. $10.00
Tall Champagne .......................... $14.00
Long Stem Champagne ................ $25.00
Long Stem Champagne, Cutting R .. $25.00
Hot Whiskey ................................ $6.00

### EMPIRE, Etching 238, Blank 858

Goblet, 10 oz. .............................. $8.00
Goblet, 9 oz. ................................ $6.00
Saucer Champagne, 5½ oz. ............ $8.00
Sherbet ........................................ $6.00
Fruit ............................................ $6.00
Parfait ........................................ $20.00
Cocktail ...................................... $6.00
Claret, 6½ oz. ............................. $12.00
Claret, 4½ oz. ............................ $10.00
Wine, 3½ oz. .............................. $10.00
Wine, 2¾ oz. ................................ $8.00
Sherry .......................................... $6.00

Crème de Menthe ........................ $6.00
Brandy ...................................... $12.00
Cordial ...................................... $20.00
Oyster Cocktail ............................ $7.00
Hollow Stem Champagne .............. $10.00
Tall Champagne .......................... $15.00
Handled Lemonade ...................... $20.00
Tumbler, 8 oz. .............................. $6.00
Tumbler, 14 oz. (701) .................. $10.00
Tumbler ...................................... $6.00

### LILY OF THE VALLEY, Etching 241, Blank 858

Goblet, 10 oz. ............................ $25.00
Saucer Champagne, 5½ oz. .......... $25.00
Sherbet ...................................... $22.00
Fruit .......................................... $22.00
Cocktail .................................... $22.00
Claret, 4½ oz. ............................ $30.00
Wine, 2¾ oz. .............................. $25.00
Sherry ........................................ $30.00
Crème de Menthe ...................... $25.00
Brandy ...................................... $45.00
Cordial ...................................... $45.00
Oyster Cocktail .......................... $20.00
Hollow Stem Champagne ............ $30.00
Tall Champagne ........................ $45.00

### NEW ADAM, Etching 252, Blank 858

Goblet, 9 oz. ................................ $8.00
Saucer Champagne ...................... $8.00
Fruit ............................................ $8.00
Cocktail ...................................... $8.00
Claret, 4½ oz. .............................. $8.00
Wine, 2¾ oz. ................................ $8.00
Sherry ........................................ $10.00
Cordial ...................................... $15.00

### FLORID, Etching 256, Blank 858

Goblet, 9 oz. .............................. $10.00
Saucer Champagne, 5½ oz. .......... $10.00
Sherbet ........................................ $8.00
Fruit .......................................... $10.00
Cocktail .................................... $10.00
Wine, 2¾ oz. .............................. $12.00
Sherry ........................................ $10.00

### CUTTING 77, Blank 858

Goblet, 11 oz. ............................ $10.00
Goblet, 10 oz. ............................ $10.00
Goblet, 9 oz. ................................ $8.00
Saucer Champagne, 7 oz. .............. $8.00
Sherbet ........................................ $6.00
Fruit ............................................ $6.00
Cocktail ...................................... $6.00
Claret, 6½ oz. ............................. $10.00
Claret, 4½ oz. ............................ $10.00
Wine, 3½ oz. ................................ $8.00

| | |
|---|---|
| Wine, 2¾ oz. | $6.00 |
| Sherry | $8.00 |
| Crème de Menthe | $6.00 |
| Brandy | $15.00 |
| Cordial | $15.00 |
| Hollow Stem Champagne, C. F. | $12.00 |
| Tall Champagne | $12.00 |
| Long Stem Champagne | $25.00 |
| Hot Whiskey | $6.00 |

### LARGE SUNBURST STAR, Cutting 81, Blank 858

| | |
|---|---|
| Goblet, 11 oz. | $10.00 |
| Goblet, 10 oz. | $9.00 |
| Goblet, 9 oz. | $9.00 |
| Saucer Champagne, 7 oz. | $9.00 |
| Sherbet | $6.00 |
| Fruit | $6.00 |
| Cocktail | $9.00 |
| Claret, 6½ oz. | $6.00 |
| Claret, 4½ oz. | $6.00 |
| Wine, 3½ oz. | $6.00 |
| Wine, 2¾ oz. | $6.00 |
| Sherry | $6.00 |
| Crème de Menthe | $6.00 |
| Brandy | $8.00 |
| Cordial | $10.00 |
| Hollow Stem Champagne | $10.00 |
| Tall Champagne | $10.00 |
| Long Stem Champagne | $25.00 |
| Hot Whiskey | $6.00 |

### CUTTING 104, Blank 858

| | |
|---|---|
| Goblet, 11 oz. | $9.00 |
| Goblet, 10 oz. | $9.00 |
| Goblet, 9 oz. | $8.00 |
| Saucer Champagne, 7 oz. | $9.00 |
| Sherbet | $8.00 |
| Fruit | $8.00 |
| Cocktail | $8.00 |
| Claret, 6½ oz. | $10.00 |
| Claret, 4½ oz. | $10.00 |
| Wine, 3½ oz. | $10.00 |
| Wine, 2¾ oz. | $10.00 |
| Sherry | $9.00 |
| Brandy | $10.00 |
| Cordial | $10.00 |
| Hollow Stem Champagne | $20.00 |
| Tall Champagne | $8.00 |
| Hot Whiskey | $8.00 |

### MISSION, Cutting 116, Blank 858

| | |
|---|---|
| Goblet, 11 oz. | $10.00 |
| Goblet, 10 oz. | $8.00 |
| Goblet, 9 oz. | $8.00 |
| Goblet, 8 oz. | $6.00 |
| Saucer Champagne, 7 oz. | $8.00 |
| Saucer Champagne, 5½ oz. | $6.00 |
| Sherbet | $6.00 |

| | |
|---|---|
| Fruit | $6.00 |
| Parfait | $14.00 |
| Cocktail | $6.00 |
| Claret, 6½ oz. | $10.00 |
| Claret, 4½ oz. | $10.00 |
| Wine, 3½ oz. | $8.00 |
| Wine, 2¾ oz. | $8.00 |
| Sherry | $8.00 |
| Crème de Menthe | $6.00 |
| Brandy | $12.00 |
| Cordial | $15.00 |
| Oyster Cocktail | $5.00 |
| Hollow Stem Champagne | $10.00 |
| Tall Champagne | $8.00 |
| Long Stem Champagne | $25.00 |
| Long Stem Champagne, Cutting R. | $25.00 |
| Bass Ale | $15.00 |
| Hot Whiskey | $6.00 |

### BILLOW, Cutting 118, Blank 858

| | |
|---|---|
| Goblet, 11 oz. | $8.00 |
| Goblet, 10 oz. | $8.00 |
| Goblet, 9 oz. | $8.00 |
| Goblet, 8 oz. | $8.00 |
| Saucer Champagne, 7 oz. | $6.00 |
| Saucer Champagne, 5½ oz. | $6.00 |
| Sherbet | $6.00 |
| Fruit | $6.00 |
| Cocktail | $8.00 |
| Claret, 6½ oz. | $8.00 |
| Claret, 4½ oz. | $8.00 |
| Wine, 3½ oz. | $8.00 |
| Wine, 2¾ oz. | $8.00 |
| Sherry | $6.00 |
| Crème de Menthe | $6.00 |
| Brandy | $12.00 |
| Cordial | $15.00 |
| Oyster Cocktail | $5.00 |
| Hollow Stem Champagne | $10.00 |
| Tall Champagne | $10.00 |
| Long Stem Champagne | $25.00 |
| Bass Ale | $15.00 |
| Hot Whiskey | $6.00 |

### COIN GOLD, Decoration 2, Blank 858

| | |
|---|---|
| Goblet, 11 oz. | $6.00 |
| Goblet, 10 oz. | $6.00 |
| Goblet, 9 oz. | $6.00 |
| Goblet, 8 oz. | $6.00 |
| Saucer Champagne, 7 oz. | $6.00 |
| Sherbet | $6.00 |
| Fruit | $6.00 |
| Cocktail | $6.00 |
| Claret, 6½ oz. | $6.00 |
| Claret, 4½ oz. | $6.00 |
| Wine, 3½ oz. | $6.00 |
| Wine, 2¾ oz. | $6.00 |
| Sherry | $6.00 |
| Crème de Menthe | $6.00 |

| | |
|---|---|
| Brandy | $12.00 |
| Cordial | $12.00 |
| Hollow Stem Champagne | $10.00 |
| Tall Champagne | $10.00 |
| Bass Ale | $15.00 |
| Hot Whiskey | $6.00 |

### COIN GOLD, Decoration 6, Blank 858

| | |
|---|---|
| Goblet, 10 oz. | $6.00 |
| Saucer Champagne, 5½ oz. | $6.00 |
| Sherbet | $6.00 |
| Fruit | $6.00 |
| Cocktail | $6.00 |
| Claret, 4½ oz. | $6.00 |
| Wine, 3½ oz. | $6.00 |
| Sherry | $6.00 |
| Crème de Menthe | $6.00 |
| Brandy (Pousse Cafe) | $10.00 |
| Cordial | $10.00 |
| Hollow Stem Champagne | $10.00 |
| Tall Champagne | $10.00 |

### COIN GOLD, Decoration 7, Blank 858

| | |
|---|---|
| Goblet, 9 oz. | $6.00 |
| Saucer Champagne, 5½ oz. | $6.00 |
| Fruit | $6.00 |
| Wine, 2¾ oz. | $6.00 |
| Oyster Cocktail | $6.00 |

### DRESDEN, Decoration 12, Blank 858

| | |
|---|---|
| Goblet, 9 oz. | $45.00 |
| Saucer Champagne, 5½ oz. | $45.00 |
| Fruit | $45.00 |
| Cocktail | $45.00 |
| Claret, 4½ oz. | $45.00 |

### DAISY, Decoration 17, Blank 858

| | |
|---|---|
| Goblet, 9 oz. | $45.00 |
| Saucer Champagne, 5½ oz. | $45.00 |
| Fruit | $45.00 |
| Cocktail | $45.00 |

### BLUE BORDER, Decoration 19, Blank 858

| | |
|---|---|
| Goblet, 9 oz. | $45.00 |
| Saucer Champagne, 5½ oz. | $45.00 |
| Fruit | $45.00 |
| Cocktail | $45.00 |

### BLACK BORDER, Decoration 20, Blank 858

| | |
|---|---|
| Goblet, 9 oz. | $45.00 |
| Saucer Champagne, 5½ oz. | $45.00 |
| Fruit | $45.00 |
| Cocktail | $45.00 |

### ENAMEL AND GOLD, Decoration 21, Blank 858

| | |
|---|---|
| Goblet, 9 oz. | $50.00 |

Saucer Champagne, 5½ oz. .......... $50.00
Fruit .............................................. $50.00

### Blank 863

Goblet, 10½ oz. ............................ $7.00
Goblet, 9 oz., Short Stem ............. $7.00
Goblet, 7 oz., Long Stem .............. $7.00
Goblet, 5½ oz. .............................. $7.00
Saucer Champagne ........................ $7.00
Fruit .............................................. $7.00
Café Parfait .................................. $22.00
Roemer (Tall Cocktail), 5½ oz. ...... $8.00
Roemer (Tall Cocktail), 4½ oz. ...... $8.00
Cocktail, 3½ oz. ............................ $7.00
Cocktail, 3 oz. ............................... $7.00
Claret ............................................ $7.00
Rhine Wine ................................... $7.00
Wine .............................................. $7.00
Sherry ............................................ $7.00
Crème de Menthe .......................... $7.00
Brandy (Pousse Café) .................... $7.00
Cordial ........................................ $15.00
Hollow Stem Champagne, C. F. ... $12.00
Tall Champagne ........................... $15.00

### BLOCK, Etching 38½, Blank 863

Goblet, 10½ oz. ............................ $7.00
Goblet, 9 oz. ................................. $7.00
Saucer Champagne, 5½ oz. ............ $7.00
Fruit .............................................. $7.00
Cocktail, 3 oz. ............................... $7.00
Claret ............................................ $7.00
Rhine Wine ................................... $7.00
Wine .............................................. $7.00
Sherry ............................................ $7.00
Crème de Menthe .......................... $7.00
Brandy (Pousse Café) .................... $7.00
Cordial .......................................... $7.00
Hollow Stem Champagne, C. F. ..... $7.00
Tall Champagne .............................. $7.00

### CHAIN, Etching 42, Blank 863

Goblet, 10½ oz. ........................... $10.00
Goblet, 9 oz .................................. $7.00
Saucer Champagne ...................... $10.00
Fruit .............................................. $7.00
Cocktail ........................................ $7.00
Wine ............................................ $10.00
Sherry ............................................ $7.00
Crème de Menthe .......................... $7.00
Cordial ........................................ $10.00

### SMALL CLOVERLEAF, Etching 67, Blank 863

Goblet, 10½ oz. ............................ $8.00
Goblet, 9 oz. ................................. $8.00
Goblet, 7 oz. ................................. $8.00
Goblet, 5½ oz. .............................. $8.00

Saucer Champagne ........................ $8.00
Fruit .............................................. $8.00
Cocktail, 3½ oz. ............................ $8.00
Cocktail, 3 oz. ............................... $8.00
Claret ............................................ $8.00
Rhine Wine ................................... $8.00
Wine .............................................. $8.00
Sherry ............................................ $8.00
Crème de Menthe .......................... $8.00
Brandy (Pousse Café) .................... $8.00
Cordial .......................................... $8.00
Hollow Stem Champagne ............... $8.00
Tall Champagne .............................. $8.00

### VINTAGE, Etching 204, Blank 863

Goblet, 10½ oz. ............................ $9.00
Goblet, 9 oz. ................................. $9.00
Goblet, 7 oz. ................................. $9.00
Saucer Champagne, 5½ oz. ............ $9.00
Fruit .............................................. $7.00
Cocktail, 3½ oz. ............................ $7.00
Claret ............................................ $9.00
Rhine Wine ................................... $9.00
Wine .............................................. $9.00
Sherry ............................................ $7.00
Crème de Menthe .......................... $7.00
Brandy (Pousse Café) .................... $9.00
Cordial .......................................... $9.00
Hollow Stem Champagne, C. F. ..... $9.00
Tall Champagne .............................. $9.00

### ETCHING 210, Blank 863

Goblet, 10½ oz. ........................... $10.00
Goblet, 9 oz. ............................... $10.00
Goblet, 7 oz. ............................... $10.00
Saucer Champagne ...................... $10.00
Fruit .............................................. $8.00
Cocktail, 3½ oz. ............................ $8.00
Claret .......................................... $10.00
Rhine Wine ................................. $10.00
Wine ............................................ $10.00
Sherry ............................................ $8.00
Crème de Menthe .......................... $8.00
Brandy (Pousse Café) .................. $10.00
Cordial ........................................ $10.00
Hollow Stem Champagne, C. F. ... $10.00
Tall Champagne ........................... $10.00

### ETCHING 212, Blank 863

Goblet, 10½ oz. ........................... $10.00
Goblet, 9 oz. ............................... $10.00
Goblet, 7 oz. ............................... $10.00
Saucer Champagne ...................... $10.00
Fruit .............................................. $8.00
Cocktail, 3½ oz. ............................ $8.00
Claret .......................................... $15.00
Rhine Wine ................................. $10.00
Wine ............................................ $10.00
Sherry ............................................ $8.00
Crème de Menthe .......................... $8.00

Brandy (Pousse Café) .................. $20.00
Cordial ........................................ $25.00
Hollow Stem Champagne, C. F. ... $15.00
Tall Champagne ........................... $20.00

### ETCHING 214, Blank 863

Goblet, 10½ oz. ........................... $10.00
Goblet, 9 oz. ............................... $10.00
Goblet, 7 oz. ............................... $10.00
Saucer Champagne ...................... $10.00
Fruit .............................................. $8.00
Cocktail, 3½ oz. ............................ $8.00
Claret .......................................... $12.00
Rhine Wine ................................. $10.00
Wine ............................................ $10.00
Sherry ............................................ $8.00
Crème de Menthe .......................... $8.00
Brandy (Pousse Café) .................. $12.00
Cordial ........................................ $15.00
Hollow Stem Champagne, C. F. ... $12.00
Tall Champagne ........................... $12.00

### NEW VINTAGE, Etching 227, Blank 863

Goblet, 10½ oz. ........................... $10.00
Goblet, 9 oz. ............................... $10.00
Goblet, 7 oz. ............................... $10.00
Goblet, 5½ oz. ............................. $10.00
Saucer Champagne ...................... $10.00
Fruit .............................................. $8.00
Cocktail, 3½ oz. ............................ $8.00
Cocktail, 3 oz. ............................... $8.00
Claret .......................................... $12.00
Rhine Wine ................................. $10.00
Wine ............................................ $10.00
Sherry ............................................ $8.00
Crème de Menthe .......................... $8.00
Brandy (Pousse Café) .................. $15.00
Cordial ........................................ $15.00
Hollow Stem Champagne, C. F. ... $10.00
Tall Champagne ........................... $12.00
Roemer, 5½ oz. ........................... $18.00
Roemer, 4½ oz. ........................... $18.00

### GARLAND, Etching 237, Blank 863

Goblet, 10½ oz. ........................... $15.00
Goblet, 9 oz. ............................... $12.00
Saucer Champagne ...................... $12.00
Fruit .............................................. $9.00
Cocktail, 3½ oz. ............................ $9.00
Claret .......................................... $15.00
Rhine Wine ................................. $15.00
Wine ............................................ $15.00
Sherry ............................................ $9.00
Crème de Menthe .......................... $9.00
Brandy (Pousse Café) .................. $20.00
Cordial ........................................ $25.00
Hollow Stem Champagne,
   C. F. ....................................... $12.00
Tall Champagne ........................... $18.00

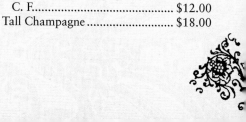

### PERSIAN, Etching 253, Blank 863

| | |
|---|---|
| Goblet, 9 oz. | $12.00 |
| Goblet, 7 oz. | $12.00 |
| Saucer Champagne | $10.00 |
| Fruit | $9.00 |
| Cocktail, 3½ oz. | $9.00 |
| Wine | $15.00 |
| Cordial | $20.00 |

### CUTTING 4, Blank 863

| | |
|---|---|
| Goblet, 10½ oz. | $10.00 |
| Goblet, 9 oz. | $10.00 |
| Goblet, 7 oz. | $10.00 |
| Saucer Champagne | $10.00 |
| Cocktail | $9.00 |
| Claret | $10.00 |
| Rhine Wine | $10.00 |
| Wine | $10.00 |
| Sherry | $10.00 |
| Crème de Menthe | $10.00 |
| Brandy (Pousse Café) | $12.00 |
| Cordial | $12.00 |
| Hollow Stem Champagne | $12.00 |
| Tall Champagne | $10.00 |
| Roemer | $15.00 |

### LARGE SUNBURST STAR, Cutting 81, Blank 863

| | |
|---|---|
| Goblet, 10½ oz. | $9.00 |
| Goblet, 9 oz. | $9.00 |
| Goblet, 7 oz. | $8.00 |
| Saucer Champagne | $9.00 |
| Fruit | $7.00 |
| Cocktail, 3½ oz. | $7.00 |
| Claret | $12.00 |
| Rhine Wine | $9.00 |
| Wine | $9.00 |
| Sherry | $8.00 |
| Crème de Menthe | $8.00 |
| Brandy (Pousse Café) | $12.00 |
| Cordial | $12.00 |
| Tall Champagne | $9.00 |

### CUTTING 110, Blank 863

| | |
|---|---|
| Goblet, 10½ oz. | $10.00 |
| Goblet, 9 oz. | $10.00 |
| Goblet, 7 oz. | $10.00 |
| Saucer Champagne | $10.00 |
| Fruit | $8.00 |
| Cocktail, 3½ oz. | $8.00 |
| Claret | $10.00 |
| Rhine Wine | $10.00 |
| Wine | $10.00 |
| Sherry | $8.00 |
| Crème de Menthe | $8.00 |
| Brandy (Pousse Café) | $10.00 |
| Cordial | $10.00 |
| Tall Champagne | $10.00 |

### MISSION, Cutting 116, Blank 863

| | |
|---|---|
| Goblet, 10½ oz. | $10.00 |
| Goblet, 9 oz. | $10.00 |
| Saucer Champagne | $10.00 |
| Fruit | $8.00 |
| Cocktail, 3½ oz. | $8.00 |
| Claret | $12.00 |
| Rhine Wine | $10.00 |
| Wine | $10.00 |
| Sherry | $8.00 |
| Crème de Menthe | $8.00 |
| Brandy (Pousse Café) | $15.00 |
| Cordial | $15.00 |
| Hollow Stem Champagne, C. F. | $12.00 |
| Tall Champagne | $12.00 |
| Roemer, 5½ oz. | $15.00 |
| Roemer, 4½ oz. | $15.00 |

### BILLOW, Cutting 118, Blank 863

| | |
|---|---|
| Goblet, 10½ oz. | $10.00 |
| Goblet, 9 oz. | $10.00 |
| Goblet, 7 oz. | $10.00 |
| Goblet, 5½ oz. | $10.00 |
| Saucer Champagne | $10.00 |
| Fruit | $8.00 |
| Cocktail, 3½ oz. | $8.00 |
| Claret | $12.00 |
| Rhine Wine | $10.00 |
| Wine | $10.00 |
| Sherry | $8.00 |
| Crème de Menthe | $12.00 |
| Brandy (Pousse Café) | $12.00 |
| Cordial | $15.00 |
| Hollow Stem Champagne, C. F. | $12.00 |
| Tall Champagne | $15.00 |
| Roemer, 5½ oz. | $18.00 |
| Roemer, 4½ oz. | $18.00 |

### CUTTING 125, Blank 863

| | |
|---|---|
| Goblet, 10½ oz. | $10.00 |
| Goblet, 9 oz. | $10.00 |
| Saucer Champagne | $10.00 |
| Fruit | $8.00 |
| Cocktail, 3½ oz. | $8.00 |
| Claret | $12.00 |
| Rhine Wine | $10.00 |
| Wine | $10.00 |
| Sherry | $8.00 |
| Crème de Menthe | $8.00 |
| Brandy (Pousse Café) | $18.00 |
| Cordial | $18.00 |
| Hollow Stem Champagne, C. F. | $15.00 |
| Tall Champagne | $15.00 |

### CUTTING 129, Blank 863

| | |
|---|---|
| Goblet, 9 oz. | $10.00 |
| Saucer Champagne | $10.00 |
| Fruit | $8.00 |

| | |
|---|---|
| Cocktail, 3½ oz. | $8.00 |
| Claret | $10.00 |
| Wine | $10.00 |

### CLOVER, Cutting 132, Blank 863

| | |
|---|---|
| Goblet, 9 oz. | $10.00 |
| Saucer Champagne | $10.00 |
| Fruit | $8.00 |
| Cocktail, 3½ oz. | $8.00 |
| Claret | $10.00 |
| Wine | $10.00 |
| Sherry | $8.00 |

### CHRYSANTHEMUM, Cutting 133, Blank 863

| | |
|---|---|
| Goblet, 9 oz. | $10.00 |
| Saucer Champagne | $10.00 |
| Fruit | $8.00 |
| Cocktail, 3½ oz. | $8.00 |
| Wine | $10.00 |

### GENEVA, Cutting 135, Blank 863

| | |
|---|---|
| Goblet, 9 oz. | $10.00 |
| Saucer Champagne | $10.00 |
| Fruit | $8.00 |

### APPLE BLOSSOM, Cutting 138, Blank 863

| | |
|---|---|
| Goblet, 9 oz. | $10.00 |
| Saucer Champagne | $10.00 |
| Fruit | $8.00 |
| Cocktail, 3½ oz. | $8.00 |
| Wine | $10.00 |

### FAIRFAX, Cutting 167, Blank 863

| | |
|---|---|
| Goblet, 9 oz. | $10.00 |
| Saucer Champagne | $10.00 |
| Fruit | $8.00 |
| Cocktail, 3½ oz. | $8.00 |
| Wine | $10.00 |
| Café Parfait | $10.00 |

### Blank 867, 867½

| | |
|---|---|
| Goblet, 10 oz. | $8.00 |
| Goblet, 9 oz. | $8.00 |
| Saucer Champagne | $8.00 |
| Fruit | $8.00 |
| Sherbet | $8.00 |
| Cocktail | $8.00 |
| Claret | $8.00 |
| Wine | $8.00 |
| Sherry | $8.00 |
| Cordial | $8.00 |

### FRESNO, Etching 78, Blank 867½

| | |
|---|---|
| Goblet, 9 oz. | $10.00 |

| | |
|---|---|
| Saucer Champagne | $10.00 |
| Fruit | $10.00 |
| Cocktail | $10.00 |
| Wine | $10.00 |

### PARISIAN, Etching 53, Blank 867½

| | |
|---|---|
| Goblet, 10 oz. | $10.00 |
| Saucer Champagne | $10.00 |
| Fruit | $8.00 |
| Sherbet | $8.00 |
| Cocktail | $8.00 |
| Claret | $10.00 |
| Wine | $10.00 |
| Sherry | $8.00 |
| Cordial | $12.00 |

### Blank 869
#### Crystal

| | |
|---|---|
| Goblet | $10.00 |
| Saucer Champagne | $10.00 |
| High Sherbet | $10.00 |
| Low Sherbet | $8.00 |
| Fruit | $8.00 |
| Parfait | $10.00 |
| Cocktail | $8.00 |
| Claret | $12.00 |
| Wine | $12.00 |
| Cordial | $15.00 |
| Oyster Cocktail | $8.00 |

#### Amber/Green

| | |
|---|---|
| Goblet | $24.00 |
| Saucer Champagne | $20.00 |
| High Sherbet | $20.00 |
| Low Sherbet | $16.00 |
| Fruit | $16.00 |
| Parfait | $20.00 |
| Cocktail | $12.00 |
| Claret | $22.00 |
| Wine | $20.00 |
| Cordial | $24.00 |
| Oyster Cocktail | $12.00 |

#### Blue

| | |
|---|---|
| Goblet | $30.00 |
| Saucer Champagne | $25.00 |
| High Sherbet | $25.00 |
| Low Sherbet | $22.00 |
| Fruit | $22.00 |
| Parfait | $30.00 |
| Cocktail | $22.00 |
| Claret | $30.00 |
| Wine | $28.00 |
| Cordial | $34.00 |
| Oyster Cocktail | $20.00 |

### SHERMAN, Etching 77, Blank 869

| | |
|---|---|
| Goblet | $15.00 |

| | |
|---|---|
| Saucer Champagne | $15.00 |
| High Sherbet | $12.00 |
| Low Sherbet | $10.00 |
| Fruit | $10.00 |
| Parfait | $18.00 |
| Cocktail | $10.00 |
| Wine | $15.00 |
| Cordial | $20.00 |
| Oyster Cocktail | $8.00 |

### ROYAL, Etching 273, Blank 869
#### Crystal

| | |
|---|---|
| Goblet | $26.00 |
| Saucer Champagne | $20.00 |
| High Sherbet | $20.00 |
| Low Sherbet | $10.00 |
| Fruit | $10.00 |
| Parfait | $20.00 |
| Cocktail | $18.00 |
| Wine | $26.00 |
| Cordial | $32.00 |
| Oyster Cocktail | $10.00 |

#### Amber/Green

| | |
|---|---|
| Goblet | $35.00 |
| Saucer Champagne | $32.00 |
| High Sherbet | $32.00 |
| Low Sherbet | $28.00 |
| Fruit | $28.00 |
| Parfait | $40.00 |
| Cocktail | $26.00 |
| Wine | $35.00 |
| Cordial | $45.00 |
| Oyster Cocktail | $24.00 |

#### Blue

| | |
|---|---|
| Goblet | $75.00 |
| Saucer Champagne | $65.00 |
| High Sherbet | $65.00 |
| Low Sherbet | $48.00 |
| Fruit | $48.00 |
| Parfait | $75.00 |
| Cocktail | $50.00 |
| Wine | $85.00 |
| Cordial | $97.00 |
| Oyster Cocktail | $45.00 |

### ARBOR, Cutting 184, Blank 869
#### Amber/Green

| | |
|---|---|
| Goblet | $35.00 |
| High Sherbet | $32.00 |
| Low Sherbet | $27.00 |
| Parfait | $38.00 |
| Cocktail | $30.00 |
| Wine | $32.00 |
| Oyster Cocktail | $24.00 |

#### Blue

| | |
|---|---|
| Goblet | $40.00 |

| | |
|---|---|
| High Sherbet | $38.00 |
| Low Sherbet | $32.00 |
| Parfait | $40.00 |
| Cocktail | $32.00 |
| Wine | $40.00 |
| Oyster Cocktail | $30.00 |

### ALASKA, Decoration 54, Blank 869

| | |
|---|---|
| Goblet | $12.00 |
| Saucer Champagne | $12.00 |
| Fruit | $10.00 |
| Parfait | $12.00 |
| Cocktail | $10.00 |
| Wine | $12.00 |

### Blank 870
#### Crystal/Mother of Pearl

| | |
|---|---|
| Goblet | $20.00 |
| High Sherbet | $16.00 |
| Low Sherbet | $12.00 |
| Parfait | $20.00 |
| Cocktail | $14.00 |
| Claret | $22.00 |
| Wine | $20.00 |
| Cordial | $25.00 |
| Oyster Cocktail | $10.00 |

#### Amber/Green

| | |
|---|---|
| Goblet | $30.00 |
| High Sherbet | $28.00 |
| Low Sherbet | $22.00 |
| Parfait | $30.00 |
| Cocktail | $22.00 |
| Claret | $30.00 |
| Wine | $28.00 |
| Cordial | $35.00 |
| Oyster Cocktail | $18.00 |

#### Rose/Blue

| | |
|---|---|
| Goblet | $34.00 |
| High Sherbet | $30.00 |
| Low Sherbet | $25.00 |
| Parfait | $35.00 |
| Cocktail | $28.00 |
| Claret | $36.00 |
| Wine | $34.00 |
| Cordial | $50.00 |
| Oyster Cocktail | $22.00 |

### BRUNSWICK, Etching 79, Blank 870
#### Crystal

| | |
|---|---|
| Goblet | $22.00 |
| High Sherbet | $20.00 |
| Low Sherbet | $18.00 |
| Parfait | $25.00 |
| Cocktail | $18.00 |

| | |
|---|---|
| Claret | $26.00 |
| Wine | $25.00 |
| Cordial | $28.00 |
| Oyster Cocktail | $14.00 |

### Amber/Green

| | |
|---|---|
| Goblet | $28.00 |
| High Sherbet | $26.00 |
| Low Sherbet | $22.00 |
| Parfait | $28.00 |
| Cocktail | $22.00 |
| Claret | $30.00 |
| Wine | $28.00 |
| Cordial | $45.00 |
| Oyster Cocktail | $18.00 |

### Blue

| | |
|---|---|
| Goblet | $34.00 |
| High Sherbet | $32.00 |
| Low Sherbet | $28.00 |
| Parfait | $38.00 |
| Cocktail | $28.00 |
| Claret | $38.00 |
| Wine | $35.00 |
| Cordial | $50.00 |
| Oyster Cocktail | $22.00 |

### BARONET, Etching 92, Blank 870

| | |
|---|---|
| Goblet | $24.00 |
| High Sherbet | $22.00 |
| Low Sherbet | $16.00 |
| Cocktail | $18.00 |
| Claret | $24.00 |
| Wine | $22.00 |
| Cordial | $28.00 |

### SEVILLE, Etching 274, Blank 870
#### Crystal

| | |
|---|---|
| Goblet | $25.00 |
| High Sherbet | $24.00 |
| Low Sherbet | $20.00 |
| Parfait | $27.00 |
| Cocktail | $20.00 |
| Wine | $26.00 |
| Cordial | $30.00 |
| Oyster Cocktail | $18.00 |

#### Amber/Green

| | |
|---|---|
| Goblet | $38.00 |
| High Sherbet | $35.00 |
| Low Sherbet | $30.00 |
| Parfait | $38.00 |
| Cocktail | $30.00 |
| Wine | $40.00 |
| Cordial | $50.00 |
| Oyster Cocktail | $28.00 |

### MONARCH, Decoration 60, Blank 870

| | |
|---|---|
| Goblet | $22.00 |

| | |
|---|---|
| High Sherbet | $20.00 |
| Low Sherbet | $16.00 |
| Parfait | $22.00 |
| Cocktail | $16.00 |
| Wine | $22.00 |
| Cordial | $28.00 |
| Oyster Cocktail | $14.00 |

### GRAPE STEM, Decorations 61, 62 & 63, Blank 870

| | |
|---|---|
| Goblet | $85.00 |
| High Sherbet | $80.00 |
| Fruit | $65.00 |
| Parfait | $85.00 |
| Wine | $85.00 |
| Cordial | $125.00 |

### Blank 877
#### Crystal/Mother of Pearl

| | |
|---|---|
| Goblet | $20.00 |
| High Sherbet | $18.00 |
| Low Sherbet | $10.00 |
| Parfait | $24.00 |
| Cocktail | $14.00 |
| Claret | $24.00 |
| Wine | $22.00 |
| Cordial | $22.00 |
| Oyster Cocktail | $10.00 |
| Grapefruit and Liner | $25.00 |
| Footed Ice Tea | $20.00 |
| Footed Tumbler, 9 oz. | $10.00 |
| Footed Juice | $10.00 |
| Footed Whiskey | $10.00 |

#### Amber/Green

| | |
|---|---|
| Goblet | $30.00 |
| High Sherbet | $28.00 |
| Low Sherbet | $16.00 |
| Parfait | $28.00 |
| Cocktail | $16.00 |
| Claret | $36.00 |
| Wine | $32.00 |
| Cordial | $38.00 |
| Oyster Cocktail | $14.00 |
| Grapefruit and Liner | $45.00 |
| Footed Ice Tea | $30.00 |
| Footed Tumbler, 9 oz. | $18.00 |
| Footed Juice | $16.00 |
| Footed Whiskey | $20.00 |

#### Orchid/Azure

| | |
|---|---|
| Goblet | $48.00 |
| High Sherbet | $45.00 |
| Low Sherbet | $28.00 |
| Parfait | $40.00 |
| Cocktail | $35.00 |
| Claret | $57.00 |

| | |
|---|---|
| Wine | $48.00 |
| Cordial | $58.00 |
| Oyster Cocktail | $28.00 |
| Grapefruit and Liner | $57.00 |
| Footed Ice Tea | $45.00 |
| Footed Tumbler, 9 oz. | $32.00 |
| Footed Juice | $30.00 |
| Footed Whiskey | $30.00 |

#### Empire Green/Regal Blue

| | |
|---|---|
| Goblet | $125.00 |
| High Sherbet | $95.00 |
| Low Sherbet | $40.00 |
| Cocktail | $45.00 |
| Claret | $125.00 |
| Cordial | $135.00 |
| Oyster Cocktail | $35.00 |
| Footed Ice Tea | $95.00 |
| Footed Tumbler, 9 oz. | $40.00 |
| Footed Juice | $40.00 |

### CORDELLA, Etching 82, Blank 877
#### Green

| | |
|---|---|
| Goblet | $42.00 |
| High Sherbet | $40.00 |
| Low Sherbet | $30.00 |
| Parfait | $40.00 |
| Cocktail | $35.00 |
| Claret | $45.00 |
| Wine | $40.00 |
| Cordial | $48.00 |
| Oyster Cocktail | $30.00 |
| Grapefruit and Liner | $48.00 |
| Footed Ice Tea | $40.00 |
| Footed Tumbler, 9 oz. | $32.00 |
| Footed Juice | $28.00 |
| Footed Whiskey | $32.00 |

#### Orchid

| | |
|---|---|
| Goblet | $42.00 |
| High Sherbet | $40.00 |
| Low Sherbet | $30.00 |
| Parfait | $42.00 |
| Cocktail | $35.00 |
| Claret | $45.00 |
| Wine | $40.00 |
| Cordial | $52.00 |
| Oyster Cocktail | $30.00 |
| Grapefruit and Liner | $58.00 |
| Footed Ice Tea | $40.00 |
| Footed Tumbler, 9 oz. | $32.00 |
| Footed Juice | $30.00 |
| Footed Whiskey | $32.00 |

### VERNON, Etching 277, Blank 877
#### Amber/Green

| | |
|---|---|
| Goblet | $48.00 |
| High Sherbet | $44.00 |
| Low Sherbet | $35.00 |

| | |
|---|---|
| Parfait | $48.00 |
| Cocktail | $40.00 |
| Claret | $50.00 |
| Wine | $47.00 |
| Cordial | $68.00 |
| Oyster Cocktail | $30.00 |
| Grapefruit and Liner | $68.00 |
| Footed Ice Tea | $45.00 |
| Footed Tumbler, 9 oz. | $35.00 |
| Footed Juice | $35.00 |
| Footed Whiskey | $38.00 |

### Orchid/Azure

| | |
|---|---|
| Goblet | $65.00 |
| High Sherbet | $50.00 |
| Low Sherbet | $35.00 |
| Parfait | $62.00 |
| Cocktail | $40.00 |
| Claret | $75.00 |
| Wine | $64.00 |
| Cordial | $110.00 |
| Oyster Cocktail | $40.00 |
| Grapefruit and Liner | $95.00 |
| Footed Ice Tea | $58.00 |
| Footed Tumbler, 9 oz. | $42.00 |
| Footed Juice | $42.00 |
| Footed Whiskey | $45.00 |

### OAK LEAF, Etching 290, Blank 877
#### Crystal/ Green

| | |
|---|---|
| Goblet | $70.00 |
| High Sherbet | $65.00 |
| Low Sherbet | $45.00 |
| Parfait | $65.00 |
| Cocktail | $55.00 |
| Claret | $75.00 |
| Wine | $65.00 |
| Cordial | $85.00 |
| Oyster Cocktail | $40.00 |
| Grapefruit and Liner | $85.00 |
| Footed Ice Tea | $65.00 |
| Footed Tumbler, 9 oz. | $45.00 |
| Footed Juice | $40.00 |
| Footed Whiskey | $55.00 |

### KINGSLEY, Cutting 192, Blank 877

| | |
|---|---|
| Goblet | $35.00 |
| High Sherbet | $32.00 |
| Low Sherbet | $30.00 |
| Parfait | $35.00 |
| Wine | $35.00 |
| Cocktail | $30.00 |
| Footed Tumbler, 12 oz. | $35.00 |
| Footed Tumbler, 9 oz. | $30.00 |
| Footed Tumbler, 5 oz. | $26.00 |
| Footed Tumbler, 2½ oz. | $24.00 |

### LATTICE, Cutting 196, Blank 877

| | |
|---|---|
| Goblet | $25.00 |
| High Sherbet | $22.00 |

| | |
|---|---|
| Low Sherbet | $18.00 |
| Parfait | $25.00 |
| Cocktail | $20.00 |
| Claret | $28.00 |
| Wine | $25.00 |
| Cordial | $32.00 |
| Oyster Cocktail | $18.00 |
| Footed Ice Tea | $24.00 |
| Footed Tumbler, 9 oz. | $18.00 |
| Footed Juice | $20.00 |
| Footed Whiskey | $20.00 |

### CHATTERIS, Cutting 197, Blank 877

| | |
|---|---|
| Goblet | $25.00 |
| High Sherbet | $22.00 |
| Low Sherbet | $18.00 |
| Parfait | $25.00 |
| Cocktail | $20.00 |
| Claret | $28.00 |
| Wine | $25.00 |
| Cordial | $32.00 |
| Oyster Cocktail | $18.00 |
| Footed Ice Tea | $24.00 |
| Footed Tumbler, 9 oz. | $18.00 |
| Footed Juice | $20.00 |
| Footed Whiskey | $20.00 |

### OAKWOOD, Decoration 72, Blank 877
#### Orchid/Azure

| | |
|---|---|
| Goblet | $195.00 |
| High Sherbet | $165.00 |
| Low Sherbet | $85.00 |
| Parfait | $175.00 |
| Cocktail | $95.00 |
| Claret | $195.00 |
| Wine | $185.00 |
| Cordial | $225.00 – Market |
| Oyster Cocktail | $85.00 |
| Grapefruit and Liner | $225.00 – Market |
| Footed Ice Tea | $165.00 |
| Footed Tumbler, 9 oz. | $95.00 |
| Footed Juice | $95.00 |
| Footed Whiskey | $95.00 |

### Blank 879
#### Crystal

| | |
|---|---|
| Goblet | $20.00 |
| Saucer Champagne | $18.00 |
| Fruit | $16.00 |
| Cocktail | $18.00 |
| Claret | $25.00 |
| Wine | $25.00 |
| Sherry | $20.00 |
| Crème de Menthe | $18.00 |
| Brandy (Pousse Café) | $25.00 |
| Cordial | $30.00 |

### Orchid

| | |
|---|---|
| Goblet | $35.00 |
| Saucer Champagne | $32.00 |
| Fruit | $30.00 |
| Cocktail | $32.00 |
| Claret | $35.00 |
| Wine | $35.00 |
| Sherry | $32.00 |
| Crème de Menthe | $32.00 |
| Brandy (Pousse Café) | $35.00 |
| Cordial | $38.00 |

### IRISH LACE, Etching 36, Blank 879

| | |
|---|---|
| Goblet | $25.00 |
| Saucer Champagne | $22.00 |
| Fruit | $20.00 |
| Cocktail | $20.00 |
| Claret | $30.00 |
| Wine | $25.00 |
| Sherry | $22.00 |
| Crème de Menthe | $20.00 |
| Brandy (Pousse Café) | $34.00 |
| Cordial | $37.00 |

### BLOCK, Etching 38½, Blank 879

| | |
|---|---|
| Goblet | $20.00 |
| Saucer Champagne | $18.00 |
| Fruit | $15.00 |
| Cocktail | $15.00 |
| Claret | $25.00 |
| Wine | $25.00 |
| Sherry | $18.00 |
| Crème de Menthe | $18.00 |
| Brandy (Pousse Café) | $28.00 |
| Cordial | $30.00 |

### LILY OF THE VALLEY, Etching 241, Blank 879

| | |
|---|---|
| Goblet | $35.00 |
| Saucer Champagne | $32.00 |
| Fruit | $27.00 |
| Cocktail | $30.00 |
| Claret | $38.00 |
| Wine | $35.00 |
| Crème de Menthe | $30.00 |
| Brandy (Pousse Café) | $42.00 |
| Cordial | $48.00 |
| Handled Footed Lemonade | $35.00 |
| Tumbler | $20.00 |

### Blank 880

| | |
|---|---|
| Goblet, 11 oz. | $8.00 |
| Goblet, 10 oz. | $8.00 |
| Goblet, 9 oz. | $8.00 |
| Goblet, 8 oz. | $8.00 |
| Saucer Champagne, 7 oz. | $8.00 |

| Saucer Champagne, 5½ oz. | $7.00 |
|---|---|
| Sherbet | $7.00 |
| Cocktail, 3½ oz. | $8.00 |
| Cocktail, 3 oz. | $8.00 |
| Claret, 6½ oz. | $8.00 |
| Claret, 4½ oz. | $8.00 |
| Rhine Wine | $8.00 |
| Wine, 3½ oz. | $8.00 |
| Wine, 2¾ oz. | $8.00 |
| Sherry | $8.00 |
| Crème de Menthe | $8.00 |
| Brandy (Pousse Café), 1 oz. | $10.00 |
| Brandy (Pousse Café), ¾ oz. | $10.00 |
| Cordial, 1 oz. | $10.00 |
| Cordial, ¾ oz. | $10.00 |
| Hollow Stem Champagne | $8.00 |
| Tall Champagne | $8.00 |
| Tall Grapefruit and Liner | $25.00 |
| Short Grapefruit and Liner | $18.00 |
| Hot Whiskey | $7.00 |
| Tall Ale | $8.00 |

### IRISH LACE, Etching 36, Blank 880

| Goblet, 9 oz. | $12.00 |
|---|---|
| Saucer Champagne, 5½ oz. | $12.00 |
| Sherbet | $10.00 |
| Cocktail, 3½ oz. | $10.00 |
| Claret, 4½ oz. | $12.00 |
| Wine, 2¾ oz. | $12.00 |
| Sherry | $10.00 |
| Crème de Menthe | $10.00 |
| Cordial, 1 oz. | $15.00 |

### GREEK, Etching 45, Blank 880

| Goblet, 11 oz. | $12.00 |
|---|---|
| Goblet, 10 oz. | $12.00 |
| Goblet, 9 oz. | $10.00 |
| Goblet, 8 oz. | $10.00 |
| Saucer Champagne, 7 oz. | $12.00 |
| Saucer Champagne, 5½ oz. | $10.00 |
| Sherbet | $10.00 |
| Cocktail, 3½ oz. | $10.00 |
| Cocktail, 3 oz. | $10.00 |
| Claret, 6½ oz. | $12.00 |
| Claret, 4½ oz. | $12.00 |
| Rhine Wine | $12.00 |
| Wine, 3½ oz. | $10.00 |
| Wine, 2¾ oz. | $10.00 |
| Sherry | $10.00 |
| Crème de Menthe | $10.00 |
| Brandy (Pousse Café), 1 oz. | $15.00 |
| Brandy (Pousse Café), ¾ oz. | $15.00 |
| Cordial, 1 oz. | $18.00 |
| Cordial, ¾ oz. | $18.00 |
| Hollow Stem Champagne | $12.00 |
| Tall Champagne | $12.00 |
| Tall Grapefruit and Liner | $30.00 |
| Short Grapefruit and Liner | $22.00 |
| Hot Whiskey | $9.00 |
| Tall Ale | $12.00 |

### NEW VINTAGE, Etching 227, Blank 880

| Goblet, 11 oz. | $12.00 |
|---|---|
| Goblet, 10 oz. | $12.00 |
| Goblet, 9 oz. | $10.00 |
| Goblet, 8 oz. | $10.00 |
| Saucer Champagne, 7 oz. | $10.00 |
| Saucer Champagne, 5½ oz. | $9.00 |
| Sherbet | $9.00 |
| Cocktail, 3½ oz. | $9.00 |
| Claret, 6½ oz. | $12.00 |
| Claret, 4½ oz. | $12.00 |
| Rhine Wine | $12.00 |
| Wine, 3½ oz. | $12.00 |
| Wine, 2¾ oz. | $12.00 |
| Sherry | $10.00 |
| Crème de Menthe | $10.00 |
| Brandy (Pousse Café), 1 oz. | $15.00 |
| Cordial, 1 oz. | $18.00 |
| Hollow Stem Champagne | $12.00 |
| Tall Champagne | $14.00 |
| Tall Grapefruit and Liner | $30.00 |
| Short Grapefruit and Liner | $20.00 |
| Hot Whiskey | $10.00 |
| Tall Ale | $12.00 |

### KORNFLOWER, Etching 234, Blank 880

| Goblet, 11 oz. | $12.00 |
|---|---|
| Goblet, 10 oz. | $12.00 |
| Goblet, 9 oz. | $12.00 |
| Goblet, 8 oz. | $12.00 |
| Saucer Champagne, 7 oz. | $12.00 |
| Saucer Champagne, 5½ oz. | $10.00 |
| Sherbet | $10.00 |
| Cocktail, 3½ oz. | $10.00 |
| Claret, 6½ oz. | $14.00 |
| Claret, 4½ oz. | $10.00 |
| Rhine Wine | $12.00 |
| Wine, 3½ oz. | $12.00 |
| Wine, 2¾ oz. | $12.00 |
| Sherry | $10.00 |
| Crème de Menthe | $10.00 |
| Brandy (Pousse Café), 1 oz. | $15.00 |
| Cordial, 1 oz. | $20.00 |
| Hollow Stem Champagne | $12.00 |
| Tall Champagne | $12.00 |
| Tall Grapefruit and Liner | $30.00 |
| Short Grapefruit and Liner | $20.00 |
| Hot Whiskey | $12.00 |
| Tall Ale | $12.00 |

### GARLAND, Etching 237, Blank 880

| Goblet, 11 oz. | $15.00 |
|---|---|
| Goblet, 10 oz. | $15.00 |
| Goblet, 9 oz. | $12.00 |
| Goblet, 8 oz. | $8.00 |
| Saucer Champagne, 7 oz. | $12.00 |
| Saucer Champagne, 5½ oz. | $12.00 |

| Sherbet | $10.00 |
|---|---|
| Cocktail, 3½ oz. | $10.00 |
| Claret, 6½ oz. | $18.00 |
| Claret, 4½ oz. | $15.00 |
| Rhine Wine | $15.00 |
| Wine, 3½ oz. | $15.00 |
| Wine, 2¾ oz. | $15.00 |
| Sherry | $12.00 |
| Crème de Menthe | $12.00 |
| Brandy (Pousse Café), 1 oz. | $20.00 |
| Cordial, 1 oz. | $28.00 |
| Hollow Stem Champagne | $18.00 |
| Tall Champagne | $15.00 |
| Tall Grapefruit and Liner | $34.00 |
| Short Grapefruit and Liner | $30.00 |
| Hot Whiskey | $12.00 |
| Tall Ale | $15.00 |

### ROSILYN, Etching 249, Blank 880

| Goblet, 10 oz. | $15.00 |
|---|---|
| Saucer Champagne, 5½ oz. | $15.00 |
| Sherbet | $12.00 |
| Cocktail, 4½ oz. | $12.00 |
| Claret, 4½ oz. | $18.00 |
| Wine, 2¾ oz. | $15.00 |
| Sherry | $12.00 |
| Cordial, 1 oz. | $25.00 |

### LARGE SUNBURST STAR, Cutting 81, Blank 880

| Goblet, 11 oz. | $8.00 |
|---|---|
| Goblet, 10 oz. | $8.00 |
| Goblet, 9 oz. | $8.00 |
| Goblet, 8 oz. | $8.00 |
| Saucer Champagne, 7 oz. | $8.00 |
| Saucer Champagne, 5½ oz. | $7.00 |
| Sherbet | $7.00 |
| Cocktail, 3½ oz. | $7.00 |
| Claret, 6½ oz. | $9.00 |
| Claret, 4½ oz. | $9.00 |
| Rhine Wine | $9.00 |
| Wine, 3½ oz. | $9.00 |
| Wine, 2¾ oz. | $9.00 |
| Sherry | $7.00 |
| Crème de Menthe | $7.00 |
| Brandy (Pousse Café), 1 oz. | $10.00 |
| Cordial, 1 oz. | $10.00 |
| Hollow Stem Champagne | $8.00 |
| Tall Champagne | $8.00 |
| Tall Grapefruit and Liner | $25.00 |
| Short Grapefruit and Liner | $20.00 |
| Hot Whiskey | $7.00 |
| Tall Ale | $8.00 |

### GENEVA, Cutting 135, Blank 880

| Goblet, 9 oz. | $10.00 |
|---|---|
| Saucer Champagne, 5½ oz. | $10.00 |
| Sherbet | $9.00 |
| Cocktail, 3½ oz. | $9.00 |

### AIRDALE, Cutting 175, Blank 880

Goblet, 10 oz. ............................... $10.00
Saucer Champagne, 5½ oz. .......... $10.00
Sherbet.......................................... $9.00
Cocktail, 3½ oz. ............................ $9.00
Wine, 2¾ oz. ................................. $10.00

### Blank 882

Goblet, 11 oz. ............................... $10.00
Goblet, 10 oz. ............................... $10.00
Goblet, 9 oz. ................................. $9.00
Goblet, 8 oz. ................................. $9.00
Saucer Champagne, 7 oz. ............. $10.00
Saucer Champagne, 5½ oz. .......... $10.00
Sherbet.......................................... $9.00
Cocktail, 3½ oz. ............................ $9.00
Cocktail, 3 oz. ............................... $9.00
Claret, 6½ oz. ............................... $12.00
Claret, 4½ oz. ............................... $12.00
Rhine Wine, 4 oz. ......................... $10.00
Wine, 3½ oz. ................................. $10.00
Wine, 2¾ oz. ................................. $10.00
Sherry, 2 oz. ................................. $10.00
Crème de Menthe, 2½ oz. .............. $9.00
Brandy (Pousse Café), 1 oz. .......... $12.00
Cordial, 1 oz. ................................ $12.00
Cordial, ¾ oz. ............................... $12.00
Hollow Stem Champagne............. $10.00
Tall Champagne ............................ $10.00
Grapefruit and Liner .................... $20.00
Custard ......................................... $8.00
Hot Whiskey.................................. $9.00
Tall Ale ......................................... $10.00

### IVY, Etching 235, Blank 882

Goblet, 11 oz. ............................... $12.00
Goblet, 10 oz. ............................... $12.00
Goblet, 9 oz. ................................. $11.00
Goblet, 8 oz. ................................. $10.00
Saucer Champagne, 7 oz. ............. $12.00
Saucer Champagne, 5½ oz. .......... $10.00
Sherbet.......................................... $9.00
Cocktail, 3½ oz. ............................ $9.00
Cocktail, 3 oz. ............................... $9.00
Claret, 6½ oz. ............................... $16.00
Claret, 4½ oz. ............................... $12.00
Rhine Wine ................................... $12.00
Wine, 3½ oz. ................................. $12.00
Wine, 2¾ oz. ................................. $12.00
Sherry............................................ $9.00
Crème de Menthe........................... $9.00
Brandy (Pousse Café) ................... $25.00
Cordial, 1 oz. ................................ $25.00
Cordial, ¾ oz. ............................... $25.00
Hollow Stem Champagne............. $12.00
Tall Champagne ............................ $12.00
Grapefruit and Liner .................... $22.00
Custard ......................................... $7.00

Hot Whiskey.................................. $9.00
Tall Ale ......................................... $12.00

### GRILLE, Etching 236, Blank 882

Goblet, 11 oz. ............................... $10.00
Goblet, 10 oz. ............................... $10.00
Goblet, 9 oz. ................................. $9.00
Goblet, 8 oz. ................................. $9.00
Saucer Champagne, 7 oz. ............. $10.00
Saucer Champagne, 5½ oz. .......... $10.00
Sherbet.......................................... $9.00
Cocktail, 3½ oz. ............................ $9.00
Cocktail, 3 oz. ............................... $9.00
Claret, 6½ oz. ............................... $15.00
Claret, 4½ oz. ............................... $10.00
Rhine Wine ................................... $10.00
Wine, 3½ oz. ................................. $10.00
Wine, 2¾ oz. ................................. $10.00
Sherry............................................ $9.00
Crème de Menthe........................... $9.00
Brandy (Pousse Café) ................... $15.00
Cordial, 1 oz. ................................ $15.00
Cordial, ¾ oz. ............................... $15.00
Hollow Stem Champagne............. $10.00
Tall Champagne ............................ $10.00
Grapefruit and Liner .................... $25.00
Custard ......................................... $7.00
Hot Whiskey.................................. $9.00
Tall Ale ......................................... $10.00

### Blank 890
#### Crystal

Goblet............................................ $20.00
Saucer Champagne........................ $16.00
Low Sherbet.................................. $12.00
Parfait........................................... $20.00
Cocktail........................................ $12.00
Claret Wine................................... $18.00
Cordial ......................................... $20.00
Oyster Cocktail............................. $7.00
Footed Ice Tea............................... $12.00
Footed Tumbler, 9 oz. ................... $8.00
Footed Juice ................................. $8.00
Footed Whiskey ............................ $8.00

#### Green/Rose

Goblet............................................ $35.00
Saucer Champagne........................ $30.00
Low Sherbet.................................. $12.00
Parfait........................................... $34.00
Cocktail........................................ $14.00
Claret Wine................................... $35.00
Cordial ......................................... $38.00
Oyster Cocktail............................. $14.00
Footed Ice Tea............................... $30.00
Footed Tumbler, 9 oz. ................... $20.00
Footed Juice ................................. $14.00
Footed Whiskey ............................ $24.00

#### Burgundy

Goblet............................................ $47.00
Saucer Champagne........................ $38.00
Low Sherbet.................................. $32.00
Parfait........................................... $42.00
Cocktail........................................ $38.00
Claret Wine................................... $50.00
Cordial ......................................... $56.00
Oyster Cocktail............................. $30.00
Footed Ice Tea............................... $45.00
Footed Tumbler, 9 oz. ................... $35.00
Footed Juice ................................. $35.00
Footed Whiskey ............................ $38.00

### VERONA, Etching 281, Blank 890
#### Crystal

Goblet............................................ $35.00
Saucer Champagne........................ $32.00
Low Sherbet.................................. $26.00
Parfait........................................... $38.00
Cocktail........................................ $30.00
Claret............................................ $44.00
Wine.............................................. $40.00
Cordial ......................................... $50.00
Oyster Cocktail............................. $22.00
Footed Ice Tea............................... $34.00
Footed Tumbler, 9 oz. ................... $24.00
Footed Juice ................................. $24.00
Footed Whiskey ............................ $28.00

#### Green/Rose

Goblet............................................ $47.00
Saucer Champagne........................ $44.00
Low Sherbet.................................. $30.00
Parfait........................................... $45.00
Cocktail........................................ $35.00
Claret............................................ $52.00
Wine.............................................. $48.00
Cordial ......................................... $65.00
Oyster Cocktail............................. $30.00
Footed Ice Tea............................... $45.00
Footed Tumbler, 9 oz. ................... $30.00
Footed Juice ................................. $30.00
Footed Whiskey ............................ $35.00

### WARWICK, Cutting 198, Blank 890

Goblet............................................ $22.00
Saucer Champagne........................ $20.00
Low Sherbet.................................. $15.00
Parfait........................................... $25.00
Cocktail........................................ $15.00
Claret Wine................................... $22.00
Cordial ......................................... $45.00
Oyster Cocktail............................. $15.00
Footed Ice Tea............................... $20.00
Footed Tumbler,
   9 oz. .......................................... $15.00
Footed Juice ................................. $18.00
Footed Whiskey ............................ $18.00

### Blank 891
#### Crystal
Goblet.................................. $20.00
High Sherbet....................... $16.00
Low Sherbet......................... $9.00
Cocktail.............................. $12.00
Claret.................................. $20.00
Cordial................................ $24.00
Oyster Cocktail.................... $7.00
Footed Ice Tea.................... $18.00
Footed Tumbler,
  9 oz. ............................... $10.00
Footed Juice ....................... $10.00

#### Topaz
Goblet.................................. $35.00
High Sherbet....................... $32.00
Low Sherbet....................... $28.00
Cocktail.............................. $30.00
Claret.................................. $38.00
Cordial................................ $45.00
Oyster Cocktail.................. $25.00
Footed Ice Tea.................... $32.00
Footed Tumbler,
  9 oz. ............................... $28.00
Footed Juice ....................... $28.00

### SPRINGTIME, Etching 318, Blank 891
#### Crystal
Goblet.................................. $35.00
High Sherbet....................... $30.00
Low Sherbet....................... $20.00
Cocktail.............................. $30.00
Claret.................................. $40.00
Cordial................................ $42.00
Oyster Cocktail.................. $20.00
Footed Ice Tea.................... $35.00
Footed Tumbler, 9 oz. ........ $30.00
Footed Juice ....................... $30.00

#### Topaz
Goblet.................................. $42.00
High Sherbet....................... $40.00
Low Sherbet....................... $28.00
Cocktail.............................. $35.00
Claret.................................. $50.00
Cordial................................ $65.00
Oyster Cocktail.................. $28.00
Footed Ice Tea.................... $40.00
Footed Tumbler, 9 oz. ........ $30.00
Footed Juice ....................... $30.00

### NORDIC, Blank 892
Goblet.................................. $22.00
Saucer Champagne............... $20.00

Low Sherbet........................ $18.00
Cocktail.............................. $20.00
Claret.................................. $25.00
Wine ................................... $22.00
Cordial................................ $34.00
Oyster Cocktail.................. $15.00
Footed Ice Tea.................... $22.00
Footed Juice ....................... $16.00

### ARIEL, Tracing 93, Blank 892
Goblet.................................. $25.00
Saucer Champagne............... $22.00
Low Sherbet........................ $20.00
Cocktail.............................. $20.00
Claret.................................. $27.00
Wine ................................... $25.00
Cordial................................ $35.00
Oyster Cocktail.................. $18.00
Footed Ice Tea.................... $22.00
Footed Juice ....................... $20.00

### RINGLET, Tracing 95, Blank 892
Goblet.................................. $25.00
Saucer Champagne............... $22.00
Low Sherbet........................ $20.00
Cocktail.............................. $20.00
Claret.................................. $25.00
Wine ................................... $22.00
Cordial................................ $35.00
Oyster Cocktail.................. $18.00
Footed Ice Tea.................... $22.00
Footed Juice ....................... $20.00

### ROSEMARY, Etching 339, Blank 892
Goblet.................................. $26.00
Saucer Champagne............... $24.00
Low Sherbet........................ $18.00
Cocktail.............................. $20.00
Claret.................................. $30.00
Wine ................................... $30.00
Cordial................................ $38.00
Oyster Cocktail.................. $18.00
Footed Ice Tea.................... $24.00
Footed Juice ....................... $20.00

### ORCHID, Carving 48, Blank 892
Goblet.................................. $65.00
Saucer Champagne............... $62.00
Low Sherbet........................ $54.00
Cocktail.............................. $60.00
Claret.................................. $75.00
Wine ................................... $70.00
Cordial................................ $110.00
Oyster Cocktail.................. $40.00
Footed Ice Tea.................... $65.00
Footed Juice ....................... $60.00

### INGRID, Cutting 794, Blank 892
Goblet.................................. $30.00
Saucer Champagne............... $27.00
Low Sherbet........................ $24.00
Cocktail.............................. $27.00
Claret.................................. $35.00
Wine ................................... $32.00
Cordial................................ $58.00
Oyster Cocktail.................. $24.00
Footed Ice Tea.................... $30.00
Footed Juice ....................... $25.00

### PAPYRUS, Cutting 795, Blank 892
Goblet.................................. $30.00
Saucer Champagne............... $27.00
Low Sherbet........................ $24.00
Cocktail.............................. $27.00
Claret.................................. $34.00
Wine ................................... $32.00
Cordial................................ $58.00
Oyster Cocktail.................. $20.00
Footed Ice Tea.................... $30.00
Footed Juice ....................... $24.00

### LYRIC, Cutting 796, Blank 892
Goblet.................................. $30.00
Saucer Champagne............... $27.00
Low Sherbet........................ $24.00
Cocktail.............................. $27.00
Claret.................................. $34.00
Wine ................................... $32.00
Cordial................................ $58.00
Oyster Cocktail.................. $20.00
Footed Ice Tea.................... $30.00
Footed Juice ....................... $24.00

### CHRISTINE, Cutting 798, Blank 892
Goblet.................................. $30.00
Saucer Champagne............... $27.00
Low Sherbet........................ $24.00
Cocktail.............................. $27.00
Claret.................................. $34.00
Wine ................................... $32.00
Cordial................................ $58.00
Oyster Cocktail.................. $20.00
Footed Ice Tea.................... $30.00
Footed Juice ....................... $24.00

### COIN, Blank 1372
#### Crystal
Goblet.................................. $45.00
Sherbet................................ $45.00
Wine ................................... $50.00
Ice Tea................................ $55.00
Ice Tea/Highball ................. $50.00
Water/Scotch and Soda........ $45.00
Juice/Old Fashioned ............ $45.00
Double Old Fashioned ......... $45.00

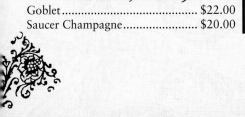

### Olive

| | |
|---|---|
| Goblet | $50.00 |
| Sherbet | $45.00 |
| Wine | $50.00 |
| Ice Tea | $50.00 |
| Double Old Fashioned | $50.00 |

### Ruby

| | |
|---|---|
| Goblet | $125.00 |
| Sherbet | $95.00 |
| Wine | $125.00 |
| Ice Tea | $125.00 |
| Double Old Fashioned | $95.00 |

## ALEXIS, Blank 1630

| | |
|---|---|
| Goblet | $15.00 |
| Cocktail | $15.00 |
| Claret | $18.00 |
| Wine, 3 oz. | $12.00 |
| Wine, 2 oz. | $12.00 |
| Crème de Menthe | $10.00 |
| Brandy (Pousse Café) | $18.00 |
| Cordial | $18.00 |
| Tall Champagne | $10.00 |
| Footed Ice Tea | $15.00 |
| Footed Tumbler | $10.00 |

## AMERICAN, Blank 2056
### Crystal

| | |
|---|---|
| Goblet | $22.00 |
| Low Goblet | $12.50 |
| Sherbet, Hexagon foot | $14.00 |
| High Sherbet, Flared | $14.00 |
| High Sherbet, Regular | $14.00 |
| Low Sherbet, Flared | $12.00 |
| Low Sherbet, Regular | $12.00 |
| Handled Sherbet | $135.00 |
| Footed Cocktail | $17.00 |
| Old Fashioned Cocktail | $18.00 |
| Claret | $55.00 |
| Footed Wine, Hexagon Foot | $22.00 |
| Oyster Cocktail | $14.00 |
| Sundae | $18.00 |
| Footed Lemonade, Handled | $175.00 |
| Footed Ice Tea | $22.00 |
| Footed Tumbler, 9 oz. | $16.00 |
| Footed Juice | $20.00 |
| Ice Tea Tumbler, Flared | $22.00 |
| Table Tumbler, Flared | $25.00 |
| Ice Tea Tumbler, Regular | $22.00 |
| Table Tumbler, Regular | $18.00 |
| Tumbler, Regular, 5 oz. | $18.00 |
| Whiskey Tumbler | $18.00 |
| Baby Tumbler | $400.00 – Market |
| Beer Mug | $80.00 |
| Beer Mug (Reintroduction) | $80.00 |

| | |
|---|---|
| Tom and Jerry Mug | $45.00 |
| Youth Mug | $45.00 |

### Green

| | |
|---|---|
| Ice Tea Tumbler, Regular | $85.00 |
| Table Tumbler, Regular | $75.00 |

## VOGUE, Blank 2106

| | |
|---|---|
| Goblet | $10.00 |
| Sherbet, 3 oz. | $8.00 |
| Sherbet, 2½ oz. | $8.00 |
| Parfait, 6¼ oz. | $10.00 |
| Parfait, 4⅜ oz. | $10.00 |
| Wine | $10.00 |
| Footed Handled Lemonade | $15.00 |
| Footed Soda, 12 oz. | $10.00 |
| Footed Soda, 10 oz. | $10.00 |
| Footed Soda, 8 oz. | $8.00 |
| Footed Soda, 6 oz. | $8.00 |
| Footed Soda, 4 oz. | $8.00 |
| Cocola | $8.00 |
| Sundae | $8.00 |

## COLONIAL PRISM, Blank 2183

| | |
|---|---|
| Table Tumbler | $8.00 |
| Ice Tea Tumbler | $8.00 |
| Handled Tumbler | $15.00 |
| Sherbet, Regular | $8.00 |
| Sherbet, Flared | $8.00 |
| Grapefruit and Liner | $15.00 |

## COLONIAL, Blank 2222
### Crystal

| | |
|---|---|
| Goblet | $10.00 |
| High Sherbet | $10.00 |
| Low Sherbet, 4½ oz. | $8.00 |
| Low Sherbet, 3 oz. | $7.00 |
| Fruit Cocktail | $8.00 |
| Wine | $10.00 |
| Wine Tumbler | $10.00 |
| Ice Tea Tumbler, 14 oz. Regular | $10.00 |
| Ice Tea Tumbler, 12 oz. Flared | $10.00 |
| Table Tumbler, Regular | $8.00 |
| Table Tumbler, Flared | $8.00 |
| Footed Oyster Cocktail | $8.00 |

### Amber/Green

| | |
|---|---|
| Goblet | $13.00 |
| High Sherbet | $12.00 |
| Low Sherbet, 4½ oz. | $10.00 |
| Fruit Cocktail | $10.00 |
| Wine Tumbler | $12.00 |
| Ice Tea Tumbler, 14 oz. Regular | $15.00 |

| | |
|---|---|
| Table Tumbler, Regular | $12.00 |
| Parfait | $18.00 |
| Footed Oyster Cocktail | $10.00 |

## Priscilla, Blank 2321
### Crystal

| | |
|---|---|
| Goblet, 9 oz. | $12.00 |
| Goblet, 7 oz. | $10.00 |
| Saucer Champagne | $10.00 |
| Sherbet | $10.00 |
| Footed Tumbler | $12.00 |
| Footed Tumbler, Handled | $12.00 |
| Footed Custard, Handled | $12.00 |

### Amber/Green

| | |
|---|---|
| Goblet, 9 oz. | $20.00 |
| Goblet, 7 oz. | $20.00 |
| Saucer Champagne | $20.00 |
| Sherbet | $20.00 |
| Footed Tumbler | $22.00 |
| Footed Tumbler, Handled | $30.00 |
| Footed Custard, Handled | $30.00 |

### Blue

| | |
|---|---|
| Goblet, 9 oz. | $30.00 |
| Goblet, 7 oz. | $25.00 |
| Saucer Champagne | $30.00 |
| Sherbet | $25.00 |
| Footed Tumbler | $30.00 |
| Footed Tumbler, Handled | $35.00 |
| Footed Custard, Handled | $30.00 |

## COLONY, Blank 2412

| | |
|---|---|
| Goblet | $22.00 |
| Sherbet | $15.00 |
| Cocktail | $15.00 |
| Wine | $23.00 |
| Oyster Cocktail | $15.00 |
| Footed Ice Tea | $25.00 |
| Footed Juice | $15.00 |
| Flat Tumbler, 12 oz. | $25.00 |
| Flat Tumbler, 9 oz. | $25.00 |
| Flat Tumbler, 5 oz. | $22.00 |

## HERMITAGE, Blank 2449
### Crystal

| | |
|---|---|
| Goblet | $24.00 |
| High Sherbet | $20.00 |
| Low Sherbet | $18.00 |
| Fruit Cocktail | $18.00 |
| Cocktail | $18.00 |
| Old Fashioned Cocktail | $20.00 |
| Claret | $25.00 |
| Footed Ice Tea | $24.00 |

Footed Table Tumbler,
9 oz. .................................. $20.00
Footed Juice ............................ $20.00
Footed Whiskey, 2 oz. .............. $20.00
Tumbler, 13 oz. ....................... $28.00
Tumbler, 9 oz. ......................... $22.00
Tumbler, 5 oz. ......................... $18.00
Tumbler, 2 oz. ......................... $16.00
Beer Mug, 12 oz. ..................... $48.00
Beer Mug, 9 oz. ....................... $42.00

### Regular Colors
Goblet ...................................... $30.00
High Sherbet ........................... $26.00
Low Sherbet ............................ $20.00
Fruit Cocktail .......................... $20.00
Cocktail ................................... $18.00
Old Fashioned Cocktail .............. $22.00
Claret ...................................... $34.00
Footed Ice Tea ......................... $30.00
Footed Table Tumbler, 9 oz. ......... $22.00
Footed Juice ............................ $20.00
Footed Whiskey, 2 oz. .................. $20.00
Tumbler, 13 oz. ....................... $34.00
Tumbler, 9 oz. ......................... $28.00
Tumbler, 5 oz. ......................... $22.00
Tumbler, 2 oz. ......................... $22.00

### Wisteria
Goblet ...................................... $65.00
High Sherbet ........................... $55.00
Low Sherbet ............................ $50.00
Fruit Cocktail .......................... $35.00
Cocktail ................................... $35.00
Old Fashioned Cocktail .............. $38.00
Footed Ice Tea ......................... $65.00
Footed Tumbler, 9 oz. ................. $48.00
Footed Juice ............................ $38.00
Tumbler, 13 oz. ....................... $57.00
Tumbler, 9 oz. ......................... $45.00
Tumbler, 5 oz. ......................... $42.00
Tumbler, 2 oz. ......................... $50.00

## BAROQUE, Blank 2496
### Crystal
Goblet ...................................... $25.00
Sherbet .................................... $20.00
Footed Cocktail ........................ $14.00
Old Fashioned Cocktail .............. $25.00
Footed Ice Tea ......................... $45.00
Footed Tumbler, 9 oz. ................. $18.00
Flat Ice Tea, 14 oz. ................... $45.00
Tumbler, 9 oz. ......................... $30.00
Tumbler, 5 oz. ......................... $20.00

### Azure
Goblet ...................................... $52.00
Sherbet .................................... $46.00
Footed Cocktail ........................ $20.00
Old Fashioned Cocktail .............. $80.00

Footed Ice Tea ......................... $50.00
Footed Tumbler,
9 oz. .................................. $45.00
Flat Ice Tea, 14 oz. ................... $85.00
Tumbler, 9 oz. ......................... $60.00
Tumbler, 5 oz. ......................... $50.00

### Gold Tint
Goblet ...................................... $54.00
Sherbet .................................... $38.00
Footed Cocktail ........................ $27.00
Old Fashioned Cocktail .............. $54.00
Footed Ice Tea ......................... $60.00
Footed Tumbler, 9 oz. ................. $40.00
Flat Ice Tea, 14 oz. ................... $80.00
Tumbler, 9 oz. ......................... $60.00
Tumbler, 5 oz. ......................... $55.00

## SUNRAY, Blank 2510
### Crystal
Goblet ...................................... $20.00
Sherbet .................................... $16.00
Fruit Cocktail .......................... $16.00
Footed Cocktail ........................ $16.00
Claret ...................................... $22.00
Footed Ice Tea ......................... $20.00
Footed Tumbler,
9 oz. .................................. $18.00
Footed Juice ............................ $18.00
Tumbler, 13 oz. ....................... $22.00
Tumbler, 9 oz. ......................... $18.00
Tumbler, 5 oz. ......................... $15.00
Old Fashioned ......................... $15.00
Whiskey Tumbler ..................... $22.00

### Azure/Green/Amber/Topaz
Goblet ...................................... $28.00
Sherbet .................................... $28.00
Footed Tumbler,
9 oz. .................................. $28.00

## GLACIER, Blank 2510
Goblet ...................................... $25.00
Sherbet .................................... $20.00
Fruit Cocktail .......................... $18.00
Footed Cocktail ........................ $16.00
Claret ...................................... $27.00
Footed Ice Tea ......................... $25.00
Footed Tumbler,
9 oz. .................................. $18.00
Footed Juice ............................ $18.00
Tumbler, 13 oz. ....................... $22.00
Tumbler, 9 oz. ......................... $20.00
Tumbler, 5 oz. ......................... $18.00
Old Fashioned ......................... $18.00
Whiskey Tumbler ..................... $24.00

## WISTAR, Blank 2620,
## BETSY ROSS, Blank 2620
Goblet ...................................... $22.00
Sherbet .................................... $20.00
Tumbler, 12 oz. ....................... $22.00
Tumbler, 5 oz. ......................... $20.00

## CENTURY,
## Blank 2630
Goblet ...................................... $22.00
Sherbet .................................... $14.00
Cocktail ................................... $14.00
Wine ........................................ $22.00
Oyster Cocktail ........................ $12.00
Footed Ice Tea ......................... $25.00
Footed Juice ............................ $14.00

## RADIANCE,
## Blank 2700
Goblet ...................................... $15.00
Sherbet .................................... $12.00
Footed Juice ............................ $12.00

## VINTAGE,
## Blank 2713
Goblet ...................................... $35.00
Sherbet .................................... $30.00
Footed Ice Tea ......................... $35.00

## FAIRMONT, Blank 2718
### Crystal
Goblet ...................................... $8.00
Sherbet .................................... $7.00
Footed Ice Tea ......................... $8.00
Footed Juice ............................ $7.00

### Colors
Goblet ...................................... $15.00
Sherbet .................................... $12.00
Footed Ice Tea ......................... $15.00
Footed Juice ............................ $12.00

## JAMESTOWN, Blank 2719
### Crystal
Goblet ...................................... $18.00
Sherbet .................................... $16.00
Wine ........................................ $18.00
Footed Ice Tea ......................... $20.00

Footed Juice ................................. $16.00
Tumbler, 12 oz. ........................... $18.00
Tumbler, 9 oz. ............................. $16.00

### Amber/Brown
Goblet ........................................... $15.00
Sherbet ......................................... $12.00
Wine .............................................. $15.00
Footed Ice Tea ............................. $15.00
Footed Juice ................................. $15.00
Tumbler, 12 oz. ........................... $15.00
Tumbler, 9 oz. ............................. $12.00

### Ruby
Goblet ........................................... $34.00
Sherbet ......................................... $28.00
Wine .............................................. $32.00
Footed Ice Tea ............................. $36.00
Footed Juice ................................. $30.00
Tumbler, 12 oz. ........................... $34.00
Tumbler, 9 oz. ............................. $32.00

### Other Colors
Goblet ........................................... $28.00
Sherbet ......................................... $22.00
Wine .............................................. $28.00
Footed Ice Tea ............................. $30.00
Footed Juice ................................. $22.00
Tumbler, 12 oz. ........................... $30.00
Tumbler, 9 oz. ............................. $28.00

## ARGUS, Blank 2770
### Crystal/Olive/Gray
Goblet ........................................... $22.00
Sherbet ......................................... $18.00
Wine .............................................. $18.00
Footed Ice Tea ............................. $22.00
Highball ........................................ $18.00
Old Fashioned .............................. $18.00
Juice Tumbler ............................... $18.00

### Cobalt/Ruby
Goblet ........................................... $30.00
Sherbet ......................................... $22.00
Wine .............................................. $22.00
Footed Ice Tea ............................. $30.00
Highball ........................................ $30.00
Old Fashioned .............................. $30.00
Juice Tumbler ............................... $30.00

## PEBBLE BEACH, Blank 2806
Goblet ........................................... $15.00
Sherbet ......................................... $12.00
Wine/On the Rocks ...................... $12.00
Ice Tea Tumbler ........................... $15.00
Juice Tumbler ............................... $12.00

## SORRENTO, Blank 2832
Goblet ........................................... $12.00
Sherbet ......................................... $10.00
Wine .............................................. $12.00
Footed Ice Tea ............................. $12.00
Double Old Fashioned ................. $10.00
Highball ........................................ $10.00

## PANELLED DIAMOND POINT, Blank 2860
Goblet ........................................... $25.00
Champagne ................................... $20.00
Wine .............................................. $25.00
Footed Ice Tea ............................. $25.00

## MOONSTONE, Blank 2882
### Crystal/Apple Green/Pink
Goblet ........................................... $15.00
Sherbet ......................................... $14.00
Wine .............................................. $15.00
Footed Ice Tea ............................. $15.00
Highball ........................................ $15.00
Old Fashioned .............................. $15.00

### Other Colors
Goblet ........................................... $12.00
Sherbet ......................................... $12.00
Wine .............................................. $12.00
Footed Ice Tea ............................. $12.00
Highball ........................................ $12.00
Old Fashioned .............................. $12.00

## STRATTON, Blank 2885
Goblet ........................................... $15.00
Sherbet ......................................... $14.00
Wine .............................................. $18.00
Footed Ice Tea ............................. $18.00
Double Old Fashioned ................. $14.00
Highball ........................................ $14.00

## HERITAGE, Blank 2887
Goblet ........................................... $16.00
Sherbet ......................................... $14.00
Wine .............................................. $16.00
Footed Ice Tea ............................. $18.00
Double Old Fashioned ................. $14.00
Highball ........................................ $14.00

## MONARCH, Blank 2903
Goblet ........................................... $12.00
Wine .............................................. $12.00
Footed Ice Tea ............................. $12.00
Double Old Fashioned ................. $10.00
Highball ........................................ $12.00

## FAIRLANE, Blank 2916
Goblet ........................................... $12.00
Champagne ................................... $12.00
Wine .............................................. $12.00
Footed Ice Tea ............................. $12.00
Cordial .......................................... $15.00
Double Old Fashioned ................. $10.00
Highball ........................................ $10.00

## GREENFIELD, Cutting 935, Blank 2916
Goblet ........................................... $15.00
Champagne ................................... $12.00
Wine .............................................. $12.00
Footed Ice Tea ............................. $15.00
Cordial .......................................... $15.00

## BRACELET, Decoration 694, Blank 2916
Goblet ........................................... $15.00
Champagne ................................... $15.00
Wine .............................................. $15.00
Footed Ice Tea ............................. $15.00
Cordial .......................................... $15.00

## WOODLAND, Blank 2921
Goblet ........................................... $15.00
Sherbet ......................................... $15.00
Wine .............................................. $15.00
Footed Ice Tea ............................. $15.00

## TRANSITION, Blank 2936
Wine/Juice .................................... $10.00
Double Old Fashioned ................. $10.00
Highball ........................................ $12.00

## VIRGINIA, Blank 2977
Goblet ........................................... $15.00
Sherbet ......................................... $15.00
Wine .............................................. $15.00
Footed Ice Tea ............................. $15.00

## KIMBERLY, *Blank 2990*

Goblet ........................................... $18.00
Sherbet .......................................... $18.00
Wine .............................................. $18.00
Wine Goblet (Magnum) ............. $25.00
Flute/Parfait ................................. $25.00

## VISION, *Blank 3008*
### Midnight Blue/White

Goblet ........................................... $25.00
Sherbet .......................................... $22.00
Claret ............................................ $25.00
Tulip Wine .................................... $26.00
Cordial ......................................... $28.00
Footed Ice Tea .............................. $25.00

### Other Colors

Goblet ........................................... $18.00
Sherbet .......................................... $18.00
Claret ............................................ $18.00
Tulip Wine .................................... $20.00
Cordial ......................................... $22.00
Footed Ice Tea .............................. $18.00

## RADIANCE, *Blank 3113*

Goblet ........................................... $15.00
Sherbet .......................................... $15.00
Wine .............................................. $15.00
Footed Ice Tea .............................. $15.00

## *Blank 4020*
### Crystal/Ebony Base

Goblet ........................................... $30.00
High Sherbet ................................. $28.00
Low Sherbet, 7 oz. ........................ $22.00
Low Sherbet, 5 oz. ........................ $22.00
Cocktail, 3½ oz. ............................ $16.00
Claret ............................................ $35.00
Wine .............................................. $35.00
Footed Ice Tea .............................. $35.00
Footed Tumbler, 13 oz. ................ $35.00
Footed Tumbler, 10 oz. ................ $26.00
Footed Juice .................................. $24.00
Footed Whiskey ............................ $22.00

### Regular Colors

Goblet ........................................... $35.00
High Sherbet ................................. $32.00
Low Sherbet, 7 oz. ........................ $28.00
Low Sherbet, 5 oz. ........................ $28.00
Cocktail, 3½ oz. ............................ $20.00
Claret ............................................ $45.00

Wine .............................................. $45.00
Footed Ice Tea .............................. $35.00
Footed Tumbler, 13 oz. ................ $40.00
Footed Tumbler, 10 oz. ................ $28.00
Footed Juice .................................. $30.00
Footed Whiskey ............................ $30.00

### Wisteria

Goblet ........................................... $55.00
High Sherbet ................................. $47.00
Low Sherbet, 7 oz. ........................ $35.00
Low Sherbet, 5 oz. ........................ $35.00
Cocktail, 3½ oz. ............................ $35.00
Claret ............................................ $65.00
Wine .............................................. $65.00
Footed Ice Tea .............................. $55.00
Footed Tumbler,
  13 oz. ........................................ $60.00
Footed Tumbler,
  10 oz. ........................................ $35.00
Footed Juice .................................. $35.00
Footed Whiskey ............................ $40.00

## KASHMIR, *Etching 283,*
*Blank 4020*

Goblet ........................................... $48.00
High Sherbet ................................. $42.00
Low Sherbet, 7 oz. ........................ $36.00
Low Sherbet, 5 oz. ........................ $32.00
Cocktail, 4 oz. (4020½) ............... $30.00
Cocktail, 3½ oz. ............................ $30.00
Footed Ice Tea .............................. $48.00
Footed Tumbler, 13 oz. ................ $45.00
Footed Tumbler, 10 oz. ................ $34.00
Footed Juice .................................. $30.00
Footed Whiskey ............................ $36.00

## NEW GARLAND, *Etching 284,*
*Blank 4020*
### Amber

Goblet ........................................... $38.00
High Sherbet ................................. $34.00
Low Sherbet, 7 oz. ........................ $30.00
Low Sherbet, 5 oz. ........................ $30.00
Cocktail, 4 oz. (4020½) ............... $30.00
Cocktail, 3½ oz. ............................ $30.00
Footed Ice Tea .............................. $38.00
Footed Tumbler, 13 oz. ................ $38.00
Footed Tumbler, 10 oz. ................ $32.00
Footed Juice .................................. $30.00
Footed Whiskey ............................ $30.00

### Rose/Topaz

Goblet ........................................... $48.00
High Sherbet ................................. $45.00
Low Sherbet, 7 oz. ........................ $30.00
Low Sherbet, 5 oz. ........................ $30.00
Cocktail, 4 oz. (4020½) ............... $30.00
Cocktail, 3½ oz. ............................ $30.00
Footed Ice Tea .............................. $48.00

Footed Tumbler, 13 oz. ................ $48.00
Footed Tumbler, 10 oz. ................ $30.00
Footed Juice .................................. $30.00
Footed Whiskey ............................ $36.00

## MINUET, *Etching 285,*
*Blank 4020*

Goblet ........................................... $65.00
High Sherbet ................................. $60.00
Low Sherbet, 7 oz. ........................ $48.00
Low Sherbet, 5 oz. ........................ $45.00
Cocktail, 4 oz. (4020½) ............... $42.00
Cocktail, 3½ oz. ............................ $42.00
Footed Ice Tea .............................. $65.00
Footed Tumbler, 13 oz. ................ $64.00
Footed Tumbler, 10 oz. ................ $48.00
Footed Juice .................................. $45.00
Footed Whiskey ............................ $54.00

## FERN, *Etching 305,*
*Blank 4020*

Goblet ........................................... $38.00
High Sherbet ................................. $35.00
Low Sherbet, 7 oz. ........................ $30.00
Low Sherbet, 5 oz. ........................ $30.00
Cocktail, 4 oz. (4020½) ............... $30.00
Cocktail, 3½ oz. ............................ $30.00
Footed Ice Tea .............................. $38.00
Footed Tumbler, 13 oz. ................ $38.00
Footed Tumbler, 10 oz. ................ $32.00
Footed Juice .................................. $32.00
Footed Whiskey ............................ $35.00

## QUEEN ANN, *Etching 306,*
*Blank 4020*
### Crystal

Goblet ........................................... $38.00
High Sherbet ................................. $35.00
Low Sherbet, 7 oz. ........................ $32.00
Low Sherbet, 5 oz. ........................ $32.00
Cocktail, 4 oz. (4020½) ............... $30.00
Cocktail, 3½ oz. ............................ $30.00
Footed Ice Tea .............................. $38.00
Footed Tumbler, 13 oz. ................ $38.00
Footed Tumbler, 10 oz. ................ $34.00
Footed Juice .................................. $30.00
Footed Whiskey ............................ $30.00

### Amber

Goblet ........................................... $40.00
High Sherbet ................................. $36.00
Low Sherbet, 7 oz. ........................ $32.00
Low Sherbet, 5 oz. ........................ $30.00
Cocktail, 4 oz. (4020½) ............... $30.00
Cocktail, 3½ oz. ............................ $30.00
Footed Ice Tea .............................. $40.00
Footed Tumbler, 13 oz. ................ $40.00
Footed Tumbler, 10 oz. ................ $32.00
Footed Juice .................................. $30.00
Footed Whiskey ............................ $34.00

### FOUNTAIN, Etching 307, Blank 4020
#### Crystal
Goblet .............................. $32.00
High Sherbet ....................... $30.00
Low Sherbet, 7 oz. ................. $28.00
Low Sherbet, 5 oz. ................. $26.00
Cocktail, 3½ oz. ................... $26.00
Footed Ice Tea ..................... $32.00
Footed Tumbler, 13 oz. ............. $32.00
Footed Tumbler, 10 oz. ............. $26.00
Footed Juice ....................... $26.00
Footed Whiskey ..................... $25.00

#### Green
Goblet .............................. $36.00
High Sherbet ....................... $34.00
Low Sherbet, 7 oz. ................. $34.00
Low Sherbet, 5 oz. ................. $34.00
Cocktail, 3½ oz. ................... $32.00
Footed Ice Tea ..................... $36.00
Footed Tumbler, 13 oz. ............. $36.00
Footed Tumbler, 10 oz. ............. $32.00
Footed Juice ....................... $32.00
Footed Whiskey ..................... $32.00

### MILLEFLEUR, Cutting 195, Blank 4020
Goblet .............................. $35.00
High Sherbet ....................... $32.00
Low Sherbet, 7 oz. ................. $30.00
Low Sherbet, 5 oz. ................. $30.00
Cocktail, 3½ oz. ................... $28.00
Claret ............................. $40.00
Wine ............................... $40.00
Footed Ice Tea ..................... $35.00
Footed Tumbler, 13 oz. ............. $35.00
Footed Tumbler, 10 oz. ............. $30.00
Footed Juice ....................... $30.00
Footed Whiskey ..................... $30.00

### FORMAL GARDEN, Cutting 700, Blank 4020
Goblet .............................. $35.00
High Sherbet ....................... $33.00
Low Sherbet, 7 oz. ................. $30.00
Low Sherbet, 5 oz. ................. $30.00
Cocktail, 3½ oz. ................... $30.00
Footed Ice Tea ..................... $35.00
Footed Tumbler, 13 oz. ............. $35.00
Footed Tumbler, 10 oz. ............. $30.00
Footed Juice ....................... $30.00
Footed Whiskey ..................... $30.00

### TAPESTRY, Cutting 701, Blank 4020
Goblet .............................. $30.00
High Sherbet ....................... $32.00
Low Sherbet, 7 oz. ................. $25.00
Low Sherbet, 5 oz. ................. $25.00
Cocktail, 3½ oz. ................... $25.00

Footed Ice Tea ..................... $30.00
Footed Tumbler, 13 oz. ............. $30.00
Footed Tumbler, 10 oz. ............. $25.00
Footed Juice ....................... $25.00
Footed Whiskey ..................... $25.00

### COMET, Cutting 702, Blank 4020
#### Crystal
Goblet .............................. $27.00
High Sherbet ....................... $27.00
Low Sherbet, 7 oz. ................. $22.00
Low Sherbet, 5 oz. ................. $22.00
Cocktail, 4 oz. (4020½) ............ $22.00
Cocktail, 3½ oz. ................... $24.00
Claret ............................. $27.00
Wine ............................... $27.00
Footed Ice Tea ..................... $27.00
Footed Tumbler, 13 oz. ............. $27.00
Footed Tumbler, 10 oz. ............. $22.00
Footed Juice ....................... $22.00
Footed Whiskey ..................... $22.00

#### Green/Ebony
Goblet .............................. $35.00
High Sherbet ....................... $35.00
Low Sherbet, 7 oz. ................. $32.00
Low Sherbet, 5 oz. ................. $32.00
Cocktail, 4 oz. (4020½) ............ $32.00
Cocktail, 3½ oz. ................... $32.00
Claret ............................. $36.00
Wine ............................... $36.00
Footed Ice Tea ..................... $35.00
Footed Tumbler, 13 oz. ............. $35.00
Footed Tumbler, 10 oz. ............. $32.00
Footed Juice ....................... $32.00
Footed Whiskey ..................... $32.00

### NEW YORKER, Cutting 703, Blank 4020
#### Crystal
Goblet .............................. $28.00
High Sherbet ....................... $26.00
Low Sherbet, 7 oz. ................. $24.00
Cocktail, 4 oz. .................... $24.00
Claret ............................. $28.00
Wine ............................... $24.00
Footed Ice Tea ..................... $28.00
Footed Tumbler, 13 oz. ............. $28.00
Footed Tumbler, 10 oz. ............. $22.00
Footed Juice ....................... $22.00
Footed Whiskey ..................... $20.00

#### Green/Ebony
Goblet .............................. $36.00
High Sherbet ....................... $34.00
Low Sherbet, 7 oz. ................. $32.00
Cocktail, 4 oz. .................... $32.00
Claret ............................. $38.00
Wine ............................... $38.00
Footed Ice Tea ..................... $36.00

Footed Tumbler, 13 oz. ............. $36.00
Footed Tumbler, 10 oz. ............. $32.00
Footed Juice ....................... $32.00
Footed Whiskey ..................... $30.00

### RHYTHM, Cutting 773, Blank 4020
Goblet .............................. $25.00
High Sherbet ....................... $20.00
Low Sherbet, 7 oz. ................. $18.00
Low Sherbet, 5 oz. ................. $18.00
Cocktail, 4 oz. .................... $18.00
Cocktail, 3½ oz. ................... $18.00
Claret ............................. $28.00
Wine ............................... $25.00
Footed Tumbler, 13 oz. ............. $28.00
Footed Tumbler, 10 oz. ............. $20.00
Footed Juice ....................... $20.00
Footed Whiskey ..................... $18.00

### CHELSEA, Cutting 783, Blank 4020
Goblet .............................. $25.00
High Sherbet ....................... $20.00
Low Sherbet, 7 oz. ................. $18.00
Low Sherbet, 5 oz. ................. $18.00
Cocktail, 4 oz. .................... $18.00
Cocktail, 3½ oz. ................... $18.00
Claret ............................. $28.00
Wine ............................... $25.00
Footed Tumbler, 13 oz. ............. $28.00
Footed Tumbler, 10 oz. ............. $20.00
Footed Juice ....................... $20.00
Footed Whiskey ..................... $18.00

### CLUB DESIGN A, Decoration 603, Blank 4020
Goblet .............................. $40.00
High Sherbet ....................... $40.00
Low Sherbet, 7 oz. ................. $40.00
Low Sherbet, 5 oz. ................. $40.00
Cocktail, 3½ oz. ................... $40.00
Footed Ice Tea ..................... $40.00
Footed Tumbler, 13 oz. ............. $40.00
Footed Tumbler, 10 oz. ............. $40.00
Footed Juice ....................... $40.00
Footed Whiskey ..................... $40.00

### CLUB DESIGN B, Decoration 604, Blank 4020
Goblet .............................. $37.00
High Sherbet ....................... $37.00
Low Sherbet, 7 oz. ................. $37.00
Low Sherbet, 5 oz. ................. $37.00
Cocktail, 3½ oz. ................... $37.00
Footed Ice Tea ..................... $37.00
Footed Tumbler, 13 oz. ............. $37.00
Footed Tumbler, 10 oz. ............. $37.00
Footed Juice ....................... $37.00
Footed Whiskey ..................... $37.00

**SATURN, *Decoration 605,***
***Blank 4020***

| | |
|---|---|
| Goblet | $40.00 |
| High Sherbet | $40.00 |
| Low Sherbet, 7 oz. | $40.00 |
| Low Sherbet, 5 oz. | $40.00 |
| Cocktail, 3½ oz. | $40.00 |
| Footed Ice Tea | $40.00 |
| Footed Tumbler, 13 oz. | $40.00 |
| Footed Tumbler, 10 oz. | $40.00 |
| Footed Juice | $40.00 |
| Footed Whiskey | $40.00 |

**POLKA DOT, *Decoration 607,***
***Blank 4020***

| | |
|---|---|
| Goblet | $45.00 |
| High Sherbet | $45.00 |
| Low Sherbet, 7 oz. | $45.00 |
| Low Sherbet, 5 oz. | $45.00 |
| Cocktail, 3½ oz. | $45.00 |
| Footed Ice Tea | $45.00 |
| Footed Tumbler, 13 oz. | $45.00 |
| Footed Tumbler, 10 oz. | $45.00 |
| Footed Juice | $45.00 |
| Footed Whiskey | $45.00 |

**CLUB DESIGN C, *Decoration 611,***
***Blank 4020***

| | |
|---|---|
| Low Sherbet, 7 oz. | $42.00 |
| Footed Ice Tea | $42.00 |
| Footed Tumbler, 13 oz. | $42.00 |
| Footed Tumbler, 10 oz. | $42.00 |
| Footed Juice | $42.00 |
| Footed Whiskey | $42.00 |

**CLUB DESIGN D, *Decoration 612,***
***Blank 4020***

| | |
|---|---|
| Low Sherbet, 7 oz. | $35.00 |
| Footed Ice Tea | $35.00 |
| Footed Tumbler, 13 oz. | $35.00 |
| Footed Tumbler, 10 oz. | $35.00 |
| Footed Juice | $35.00 |
| Footed Whiskey | $35.00 |

**VICTORIAN,**
***Blank 4024***
Crystal

| | |
|---|---|
| Goblet, 11 oz. | $25.00 |
| Goblet, 10 oz. | $25.00 |
| Saucer Champagne | $22.00 |
| Sherbet | $20.00 |
| Cocktail | $20.00 |
| Claret-Wine | $25.00 |
| Rhine Wine | $25.00 |
| Sherry | $25.00 |
| Cordial | $25.00 |
| Oyster Cocktail | $20.00 |
| Footed Ice Tea | $25.00 |

| | |
|---|---|
| Footed Tumbler, 8 oz. | $20.00 |
| Footed Juice | $20.00 |
| Footed Whiskey | $20.00 |

Burgundy/Empire Green

| | |
|---|---|
| Goblet, 11 oz. | $35.00 |
| Goblet, 10 oz. | $35.00 |
| Saucer Champagne | $30.00 |
| Sherbet | $22.00 |
| Cocktail | $22.00 |
| Claret-Wine | $35.00 |
| Rhine Wine | $35.00 |
| Sherry | $35.00 |
| Cordial | $40.00 |
| Oyster Cocktail | $22.00 |
| Footed Ice Tea | $35.00 |
| Footed Tumbler, 8 oz. | $28.00 |
| Footed Juice | $28.00 |
| Footed Whiskey | $30.00 |

Regal Blue

| | |
|---|---|
| Goblet, 11 oz. | $45.00 |
| Goblet, 10 oz. | $45.00 |
| Saucer Champagne | $40.00 |
| Sherbet | $32.00 |
| Cocktail | $32.00 |
| Claret-Wine | $45.00 |
| Rhine Wine | $50.00 |
| Sherry | $45.00 |
| Cordial | $55.00 |
| Oyster Cocktail | $32.00 |
| Footed Ice Tea | $45.00 |
| Footed Tumbler, 8 oz. | $30.00 |
| Footed Juice | $30.00 |
| Footed Whiskey | $34.00 |

Silver Mist

| | |
|---|---|
| Goblet, 11 oz. | $26.00 |
| Goblet, 10 oz. | $26.00 |
| Saucer Champagne | $24.00 |
| Sherbet | $22.00 |
| Cocktail | $22.00 |
| Claret-Wine | $26.00 |
| Rhine Wine | $26.00 |
| Sherry | $26.00 |
| Cordial | $30.00 |
| Oyster Cocktail | $22.00 |
| Footed Ice Tea | $26.00 |
| Footed Tumbler, 8 oz. | $22.00 |
| Footed Juice | $22.00 |
| Footed Whiskey | $22.00 |

Ruby

| | |
|---|---|
| Rhine Wine | $55.00 |
| Sherry | $60.00 |
| Cordial | $65.00 |

**ELSINORE, *Etching 89, Blank 4024***

| | |
|---|---|
| Goblet, 10 oz. | $20.00 |
| Saucer Champagne | $20.00 |

| | |
|---|---|
| Sherbet | $18.00 |
| Cordial | $22.00 |
| Oyster Cocktail | $15.00 |
| Footed Ice Tea | $20.00 |
| Footed Tumbler, 8 oz. | $15.00 |
| Footed Juice | $15.00 |

**MANHATTAN, *Cutting 725,***
***Blank 4024***

| | |
|---|---|
| Goblet, 11 oz. | $22.00 |
| Goblet, 10 oz. | $22.00 |
| Saucer Champagne | $22.00 |
| Sherbet | $20.00 |
| Cocktail | $20.00 |
| Claret-Wine | $22.00 |
| Rhine Wine | $22.00 |
| Sherry | $20.00 |
| Cordial | $25.00 |
| Oyster Cocktail | $18.00 |
| Footed Ice Tea | $22.00 |
| Footed Tumbler, 8 oz. | $18.00 |
| Footed Juice | $18.00 |
| Footed Whiskey | $18.00 |

**METEOR, *Cutting 726,***
***Blank 4024***

| | |
|---|---|
| Goblet, 11 oz. | $22.00 |
| Goblet, 10 oz. | $22.00 |
| Saucer Champagne | $22.00 |
| Sherbet | $18.00 |
| Cocktail | $18.00 |
| Claret-Wine | $22.00 |
| Rhine Wine | $25.00 |
| Sherry | $20.00 |
| Cordial | $25.00 |
| Oyster Cocktail | $15.00 |
| Footed Ice Tea | $22.00 |
| Footed Tumbler, 8 oz. | $15.00 |
| Footed Juice | $15.00 |
| Footed Whiskey | $15.00 |

**NATIONAL, *Cutting 727, Blank 4024***

| | |
|---|---|
| Goblet, 11 oz. | $22.00 |
| Goblet, 10 oz. | $22.00 |
| Saucer Champagne | $22.00 |
| Sherbet | $20.00 |
| Cocktail | $20.00 |
| Claret-Wine | $22.00 |
| Rhine Wine | $22.00 |
| Sherry | $20.00 |
| Cordial | $25.00 |
| Oyster Cocktail | $18.00 |
| Footed Ice Tea | $22.00 |
| Footed Tumbler, 8 oz. | $18.00 |
| Footed Juice | $18.00 |
| Footed Whiskey | $18.00 |

**EMBASSY, *Cutting 728, Blank 4024***

| | |
|---|---|
| Goblet, 11 oz. | $22.00 |
| Goblet, 10 oz. | $22.00 |

Saucer Champagne ...................... $22.00
Sherbet .................................... $20.00
Cocktail .................................... $20.00
Claret-Wine .............................. $25.00
Rhine Wine ............................... $25.00
Sherry...................................... $22.00
Cordial .................................... $25.00
Oyster Cocktail ......................... $15.00
Footed Ice Tea .......................... $22.00
Footed Tumbler, 8 oz. ................ $15.00
Footed Juice ............................. $15.00
Footed Whiskey ......................... $15.00

### SEAWEED, Cutting 732, Blank 4024
Goblet, 11 oz. ........................... $22.00
Goblet, 10 oz. ........................... $22.00
Saucer Champagne ...................... $22.00
Sherbet .................................... $20.00
Cocktail .................................... $20.00
Claret-Wine .............................. $22.00
Rhine Wine ............................... $22.00
Sherry...................................... $20.00
Cordial .................................... $25.00
Oyster Cocktail ......................... $18.00
Footed Ice Tea .......................... $22.00
Footed Tumbler, 8 oz. ................ $18.00
Footed Juice ............................. $18.00
Footed Whiskey ......................... $18.00

### MARQUETTE, Cutting 733, Blank 4024
Goblet, 11 oz. ........................... $22.00
Goblet, 10 oz. ........................... $22.00
Saucer Champagne ...................... $22.00
Sherbet .................................... $20.00
Cocktail .................................... $20.00
Claret-Wine .............................. $22.00
Rhine Wine ............................... $22.00
Sherry...................................... $20.00
Cordial .................................... $25.00
Oyster Cocktail ......................... $18.00
Footed Ice Tea .......................... $22.00
Footed Tumbler, 8 oz. ................ $18.00
Footed Juice ............................. $18.00
Footed Whiskey ......................... $18.00

### MESA, Blank 4186
Crystal/Regular Colors
Goblet...................................... $20.00
Sherbet..................................... $15.00
Wine/On the Rocks ..................... $20.00
Ice Tea...................................... $20.00
Double Old Fashioned Cocktail ... $18.00
Juice......................................... $15.00

#### Ruby
Goblet...................................... $35.00
Sherbet..................................... $30.00
Wine/On the Rocks ..................... $35.00

Ice Tea...................................... $35.00
Double Old Fashioned Cocktail ... $30.00
Juice......................................... $30.00

### Blank 5001
Goblet, 11 oz. ........................... $16.00
Goblet, 8¾ oz. ........................... $14.00
Goblet, 7½ oz. ........................... $10.00
Saucer Champagne ...................... $10.00
Cocktail, 4 oz. ........................... $10.00
Cocktail, 3 oz. ........................... $10.00
Cocktail, 2½ oz. ........................ $10.00
Claret, 5½ oz. ........................... $16.00
Claret, 4¾ oz. ........................... $16.00
Rhine Wine, 4 oz. ...................... $14.00
Rhine Wine, 2½ oz. .................... $14.00
Wine, 3½ oz. ............................. $12.00
Wine, 2 oz. ............................... $12.00
Sherry, 2½ oz. ........................... $10.00
Sherry, 2 oz. ............................. $10.00
Sherry, 1½ oz. ........................... $10.00
Brandy, ¾ oz. ............................ $15.00
Cordial, 1 oz. ............................ $16.00
Cordial, ¾ oz. ........................... $18.00
Tall Champagne, 5¾ oz. .............. $15.00
Hot Whiskey, 5 oz....................... $10.00

### LARGE CLOVERLEAF, Etching 47, Blank 5001
Goblet, 11 oz. ........................... $16.00
Goblet, 8¾ oz. ........................... $14.00
Goblet, 7½ oz. ........................... $10.00
Saucer Champagne ...................... $10.00
Cocktail, 4 oz. ........................... $10.00
Cocktail, 3 oz. ........................... $10.00
Cocktail, 2½ oz. ........................ $10.00
Claret, 5½ oz. ........................... $16.00
Claret, 4¾ oz. ........................... $16.00
Rhine Wine, 4 oz. ...................... $14.00
Rhine Wine, 2½ oz. .................... $14.00
Wine, 3½ oz. ............................. $12.00
Wine, 2 oz. ............................... $12.00
Sherry, 2½ oz. ........................... $12.00
Sherry, 2 oz. ............................. $12.00
Sherry, 1½ oz. ........................... $12.00
Brandy, ¾ oz. ............................ $15.00
Cordial, 1 oz. ............................ $16.00
Cordial, ¾ oz. ........................... $18.00
Tall Champagne, 5¾ oz. .............. $14.00
Hot Whiskey, 5 oz....................... $10.00

### AMERICAN LADY, Blank 5056
Crystal
Goblet...................................... $25.00
Sherbet..................................... $16.00
Cocktail .................................... $16.00

Claret....................................... $35.00
Wine ........................................ $32.00
Cordial .................................... $48.00
Oyster Cocktail ......................... $20.00
Footed Ice Tea .......................... $25.00
Footed Juice .............................. $20.00

#### Burgundy/Amethyst
Goblet...................................... $58.00
Sherbet..................................... $54.00
Cocktail .................................... $54.00
Claret....................................... $65.00
Wine ........................................ $60.00
Cordial .................................... $78.00
Oyster Cocktail ......................... $47.00
Footed Ice Tea .......................... $58.00
Footed Juice .............................. $52.00

#### Regal Blue/Empire Green
Goblet...................................... $125.00
Sherbet..................................... $95.00
Cocktail .................................... $85.00
Claret....................................... $150.00
Wine ........................................ $150.00
Cordial .................................... $179.00
Footed Ice Tea .......................... $135.00
Footed Juice .............................. $85.00

### Blank 5061
Goblet, 11 oz. ........................... $10.00
Goblet, 10 oz. ........................... $10.00
Goblet, 9 oz. ............................. $8.00
Goblet, 8 oz. ............................. $8.00
Saucer Champagne ...................... $10.00
Sherbet .................................... $8.00
Cocktail .................................... $8.00
Claret, 6½ oz. ........................... $10.00
Claret, 4½ oz. ........................... $10.00
Rhine Wine ............................... $10.00
Wine ........................................ $10.00
Sherry...................................... $10.00
Crème de Menthe........................ $8.00
Brandy (Pousse Café) .................. $10.00
Cordial .................................... $10.00
Hollow Stem Champagne.............. $10.00
Tall Champagne .......................... $10.00
Hot Whiskey .............................. $10.00

### Cutting 4, Blank 5061
Goblet, 9 oz. ............................. $12.00
Saucer Champagne ...................... $12.00
Sherbet .................................... $10.00
Cocktail .................................... $10.00

### Blank 5070
Goblet, 10 oz. ........................... $10.00

Goblet, 9 oz. ...................................... $9.00
Goblet, 8 oz. ...................................... $9.00
Saucer Champagne ...................... $10.00
Sherbet ............................................... $8.00
Cocktail, 3½ oz. ............................... $8.00
Cocktail, 3 oz. ................................... $8.00
Claret, 6 oz. ..................................... $10.00
Claret, 4½ oz. ................................. $10.00
Rhine Wine ..................................... $10.00
Wine .................................................. $10.00
Sherry ............................................... $10.00
Crème de Menthe ............................ $9.00
Brandy (Pousse Café), 1 oz. ......... $12.00
Brandy (Pousse Café), ¾ oz. ......... $12.00
Cordial, 1 oz. .................................. $12.00
Cordial, ¾ oz. .................................. $12.00
Hollow Stem Champagne ............. $10.00
Tall Champagne ................................ $9.00
Hot Whiskey ...................................... $8.00

### POUPEE, Etching 231, Blank 5070
Goblet, 10 oz. .................................. $14.00
Goblet, 9 oz. .................................... $12.00
Goblet, 8 oz. .................................... $12.00
Saucer Champagne ........................ $12.00
Sherbet ............................................. $10.00
Cocktail, 3½ oz. ............................. $10.00
Cocktail, 3 oz. ................................. $10.00
Claret, 6 oz. ..................................... $18.00
Claret, 4½ oz. ................................. $18.00
Rhine Wine ..................................... $16.00
Wine .................................................. $16.00
Sherry ............................................... $14.00
Crème de Menthe .......................... $12.00
Brandy (Pousse Café), 1 oz. ......... $18.00
Brandy (Pousse Café), ¾ oz. ......... $18.00
Cordial, 1 oz. .................................. $20.00
Cordial, ¾ oz. .................................. $22.00
Hollow Stem Champagne ............. $18.00
Tall Champagne .............................. $18.00
Hot Whiskey .................................... $10.00

### LOTUS, Etching 232, Blank 5070
Goblet, 10 oz. .................................. $14.00
Goblet, 9 oz. .................................... $12.00
Goblet, 8 oz. .................................... $12.00
Saucer Champagne ........................ $12.00
Sherbet ............................................. $10.00
Cocktail, 3½ oz. ............................. $10.00
Cocktail, 3 oz. ................................. $10.00
Claret, 6 oz. ..................................... $16.00
Claret, 4½ oz. ................................. $16.00
Rhine Wine ..................................... $16.00
Wine .................................................. $16.00
Sherry ............................................... $16.00
Crème de Menthe .......................... $12.00
Brandy (Pousse Café), 1 oz. ......... $18.00
Brandy (Pousse Café), ¾ oz. ......... $18.00
Cordial, 1 oz. .................................. $20.00

Cordial, ¾ oz. .................................. $22.00
Hollow Stem Champagne ............. $16.00
Tall Champagne .............................. $16.00
Hot Whiskey .................................... $12.00

### Blank 5082
Crystal/Amber/Green
Goblet .............................................. $34.00
High Sherbet ................................... $30.00
Low Sherbet .................................... $28.00
Parfait .............................................. $34.00
Cocktail ........................................... $28.00
Claret ............................................... $35.00
Wine ................................................. $32.00
Cordial ............................................. $36.00
Grapefruit ........................................ $38.00

Rose/Azure
Goblet .............................................. $36.00
High Sherbet ................................... $34.00
Low Sherbet .................................... $28.00
Parfait .............................................. $35.00
Cocktail ........................................... $32.00
Claret ............................................... $38.00
Wine ................................................. $32.00
Cordial ............................................. $38.00
Grapefruit ........................................ $42.00

Blue
Goblet .............................................. $36.00
High Sherbet ................................... $34.00
Low Sherbet .................................... $30.00
Parfait .............................................. $34.00
Cocktail ........................................... $30.00
Claret ............................................... $38.00
Wine ................................................. $35.00
Cordial ............................................. $48.00
Grapefruit ........................................ $40.00

### RICHMOND, Etching 74, Blank 5082
Goblet .............................................. $20.00
High Sherbet ................................... $15.00
Low Sherbet .................................... $12.00
Parfait .............................................. $20.00
Cocktail ........................................... $12.00
Claret ............................................... $22.00
Wine ................................................. $20.00
Cordial ............................................. $22.00

### EILENE, Etching 83, Blank 5082
Crystal/Green
Goblet .............................................. $35.00
High Sherbet ................................... $33.00
Low Sherbet .................................... $30.00
Parfait .............................................. $34.00
Cocktail ........................................... $30.00
Claret ............................................... $38.00
Wine ................................................. $35.00

Cordial, ¾ oz. .................................. $22.00
Hollow Stem Champagne ............. $16.00
Tall Champagne .............................. $16.00
Hot Whiskey .................................... $12.00

Cordial ............................................. $40.00
Grapefruit ........................................ $35.00

Rose/Azure
Goblet .............................................. $45.00
High Sherbet ................................... $40.00
Low Sherbet .................................... $34.00
Parfait .............................................. $45.00
Cocktail ........................................... $34.00
Claret ............................................... $48.00
Wine ................................................. $45.00
Cordial ............................................. $48.00
Grapefruit ........................................ $50.00

### ROGENE, Etching 269, Blank 5082
Goblet .............................................. $35.00
High Sherbet ................................... $32.00
Low Sherbet .................................... $28.00
Parfait .............................................. $35.00
Cocktail ........................................... $28.00
Claret ............................................... $38.00
Wine ................................................. $35.00
Cordial ............................................. $42.00
Grapefruit and Liner ...................... $48.00

### MYSTIC, Etching 270½, Blank 5082
Goblet .............................................. $48.00
High Sherbet ................................... $40.00
Low Sherbet .................................... $38.00
Parfait .............................................. $48.00
Cocktail ........................................... $38.00
Wine ................................................. $48.00

### DELPHIAN, Etching 272, Blank 5082
Goblet .............................................. $54.00
High Sherbet ................................... $45.00
Low Sherbet .................................... $35.00
Parfait .............................................. $48.00
Cocktail ........................................... $40.00
Wine ................................................. $55.00
Cordial ............................................. $75.00

### KENMORE, Cutting 176, Blank 5082
Goblet .............................................. $48.00
High Sherbet ................................... $40.00
Low Sherbet .................................... $35.00
Parfait .............................................. $45.00
Cocktail ........................................... $38.00
Wine ................................................. $54.00

### PRINCESS, Decoration 43, Blank 5082
Goblet .............................................. $20.00
High Sherbet ................................... $15.00
Low Sherbet .................................... $12.00
Parfait .............................................. $20.00
Cocktail ........................................... $15.00
Claret ............................................... $22.00
Wine ................................................. $22.00
Cordial ............................................. $24.00

## DUCHESS, Decoration 51, Blank 5082

| | |
|---|---|
| Goblet | $65.00 |
| High Sherbet | $55.00 |
| Low Sherbet | $47.00 |
| Parfait | $60.00 |
| Cocktail | $47.00 |
| Wine | $60.00 |
| Cordial | $125.00 |

## Blank 5083
### Crystal/Green/Amber

| | |
|---|---|
| Goblet | $20.00 |
| High Sherbet | $20.00 |
| Low Sherbet | $18.00 |
| Parfait | $20.00 |
| Cocktail | $18.00 |
| Wine | $22.00 |

### Blue

| | |
|---|---|
| Goblet | $25.00 |
| High Sherbet | $22.00 |
| Low Sherbet | $20.00 |
| Parfait | $25.00 |
| Cocktail | $20.00 |
| Wine | $20.00 |

## LYNN, Cutting 180, Blank 5083

| | |
|---|---|
| Goblet | $18.00 |
| High Sherbet | $18.00 |
| Low Sherbet | $15.00 |
| Parfait | $18.00 |
| Cocktail | $15.00 |
| Wine | $20.00 |

## Blank 5093
### Amber/Green/Mother of Pearl

| | |
|---|---|
| Goblet | $30.00 |
| High Sherbet | $28.00 |
| Low Sherbet | $25.00 |
| Parfait | $30.00 |
| Cocktail | $25.00 |
| Claret | $34.00 |
| Wine | $30.00 |
| Cordial | $35.00 |

### Rose/Azure

| | |
|---|---|
| Goblet | $35.00 |
| High Sherbet | $30.00 |
| Low Sherbet | $28.00 |
| Parfait | $35.00 |
| Cocktail | $30.00 |
| Claret | $37.00 |
| Wine | $34.00 |
| Cordial | $60.00 |

### Blue

| | |
|---|---|
| Goblet | $42.00 |
| High Sherbet | $37.00 |
| Low Sherbet | $28.00 |
| Parfait | $40.00 |
| Cocktail | $32.00 |
| Claret | $45.00 |
| Wine | $38.00 |
| Cordial | $60.00 |

## AVALON, Etching 85, Blank 5093

| | |
|---|---|
| Goblet | $38.00 |
| High Sherbet | $34.00 |
| Low Sherbet | $30.00 |
| Parfait | $45.00 |
| Cocktail | $34.00 |
| Claret | $48.00 |
| Wine | $45.00 |
| Cordial | $75.00 |

## VESPER, Etching 275, Blank 5093
### Amber/Green

| | |
|---|---|
| Goblet | $45.00 |
| High Sherbet | $45.00 |
| Low Sherbet | $35.00 |
| Parfait | $50.00 |
| Cocktail | $34.00 |
| Wine | $55.00 |
| Cordial | $75.00 |

### Blue

| | |
|---|---|
| Goblet | $110.00 |
| High Sherbet | $85.00 |
| Low Sherbet | $55.00 |
| Parfait | $95.00 |
| Cocktail | $68.00 |
| Wine | $125.00 |
| Cordial | $150.00 |

## Blank 5097
### Crystal

| | |
|---|---|
| Goblet | $32.00 |
| High Sherbet | $27.00 |
| Low Sherbet | $24.00 |
| Parfait | $30.00 |
| Cocktail | $24.00 |
| Claret | $34.00 |
| Wine | $32.00 |
| Cordial | $36.00 |

### Amber/Green/Mother of Pearl

| | |
|---|---|
| Goblet | $36.00 |
| High Sherbet | $30.00 |
| Low Sherbet | $27.00 |
| Parfait | $38.00 |
| Cocktail | $30.00 |
| Claret | $38.00 |

| | |
|---|---|
| Wine | $34.00 |
| Cordial | $45.00 |

### Rose

| | |
|---|---|
| Goblet | $45.00 |
| High Sherbet | $40.00 |
| Low Sherbet | $30.00 |
| Parfait | $42.00 |
| Cocktail | $32.00 |
| Claret | $45.00 |
| Wine | $40.00 |
| Cordial | $58.00 |

### Orchid

| | |
|---|---|
| Goblet | $45.00 |
| High Sherbet | $40.00 |
| Low Sherbet | $30.00 |
| Parfait | $40.00 |
| Cocktail | $32.00 |
| Claret | $45.00 |
| Wine | $40.00 |
| Cordial | $58.00 |

## GREEK, Etching 45, Blank 5097
### Amber/Green

| | |
|---|---|
| Goblet | $38.00 |
| High Sherbet | $35.00 |
| Low Sherbet | $28.00 |
| Parfait | $38.00 |
| Cocktail | $30.00 |
| Claret | $40.00 |
| Wine | $40.00 |
| Cordial | $57.00 |
| Oyster Cocktail | $25.00 |

### Rose

| | |
|---|---|
| Goblet | $44.00 |
| High Sherbet | $40.00 |
| Low Sherbet | $32.00 |
| Parfait | $42.00 |
| Cocktail | $35.00 |
| Claret | $45.00 |
| Wine | $42.00 |
| Cordial | $58.00 |

## SPARTAN, Etching 80, Blank 5097
### Crystal

| | |
|---|---|
| Goblet | $30.00 |
| High Sherbet | $28.00 |
| Low Sherbet | $25.00 |
| Parfait | $30.00 |
| Cocktail | $27.00 |
| Claret | $35.00 |
| Wine | $32.00 |
| Cordial | $36.00 |

### Amber/Green

| | |
|---|---|
| Goblet | $35.00 |
| High Sherbet | $30.00 |
| Low Sherbet | $25.00 |

| | |
|---|---|
| Parfait | $37.00 |
| Cocktail | $30.00 |
| Claret | $38.00 |
| Wine | $35.00 |
| Cordial | $55.00 |

### Orchid

| | |
|---|---|
| Goblet | $40.00 |
| High Sherbet | $36.00 |
| Low Sherbet | $32.00 |
| Parfait | $40.00 |
| Cocktail | $35.00 |
| Claret | $45.00 |
| Wine | $40.00 |
| Cordial | $58.00 |

### BEVERLY, Etching 276, Blank 5097
#### Crystal

| | |
|---|---|
| Goblet | $30.00 |
| High Sherbet | $28.00 |
| Low Sherbet | $24.00 |
| Parfait | $30.00 |
| Cocktail | $28.00 |
| Claret | $35.00 |
| Wine | $34.00 |
| Cordial | $38.00 |

#### Amber/Green

| | |
|---|---|
| Goblet | $40.00 |
| High Sherbet | $35.00 |
| Low Sherbet | $28.00 |
| Parfait | $42.00 |
| Cocktail | $30.00 |
| Claret | $36.00 |
| Wine | $34.00 |
| Cordial | $58.00 |

### Blank 5098
#### Crystal

| | |
|---|---|
| Goblet | $30.00 |
| High Sherbet | $25.00 |
| Low Sherbet | $20.00 |
| Parfait | $30.00 |
| Cocktail | $25.00 |
| Claret | $30.00 |
| Wine | $28.00 |
| Cordial | $32.00 |
| Oyster Cocktail | $18.00 |
| Footed Ice Tea | $30.00 |
| Footed Tumbler, 9 oz. | $22.00 |
| Footed Juice | $22.00 |
| Footed Whiskey | $22.00 |

#### Amber/Green/Topaz/Gold Tint

| | |
|---|---|
| Goblet | $38.00 |
| High Sherbet | $35.00 |
| Low Sherbet | $28.00 |
| Parfait | $35.00 |

| | |
|---|---|
| Cocktail | $34.00 |
| Claret | $45.00 |
| Wine | $45.00 |
| Cordial | $48.00 |
| Oyster Cocktail | $25.00 |
| Footed Ice Tea | $35.00 |
| Footed Tumbler, 9 oz. | $30.00 |
| Footed Juice | $30.00 |
| Footed Whiskey | $32.00 |

### Rose/Azure

| | |
|---|---|
| Goblet | $45.00 |
| High Sherbet | $42.00 |
| Low Sherbet | $32.00 |
| Parfait | $45.00 |
| Cocktail | $35.00 |
| Claret | $50.00 |
| Wine | $44.00 |
| Cordial | $56.00 |
| Oyster Cocktail | $30.00 |
| Footed Ice Tea | $42.00 |
| Footed Tumbler, 9 oz. | $32.00 |
| Footed Juice | $30.00 |
| Footed Whiskey | $35.00 |

### Wisteria

| | |
|---|---|
| Goblet | $95.00 |
| High Sherbet | $75.00 |
| Low Sherbet | $50.00 |
| Cocktail | $65.00 |
| Claret | $125.00 |
| Wine | $95.00 |
| Cordial | $150.00 |
| Oyster Cocktail | $45.00 |
| Footed Ice Tea | $85.00 |
| Footed Tumbler, 9 oz. | $55.00 |
| Footed Juice | $55.00 |
| Footed Whiskey | $75.00 |

### CAMDEN, Etching 84, Blank 5098

| | |
|---|---|
| Goblet | $40.00 |
| High Sherbet | $35.00 |
| Low Sherbet | $30.00 |
| Parfait | $40.00 |
| Cocktail | $35.00 |
| Claret | $45.00 |
| Wine | $40.00 |
| Cordial | $50.00 |
| Oyster Cocktail | $30.00 |
| Footed Ice Tea | $40.00 |
| Footed Tumbler, 9 oz. | $30.00 |
| Footed Juice | $30.00 |
| Footed Whiskey | $32.00 |

### VERSAILLES, Etching 278, Blank 5098
#### Green/Rose

| | |
|---|---|
| Goblet | $95.00 |
| High Sherbet | $82.00 |
| Low Sherbet | $57.00 |
| Parfait | $95.00 |

| | |
|---|---|
| Cocktail | $58.00 |
| Claret | $125.00 |
| Wine | $110.00 |
| Cordial | $150.00 |
| Oyster Cocktail | $48.00 |
| Footed Ice Tea | $80.00 |
| Footed Tumbler, 9 oz. | $50.00 |
| Footed Juice | $52.00 |
| Footed Whiskey | $60.00 |

### Azure

| | |
|---|---|
| Goblet | $110.00 |
| High Sherbet | $75.00 |
| Low Sherbet | $60.00 |
| Parfait | $125.00 |
| Cocktail | $62.00 |
| Claret | $135.00 |
| Wine | $115.00 |
| Cordial | $175.00 |
| Oyster Cocktail | $55.00 |
| Footed Ice Tea | $95.00 |
| Footed Tumbler, 9 oz. | $65.00 |
| Footed Juice | $65.00 |
| Footed Whiskey | $85.00 |

### JUNE, Etching 279, Blank 5098
#### Crystal

| | |
|---|---|
| Goblet | $40.00 |
| High Sherbet | $34.00 |
| Low Sherbet | $25.00 |
| Parfait | $58.00 |
| Cocktail | $32.00 |
| Claret | $58.00 |
| Wine | $55.00 |
| Cordial | $85.00 |
| Oyster Cocktail | $30.00 |
| Footed Ice Tea | $40.00 |
| Footed Tumbler, 9 oz. | $28.00 |
| Footed Juice | $34.00 |
| Footed Whiskey | $42.00 |

### Rose/Azure

| | |
|---|---|
| Goblet | $95.00 |
| High Sherbet | $70.00 |
| Low Sherbet | $62.00 |
| Parfait | $125.00 |
| Cocktail | $65.00 |
| Claret | $135.00 |
| Wine | $125.00 |
| Cordial | $175.00 |
| Oyster Cocktail | $55.00 |
| Footed Ice Tea | $85.00 |
| Footed Tumbler, 9 oz. | $58.00 |
| Footed Juice | $60.00 |
| Footed Whiskey | $70.00 |

### Topaz/Gold Tint

| | |
|---|---|
| Goblet | $75.00 |
| High Sherbet | $58.00 |
| Low Sherbet | $45.00 |

| | |
|---|---|
| Parfait | $85.00 |
| Cocktail | $55.00 |
| Claret | $95.00 |
| Wine | $85.00 |
| Cordial | $125.00 |
| Oyster Cocktail | $40.00 |
| Footed Ice Tea | $65.00 |
| Footed Tumbler, 9 oz. | $45.00 |
| Footed Juice | $48.00 |
| Footed Whiskey | $65.00 |

### ACANTHUS, Etching 282, Blank 5098

| | |
|---|---|
| Goblet | $40.00 |
| High Sherbet | $35.00 |
| Low Sherbet | $25.00 |
| Parfait | $40.00 |
| Cocktail | $35.00 |
| Claret | $45.00 |
| Wine | $40.00 |
| Cordial | $70.00 |
| Oyster Cocktail | $22.00 |
| Footed Ice Tea | $40.00 |
| Footed Tumbler, 9 oz. | $30.00 |
| Footed Juice | $30.00 |
| Footed Whiskey | $40.00 |

### FERN, Etching 305, Blank 5098
#### Crystal

| | |
|---|---|
| Goblet | $35.00 |
| High Sherbet | $32.00 |
| Low Sherbet | $25.00 |
| Parfait | $35.00 |
| Cocktail | $32.00 |
| Claret | $38.00 |
| Wine | $35.00 |
| Cordial | $45.00 |
| Oyster Cocktail | $22.00 |
| Footed Ice Tea | $35.00 |
| Footed Tumbler, 9 oz. | $28.00 |
| Footed Juice | $28.00 |
| Footed Whiskey | $32.00 |

#### Rose

| | |
|---|---|
| Goblet | $48.00 |
| High Sherbet | $45.00 |
| Low Sherbet | $30.00 |
| Parfait | $50.00 |
| Cocktail | $42.00 |
| Claret | $50.00 |
| Wine | $45.00 |
| Cordial | $75.00 |
| Oyster Cocktail | $25.00 |
| Footed Ice Tea | $45.00 |
| Footed Tumbler, 9 oz. | $30.00 |
| Footed Juice | $32.00 |
| Footed Whiskey | $46.00 |

### BERRY, Cutting 188, Blank 5098

| | |
|---|---|
| Goblet | $45.00 |

| | |
|---|---|
| High Sherbet | $40.00 |
| Low Sherbet | $30.00 |
| Parfait | $45.00 |
| Cocktail | $35.00 |
| Wine | $48.00 |
| Oyster Cocktail | $30.00 |
| Footed Ice Tea | $45.00 |
| Footed Tumbler, 9 oz. | $30.00 |
| Footed Juice | $30.00 |
| Footed Whiskey | $38.00 |

### DELPHINE, Cutting 199, Blank 5098

| | |
|---|---|
| Goblet | $24.00 |
| High Sherbet | $22.00 |
| Low Sherbet | $18.00 |
| Parfait | $24.00 |
| Cocktail | $22.00 |
| Claret | $28.00 |
| Wine | $28.00 |
| Cordial | $32.00 |
| Footed Ice Tea | $24.00 |
| Footed Tumbler, 9 oz. | $16.00 |
| Footed Juice | $18.00 |
| Footed Whiskey | $22.00 |

### KINGSTON, Decoration 41, Blank 5098

| | |
|---|---|
| Goblet | $35.00 |
| High Sherbet | $30.00 |
| Low Sherbet | $24.00 |
| Parfait | $35.00 |
| Cocktail | $25.00 |
| Claret | $38.00 |
| Wine | $38.00 |
| Cordial | $45.00 |
| Oyster Cocktail | $22.00 |
| Footed Ice Tea | $34.00 |
| Footed Tumbler, 9 oz. | $25.00 |
| Footed Juice | $25.00 |
| Footed Whiskey | $28.00 |

### Blank 5099
#### Regular Colors

| | |
|---|---|
| Goblet | $45.00 |
| High Sherbet | $40.00 |
| Low Sherbet | $32.00 |
| Parfait | $42.00 |
| Cocktail | $38.00 |
| Claret | $50.00 |
| Wine | $45.00 |
| Cordial | $65.00 |
| Oyster Cocktail | $30.00 |
| Footed Ice Tea | $42.00 |
| Footed Tumbler, 9 oz. | $32.00 |
| Footed Juice | $34.00 |
| Footed Whiskey | $38.00 |

#### Wisteria

| | |
|---|---|
| Goblet | $95.00 |
| High Sherbet | $75.00 |
| Low Sherbet | $48.00 |
| Cocktail | $54.00 |
| Claret | $110.00 |
| Wine | $95.00 |
| Cordial | $125.00 |
| Oyster Cocktail | $38.00 |
| Footed Ice Tea | $85.00 |
| Footed Tumbler, 9 oz. | $48.00 |
| Footed Juice | $48.00 |
| Footed Whiskey | $64.00 |

### VERSAILLES, Etching 278, Blank 5099
#### Topaz

| | |
|---|---|
| Goblet | $85.00 |
| High Sherbet | $70.00 |
| Low Sherbet | $50.00 |
| Parfait | $75.00 |
| Cocktail | $54.00 |
| Claret | $110.00 |
| Wine | $100.00 |
| Cordial | $125.00 |
| Oyster Cocktail | $38.00 |
| Footed Ice Tea | $75.00 |
| Footed Tumbler, 9 oz. | $38.00 |
| Footed Juice | $40.00 |
| Footed Whiskey | $54.00 |

### TROJAN, Etching 280, Blank 5099
#### Topaz

| | |
|---|---|
| Goblet | $75.00 |
| High Sherbet | $55.00 |
| Low Sherbet | $45.00 |
| Parfait | $75.00 |
| Cocktail | $55.00 |
| Claret | $85.00 |
| Wine | $75.00 |
| Cordial | $95.00 |
| Oyster Cocktail | $35.00 |
| Footed Ice Tea | $60.00 |
| Footed Tumbler, 9 oz. | $45.00 |
| Footed Juice | $47.00 |
| Footed Whiskey | $50.00 |
| Add 30% for Rose | |

### KASHMIR, Etching 283, Blank 5099
#### Topaz

| | |
|---|---|
| Goblet | $75.00 |
| High Sherbet | $55.00 |
| Low Sherbet | $45.00 |
| Parfait | $65.00 |
| Cocktail | $55.00 |
| Claret | $84.00 |
| Wine | $76.00 |
| Cordial | $95.00 |
| Oyster Cocktail | $35.00 |

| | |
|---|---|
| Footed Ice Tea | $60.00 |
| Footed Tumbler, 9 oz. | $45.00 |
| Footed Juice | $45.00 |
| Footed Whiskey | $48.00 |

### Azure

| | |
|---|---|
| Goblet | $85.00 |
| High Sherbet | $70.00 |
| Low Sherbet | $50.00 |
| Parfait | $85.00 |
| Cocktail | $68.00 |
| Claret | $110.00 |
| Wine | $95.00 |
| Cordial | $150.00 |
| Oyster Cocktail | $44.00 |
| Footed Ice Tea | $78.00 |
| Footed Tumbler, 9 oz. | $54.00 |
| Footed Juice | $54.00 |
| Footed Whiskey | $58.00 |

### COLONIAL DAME, Blank 5412

| | |
|---|---|
| Goblet | $35.00 |
| Sherbet | $25.00 |
| Cocktail | $25.00 |
| Claret-Wine | $38.00 |
| Cordial | $38.00 |
| Oyster Cocktail | $25.00 |
| Footed Ice Tea | $35.00 |
| Footed Juice | $35.00 |

### Blank 6000
#### Crystal

| | |
|---|---|
| Goblet | $22.00 |
| High Sherbet | $18.00 |
| Low Sherbet | $14.00 |
| Cocktail | $16.00 |
| Wine | $24.00 |
| Oyster Cocktail | $12.00 |
| Footed Ice Tea | $22.00 |
| Footed Juice | $14.00 |

#### Colors

| | |
|---|---|
| Goblet | $34.00 |
| High Sherbet | $30.00 |
| Low Sherbet | $24.00 |
| Cocktail | $25.00 |
| Wine | $34.00 |
| Oyster Cocktail | $20.00 |
| Footed Ice Tea | $32.00 |
| Footed Juice | $25.00 |

### MONROE, Etching 86, Blank 6000

| | |
|---|---|
| Goblet | $24.00 |
| High Sherbet | $20.00 |

| | |
|---|---|
| Low Sherbet | $18.00 |
| Cocktail | $20.00 |
| Wine | $24.00 |
| Oyster Cocktail | $14.00 |
| Footed Ice Tea | $22.00 |
| Footed Juice | $18.00 |

### LEGION, Etching 309, Blank 6000

| | |
|---|---|
| Goblet | $32.00 |
| High Sherbet | $28.00 |
| Low Sherbet | $22.00 |
| Cocktail | $27.00 |
| Wine | $34.00 |
| Oyster Cocktail | $18.00 |
| Footed Ice Tea | $32.00 |
| Footed Juice | $25.00 |

### WATERBURY, Cutting 712, Blank 6000

| | |
|---|---|
| Goblet | $16.00 |
| High Sherbet | $14.00 |
| Low Sherbet | $12.00 |
| Cocktail | $15.00 |
| Wine | $20.00 |
| Oyster Cocktail | $10.00 |
| Footed Ice Tea | $15.00 |
| Footed Juice | $14.00 |

### CELEBRITY, Cutting 749, Blank 6000

| | |
|---|---|
| Goblet | $16.00 |
| High Sherbet | $14.00 |
| Low Sherbet | $12.00 |
| Cocktail | $15.00 |
| Wine | $20.00 |
| Oyster Cocktail | $10.00 |
| Footed Ice Tea | $15.00 |
| Footed Juice | $14.00 |

### MEMORIES, Cutting 750, Blank 6000

| | |
|---|---|
| Goblet | $16.00 |
| High Sherbet | $14.00 |
| Low Sherbet | $12.00 |
| Cocktail | $14.00 |
| Wine | $20.00 |

### Blank 6002

| | |
|---|---|
| Goblet | $65.00 |
| High Sherbet | $58.00 |
| Low Sherbet | $50.00 |
| Claret | $75.00 |
| Wine | $70.00 |
| Cordial | $95.00 |
| Oyster Cocktail | $45.00 |
| Footed Ice Tea | $65.00 |
| Footed Tumbler, 10 oz. | $50.00 |

| | |
|---|---|
| Footed Juice | $48.00 |
| Footed Whiskey | $50.00 |

### New Garland, Etching 284, Blank 6002

| | |
|---|---|
| Goblet | $75.00 |
| High Sherbet | $65.00 |
| Low Sherbet | $52.00 |
| Claret | $87.00 |
| Wine | $82.00 |
| Cordial | $110.00 |
| Oyster Cocktail | $48.00 |
| Footed Ice Tea | $75.00 |
| Footed Tumbler, 10 oz. | $57.00 |
| Footed Juice | $52.00 |
| Footed Whiskey | $55.00 |

### MINUET, Etching 285, Blank 6002

| | |
|---|---|
| Goblet | $75.00 |
| High Sherbet | $65.00 |
| Low Sherbet | $52.00 |
| Claret | $87.00 |
| Wine | $82.00 |
| Cordial | $110.00 |
| Oyster Cocktail | $48.00 |
| Footed Ice Tea | $75.00 |
| Footed Tumbler, 10 oz. | $57.00 |
| Footed Juice | $58.00 |
| Footed Whiskey | $55.00 |

### Blank 6003
#### Crystal

| | |
|---|---|
| Goblet | $30.00 |
| High Sherbet | $26.00 |
| Low Sherbet | $20.00 |
| Cocktail | $26.00 |
| Cordial | $32.00 |
| Oyster Cocktail | $18.00 |
| Footed Ice Tea | $30.00 |
| Footed Tumbler, 10 oz. | $22.00 |
| Footed Juice | $20.00 |
| Footed Whiskey | $20.00 |

#### Wisteria

| | |
|---|---|
| Goblet | $70.00 |
| High Sherbet | $65.00 |
| Low Sherbet | $40.00 |
| Cocktail | $45.00 |
| Cordial | $125.00 |
| Oyster Cocktail | $30.00 |
| Footed Ice Tea | $70.00 |
| Footed Tumbler, 10 oz. | $38.00 |
| Footed Juice | $38.00 |
| Footed Whiskey | $62.00 |

#### Other Colors

| | |
|---|---|
| Goblet | $35.00 |
| High Sherbet | $30.00 |
| Low Sherbet | $20.00 |

Cocktail ............................... $25.00
Cordial ................................ $68.00
Oyster Cocktail ..................... $22.00
Footed Ice Tea ...................... $35.00
Footed Tumbler, 10 oz. ........ $28.00
Footed Juice ......................... $25.00
Footed Whiskey .................... $38.00

### MANOR, Etching 286, Blank 6003
#### Crystal
Goblet .................................. $38.00
High Sherbet ........................ $35.00
Low Sherbet ......................... $26.00
Cocktail ............................... $34.00
Cordial ................................ $50.00
Oyster Cocktail ..................... $25.00
Footed Ice Tea ...................... $40.00
Footed Tumbler, 10 oz. ........ $30.00
Footed Juice ......................... $30.00
Footed Whiskey .................... $34.00

#### Green/Topaz
Goblet .................................. $54.00
High Sherbet ........................ $50.00
Low Sherbet ......................... $38.00
Cocktail ............................... $45.00
Cordial ................................ $85.00
Oyster Cocktail ..................... $34.00
Footed Ice Tea ...................... $54.00
Footed Tumbler, 10 oz. ........ $38.00
Footed Juice ......................... $40.00
Footed Whiskey .................... $52.00

#### Wisteria
Goblet .................................. $125.00
High Sherbet ........................ $110.00
Low Sherbet ......................... $60.00
Cocktail ............................... $85.00
Cordial ................................ $145.00
Oyster Cocktail ..................... $48.00
Footed Ice Tea ...................... $125.00
Footed Tumbler, 10 oz. ........ $62.00
Footed Juice ......................... $60.00
Footed Whiskey .................... $110.00

### Blank 6004
#### Crystal
Goblet .................................. $34.00
High Sherbet ........................ $30.00
Low Sherbet ......................... $20.00
Parfait ................................. $38.00
Cocktail ............................... $30.00
Claret .................................. $40.00
Wine .................................... $40.00
Cordial ................................ $42.00
Oyster Cocktail ..................... $20.00
Footed Ice Tea ...................... $35.00
Footed Tumbler, 9 oz. .......... $25.00

Footed Juice ......................... $22.00
Footed Whiskey .................... $28.00
#### Add 25% for Green

#### Wisteria
Goblet .................................. $95.00
High Sherbet ........................ $85.00
Low Sherbet ......................... $60.00
Parfait ................................. $85.00
Cocktail ............................... $80.00
Claret .................................. $110.00
Wine .................................... $95.00
Cordial ................................ $125.00
Oyster Cocktail ..................... $55.00
Footed Ice Tea ...................... $95.00
Footed Tumbler, 9 oz. .......... $60.00
Footed Juice ......................... $60.00
Footed Whiskey .................... $75.00

### FUCHSIA, Etching 310, Blank 6004
#### Crystal
Goblet .................................. $55.00
High Sherbet ........................ $50.00
Low Sherbet ......................... $40.00
Parfait ................................. $65.00
Cocktail ............................... $48.00
Claret .................................. $65.00
Wine .................................... $60.00
Cordial ................................ $85.00
Oyster Cocktail ..................... $38.00
Footed Ice Tea ...................... $55.00
Footed Tumbler, 9 oz. .......... $45.00
Footed Juice ......................... $40.00
Footed Whiskey .................... $47.00

#### Wisteria
Goblet .................................. $165.00
High Sherbet ........................ $125.00
Low Sherbet ......................... $75.00
Parfait ................................. $135.00
Cocktail ............................... $84.00
Claret .................................. $175.00
Wine .................................... $150.00
Cordial ................................ $185.00
Oyster Cocktail ..................... $64.00
Footed Ice Tea ...................... $160.00
Footed Tumbler,
  9 oz. ................................. $75.00
Footed Juice ......................... $75.00
Footed Whiskey .................... $125.00

### STAUNTON, Cutting 707, Blank 6004
Goblet .................................. $34.00
High Sherbet ........................ $30.00
Low Sherbet ......................... $20.00
Cocktail ............................... $38.00
Claret .................................. $40.00
Wine .................................... $40.00
Oyster Cocktail ..................... $20.00

Footed Ice Tea ...................... $34.00
Footed Tumbler, 9 oz. .......... $25.00
Footed Juice ......................... $22.00
Footed Whiskey .................... $25.00

### NAIRN, Cutting 708, Blank 6004
Goblet .................................. $34.00
High Sherbet ........................ $30.00
Low Sherbet ......................... $20.00
Cocktail ............................... $38.00
Claret .................................. $40.00
Wine .................................... $40.00
Oyster Cocktail ..................... $20.00
Footed Ice Tea ...................... $34.00
Footed Tumbler,
  9 oz. ................................. $25.00
Footed Juice ......................... $22.00
Footed Whiskey .................... $25.00

### Blank 6005
#### Crystal
Goblet .................................. $30.00
High Sherbet ........................ $28.00
Low Sherbet ......................... $20.00
Parfait ................................. $30.00
Cocktail ............................... $25.00
Claret .................................. $35.00
Wine .................................... $32.00
Cordial ................................ $40.00
Oyster Cocktail ..................... $15.00
Footed Ice Tea ...................... $30.00
Footed Tumbler, 9 oz. .......... $16.00
Footed Juice ......................... $16.00
Footed Whiskey .................... $25.00

#### Colors
Goblet .................................. $45.00
High Sherbet ........................ $40.00
Low Sherbet ......................... $34.00
Parfait ................................. $48.00
Cocktail ............................... $40.00
Claret .................................. $50.00
Wine .................................... $45.00
Cordial ................................ $65.00
Oyster Cocktail ..................... $30.00
Footed Ice Tea ...................... $42.00
Footed Tumbler, 9 oz. .......... $34.00
Footed Juice ......................... $34.00
Footed Whiskey .................... $42.00

### FLORENTINE, Etching 311, Blank 6005
#### Crystal
Goblet .................................. $38.00
High Sherbet ........................ $34.00
Low Sherbet ......................... $25.00
Parfait ................................. $38.00

| | |
|---|---|
| Cocktail | $32.00 |
| Claret | $46.00 |
| Wine | $44.00 |
| Cordial | $56.00 |
| Oyster Cocktail | $25.00 |
| Footed Ice Tea | $40.00 |
| Footed Tumbler, 9 oz. | $30.00 |
| Footed Juice | $28.00 |
| Footed Whiskey | $34.00 |

### Topaz/Gold Tint

| | |
|---|---|
| Goblet | $65.00 |
| High Sherbet | $58.00 |
| Low Sherbet | $38.00 |
| Parfait | $65.00 |
| Cocktail | $56.00 |
| Claret | $68.00 |
| Wine | $65.00 |
| Cordial | $85.00 |
| Oyster Cocktail | $35.00 |
| Footed Ice Tea | $62.00 |
| Footed Tumbler, 9 oz. | $42.00 |
| Footed Juice | $42.00 |
| Footed Whiskey | $52.00 |

### MAYDAY, Etching 312, Blank 6005

| | |
|---|---|
| Goblet | $30.00 |
| High Sherbet | $28.00 |
| Low Sherbet | $20.00 |
| Parfait | $28.00 |
| Cocktail | $26.00 |
| Claret | $32.00 |
| Wine | $30.00 |
| Cordial | $38.00 |
| Oyster Cocktail | $18.00 |
| Footed Ice Tea | $30.00 |
| Footed Tumbler, 9 oz. | $24.00 |
| Footed Juice | $20.00 |
| Footed Whiskey | $25.00 |

### Blank 6007
#### Crystal

| | |
|---|---|
| Goblet | $35.00 |
| High Sherbet | $32.00 |
| Low Sherbet | $27.00 |
| Cocktail | $28.00 |
| Claret | $40.00 |
| Wine | $40.00 |
| Cordial | $45.00 |
| Oyster Cocktail | $25.00 |
| Footed Ice Tea | $35.00 |
| Footed Tumbler, 9 oz. | $27.00 |
| Footed Juice | $28.00 |
| Footed Whiskey | $32.00 |

#### Wisteria

| | |
|---|---|
| Goblet | $125.00 |

| | |
|---|---|
| High Sherbet | $85.00 |
| Low Sherbet | $68.00 |
| Cocktail | $75.00 |
| Claret | $135.00 |
| Wine | $125.00 |
| Cordial | $150.00 |
| Oyster Cocktail | $56.00 |
| Footed Ice Tea | $100.00 |
| Footed Tumbler, 9 oz. | $68.00 |
| Footed Juice | $68.00 |
| Footed Whiskey | $75.00 |

#### Other Colors

| | |
|---|---|
| Goblet | $55.00 |
| High Sherbet | $50.00 |
| Low Sherbet | $40.00 |
| Cocktail | $42.00 |
| Claret | $58.00 |
| Wine | $55.00 |
| Cordial | $75.00 |
| Oyster Cocktail | $38.00 |
| Footed Ice Tea | $54.00 |
| Footed Tumbler, 9 oz. | $40.00 |
| Footed Juice | $42.00 |
| Footed Whiskey | $47.00 |

### CASTLE, Etching 87, Blank 6007

| | |
|---|---|
| Goblet | $30.00 |
| High Sherbet | $26.00 |
| Low Sherbet | $21.00 |
| Cocktail | $25.00 |
| Claret | $34.00 |
| Wine | $34.00 |
| Cordial | $42.00 |
| Oyster Cocktail | $21.00 |
| Footed Ice Tea | $30.00 |
| Footed Tumbler, 9 oz. | $24.00 |
| Footed Juice | $27.00 |
| Footed Whiskey | $28.00 |

### MANOR, Etching 286, Blank 6007

| | |
|---|---|
| Goblet | $45.00 |
| High Sherbet | $42.00 |
| Low Sherbet | $34.00 |
| Cocktail | $40.00 |
| Claret | $54.00 |
| Wine | $54.00 |
| Cordial | $75.00 |
| Oyster Cocktail | $30.00 |
| Footed Ice Tea | $45.00 |
| Footed Tumbler, 9 oz. | $34.00 |
| Footed Juice | $34.00 |
| Footed Whiskey | $47.00 |

### MORNING GLORY, Etching 313, Blank 6007
#### Crystal

| | |
|---|---|
| Goblet | $36.00 |
| High Sherbet | $34.00 |

| | |
|---|---|
| Low Sherbet | $24.00 |
| Cocktail | $34.00 |
| Claret | $42.00 |
| Wine | $42.00 |
| Cordial | $55.00 |
| Oyster Cocktail | $20.00 |
| Footed Ice Tea | $35.00 |
| Footed Tumbler, 9 oz. | $25.00 |
| Footed Juice | $25.00 |
| Footed Whiskey | $38.00 |

#### Amber

| | |
|---|---|
| Goblet | $48.00 |
| High Sherbet | $45.00 |
| Low Sherbet | $37.00 |
| Cocktail | $42.00 |
| Claret | $56.00 |
| Wine | $54.00 |
| Cordial | $75.00 |
| Oyster Cocktail | $35.00 |
| Footed Ice Tea | $48.00 |
| Footed Tumbler, 9 oz. | $38.00 |
| Footed Juice | $38.00 |
| Footed Whiskey | $47.00 |

### YORK, Cutting 709, Blank 6007

| | |
|---|---|
| Goblet | $21.00 |
| High Sherbet | $18.00 |
| Low Sherbet | $12.00 |
| Cocktail | $18.00 |
| Claret | $25.00 |
| Wine | $25.00 |
| Cordial | $30.00 |
| Oyster Cocktail | $14.00 |
| Footed Ice Tea | $18.00 |
| Footed Tumbler, 9 oz. | $12.00 |
| Footed Juice | $12.00 |
| Footed Whiskey | $20.00 |

### BRISTOL, Cutting 710, Blank 6007

| | |
|---|---|
| Goblet | $21.00 |
| High Sherbet | $18.00 |
| Low Sherbet | $12.00 |
| Cocktail | $18.00 |
| Claret | $25.00 |
| Wine | $25.00 |
| Cordial | $30.00 |
| Oyster Cocktail | $14.00 |
| Footed Ice Tea | $18.00 |
| Footed Tumbler, 9 oz. | $12.00 |
| Footed Juice | $12.00 |
| Footed Whiskey | $20.00 |

### INVERNESS, Cutting 711, Blank 6007

| | |
|---|---|
| Goblet | $21.00 |
| High Sherbet | $18.00 |
| Low Sherbet | $12.00 |
| Cocktail | $18.00 |

Claret .......................................... $25.00
Wine ........................................... $25.00
Cordial ....................................... $30.00
Oyster Cocktail............................ $14.00
Footed Ice Tea.............................. $18.00
Footed Tumbler, 9 oz. .................. $12.00
Footed Juice ................................ $12.00
Footed Whiskey ........................... $20.00

### EATON, Cutting 713, Blank 6007
Goblet ......................................... $21.00
High Sherbet ............................... $18.00
Low Sherbet ................................ $12.00
Cocktail ...................................... $18.00
Claret .......................................... $25.00
Wine ........................................... $25.00
Cordial ....................................... $30.00
Oyster Cocktail............................ $14.00
Footed Ice Tea.............................. $18.00
Footed Tumbler, 9 oz. .................. $12.00
Footed Juice ................................ $12.00
Footed Whiskey ........................... $20.00

### OXFORD, Cutting 714, Blank 6007
Goblet ......................................... $21.00
High Sherbet ............................... $18.00
Low Sherbet ................................ $12.00
Cocktail ...................................... $18.00
Claret .......................................... $25.00
Wine ........................................... $25.00
Cordial ....................................... $30.00
Oyster Cocktail............................ $14.00
Footed Ice Tea.............................. $18.00
Footed Tumbler, 9 oz. .................. $12.00
Footed Juice ................................ $12.00
Footed Whiskey ........................... $20.00

### Blank 6008
Crystal
Goblet ......................................... $35.00
High Sherbet ............................... $32.00
Low Sherbet ................................ $28.00
Cocktail ...................................... $30.00
Wine ........................................... $40.00
Cordial ....................................... $48.00
Oyster Cocktail............................ $24.00
Footed Ice Tea.............................. $35.00
Footed Tumbler, 9 oz. .................. $28.00
Footed Juice ................................ $28.00

Topaz/Gold Tint
Goblet ......................................... $47.00
High Sherbet ............................... $42.00
Low Sherbet ................................ $30.00
Cocktail ...................................... $38.00
Wine ........................................... $52.00
Oyster Cocktail............................ $30.00

Footed Ice Tea.............................. $45.00
Footed Tumbler, 9 oz. .................. $35.00
Cordial ....................................... $55.00
Footed Juice ................................ $35.00

### Wisteria
Goblet ......................................... $125.00
High Sherbet ............................... $85.00
Low Sherbet ................................ $57.00
Cocktail ...................................... $74.00
Wine ........................................... $125.00
Cordial ....................................... $145.00
Oyster Cocktail............................ $60.00
Footed Ice Tea.............................. $100.00
Footed Tumbler, 9 oz. .................. $57.00
Footed Juice ................................ $57.00

### CHATEAU, Etching 315, Blank 6008
Goblet ......................................... $48.00
High Sherbet ............................... $55.00
Low Sherbet ................................ $32.00
Cocktail ...................................... $32.00
Wine ........................................... $45.00
Cordial ....................................... $54.00
Oyster Cocktail............................ $30.00
Footed Ice Tea.............................. $40.00
Footed Tumbler, 9 oz. .................. $32.00
Footed Juice ................................ $32.00

### CARLISLE, Cutting 715, Blank 6008
Goblet ......................................... $22.00
High Sherbet ............................... $20.00
Low Sherbet ................................ $16.00
Cocktail ...................................... $20.00
Wine ........................................... $25.00
Cordial ....................................... $30.00
Oyster Cocktail............................ $14.00
Footed Ice Tea.............................. $18.00
Footed Tumbler, 9 oz. .................. $14.00
Footed Juice ................................ $14.00

### CANTERBURY, Cutting 716, Blank 6008
Goblet ......................................... $22.00
High Sherbet ............................... $20.00
Low Sherbet ................................ $16.00
Cocktail ...................................... $20.00
Wine ........................................... $25.00
Cordial ....................................... $30.00
Oyster Cocktail............................ $14.00
Footed Ice Tea.............................. $18.00
Footed Tumbler, 9 oz. .................. $14.00
Footed Juice ................................ $14.00

### MARLBORO, Cutting 717, Blank 6008
Goblet ......................................... $22.00
High Sherbet ............................... $20.00

Low Sherbet ................................ $16.00
Cocktail ...................................... $20.00
Wine ........................................... $25.00
Cordial ....................................... $30.00
Oyster Cocktail............................ $14.00
Footed Ice Tea.............................. $18.00
Footed Tumbler, 9 oz. .................. $14.00
Footed Juice ................................ $14.00

### Blank 6009
Crystal
Goblet ......................................... $32.00
High Sherbet ............................... $30.00
Low Sherbet ................................ $24.00
Cocktail ...................................... $30.00
Claret-Wine ................................ $36.00
Cordial ....................................... $38.00
Oyster Cocktail............................ $22.00
Footed Ice Tea.............................. $30.00
Footed Tumbler, 9 oz. .................. $25.00
Footed Juice ................................ $24.00

Amber/Rose
Goblet ......................................... $40.00
High Sherbet ............................... $36.00
Low Sherbet ................................ $30.00
Cocktail ...................................... $32.00
Claret-Wine ................................ $45.00
Cordial ....................................... $48.00
Oyster Cocktail............................ $25.00
Footed Ice Tea.............................. $40.00
Footed Tumbler, 9 oz. .................. $30.00
Footed Juice ................................ $30.00

### CAMELOT, CA13/CA14, Blank 6009
Crystal
Goblet ......................................... $32.00
Dessert/Champagne...................... $30.00
Wine ........................................... $34.00
Magnum ...................................... $48.00
Footed Ice Tea, 16 oz. .................. $35.00

Blue
Goblet ......................................... $40.00
Dessert/Champagne...................... $36.00
Wine ........................................... $42.00
Magnum ...................................... $58.00
Footed Ice Tea, 16 oz. .................. $40.00

### CAMEO, Etching 88, Blank 6009
Goblet ......................................... $34.00
High Sherbet ............................... $30.00
Low Sherbet ................................ $25.00
Cocktail ...................................... $28.00
Claret-Wine ................................ $36.00
Cordial ....................................... $40.00
Oyster Cocktail............................ $22.00

Footed Ice Tea ............................ $34.00
Footed Tumbler, 9 oz. ................. $27.00
Footed Juice ............................... $27.00

### GRAND MAJESTY,
*Etching GR03/GR04, Blank 6009*
Crystal

Goblet ........................................ $34.00
Dessert/Champagne ..................... $32.00
Wine .......................................... $38.00
Magnum ..................................... $52.00
Footed Ice Tea, 16 oz. ................. $44.00

Blue

Goblet ........................................ $44.00
Dessert/Champagne ..................... $40.00
Wine .......................................... $45.00
Magnum ..................................... $65.00
Footed Ice Tea, 16 oz. ................. $44.00

### MIDNIGHT ROSE, Etching 316,
*Blank 6009*

Goblet ........................................ $38.00
High Sherbet .............................. $35.00
Low Sherbet ............................... $30.00
Cocktail ..................................... $34.00
Claret-Wine ................................ $45.00
Cordial ...................................... $68.00
Oyster Cocktail .......................... $26.00
Footed Ice Tea ............................ $38.00
Footed Tumbler, 9 oz. ................. $30.00
Footed Juice ............................... $30.00

### DONCASTER,
*Cutting 718,*
*Blank 6009*

Goblet ........................................ $24.00
High Sherbet .............................. $20.00
Low Sherbet ............................... $18.00
Cocktail ..................................... $20.00
Claret-Wine ................................ $28.00
Cordial ...................................... $35.00
Oyster Cocktail .......................... $14.00
Footed Ice Tea ............................ $20.00
Footed Tumbler, 9 oz. ................. $14.00
Footed Juice ............................... $14.00

### LANCASTER,
*Cutting 719,*
*Blank 6009*

Goblet ........................................ $24.00
High Sherbet .............................. $20.00
Low Sherbet ............................... $18.00
Cocktail ..................................... $20.00
Claret-Wine ................................ $28.00
Cordial ...................................... $35.00
Oyster Cocktail .......................... $14.00
Footed Ice Tea ............................ $20.00
Footed Tumbler, 9 oz. ................. $14.00
Footed Juice ............................... $14.00

### NOTTINGHAM, Cutting 720,
*Blank 6009*

Goblet ........................................ $24.00
High Sherbet .............................. $20.00
Low Sherbet ............................... $18.00
Cocktail ..................................... $20.00
Claret-Wine ................................ $28.00
Cordial ...................................... $35.00
Oyster Cocktail .......................... $14.00
Footed Ice Tea ............................ $20.00
Footed Tumbler, 9 oz. ................. $14.00
Footed Juice ............................... $14.00

### BUCKINGHAM, Cutting 721,
*Blank 6009*

Goblet ........................................ $24.00
High Sherbet .............................. $20.00
Low Sherbet ............................... $18.00
Cocktail ..................................... $20.00
Claret-Wine ................................ $28.00
Cordial ...................................... $35.00
Oyster Cocktail .......................... $14.00
Footed Ice Tea ............................ $20.00
Footed Tumbler, 9 oz. ................. $14.00
Footed Juice ............................... $14.00

### Blank 6010

Goblet ........................................ $32.00
High Sherbet .............................. $26.00
Low Sherbet ............................... $22.00
Cocktail ..................................... $26.00
Claret-Wine ................................ $35.00
Cordial ...................................... $48.00
Oyster Cocktail .......................... $20.00
Footed Ice Tea ............................ $32.00
Footed Tumbler, 9 oz. ................. $22.00
Footed Juice ............................... $22.00

### SHERATON, Etching 317, Blank 6010

Goblet ........................................ $34.00
High Sherbet .............................. $28.00
Low Sherbet ............................... $26.00
Cocktail ..................................... $27.00
Claret-Wine ................................ $38.00
Cordial ...................................... $48.00
Oyster Cocktail .......................... $24.00
Footed Ice Tea ............................ $34.00
Footed Tumbler, 9 oz. ................. $25.00
Footed Juice ............................... $25.00

### WELLINGTON, Cutting 722,
*Blank 6010*

Goblet ........................................ $24.00
High Sherbet .............................. $20.00
Low Sherbet ............................... $18.00
Cocktail ..................................... $20.00
Claret-Wine ................................ $28.00
Cordial ...................................... $35.00

Oyster Cocktail .......................... $14.00
Footed Ice Tea ............................ $22.00
Footed Tumbler, 9 oz. ................. $14.00
Footed Juice ............................... $14.00

### LEICESTER, Cutting 722½,
*Blank 6010*

Goblet ........................................ $24.00
High Sherbet .............................. $20.00
Low Sherbet ............................... $18.00
Cocktail ..................................... $20.00
Claret-Wine ................................ $28.00
Cordial ...................................... $35.00
Oyster Cocktail .......................... $14.00
Footed Ice Tea ............................ $22.00
Footed Tumbler, 9 oz. ................. $14.00
Footed Juice ............................... $14.00

### WESTMINSTER, Cutting 723,
*Blank 6010*

Goblet ........................................ $24.00
High Sherbet .............................. $20.00
Low Sherbet ............................... $18.00
Cocktail ..................................... $20.00
Claret-Wine ................................ $28.00
Cordial ...................................... $35.00
Oyster Cocktail .......................... $14.00
Footed Ice Tea ............................ $22.00
Footed Tumbler, 9 oz. ................. $14.00
Footed Juice ............................... $14.00

### NEO CLASSIC, Blank 6011
Crystal

Goblet ........................................ $22.00
Saucer Champagne ...................... $18.00
Low Sherbet ............................... $14.00
Cocktail ..................................... $18.00
Claret ........................................ $22.00
Rhine Wine ................................ $24.00
Wine .......................................... $24.00
Sherry ........................................ $23.00
Crème de Menthe ....................... $18.00
Brandy ....................................... $25.00
Cordial ...................................... $28.00
Oyster Cocktail .......................... $14.00
Footed Ice Tea ............................ $20.00
Footed Tumbler, 10 oz. ............... $14.00
Footed Juice ............................... $16.00
Footed Whiskey .......................... $20.00

Regal Blue/Ruby

Goblet ........................................ $65.00
Saucer Champagne ...................... $54.00
Low Sherbet ............................... $42.00
Cocktail ..................................... $45.00
Claret ........................................ $69.00
Rhine Wine ................................ $60.00
Wine .......................................... $60.00

| | |
|---|---|
| Sherry | $54.00 |
| Crème de Menthe | $47.00 |
| Brandy | $55.00 |
| Cordial | $65.00 |
| Oyster Cocktail | $35.00 |
| Footed Ice Tea | $60.00 |
| Footed Tumbler, 10 oz. | $45.00 |
| Footed Juice | $42.00 |
| Footed Whiskey | $50.00 |

### Burgundy/Amethyst/Empire Green

| | |
|---|---|
| Goblet | $65.00 |
| Saucer Champagne | $54.00 |
| Low Sherbet | $42.00 |
| Cocktail | $45.00 |
| Claret | $68.00 |
| Rhine Wine | $60.00 |
| Wine | $60.00 |
| Sherry | $54.00 |
| Crème de Menthe | $44.00 |
| Brandy | $55.00 |
| Cordial | $68.00 |
| Oyster Cocktail | $35.00 |
| Footed Ice Tea | $64.00 |
| Footed Tumbler, 10 oz. | $38.00 |
| Footed Juice | $42.00 |
| Footed Whiskey | $48.00 |

### Amber/Silver Mist

| | |
|---|---|
| Goblet | $35.00 |
| Saucer Champagne | $30.00 |
| Low Sherbet | $26.00 |
| Cocktail | $28.00 |
| Claret | $40.00 |
| Rhine Wine | $40.00 |
| Wine | $38.00 |
| Sherry | $35.00 |
| Crème de Menthe | $30.00 |
| Brandy | $36.00 |
| Cordial | $40.00 |
| Oyster Cocktail | $25.00 |
| Footed Ice Tea | $35.00 |
| Footed Tumbler, 10 oz. | $26.00 |
| Footed Juice | $26.00 |
| Footed Whiskey | $32.00 |

### NECTAR, Etching 322, Blank 6011

| | |
|---|---|
| Goblet | $25.00 |
| Saucer Champagne | $20.00 |
| Low Sherbet | $15.00 |
| Cocktail | $18.00 |
| Claret | $27.00 |
| Rhine Wine | $27.00 |
| Wine | $27.00 |
| Sherry | $25.00 |
| Crème de Menthe | $24.00 |
| Brandy | $28.00 |
| Cordial | $30.00 |
| Oyster Cocktail | $16.00 |
| Footed Ice Tea | $20.00 |

| | |
|---|---|
| Footed Tumbler, 10 oz. | $18.00 |
| Footed Juice | $18.00 |
| Footed Whiskey | $22.00 |

### ROCKET, Cutting 729, Blank 6011

| | |
|---|---|
| Goblet | $27.00 |
| Saucer Champagne | $24.00 |
| Low Sherbet | $20.00 |
| Cocktail | $22.00 |
| Claret | $32.00 |
| Rhine Wine | $30.00 |
| Wine | $30.00 |
| Sherry | $28.00 |
| Crème de Menthe | $22.00 |
| Brandy | $35.00 |
| Cordial | $38.00 |
| Oyster Cocktail | $18.00 |
| Footed Ice Tea | $25.00 |
| Footed Tumbler, 10 oz. | $22.00 |
| Footed Juice | $20.00 |
| Footed Whiskey | $25.00 |

### WHIRLPOOL, Cutting 730, Blank 6011

| | |
|---|---|
| Goblet | $27.00 |
| Saucer Champagne | $24.00 |
| Low Sherbet | $20.00 |
| Cocktail | $22.00 |
| Claret | $32.00 |
| Rhine Wine | $30.00 |
| Wine | $30.00 |
| Sherry | $25.00 |
| Crème de Menthe | $22.00 |
| Brandy | $35.00 |
| Cordial | $38.00 |
| Oyster Cocktail | $18.00 |
| Footed Ice Tea | $25.00 |
| Footed Tumbler, 10 oz. | $22.00 |
| Footed Juice | $20.00 |
| Footed Whiskey | $25.00 |

### CELESTIAL, Cutting 731, Blank 6011

| | |
|---|---|
| Goblet | $27.00 |
| Saucer Champagne | $24.00 |
| Low Sherbet | $20.00 |
| Cocktail | $22.00 |
| Claret | $32.00 |
| Rhine Wine | $30.00 |
| Wine | $30.00 |
| Sherry | $25.00 |
| Crème de Menthe | $22.00 |
| Brandy | $35.00 |
| Cordial | $38.00 |
| Oyster Cocktail | $18.00 |
| Footed Ice Tea | $25.00 |
| Footed Tumbler, 10 oz. | $22.00 |
| Footed Juice | $20.00 |
| Footed Whiskey | $25.00 |

### PLANET, Cutting 734, Blank 6011

| | |
|---|---|
| Goblet | $27.00 |
| Saucer Champagne | $24.00 |
| Low Sherbet | $20.00 |
| Cocktail | $22.00 |
| Claret | $32.00 |
| Rhine Wine | $30.00 |
| Wine | $30.00 |
| Sherry | $28.00 |
| Crème de Menthe | $22.00 |
| Brandy | $35.00 |
| Cordial | $38.00 |
| Oyster Cocktail | $18.00 |
| Footed Ice Tea | $25.00 |
| Footed Tumbler, 10 oz. | $22.00 |
| Footed Juice | $20.00 |
| Footed Whiskey | $25.00 |

### SHOOTING STARS, Cutting 735, Blank 6011

| | |
|---|---|
| Goblet | $27.00 |
| Saucer Champagne | $24.00 |
| Low Sherbet | $20.00 |
| Cocktail | $22.00 |
| Claret | $32.00 |
| Rhine Wine | $30.00 |
| Wine | $30.00 |
| Sherry | $28.00 |
| Crème de Menthe | $22.00 |
| Brandy | $35.00 |
| Cordial | $38.00 |
| Oyster Cocktail | $18.00 |
| Footed Ice Tea | $25.00 |
| Footed Tumbler, 10 oz. | $22.00 |
| Footed Juice | $20.00 |
| Footed Whiskey | $25.00 |

### DIRECTOIRE, Cutting 736, Blank 6011

| | |
|---|---|
| Goblet | $27.00 |
| Saucer Champagne | $24.00 |
| Low Sherbet | $20.00 |
| Cocktail | $22.00 |
| Claret | $32.00 |
| Rhine Wine | $30.00 |
| Wine | $30.00 |
| Sherry | $28.00 |
| Crème de Menthe | $22.00 |
| Brandy | $35.00 |
| Cordial | $38.00 |
| Oyster Cocktail | $18.00 |
| Footed Ice Tea | $25.00 |
| Footed Tumbler, 10 oz. | $22.00 |
| Footed Juice | $20.00 |
| Footed Whiskey | $25.00 |

### QUINFOIL, Cutting 737, Blank 6011

| | |
|---|---|
| Goblet | $27.00 |
| Saucer Champagne | $24.00 |

Low Sherbet ...................... $20.00
Cocktail ............................. $22.00
Claret ................................ $32.00
Rhine Wine ....................... $30.00
Wine .................................. $30.00
Sherry ................................ $28.00
Crème de Menthe ............. $22.00
Brandy ............................... $35.00
Cordial .............................. $38.00
Oyster Cocktail ................. $18.00
Footed Ice Tea .................. $25.00
Footed Tumbler, 10 oz. ..... $22.00
Footed Juice ...................... $20.00
Footed Whiskey ................. $25.00

### MARDI GRAS, Cutting 765, Blank 6011

Goblet ................................ $27.00
Saucer Champagne ............. $24.00
Low Sherbet ...................... $20.00
Cocktail ............................. $22.00
Claret ................................ $32.00
Wine .................................. $30.00
Cordial .............................. $35.00
Oyster Cocktail ................. $18.00
Footed Ice Tea .................. $25.00
Footed Tumbler, 10 oz. ..... $22.00
Footed Juice ...................... $20.00

### ATHENIAN, Cutting 770, Blank 6011

Goblet ................................ $27.00
Saucer Champagne ............. $24.00
Low Sherbet ...................... $20.00
Cocktail ............................. $22.00
Claret ................................ $32.00
Wine .................................. $30.00
Brandy ............................... $32.00
Cordial .............................. $35.00
Oyster Cocktail ................. $18.00
Footed Ice Tea .................. $25.00
Footed Tumbler, 10 oz. ..... $20.00
Footed Juice ...................... $20.00

### GOLDEN SWIRL, Decoration 614, Blank 6011

Goblet ................................ $27.00
Saucer Champagne ............. $24.00
Low Sherbet ...................... $20.00
Cocktail ............................. $22.00
Claret ................................ $32.00
Rhine Wine ....................... $30.00
Wine .................................. $30.00
Crème de Menthe ............. $22.00
Brandy ............................... $35.00
Cordial .............................. $38.00
Footed Ice Tea .................. $25.00
Footed Tumbler, 10 oz. ..... $22.00
Footed Whiskey ................. $25.00

### WESTCHESTER, Blank 6012
Crystal/Mother of Pearl

Goblet ................................ $26.00
High Sherbet ..................... $22.00
Low Sherbet ...................... $16.00
Cocktail ............................. $20.00
Claret ................................ $28.00
Rhine Wine ....................... $25.00
Wine .................................. $25.00
Sherry ................................ $22.00
Crème de Menthe ............. $22.00
Brandy ............................... $27.00
Cordial .............................. $30.00
Oyster Cocktail ................. $14.00
Footed Ice Tea .................. $24.00
Footed Tumbler, 10 oz. ..... $16.00
Footed Juice ...................... $16.00

#### Colors
Goblet ................................ $65.00
High Sherbet ..................... $45.00
Low Sherbet ...................... $34.00
Cocktail ............................. $42.00
Claret ................................ $70.00
Rhine Wine ....................... $60.00
Wine .................................. $62.00
Sherry ................................ $45.00
Crème de Menthe ............. $42.00
Brandy ............................... $65.00
Cordial .............................. $70.00
Oyster Cocktail ................. $32.00
Footed Ice Tea .................. $60.00
Footed Tumbler, 10 oz. ..... $35.00
Footed Juice ...................... $38.00

### SPRINGTIME, Etching 318, Blank 6012

Goblet ................................ $35.00
High Sherbet ..................... $32.00
Low Sherbet ...................... $28.00
Cocktail ............................. $32.00
Claret ................................ $40.00
Rhine Wine ....................... $35.00
Wine .................................. $40.00
Sherry ................................ $35.00
Crème de Menthe ............. $32.00
Brandy ............................... $36.00
Cordial .............................. $42.00
Oyster Cocktail ................. $25.00
Footed Ice Tea .................. $35.00
Footed Tumbler, 10 oz. ..... $22.00
Footed Juice ...................... $22.00

### RAMBLER, Etching 323, Blank 6012

Goblet ................................ $38.00
High Sherbet ..................... $32.00
Low Sherbet ...................... $28.00

Cocktail ............................. $32.00
Claret ................................ $45.00
Rhine Wine ....................... $42.00
Wine .................................. $45.00
Sherry ................................ $34.00
Crème de Menthe ............. $32.00
Brandy ............................... $42.00
Cordial .............................. $48.00
Oyster Cocktail ................. $28.00
Footed Ice Tea .................. $36.00
Footed Tumbler, 10 oz. ..... $28.00
Footed Juice ...................... $28.00

### FESTOON, Cutting 738, Blank 6012

Goblet ................................ $22.00
High Sherbet ..................... $28.00
Low Sherbet ...................... $16.00
Cocktail ............................. $18.00
Claret ................................ $24.00
Rhine Wine ....................... $24.00
Wine .................................. $24.00
Sherry ................................ $18.00
Crème de Menthe ............. $18.00
Brandy ............................... $26.00
Cordial .............................. $28.00
Oyster Cocktail ................. $16.00
Footed Ice Tea .................. $18.00
Footed Tumbler, 10 oz. ..... $10.00
Footed Juice ...................... $14.00

### ROCK GARDEN, Cutting 739, Blank 6012

Goblet ................................ $25.00
High Sherbet ..................... $22.00
Low Sherbet ...................... $18.00
Cocktail ............................. $22.00
Claret ................................ $28.00
Rhine Wine ....................... $28.00
Wine .................................. $28.00
Sherry ................................ $22.00
Crème de Menthe ............. $22.00
Brandy ............................... $32.00
Cordial .............................. $34.00
Oyster Cocktail ................. $14.00
Footed Ice Tea .................. $22.00
Footed Tumbler, 10 oz. ..... $12.00
Footed Juice ...................... $14.00

### RONDEAU, Cutting 740, Blank 6012

Goblet ................................ $25.00
High Sherbet ..................... $22.00
Low Sherbet ...................... $18.00
Cocktail ............................. $22.00
Claret ................................ $28.00
Rhine Wine ....................... $28.00
Wine .................................. $28.00
Sherry ................................ $22.00
Crème de Menthe ............. $22.00
Brandy ............................... $32.00
Cordial .............................. $34.00

Oyster Cocktail ...........................$14.00
Footed Ice Tea ...........................$22.00

### WATERCRESS, Cutting 741, Blank 6012

Goblet.........................................$25.00
High Sherbet ..............................$22.00
Low Sherbet ...............................$18.00
Cocktail .....................................$22.00
Claret ........................................$28.00
Rhine Wine ................................$28.00
Wine ..........................................$28.00
Sherry.........................................$22.00
Crème de Menthe........................$22.00
Brandy .......................................$32.00
Cordial ......................................$34.00
Oyster Cocktail ..........................$14.00
Footed Ice Tea ...........................$22.00
Footed Tumbler, 10 oz. ..............$12.00
Footed Juice ...............................$14.00

### ORBIT, Cutting 742, Blank 6012

Goblet.........................................$25.00
High Sherbet ..............................$22.00
Low Sherbet ...............................$16.00
Cocktail .....................................$20.00
Claret ........................................$28.00
Rhine Wine ................................$25.00
Wine ..........................................$28.00
Sherry.........................................$24.00
Crème de Menthe........................$20.00
Brandy .......................................$32.00
Cordial ......................................$32.00
Oyster Cocktail ..........................$12.00
Footed Ice Tea ...........................$25.00

### HERALDRY, Cutting 743, Blank 6012

Goblet.........................................$32.00
High Sherbet ..............................$28.00
Low Sherbet ...............................$22.00
Cocktail .....................................$25.00
Claret ........................................$35.00
Rhine Wine ................................$32.00
Wine ..........................................$35.00
Sherry.........................................$25.00
Crème de Menthe........................$22.00
Brandy .......................................$35.00
Cordial ......................................$38.00
Oyster Cocktail ..........................$18.00
Footed Ice Tea ...........................$32.00
Footed Tumbler,
   10 oz. ....................................$22.00
Footed Juice ...............................$22.00

### REGENCY, Cutting 744, Blank 6012

Goblet.........................................$25.00
High Sherbet ..............................$22.00
Low Sherbet ...............................$18.00

Cocktail .....................................$22.00
Claret ........................................$28.00
Rhine Wine ................................$28.00
Wine ..........................................$28.00
Sherry.........................................$22.00
Crème de Menthe........................$22.00
Brandy .......................................$32.00
Cordial ......................................$34.00
Oyster Cocktail ..........................$14.00
Footed Ice Tea ...........................$22.00
Footed Tumbler, 10 oz. ..............$12.00
Footed Juice ...............................$14.00

### IVY, Cutting 745, Blank 6012

Goblet.........................................$22.00
High Sherbet ..............................$20.00
Low Sherbet ...............................$16.00
Cocktail .....................................$20.00
Claret ........................................$25.00
Rhine Wine ................................$25.00
Wine ..........................................$25.00
Sherry.........................................$20.00
Crème de Menthe........................$20.00
Brandy .......................................$28.00
Cordial ......................................$30.00
Oyster Cocktail ..........................$12.00
Footed Ice Tea ...........................$20.00
Footed Tumbler, 10 oz. ..............$10.00
Footed Juice ...............................$12.00

### GOSSAMER, Cutting 746, Blank 6012

Goblet.........................................$22.00
High Sherbet ..............................$20.00
Low Sherbet ...............................$16.00
Cocktail .....................................$20.00
Claret ........................................$25.00
Wine ..........................................$25.00
Cordial ......................................$30.00
Oyster Cocktail ..........................$14.00
Footed Ice Tea ...........................$20.00
Footed Tumbler, 10 oz. ..............$10.00
Footed Juice ...............................$12.00

### CYRENE, Cutting 763, Blank 6012

Goblet.........................................$25.00
High Sherbet ..............................$22.00
Low Sherbet ...............................$18.00
Cocktail .....................................$22.00
Claret ........................................$28.00
Wine ..........................................$28.00
Cordial ......................................$34.00
Oyster Cocktail ..........................$16.00
Footed Ice Tea ...........................$22.00
Footed Tumbler, 10 oz. ..............$12.00
Footed Juice ...............................$14.00

### PIERETTE, Cutting 764, Blank 6012

Goblet.........................................$22.00
High Sherbet ..............................$20.00

Low Sherbet ...............................$16.00
Cocktail .....................................$20.00
Claret ........................................$25.00
Wine ..........................................$25.00
Cordial ......................................$30.00
Oyster Cocktail ..........................$14.00
Footed Ice Tea ...........................$20.00
Footed Tumbler, 10 oz. ..............$10.00
Footed Juice ...............................$12.00

### DECORATION, 615, Blank 6012

Goblet.........................................$25.00
High Sherbet ..............................$22.00
Low Sherbet ...............................$18.00
Cocktail .....................................$22.00
Claret ........................................$28.00
Rhine Wine ................................$28.00
Wine ..........................................$28.00
Sherry.........................................$22.00
Crème de Menthe........................$22.00
Brandy .......................................$30.00
Cordial ......................................$34.00
Oyster Cocktail ..........................$16.00
Footed Ice Tea ...........................$22.00
Footed Tumbler, 10 oz. ..............$12.00
Footed Juice ...............................$14.00

### ST. REGIS, Decoration 616, Blank 6012

Goblet.........................................$38.00
High Sherbet ..............................$34.00
Low Sherbet ...............................$28.00
Cocktail .....................................$34.00
Claret ........................................$42.00
Wine ..........................................$42.00
Cordial ......................................$45.00
Oyster Cocktail ..........................$26.00
Footed Ice Tea ...........................$38.00
Footed Tumbler, 10 oz. ..............$28.00
Footed Juice ...............................$30.00

### Blank 6013
#### Crystal

Goblet.........................................$30.00
Low Goblet.................................$25.00
Saucer Champagne......................$25.00
Low Sherbet ...............................$20.00
Cocktail .....................................$24.00
Claret ........................................$35.00
Wine ..........................................$35.00
Cordial ......................................$45.00
Oyster Cocktail ..........................$18.00
Footed Ice Tea ...........................$28.00
Footed Juice ...............................$20.00

#### Colors

Goblet.........................................$70.00
Saucer Champagne......................$62.00

| | |
|---|---|
| Cocktail | $50.00 |
| Wine | $75.00 |
| Footed Ice Tea | $65.00 |

### DAISY, Etching 324, Blank 6013

| | |
|---|---|
| Goblet | $40.00 |
| Low Goblet | $35.00 |
| Saucer Champagne | $35.00 |
| Low Sherbet | $28.00 |
| Cocktail | $32.00 |
| Claret | $47.00 |
| Wine | $45.00 |
| Cordial | $54.00 |
| Oyster Cocktail | $25.00 |
| Footed Ice Tea | $38.00 |
| Footed Juice | $25.00 |

### FANTASY, Cutting 747, Blank 6013

| | |
|---|---|
| Goblet | $32.00 |
| Low Goblet | $30.00 |
| Saucer Champagne | $30.00 |
| Low Sherbet | $26.00 |
| Cocktail | $30.00 |
| Claret | $45.00 |
| Wine | $42.00 |
| Cordial | $56.00 |
| Oyster Cocktail | $24.00 |
| Footed Ice Tea | $30.00 |
| Footed Juice | $24.00 |

### ALLEGRO, Cutting 748, Blank 6013

| | |
|---|---|
| Goblet | $32.00 |
| Low Goblet | $30.00 |
| Saucer Champagne | $30.00 |
| Low Sherbet | $26.00 |
| Cocktail | $28.00 |
| Claret | $45.00 |
| Wine | $42.00 |
| Cordial | $55.00 |
| Oyster Cocktail | $24.00 |
| Footed Ice Tea | $32.00 |
| Footed Juice | $24.00 |

### BOUQUET, Cutting 756, Blank 6013

| | |
|---|---|
| Goblet | $30.00 |
| Low Goblet | $25.00 |
| Saucer Champagne | $27.00 |
| Low Sherbet | $20.00 |
| Cocktail | $25.00 |
| Claret | $35.00 |
| Wine | $32.00 |
| Cordial | $48.00 |
| Oyster Cocktail | $20.00 |
| Footed Ice Tea | $28.00 |
| Footed Juice | $20.00 |

### SOCIETY, Cutting 757, Blank 6013

| | |
|---|---|
| Goblet | $25.00 |
| Low Goblet | $20.00 |

| | |
|---|---|
| Saucer Champagne | $22.00 |
| Low Sherbet | $20.00 |
| Cocktail | $22.00 |
| Claret | $30.00 |
| Wine | $30.00 |
| Cordial | $40.00 |
| Oyster Cocktail | $18.00 |
| Footed Ice Tea | $22.00 |
| Footed Juice | $18.00 |

### Blank 6014, 6014½
#### Crystal

| | |
|---|---|
| Goblet | $30.00 |
| Saucer Champagne | $28.00 |
| Low Sherbet | $24.00 |
| Cocktail | $28.00 |
| Claret | $35.00 |
| Wine | $32.00 |
| Cordial | $38.00 |
| Oyster Cocktail | $18.00 |
| Footed Ice Tea | $28.00 |
| Footed Tumbler, 9 oz. | $22.00 |
| Footed Juice | $20.00 |

#### Azure/Gold Tint

| | |
|---|---|
| Goblet | $38.00 |
| Saucer Champagne | $34.00 |
| Low Sherbet | $30.00 |
| Cocktail | $32.00 |
| Claret | $42.00 |
| Wine | $40.00 |
| Cordial | $52.00 |
| Oyster Cocktail | $28.00 |
| Footed Ice Tea | $35.00 |
| Footed Tumbler, 9 oz. | $30.00 |
| Footed Juice | $30.00 |

### CORSAGE, Etching 325, Blank 6014

| | |
|---|---|
| Goblet | $35.00 |
| Saucer Champagne | $32.00 |
| Low Sherbet | $24.00 |
| Cocktail | $27.00 |
| Claret | $45.00 |
| Wine | $42.00 |
| Cordial | $50.00 |
| Oyster Cocktail | $14.00 |
| Footed Ice Tea | $35.00 |
| Footed Tumbler, 9 oz. | $28.00 |
| Footed Juice | $24.00 |

### ARCADY, Etching 326, Blank 6014

| | |
|---|---|
| Goblet | $35.00 |
| Saucer Champagne | $32.00 |
| Low Sherbet | $25.00 |
| Cocktail | $30.00 |
| Claret | $46.00 |

| | |
|---|---|
| Wine | $42.00 |
| Cordial | $55.00 |
| Oyster Cocktail | $20.00 |
| Footed Ice Tea | $35.00 |
| Footed Tumbler, 9 oz. | $26.00 |
| Footed Juice | $25.00 |

### CAVENDISH, Cutting 754, Blank 6014

| | |
|---|---|
| Goblet | $25.00 |
| Saucer Champagne | $22.00 |
| Low Sherbet | $18.00 |
| Cocktail | $22.00 |
| Claret | $30.00 |
| Wine | $30.00 |
| Cordial | $36.00 |
| Oyster Cocktail | $18.00 |
| Footed Ice Tea | $22.00 |
| Footed Tumbler, 9 oz. | $18.00 |
| Footed Juice | $18.00 |

### PALMETTO, Cutting 755, Blank 6014

| | |
|---|---|
| Goblet | $25.00 |
| Saucer Champagne | $22.00 |
| Low Sherbet | $18.00 |
| Cocktail | $22.00 |
| Claret | $30.00 |
| Wine | $30.00 |
| Cordial | $36.00 |
| Oyster Cocktail | $18.00 |
| Footed Ice Tea | $22.00 |
| Footed Tumbler, 9 oz. | $18.00 |
| Footed Juice | $18.00 |

### BORDEAUX, Cutting 758, Blank 6014

| | |
|---|---|
| Goblet | $25.00 |
| Saucer Champagne | $22.00 |
| Low Sherbet | $18.00 |
| Cocktail | $22.00 |
| Claret | $30.00 |
| Wine | $30.00 |
| Cordial | $35.00 |
| Oyster Cocktail | $18.00 |
| Footed Ice Tea | $22.00 |
| Footed Tumbler, 9 oz. | $18.00 |
| Footed Juice | $18.00 |

### WEYLIN, Cutting 759, Blank 6014

| | |
|---|---|
| Goblet | $24.00 |
| Saucer Champagne | $22.00 |
| Low Sherbet | $18.00 |
| Cocktail | $22.00 |
| Claret | $28.00 |
| Wine | $28.00 |
| Cordial | $35.00 |
| Oyster Cocktail | $18.00 |
| Footed Ice Tea | $22.00 |

Footed Tumbler, 9 oz. .................. $18.00
Footed Juice ................................. $18.00

### WILMA, Blank 6016
#### Crystal

Goblet ......................................... $25.00
Saucer Champagne ....................... $23.00
Low Sherbet ................................ $17.00
Cocktail ...................................... $23.00
Claret ......................................... $30.00
Wine ........................................... $28.00
Cordial ....................................... $38.00
Oyster Cocktail ........................... $17.00
Footed Ice Tea ............................ $24.00
Footed Tumbler, 10 oz. ............... $23.00
Footed Juice ................................ $23.00
Large Claret ................................ $32.00
Continental Champagne ............... $40.00

#### Azure/Pink/Blue

Goblet ......................................... $45.00
Saucer Champagne ....................... $42.00
Low Sherbet ................................ $30.00
Cocktail ...................................... $40.00
Claret ......................................... $52.00
Wine ........................................... $50.00
Cordial ....................................... $57.00
Oyster Cocktail ........................... $30.00
Footed Ice Tea ............................ $45.00
Footed Tumbler, 10 oz. ............... $35.00
Footed Juice ................................ $35.00
Large Claret ................................ $56.00

### NAVARRE, Etching 327, Blank 6016
#### Crystal

Goblet ......................................... $38.00
Saucer Champagne ....................... $32.00
Low Sherbet ................................ $28.00
Cocktail ...................................... $32.00
Claret ......................................... $70.00
Cordial ....................................... $95.00
Oyster Cocktail ........................... $30.00
Footed Ice Tea ............................ $35.00
Footed Tumbler, 10 oz. ............... $32.00
Footed Juice ................................ $32.00
Large Claret ................................ $75.00
Magnum ..................... $135.00 – Market
Continental Champagne
........................... $135.00 – Market
Brandy Inhaler ........... $150.00 – Market
Cocktail/Sherry .......... $150.00 – Market
Double Old Fashioned ................. $65.00
Highball ...................................... $68.00
Wine ........................................... $68.00

#### Pink

Goblet ......................................... $125.00
Saucer Champagne ....................... $85.00

Claret ......................................... $135.00
Footed Ice Tea ............................ $125.00
Large Claret ................................ $150.00

#### Blue

Goblet ......................................... $125.00
Saucer Champagne ....................... $78.00
Claret ......................................... $125.00
Footed Ice Tea ............................ $85.00
Large Claret ................................ $135.00
Magnum ..................... $195.00 – Market

### MEADOW ROSE, Etching 328, Blank 6016
#### Crystal

Goblet ......................................... $38.00
Saucer Champagne ....................... $34.00
Low Sherbet ................................ $30.00
Cocktail ...................................... $34.00
Claret ......................................... $45.00
Wine ........................................... $45.00
Cordial ....................................... $65.00
Oyster Cocktail ........................... $30.00
Footed Ice Tea ............................ $38.00
Footed Tumbler, 10 oz. ............... $30.00
Footed Juice ................................ $32.00

#### Azure

Goblet ......................................... $130.00
Saucer Champagne ....................... $95.00
Low Sherbet ................................ $65.00
Cocktail ...................................... $75.00
Claret ......................................... $135.00
Wine ........................................... $135.00
Cordial ....................... $165.00 – Market
Oyster Cocktail ........................... $65.00
Footed Ice Tea ............................ $125.00
Footed Tumbler, 10 oz. ............... $60.00
Footed Juice ................................ $65.00

### MELBA, Cutting 761, Blank 6016

Goblet ......................................... $23.00
Saucer Champagne ....................... $21.00
Low Sherbet ................................ $16.00
Cocktail ...................................... $21.00
Claret ......................................... $27.00
Wine ........................................... $27.00
Cordial ....................................... $32.00
Oyster Cocktail ........................... $16.00
Footed Ice Tea ............................ $20.00
Footed Tumbler, 10 oz. ............... $12.00
Footed Juice ................................ $16.00

### CUMBERLAND, Cutting 762, Blank 6016

Goblet ......................................... $23.00
Saucer Champagne ....................... $20.00
Low Sherbet ................................ $16.00
Cocktail ...................................... $20.00
Claret ......................................... $25.00

Wine ........................................... $25.00
Cordial ....................................... $32.00
Oyster Cocktail ........................... $14.00
Footed Ice Tea ............................ $20.00
Footed Tumbler, 10 oz. ............... $12.00
Footed Juice ................................ $16.00

### RICHELIEU, Decoration 515, Blank 6016

Goblet ......................................... $65.00
Saucer Champagne ....................... $50.00
Low Sherbet ................................ $40.00
Cocktail ...................................... $48.00
Claret ......................................... $75.00
Wine ........................................... $70.00
Cordial ....................................... $125.00
Oyster Cocktail ........................... $40.00
Footed Ice Tea ............................ $65.00
Footed Tumbler, 10 oz. ............... $50.00
Footed Juice ................................ $42.00

### VICTORIA, Decoration 696, Blank 6016

Goblet ......................................... $25.00
Saucer Champagne ....................... $22.00
Large Claret ................................ $25.00
Footed Ice Tea ............................ $25.00

### REGIS, Decoration 697, Blank 6016

Goblet ......................................... $25.00
Saucer Champagne ....................... $22.00
Large Claret ................................ $25.00
Footed Ice Tea ............................ $25.00

### SCEPTRE, Blank 6017
#### Crystal

Goblet ......................................... $25.00
High Sherbet ................................ $23.00
Low Sherbet ................................ $17.00
Cocktail ...................................... $23.00
Claret ......................................... $28.00
Wine ........................................... $28.00
Cordial ....................................... $35.00
Oyster Cocktail ........................... $16.00
Footed Tumbler, 14 oz. ............... $24.00
Footed Ice Tea ............................ $24.00
Footed Tumbler, 9 oz. ................. $18.00
Footed Juice ................................ $20.00

#### Azure/Gold Tint

Goblet ......................................... $40.00
High Sherbet ................................ $37.00
Low Sherbet ................................ $34.00
Cocktail ...................................... $37.00
Claret ......................................... $48.00
Wine ........................................... $45.00
Cordial ....................................... $65.00
Oyster Cocktail ........................... $30.00

Footed Ice Tea ............................ $40.00
Footed Tumbler, 9 oz. ............... $34.00
Footed Juice ............................... $35.00

### LIDO, Etching 329, Blank 6017
#### Crystal
Goblet ......................................... $32.00
High Sherbet ............................. $30.00
Low Sherbet ............................... $22.00
Cocktail ...................................... $30.00
Claret ......................................... $38.00
Wine ........................................... $35.00
Cordial ....................................... $44.00
Oyster Cocktail .......................... $22.00
Footed Tumbler, 14 oz. ............. $36.00
Footed Ice Tea ........................... $32.00
Footed Tumbler, 9 oz. ............... $25.00
Footed Juice ............................... $25.00

#### Azure
Goblet ......................................... $75.00
High Sherbet ............................. $70.00
Low Sherbet ............................... $55.00
Cocktail ...................................... $65.00
Claret ......................................... $85.00
Wine ........................................... $75.00
Cordial ..................................... $110.00
Oyster Cocktail .......................... $50.00
Footed Ice Tea ........................... $75.00
Footed Tumbler, 9 oz. ............... $55.00
Footed Juice ............................... $55.00
Tumbler, 14 oz. .......................... $55.00

### LENOX, Etching 330, Blank 6017
Goblet ......................................... $24.00
High Sherbet ............................. $20.00
Low Sherbet ............................... $16.00
Cocktail ...................................... $20.00
Claret ......................................... $25.00
Wine ........................................... $27.00
Cordial ....................................... $38.00
Oyster Cocktail .......................... $16.00
Footed Tumbler, 14 oz. ............. $20.00
Footed Ice Tea ........................... $18.00
Footed Tumbler, 9 oz. ............... $14.00
Footed Juice ............................... $16.00

### SHIRLEY, Etching 331, Blank 6017
Goblet ......................................... $35.00
High Sherbet ............................. $32.00
Low Sherbet ............................... $28.00
Cocktail ...................................... $32.00
Claret ......................................... $45.00
Wine ........................................... $45.00
Cordial ....................................... $55.00
Oyster Cocktail .......................... $25.00
Footed Tumbler, 14 oz. ............. $40.00
Footed Ice Tea ........................... $35.00
Footed Tumbler, 9 oz. ............... $28.00
Footed Juice ............................... $28.00

### ROMANCE, Etching 341, Blank 6017
Goblet ......................................... $35.00
High Sherbet ............................. $32.00
Low Sherbet ............................... $28.00
Cocktail ...................................... $32.00
Claret ......................................... $45.00
Wine ........................................... $42.00
Cordial ....................................... $55.00
Oyster Cocktail .......................... $25.00
Footed Ice Tea ........................... $35.00
Footed Tumbler, 9 oz. ............... $28.00
Footed Juice ............................... $28.00

### RIPPLE, Cutting 766, Blank 6017
Goblet ......................................... $22.00
High Sherbet ............................. $20.00
Low Sherbet ............................... $16.00
Cocktail ...................................... $20.00
Claret ......................................... $27.00
Wine ........................................... $27.00
Cordial ....................................... $32.00
Oyster Cocktail .......................... $16.00
Footed Tumbler, 14 oz. ............. $20.00
Footed Ice Tea ........................... $20.00
Footed Tumbler, 9 oz. ............... $16.00
Footed Juice ............................... $16.00

### BEACON, Cutting 767, Blank 6017
Goblet ......................................... $25.00
High Sherbet ............................. $22.00
Low Sherbet ............................... $18.00
Cocktail ...................................... $20.00
Claret ......................................... $28.00
Wine ........................................... $28.00
Cordial ....................................... $38.00
Oyster Cocktail .......................... $20.00
Footed Tumbler, 14 oz. ............. $22.00
Footed Ice Tea ........................... $25.00
Footed Tumbler, 9 oz. ............... $20.00
Footed Juice ............................... $18.00

### BRIDAL SHOWER, Cutting 768, Blank 6017
Goblet ......................................... $22.00
High Sherbet ............................. $20.00
Low Sherbet ............................... $16.00
Cocktail ...................................... $20.00
Claret ......................................... $27.00
Wine ........................................... $27.00
Cordial ....................................... $32.00
Oyster Cocktail .......................... $14.00
Footed Tumbler, 14 oz. ............. $20.00
Footed Ice Tea ........................... $20.00
Footed Tumbler, 9 oz. ............... $14.00
Footed Juice ............................... $14.00

### LAUREL, Cutting 776, Blank 6017
Goblet ......................................... $30.00
High Sherbet ............................. $26.00
Low Sherbet ............................... $22.00

Cocktail ...................................... $25.00
Claret ......................................... $36.00
Wine ........................................... $34.00
Cordial ....................................... $40.00
Oyster Cocktail .......................... $20.00
Footed Ice Tea ........................... $30.00
Footed Tumbler, 9 oz. ............... $24.00
Footed Juice ............................... $24.00

### RAYNEL, Cutting 777, Blank 6017
Goblet ......................................... $22.00
High Sherbet ............................. $18.00
Low Sherbet ............................... $14.00
Cocktail ...................................... $18.00
Claret ......................................... $25.00
Wine ........................................... $25.00
Cordial ....................................... $30.00
Oyster Cocktail .......................... $12.00
Footed Ice Tea ........................... $18.00
Footed Tumbler, 9 oz. ............... $12.00
Footed Juice ............................... $12.00

### LUCERNE, Cutting 778, Blank 6017
Goblet ......................................... $22.00
High Sherbet ............................. $18.00
Low Sherbet ............................... $14.00
Cocktail ...................................... $18.00
Claret ......................................... $25.00
Wine ........................................... $25.00
Cordial ....................................... $30.00
Oyster Cocktail .......................... $12.00
Footed Ice Tea ........................... $18.00
Footed Tumbler, 9 oz. ............... $12.00
Footed Juice ............................... $12.00

### DRAPE, Cutting 784, Blank 6017
Goblet ......................................... $22.00
High Sherbet ............................. $18.00
Low Sherbet ............................... $14.00
Cocktail ...................................... $18.00
Claret ......................................... $25.00
Wine ........................................... $25.00
Cordial ....................................... $30.00
Oyster Cocktail .......................... $12.00
Footed Ice Tea ........................... $18.00
Footed Tumbler, 9 oz. ............... $12.00
Footed Juice ............................... $12.00

### CYNTHIA, Cutting 785, Blank 6017
Goblet ......................................... $32.00
High Sherbet ............................. $28.00
Low Sherbet ............................... $22.00
Cocktail ...................................... $28.00
Claret ......................................... $38.00
Wine ........................................... $36.00
Cordial ....................................... $45.00
Oyster Cocktail .......................... $20.00
Footed Ice Tea ........................... $32.00
Footed Tumbler, 9 oz. ............... $24.00
Footed Juice ............................... $24.00

### SIMPLICITY, Decoration 618, Blank 6017

| | |
|---|---|
| Goblet | $35.00 |
| High Sherbet | $32.00 |
| Low Sherbet | $24.00 |
| Cocktail | $32.00 |
| Claret | $40.00 |
| Wine | $40.00 |
| Cordial | $45.00 |
| Oyster Cocktail | $22.00 |
| Footed Ice Tea | $35.00 |
| Footed Tumbler, 9 oz. | $24.00 |
| Footed Juice | $24.00 |

### RONDEL, Blank 6019
#### Crystal

| | |
|---|---|
| Goblet | $20.00 |
| Sherbet | $18.00 |
| Parfait | $18.00 |
| Cocktail | $10.00 |
| Claret | $20.00 |
| Wine | $20.00 |
| Oyster Cocktail | $8.00 |
| Footed Ice Tea | $18.00 |
| Footed Juice | $10.00 |

#### Azure/Gold Tint

| | |
|---|---|
| Goblet | $35.00 |
| Sherbet | $32.00 |
| Cocktail | $30.00 |
| Claret | $35.00 |
| Wine | $35.00 |
| Oyster Cocktail | $25.00 |
| Footed Ice Tea | $35.00 |
| Footed Juice | $30.00 |

### FEDERAL, Cutting 771, Blank 6019

| | |
|---|---|
| Goblet | $26.00 |
| Sherbet | $23.00 |
| Parfait | $26.00 |
| Cocktail | $23.00 |
| Claret | $28.00 |
| Wine | $28.00 |
| Oyster Cocktail | $20.00 |
| Footed Ice Tea | $26.00 |
| Footed Juice | $22.00 |

### TULIP, Cutting 772, Blank 6019

| | |
|---|---|
| Goblet | $20.00 |
| Sherbet | $16.00 |
| Parfait | $16.00 |
| Cocktail | $16.00 |
| Claret | $20.00 |
| Wine | $20.00 |
| Oyster Cocktail | $8.00 |
| Footed Ice Tea | $16.00 |
| Footed Juice | $10.00 |

### LAUREL, Cutting 776, Blank 6019

| | |
|---|---|
| Goblet | $20.00 |
| Sherbet | $16.00 |
| Parfait | $16.00 |
| Cocktail | $16.00 |
| Claret | $20.00 |
| Wine | $20.00 |
| Oyster Cocktail | $8.00 |
| Footed Ice Tea | $16.00 |
| Footed Juice | $10.00 |

### MELODY, Blank 6020

| | |
|---|---|
| Goblet | $30.00 |
| Saucer Champagne | $28.00 |
| Low Sherbet | $24.00 |
| Parfait | $32.00 |
| Cocktail | $28.00 |
| Claret | $35.00 |
| Wine | $35.00 |
| Cordial | $42.00 |
| Oyster Cocktail | $20.00 |
| Footed Ice Tea | $30.00 |
| Footed Tumbler, 9 oz. | $24.00 |
| Footed Juice | $24.00 |

### MAYFLOWER, Etching 332, Blank 6020

| | |
|---|---|
| Goblet | $40.00 |
| Saucer Champagne | $36.00 |
| Low Sherbet | $30.00 |
| Parfait | $40.00 |
| Cocktail | $36.00 |
| Claret | $48.00 |
| Wine | $45.00 |
| Cordial | $65.00 |
| Oyster Cocktail | $28.00 |
| Footed Ice Tea | $40.00 |
| Footed Tumbler, 9 oz. | $30.00 |
| Footed Juice | $30.00 |

### GOTHIC, Cutting 774, Blank 6020

| | |
|---|---|
| Goblet | $28.00 |
| Saucer Champagne | $25.00 |
| Low Sherbet | $20.00 |
| Parfait | $28.00 |
| Cocktail | $25.00 |
| Claret | $32.00 |
| Wine | $30.00 |
| Cordial | $36.00 |
| Oyster Cocktail | $20.00 |
| Footed Ice Tea | $28.00 |
| Footed Tumbler, 9 oz. | $20.00 |
| Footed Juice | $22.00 |

### KIMBERLEY, Cutting 775, Blank 6020

| | |
|---|---|
| Goblet | $28.00 |
| Saucer Champagne | $25.00 |
| Low Sherbet | $20.00 |

| | |
|---|---|
| Parfait | $28.00 |
| Cocktail | $25.00 |
| Claret | $32.00 |
| Wine | $30.00 |
| Cordial | $36.00 |
| Oyster Cocktail | $20.00 |
| Footed Ice Tea | $28.00 |
| Footed Tumbler, 9 oz. | $20.00 |
| Footed Juice | $20.00 |

### COLFAX, Blank 6023

| | |
|---|---|
| Goblet | $16.00 |
| Saucer Champagne | $14.00 |
| Low Sherbet | $10.00 |
| Cocktail | $10.00 |
| Claret-Wine | $16.00 |
| Cordial | $20.00 |
| Oyster Cocktail | $8.00 |
| Footed Ice Tea | $14.00 |
| Footed Tumbler, 9 oz. | $10.00 |
| Footed Juice | $10.00 |

### SPENCERIAN, Tracing 94, Blank 6023

| | |
|---|---|
| Goblet | $16.00 |
| Saucer Champagne | $14.00 |
| Low Sherbet | $10.00 |
| Cocktail | $10.00 |
| Claret-Wine | $16.00 |
| Cordial | $20.00 |
| Oyster Cocktail | $8.00 |
| Footed Ice Tea | $14.00 |
| Footed Tumbler, 9 oz. | $10.00 |
| Footed Juice | $10.00 |

### COLONIAL MIRROR, Etching 334, 6023

| | |
|---|---|
| Goblet | $32.00 |
| Saucer Champagne | $30.00 |
| Low Sherbet | $27.00 |
| Cocktail | $30.00 |
| Claret-Wine | $38.00 |
| Cordial | $50.00 |
| Oyster Cocktail | $22.00 |
| Footed Ice Tea | $32.00 |
| Footed Tumbler, 9 oz. | $26.00 |
| Footed Juice | $28.00 |

### WILLOW, Etching 335, Blank 6023

| | |
|---|---|
| Goblet | $45.00 |
| Saucer Champagne | $40.00 |
| Low Sherbet | $34.00 |
| Cocktail | $38.00 |
| Claret-Wine | $52.00 |
| Cordial | $68.00 |
| Oyster Cocktail | $30.00 |
| Footed Ice Tea | $45.00 |

Footed Tumbler, 9 oz. .................. $34.00
Footed Juice .......................... $36.00

### DOLLY MADISON, Cutting 786, Blank 6023

Goblet .................................. $20.00
Saucer Champagne ..................... $18.00
Low Sherbet ........................... $14.00
Cocktail ............................... $14.00
Claret-Wine ........................... $22.00
Cordial ................................ $30.00
Oyster Cocktail ....................... $12.00
Footed Ice Tea ........................ $20.00
Footed Tumbler, 9 oz. ................. $14.00
Footed Juice .......................... $14.00

### PILGRIM, Cutting 787, Blank 6023

Goblet .................................. $35.00
Saucer Champagne ..................... $32.00
Low Sherbet ........................... $30.00
Cocktail ............................... $32.00
Claret-Wine ........................... $38.00
Cordial ................................ $45.00
Oyster Cocktail ....................... $30.00
Footed Ice Tea ........................ $35.00
Footed Tumbler, 9 oz. ................. $30.00
Footed Juice .......................... $30.00

### CHIPPENDALE, Cutting 788, Blank 6023

Goblet .................................. $20.00
Saucer Champagne ..................... $18.00
Low Sherbet ........................... $14.00
Cocktail ............................... $16.00
Claret-Wine ........................... $22.00
Cordial ................................ $30.00
Oyster Cocktail ....................... $12.00
Footed Ice Tea ........................ $20.00
Footed Tumbler, 9 oz. ................. $14.00
Footed Juice .......................... $14.00

### CATHEDRAL, Cutting 792, Blank 6023

Goblet .................................. $20.00
Saucer Champagne ..................... $18.00
Low Sherbet ........................... $14.00
Cocktail ............................... $16.00
Claret-Wine ........................... $22.00
Cordial ................................ $30.00
Oyster Cocktail ....................... $12.00
Footed Ice Tea ........................ $20.00
Footed Tumbler, 9 oz. ................. $14.00
Footed Juice .......................... $14.00

### SPIRE, Cutting 793, Blank 6023

Goblet .................................. $20.00
Saucer Champagne ..................... $18.00
Low Sherbet ........................... $14.00
Cocktail ............................... $16.00
Claret-Wine ........................... $22.00

Cordial ................................ $30.00
Oyster Cocktail ....................... $12.00
Footed Ice Tea ........................ $20.00
Footed Tumbler, 9 oz. ................. $14.00
Footed Juice .......................... $14.00

### BRIGHTON, Cutting 801, Blank 6023

Goblet .................................. $20.00
Saucer Champagne ..................... $18.00
Low Sherbet ........................... $14.00
Cocktail ............................... $16.00
Claret-Wine ........................... $22.00
Cordial ................................ $30.00
Oyster Cocktail ....................... $12.00
Footed Ice Tea ........................ $20.00
Footed Tumbler, 9 oz. ................. $14.00
Footed Juice .......................... $14.00

### WENTWORTH, Cutting 802, Blank 6023

Goblet .................................. $20.00
Saucer Champagne ..................... $18.00
Low Sherbet ........................... $14.00
Cocktail ............................... $18.00
Claret-Wine ........................... $22.00
Cordial ................................ $30.00
Oyster Cocktail ....................... $12.00
Footed Ice Tea ........................ $20.00
Footed Tumbler, 9 oz. ................. $14.00
Footed Juice .......................... $14.00

### WAKEFIELD, Cutting 820, Blank 6023

Goblet .................................. $26.00
Saucer Champagne ..................... $22.00
Low Sherbet ........................... $14.00
Cocktail ............................... $22.00
Claret-Wine ........................... $28.00
Cordial ................................ $40.00
Oyster Cocktail ....................... $14.00
Footed Ice Tea ........................ $26.00
Footed Tumbler, 9 oz. ................. $20.00
Footed Juice .......................... $20.00

### REVERE, Cutting 825, Blank 6023

Goblet .................................. $20.00
Saucer Champagne ..................... $18.00
Low Sherbet ........................... $14.00
Cocktail ............................... $16.00
Claret-Wine ........................... $22.00
Cordial ................................ $30.00
Oyster Cocktail ....................... $12.00
Footed Ice Tea ........................ $20.00
Footed Juice .......................... $14.00

### CELLINI, Blank 6024

Goblet .................................. $35.00

Saucer Champagne ..................... $30.00
Low Sherbet ........................... $24.00
Cocktail ............................... $30.00
Claret ................................. $40.00
Wine ................................... $40.00
Cordial ................................ $48.00
Oyster Cocktail ....................... $26.00
Footed Ice Tea ........................ $35.00
Footed Tumbler, 9 oz. ................. $26.00
Footed Juice .......................... $26.00

### WILLOWMERE, Etching 333, Blank 6024

Goblet .................................. $45.00
Saucer Champagne ..................... $40.00
Low Sherbet ........................... $30.00
Cocktail ............................... $38.00
Claret ................................. $50.00
Wine ................................... $48.00
Cordial ................................ $65.00
Oyster Cocktail ....................... $28.00
Footed Ice Tea ........................ $45.00
Footed Tumbler, 9 oz. ................. $30.00
Footed Juice .......................... $30.00

### REGAL, Cutting 782, Blank 6024

Goblet .................................. $35.00
Saucer Champagne ..................... $30.00
Low Sherbet ........................... $24.00
Cocktail ............................... $30.00
Claret ................................. $40.00
Wine ................................... $40.00
Cordial ................................ $48.00
Oyster Cocktail ....................... $22.00
Footed Ice Tea ........................ $35.00
Footed Tumbler, 9 oz. ................. $26.00
Footed Juice .......................... $26.00

### CORAL PEARL, Decoration 623, Blank 6024

Goblet .................................. $35.00
Saucer Champagne ..................... $32.00
Low Sherbet ........................... $24.00
Cocktail ............................... $26.00
Claret ................................. $40.00
Wine ................................... $38.00
Cordial ................................ $45.00
Oyster Cocktail ....................... $22.00
Footed Ice Tea ........................ $35.00
Footed Tumbler, 9 oz. ................. $26.00
Footed Juice .......................... $28.00

### CABOT, Blank 6025, 6025/1
No Optic

Goblet .................................. $16.00
Sherbet ................................ $10.00
Cocktail ............................... $10.00

Claret-Wine.............................. $14.00
Cordial .................................... $20.00
Oyster Cocktail......................... $8.00
Footed Ice Tea.......................... $14.00
Footed Juice ............................. $8.00

### Dimple Optic
Goblet...................................... $16.00
Sherbet..................................... $12.00
Cocktail ................................... $12.00
Claret-Wine.............................. $16.00
Cordial .................................... $20.00
Oyster Cocktail......................... $10.00
Footed Ice Tea.......................... $16.00
Footed Juice ............................. $12.00

### PLYMOUTH, *Etching 336, Blank 6025*
Goblet...................................... $38.00
Sherbet..................................... $34.00
Cocktail ................................... $32.00
Claret-Wine.............................. $45.00
Cordial .................................... $65.00
Oyster Cocktail......................... $30.00
Footed Ice Tea.......................... $38.00
Footed Juice ............................. $30.00

### SAMPLER, *Etching 337, Blank 6025*
Goblet...................................... $34.00
Sherbet..................................... $32.00
Cocktail ................................... $32.00
Claret-Wine.............................. $36.00
Cordial .................................... $45.00
Oyster Cocktail......................... $28.00
Footed Ice Tea.......................... $34.00
Footed Juice ............................. $30.00

### SUFFOLK, *Cutting 789, Blank 6025*
Goblet...................................... $20.00
Sherbet..................................... $16.00
Cocktail ................................... $16.00
Claret-Wine.............................. $25.00
Cordial .................................... $30.00
Oyster Cocktail......................... $12.00
Footed Ice Tea.......................... $18.00
Footed Juice ............................. $14.00

### HAWTHORN, *Cutting 790, Blank 6025*
Goblet...................................... $16.00
Sherbet..................................... $12.00
Cocktail ................................... $12.00
Claret-Wine.............................. $18.00
Cordial .................................... $22.00
Oyster Cocktail......................... $10.00
Footed Ice Tea.......................... $16.00
Footed Juice ............................. $10.00

### GEORGIAN, *Cutting 791, Blank 6025*
Goblet...................................... $20.00

Sherbet..................................... $16.00
Cocktail ................................... $16.00
Claret-Wine.............................. $25.00
Cordial .................................... $30.00
Oyster Cocktail......................... $12.00
Footed Ice Tea.......................... $18.00
Footed Juice ............................. $14.00

### MINUET, *Cutting 826, Blank 6025*
Goblet...................................... $30.00
Sherbet..................................... $26.00
Cocktail ................................... $26.00
Claret-Wine.............................. $36.00
Cordial .................................... $40.00
Oyster Cocktail......................... $22.00
Footed Ice Tea.......................... $30.00
Footed Juice ............................. $24.00

### GREENBRIAR, *Blank 6026*
#### Regular Optic
Goblet...................................... $25.00
Low Goblet............................... $22.00
Saucer Champagne..................... $24.00
Low Sherbet.............................. $20.00
Cocktail ................................... $23.00
Claret-Wine.............................. $30.00
Cordial .................................... $35.00
Oyster Cocktail......................... $18.00
Footed Ice Tea.......................... $25.00
Footed Juice ............................. $18.00

#### Niagara Optic
Goblet...................................... $25.00
Low Goblet............................... $22.00
Saucer Champagne..................... $24.00
Low Sherbet.............................. $20.00
Cocktail ................................... $22.00
Claret-Wine.............................. $30.00
Cordial .................................... $38.00
Oyster Cocktail......................... $18.00
Footed Ice Tea.......................... $34.00
Footed Juice ............................. $18.00

### CHINTZ, *Etching 338, Blank 6026*
Goblet...................................... $38.00
Low Goblet............................... $30.00
Saucer Champagne..................... $34.00
Low Sherbet.............................. $26.00
Cocktail ................................... $34.00
Claret-Wine.............................. $42.00
Cordial .................................... $52.00
Oyster Cocktail......................... $26.00
Footed Ice Tea.......................... $38.00
Footed Juice ............................. $30.00

### MULBERRY, *Cutting 799, Blank 6026*
Goblet...................................... $30.00
Low Goblet............................... $22.00

Saucer Champagne..................... $26.00
Low Sherbet.............................. $20.00
Cocktail ................................... $26.00
Claret-Wine.............................. $38.00
Cordial .................................... $50.00
Oyster Cocktail......................... $18.00
Footed Ice Tea.......................... $30.00
Footed Juice ............................. $22.00

### SELMA, *Cutting 800, Blank 6026*
Goblet...................................... $25.00
Low Goblet............................... $22.00
Saucer Champagne..................... $24.00
Low Sherbet.............................. $18.00
Cocktail ................................... $22.00
Claret-Wine.............................. $30.00
Cordial .................................... $35.00
Oyster Cocktail......................... $16.00
Footed Ice Tea.......................... $25.00
Footed Juice ............................. $20.00

### RHEIMS, *Cutting 803, Blank 6026*
Goblet...................................... $25.00
Low Goblet............................... $20.00
Saucer Champagne..................... $24.00
Low Sherbet.............................. $18.00
Cocktail ................................... $22.00
Claret-Wine.............................. $30.00
Cordial .................................... $38.00
Oyster Cocktail......................... $18.00
Footed Ice Tea.......................... $25.00
Footed Juice ............................. $20.00

### ENVOY, *Blank 6027*
Goblet...................................... $24.00
Saucer Champagne..................... $22.00
Low Sherbet.............................. $18.00
Cocktail ................................... $22.00
Wine ....................................... $28.00
Cordial .................................... $35.00
Oyster Cocktail......................... $16.00
Footed Ice Tea.......................... $22.00
Footed Juice ............................. $16.00

### SALON, *Cutting 804, Blank 6027*
Goblet...................................... $25.00
Saucer Champagne..................... $24.00
Low Sherbet.............................. $20.00
Cocktail ................................... $22.00
Wine ....................................... $28.00
Cordial .................................... $38.00
Oyster Cocktail......................... $16.00
Footed Ice Tea.......................... $24.00
Footed Juice ............................. $16.00

### ALOHA, *Cutting 805, Blank 6027*
Goblet...................................... $24.00

Saucer Champagne......................... $22.00
Low Sherbet.................................. $18.00
Cocktail ....................................... $22.00
Wine ............................................ $28.00
Cordial ........................................ $38.00
Oyster Cocktail ............................ $16.00
Footed Ice Tea ............................. $34.00
Footed Juice ................................ $16.00

### CADENCE, Cutting 806, Blank 6027
Goblet.......................................... $24.00
Saucer Champagne......................... $22.00
Low Sherbet.................................. $18.00
Cocktail ....................................... $22.00
Wine ............................................ $28.00
Cordial ........................................ $38.00
Oyster Cocktail ............................ $16.00
Footed Ice Tea ............................. $24.00
Footed Juice ................................ $16.00

### PRINCESS, Cutting 824, Blank 6027
Goblet.......................................... $25.00
Low Sherbet.................................. $18.00
Cocktail ....................................... $20.00
Wine ............................................ $28.00
Cordial ........................................ $35.00
Oyster Cocktail ............................ $16.00
Footed Ice Tea ............................. $24.00
Footed Juice ................................ $16.00

### FLORIN, Decoration 619, Blank 6027
Goblet.......................................... $25.00
Saucer Champagne......................... $22.00
Low Sherbet.................................. $18.00
Cocktail ....................................... $20.00
Wine ............................................ $28.00
Cordial ........................................ $35.00
Oyster Cocktail ............................ $16.00
Footed Ice Tea ............................. $24.00
Footed Juice ................................ $16.00

### CHALICE, Blank 6029
Goblet.......................................... $30.00
Saucer Champagne......................... $28.00
Cocktail ....................................... $30.00
Claret........................................... $30.00
Wine ............................................ $30.00
Cordial ........................................ $35.00
Oyster Cocktail ............................ $28.00

### SAYBROOKE, Cutting 813, Blank 6029
Goblet.......................................... $30.00
Saucer Champagne......................... $30.00
Cocktail ....................................... $30.00
Claret........................................... $30.00
Wine ............................................ $30.00

Cordial ........................................ $35.00
Oyster Cocktail ............................ $28.00

### ASTRID, Blank 6030, WAVEMERE, Blank 6030/3
Goblet.......................................... $30.00
Low Goblet ................................... $28.00
Saucer Champagne......................... $28.00
Low Sherbet.................................. $25.00
Cocktail ....................................... $26.00
Claret-Wine.................................. $30.00
Cordial ........................................ $35.00
Oyster Cocktail ............................ $20.00
Footed Ice Tea ............................. $30.00
Footed Juice ................................ $20.00

### BUTTERCUP, Etching 340, Blank 6030
Goblet.......................................... $38.00
Low Goblet ................................... $34.00
Saucer Champagne......................... $36.00
Low Sherbet.................................. $26.00
Cocktail ....................................... $34.00
Claret-Wine.................................. $48.00
Cordial ........................................ $58.00
Oyster Cocktail ............................ $24.00
Footed Ice Tea ............................. $38.00
Footed Juice ................................ $28.00

### CHRISTIANA, Cutting 814, Blank 6030
Goblet.......................................... $34.00
Low Goblet ................................... $30.00
Saucer Champagne......................... $32.00
Low Sherbet.................................. $22.00
Cocktail ....................................... $30.00
Claret-Wine.................................. $38.00
Cordial ........................................ $54.00
Oyster Cocktail ............................ $20.00
Footed Ice Tea ............................. $34.00
Footed Juice ................................ $22.00

### HOLLY, Cutting 815, Blank 6030
Goblet.......................................... $34.00
Low Goblet ................................... $30.00
Saucer Champagne......................... $30.00
Low Sherbet.................................. $22.00
Cocktail ....................................... $30.00
Claret-Wine.................................. $38.00
Cordial ........................................ $52.00
Oyster Cocktail ............................ $20.00
Footed Ice Tea ............................. $34.00
Footed Juice ................................ $24.00

### GADROON, Cutting 816, Blank 6030
Goblet.......................................... $30.00

Cordial ........................................ $35.00
Oyster Cocktail ............................ $28.00

Low Goblet ................................... $28.00
Saucer Champagne......................... $28.00
Low Sherbet.................................. $25.00
Cocktail ....................................... $27.00
Claret-Wine.................................. $32.00
Cordial ........................................ $38.00
Oyster Cocktail ............................ $20.00
Footed Ice Tea ............................. $30.00
Footed Juice ................................ $20.00

### TRELLIS, Cutting 822, Blank 6030
Goblet.......................................... $30.00
Low Goblet ................................... $28.00
Saucer Champagne......................... $28.00
Low Sherbet.................................. $25.00
Cocktail ....................................... $26.00
Claret-Wine.................................. $30.00
Cordial ........................................ $38.00
Oyster Cocktail ............................ $20.00
Footed Ice Tea ............................. $30.00
Footed Juice ................................ $20.00

### Blank 6031
Goblet.......................................... $25.00
Low Goblet ................................... $23.00
Saucer Champagne......................... $23.00
Low Sherbet.................................. $20.00
Cocktail ....................................... $22.00
Claret-Wine.................................. $28.00
Cordial ........................................ $35.00
Oyster Cocktail ............................ $20.00
Footed Ice Tea ............................. $25.00
Footed Juice ................................ $20.00

### MOUNT VERNON, Cutting 817, Blank 6031
Goblet.......................................... $24.00
Low Goblet ................................... $20.00
Saucer Champagne......................... $20.00
Low Sherbet.................................. $16.00
Cocktail ....................................... $16.00
Claret-Wine.................................. $26.00
Cordial ........................................ $35.00
Oyster Cocktail ............................ $16.00
Footed Ice Tea ............................. $22.00
Footed Juice ................................ $16.00

### TEMPO, Blank 6032
Goblet.......................................... $25.00
Saucer Champagne......................... $23.00
Low Sherbet.................................. $20.00
Cocktail ....................................... $22.00
Claret-Wine.................................. $28.00
Cordial ........................................ $35.00
Oyster Cocktail ............................ $20.00

Footed Ice Tea ................................ $25.00
Footed Juice ................................... $20.00

### FORMALITY, Cutting 818, Blank 6032

Goblet ............................................. $25.00
Saucer Champagne ....................... $23.00
Low Sherbet .................................. $20.00
Cocktail ......................................... $22.00
Claret ............................................. $30.00
Wine ............................................... $30.00
Cordial ........................................... $35.00
Oyster Cocktail ............................ $20.00
Footed Ice Tea .............................. $25.00
Footed Juice .................................. $20.00

### GREEK KEY, Cutting 819, Blank 6032

Goblet ............................................. $30.00
Saucer Champagne ....................... $28.00
Low Sherbet .................................. $25.00
Cocktail ......................................... $25.00
Claret ............................................. $34.00
Wine ............................................... $34.00
Cordial ........................................... $40.00
Oyster Cocktail ............................ $20.00
Footed Ice Tea .............................. $28.00
Footed Juice .................................. $20.00

### MADEMOISELLE, Blank 6033

Goblet ............................................. $20.00
High Sherbet ................................. $18.00
Low Sherbet .................................. $14.00
Parfait ............................................ $18.00
Cocktail ......................................... $18.00
Claret-Wine .................................. $23.00
Cordial ........................................... $25.00
Oyster Cocktail ............................ $10.00
Footed Ice Tea .............................. $18.00
Footed Juice .................................. $10.00

### BOUQUET, Etching 342, Blank 6033

Goblet ............................................. $32.00
High Sherbet ................................. $28.00
Low Sherbet .................................. $22.00
Parfait ............................................ $28.00
Cocktail ......................................... $24.00
Claret-Wine .................................. $34.00
Cordial ........................................... $40.00
Oyster Cocktail ............................ $20.00
Footed Ice Tea .............................. $32.00
Footed Juice .................................. $23.00

### SPINET, Cutting 821, Blank 6033

Goblet ............................................. $22.00
High Sherbet ................................. $20.00
Low Sherbet .................................. $16.00
Parfait ............................................ $20.00

Cocktail ......................................... $20.00
Claret-Wine .................................. $26.00
Cordial ........................................... $35.00
Oyster Cocktail ............................ $14.00
Footed Ice Tea .............................. $20.00
Footed Juice .................................. $14.00

### SPRITE, Cutting 823, Blank 6033

Goblet ............................................. $22.00
High Sherbet ................................. $20.00
Low Sherbet .................................. $16.00
Parfait ............................................ $20.00
Cocktail ......................................... $20.00
Claret-Wine .................................. $26.00
Cordial ........................................... $35.00
Oyster Cocktail ............................ $14.00
Footed Ice Tea .............................. $20.00
Footed Juice .................................. $14.00

### REFLECTION, Decoration 625, Blank 6033

Goblet ............................................. $20.00
High Sherbet ................................. $18.00
Low Sherbet .................................. $14.00
Parfait ............................................ $18.00
Cocktail ......................................... $14.00
Claret-Wine .................................. $25.00
Cordial ........................................... $28.00
Oyster Cocktail ............................ $10.00
Footed Ice Tea .............................. $18.00
Footed Juice .................................. $10.00

### RUTLEDGE, Blank 6036

Goblet ............................................. $20.00
High Sherbet ................................. $18.00
Low Sherbet .................................. $14.00
Parfait ............................................ $18.00
Cocktail ......................................... $18.00
Claret-Wine .................................. $23.00
Cordial ........................................... $25.00
Oyster Cocktail ............................ $10.00
Footed Ice Tea .............................. $20.00
Footed Juice .................................. $10.00

### CAMELIA, Etching 344, Blank 6036

Goblet ............................................. $32.00
High Sherbet ................................. $28.00
Low Sherbet .................................. $20.00
Parfait ............................................ $30.00
Cocktail ......................................... $26.00
Claret-Wine .................................. $35.00
Cordial ........................................... $40.00
Oyster Cocktail ............................ $20.00
Footed Ice Tea .............................. $32.00
Footed Juice .................................. $22.00

### ROSE, Cutting 827, Blank 6036

Goblet ............................................. $32.00

High Sherbet ................................. $28.00
Low Sherbet .................................. $20.00
Parfait ............................................ $30.00
Cocktail ......................................... $27.00
Claret-Wine .................................. $34.00
Cordial ........................................... $40.00
Oyster Cocktail ............................ $20.00
Footed Ice Tea .............................. $32.00
Footed Juice .................................. $24.00

### BALLET, Cutting 828, Blank 6036

Goblet ............................................. $24.00
High Sherbet ................................. $20.00
Low Sherbet .................................. $16.00
Parfait ............................................ $22.00
Cocktail ......................................... $20.00
Claret-Wine .................................. $25.00
Cordial ........................................... $30.00
Oyster Cocktail ............................ $12.00
Footed Ice Tea .............................. $20.00
Footed Juice .................................. $14.00

### CHATHAM, Cutting 829, Blank 6036

Goblet ............................................. $24.00
High Sherbet ................................. $20.00
Low Sherbet .................................. $16.00
Parfait ............................................ $22.00
Cocktail ......................................... $20.00
Claret-Wine .................................. $25.00
Cordial ........................................... $30.00
Oyster Cocktail ............................ $12.00
Footed Ice Tea .............................. $20.00
Footed Juice .................................. $14.00

### SILVER FLUTES, Blank 6037

Goblet ............................................. $32.00
Low Goblet .................................... $28.00
High Sherbet ................................. $28.00
Low Sherbet .................................. $24.00
Parfait ............................................ $34.00
Cocktail ......................................... $26.00
Claret-Wine .................................. $38.00
Cordial ........................................... $47.00
Oyster Cocktail ............................ $22.00
Footed Ice Tea .............................. $30.00
Footed Juice .................................. $22.00

### HEATHER, Etching 343, Blank 6037

Goblet ............................................. $36.00
Low Goblet .................................... $30.00
High Sherbet ................................. $32.00
Low Sherbet .................................. $25.00
Parfait ............................................ $38.00
Cocktail ......................................... $30.00
Claret-Wine .................................. $47.00
Cordial ........................................... $54.00
Oyster Cocktail ............................ $24.00

Footed Ice Tea ............................ $36.00
Footed Juice ............................... $27.00

### CAPRI, Blank 6045

Goblet ........................................ $22.00
Sherbet ...................................... $20.00
Cocktail ..................................... $20.00
Claret-Wine ............................... $22.00
Cordial ...................................... $25.00
Footed Ice Tea ........................... $22.00
Footed Juice ............................... $20.00

### RONDO, Cutting 830, Blank 6045

Goblet ........................................ $22.00
Sherbet ...................................... $20.00
Cocktail ..................................... $20.00
Claret-Wine ............................... $22.00
Cordial ...................................... $25.00
Footed Ice Tea ........................... $22.00
Footed Juice ............................... $20.00

### MARQUISE, Cutting 831, Blank 6045

Goblet ........................................ $22.00
Sherbet ...................................... $20.00
Cocktail ..................................... $20.00
Claret-Wine ............................... $22.00
Cordial ...................................... $25.00
Footed Ice Tea ........................... $22.00
Footed Juice ............................... $20.00

### WINDSOR, Blank 6049

Goblet ........................................ $20.00
High Sherbet .............................. $18.00
Low Sherbet ............................... $14.00
Parfait ....................................... $18.00
Cocktail ..................................... $16.00
Claret ........................................ $20.00
Wine .......................................... $20.00
Cordial ...................................... $22.00
Oyster Cocktail .......................... $12.00
Footed Ice Tea ........................... $18.00
Footed Juice ............................... $12.00

### STARFLOWER, Etching 345, Blank 6049

Goblet ........................................ $22.00
High Sherbet .............................. $20.00
Low Sherbet ............................... $18.00
Parfait ....................................... $20.00
Cocktail ..................................... $18.00
Claret ........................................ $25.00
Wine .......................................... $25.00
Cordial ...................................... $30.00
Oyster Cocktail .......................... $14.00
Footed Ice Tea ........................... $20.00
Footed Juice ............................... $14.00

### AVALON, Cutting 832, Blank 6049

Goblet ........................................ $22.00
High Sherbet .............................. $20.00
Low Sherbet ............................... $18.00
Parfait ....................................... $20.00
Cocktail ..................................... $18.00
Claret ........................................ $25.00
Wine .......................................... $25.00
Cordial ...................................... $30.00
Oyster Cocktail .......................... $14.00
Footed Ice Tea ........................... $20.00
Footed Juice ............................... $14.00

### BRIDAL WREATH, Cutting 833, Blank 6049

Goblet ........................................ $25.00
High Sherbet .............................. $22.00
Low Sherbet ............................... $18.00
Parfait ....................................... $25.00
Cocktail ..................................... $18.00
Claret ........................................ $28.00
Wine .......................................... $28.00
Cordial ...................................... $38.00
Oyster Cocktail .......................... $16.00
Footed Ice Tea ........................... $22.00
Footed Juice ............................... $16.00

### RINGLET, Blank 6051
### COURTSHIP, Blank 6051½

Goblet ........................................ $18.00
Sherbet ...................................... $14.00
Cocktail ..................................... $14.00
Claret-Wine ............................... $18.00
Cordial ...................................... $20.00
Oyster Cocktail .......................... $10.00
Footed Ice Tea ........................... $18.00
Footed Juice ............................... $10.00

### NOSEGAY, Cutting 834, Blank 6051½

Goblet ........................................ $30.00
Sherbet ...................................... $24.00
Cocktail ..................................... $22.00
Claret-Wine ............................... $35.00
Cordial ...................................... $38.00
Oyster Cocktail .......................... $20.00
Footed Ice Tea ........................... $32.00
Footed Juice ............................... $22.00

### FOSTORIA WHEAT, Cutting 837, Blank 6051½

Goblet ........................................ $30.00
Sherbet ...................................... $24.00
Cocktail ..................................... $22.00
Claret-Wine ............................... $35.00
Cordial ...................................... $38.00
Oyster Cocktail .......................... $20.00

### Footed Ice Tea ............................ $30.00
Footed Juice ............................... $24.00

### BRACELET, Cutting 838, Blank 6051½

Goblet ........................................ $22.00
Sherbet ...................................... $20.00
Cocktail ..................................... $18.00
Claret-Wine ............................... $25.00
Cordial ...................................... $30.00
Oyster Cocktail .......................... $14.00
Footed Ice Tea ........................... $22.00
Footed Juice ............................... $14.00

### PLUME, Cutting 839, Blank 6051½

Goblet ........................................ $20.00
Sherbet ...................................... $18.00
Cocktail ..................................... $18.00
Claret-Wine ............................... $23.00
Cordial ...................................... $28.00
Oyster Cocktail .......................... $12.00
Footed Ice Tea ........................... $20.00
Footed Juice ............................... $12.00

### WEDDING RING, Decoration 626, Blank 6051½

Goblet ........................................ $30.00
Sherbet ...................................... $24.00
Cocktail ..................................... $24.00
Claret-Wine ............................... $35.00
Cordial ...................................... $38.00
Oyster Cocktail .......................... $22.00
Footed Ice Tea ........................... $30.00
Footed Juice ............................... $24.00

### MOON RING, Blank 6052
### CONTINENTAL, Blank 6052½

Goblet ........................................ $18.00
Sherbet ...................................... $14.00
Cocktail ..................................... $14.00
Claret-Wine ............................... $18.00
Cordial ...................................... $20.00
Oyster Cocktail .......................... $10.00
Footed Ice Tea ........................... $18.00
Footed Juice ............................... $10.00

### THISTLE, Etching 346, Blank 6052½

Goblet ........................................ $25.00
Sherbet ...................................... $22.00
Cocktail ..................................... $22.00
Claret-Wine ............................... $28.00
Cordial ...................................... $35.00
Oyster Cocktail .......................... $20.00
Footed Ice Tea ........................... $25.00
Footed Juice ............................... $20.00

### PINE, Cutting 835, Blank 6052½

Goblet ........................................ $20.00

Sherbet ................................. $18.00
Cocktail ................................ $18.00
Claret-Wine ......................... $28.00
Cordial ................................. $22.00
Oyster Cocktail .................... $14.00
Footed Ice Tea ..................... $20.00
Footed Juice ......................... $14.00

### INGRID, Cutting 836,
### Blank 6052½

Goblet ................................. $20.00
Sherbet ................................. $18.00
Cocktail ................................ $16.00
Claret-Wine ......................... $28.00
Cordial ................................. $30.00
Oyster Cocktail .................... $14.00
Footed Ice Tea ..................... $20.00
Footed Juice ......................... $14.00

### MARILYN,
### Blank 6055

Goblet ................................. $20.00
Sherbet ................................. $18.00
Cocktail ................................ $16.00
Claret-Wine ......................... $24.00
Cordial ................................. $25.00
Oyster Cocktail .................... $12.00
Footed Ice Tea ..................... $20.00
Footed Juice ......................... $12.00

### RHAPSODY, Blank 6055½
Crystal

Goblet ................................. $18.00
Sherbet ................................. $16.00
Cocktail ................................ $16.00
Claret-Wine ......................... $22.00
Cordial ................................. $24.00
Oyster Cocktail .................... $12.00
Footed Ice Tea ..................... $18.00
Footed Juice ......................... $12.00

Turquoise

Goblet ................................. $24.00
Sherbet ................................. $20.00
Cocktail ................................ $20.00
Claret-Wine ......................... $28.00
Cordial ................................. $35.00
Oyster Cocktail .................... $18.00
Footed Ice Tea ..................... $24.00
Footed Juice ......................... $18.00

### CIRCLET, Cutting 840,
### Blank 6055½

Goblet ................................. $18.00
Sherbet ................................. $14.00
Cocktail ................................ $16.00
Claret-Wine ......................... $25.00
Cordial ................................. $25.00

Oyster Cocktail .................... $12.00
Footed Ice Tea ..................... $18.00
Footed Juice ......................... $12.00

### SPRAY, Cutting 841,
### Blank 6055½

Goblet ................................. $30.00
Sherbet ................................. $25.00
Cocktail ................................ $25.00
Claret-Wine ......................... $35.00
Cordial ................................. $40.00
Oyster Cocktail .................... $22.00
Footed Ice Tea ..................... $30.00
Footed Juice ......................... $24.00

### SHELL PEARL, Decoration 633,
### Blank 6055

Goblet ................................. $30.00
Sherbet ................................. $25.00
Cocktail ................................ $25.00
Claret-Wine ......................... $35.00
Cordial ................................. $40.00
Oyster Cocktail .................... $22.00
Footed Ice Tea ..................... $30.00
Footed Juice ......................... $24.00

### ANNIVERSARY, Decoration 634,
### Blank 6055½

Goblet ................................. $22.00
Sherbet ................................. $18.00
Cocktail ................................ $18.00
Claret-Wine ......................... $25.00
Cordial ................................. $26.00
Oyster Cocktail .................... $16.00
Footed Ice Tea ..................... $22.00
Footed Juice ......................... $16.00

### DIADEM,
### Blank 6056

Goblet ................................. $22.00
Sherbet ................................. $20.00
Cocktail ................................ $20.00
Claret-Wine ......................... $24.00
Cordial ................................. $28.00
Oyster Cocktail .................... $16.00
Footed Ice Tea ..................... $22.00
Footed Juice ......................... $16.00

### CHALICE, Blank 6059
Crystal

Goblet ................................. $22.00
Sherbet ................................. $20.00
Cocktail/Wine/Seafood .......... $22.00
Cordial ................................. $25.00
Footed Ice Tea ..................... $22.00
Footed Juice ......................... $20.00

Ebony

Goblet ................................. $26.00
Sherbet ................................. $22.00
Cocktail/Wine/Seafood .......... $24.00
Cordial ................................. $38.00
Footed Ice Tea ..................... $26.00
Footed Juice ......................... $22.00

### CONTOUR, Blank 6060
Crystal

Goblet ................................. $18.00
Sherbet ................................. $16.00
Cocktail/Wine/Seafood .......... $20.00
Cordial ................................. $20.00
Footed Ice Tea ..................... $18.00
Footed Juice ......................... $16.00

Pink

Goblet ................................. $35.00
Sherbet ................................. $30.00
Cocktail/Wine/Seafood .......... $40.00
Cordial ................................. $45.00
Footed Ice Tea ..................... $35.00
Footed Juice ......................... $30.00

### SYLVAN, Crystal Print 1,
### Blank 6060

Goblet ................................. $20.00
Sherbet ................................. $18.00
Cocktail/Wine/Seafood .......... $22.00
Cordial ................................. $25.00
Footed Ice Tea ..................... $20.00
Footed Juice ......................... $18.00

### SPRING, Cutting 844, Blank 6060

Goblet ................................. $20.00
Sherbet ................................. $18.00
Cocktail/Wine/Seafood .......... $22.00
Cordial ................................. $25.00
Footed Ice Tea ..................... $20.00
Footed Juice ......................... $18.00

### WINDFALL, Cutting 870, Blank 6060

Goblet ................................. $20.00
Sherbet ................................. $18.00
Cocktail/Wine/Seafood .......... $22.00
Cordial ................................. $25.00
Footed Ice Tea ..................... $20.00
Footed Juice ......................... $18.00

### LYRIC, Blank 6061
Crystal

Goblet ................................. $22.00
Sherbet ................................. $20.00
Cocktail/Wine/Seafood .......... $22.00
Cordial ................................. $25.00

| | |
|---|---|
| Footed Ice Tea | $22.00 |
| Footed Juice | $20.00 |

### Pink

| | |
|---|---|
| Goblet | $38.00 |
| Sherbet | $34.00 |
| Cocktail/Wine/Seafood | $43.00 |
| Cordial | $44.00 |
| Footed Ice Tea | $38.00 |
| Footed Juice | $34.00 |

### SKYFLOWER, Crystal Print 2, Blank 6061

| | |
|---|---|
| Goblet | $22.00 |
| Sherbet | $20.00 |
| Cocktail/Wine/Seafood | $22.00 |
| Cordial | $25.00 |
| Footed Ice Tea | $22.00 |
| Footed Juice | $20.00 |

### REGAL, Cutting 842, Blank 6061

| | |
|---|---|
| Goblet | $22.00 |
| Sherbet | $20.00 |
| Cocktail/Wine/Seafood | $22.00 |
| Cordial | $25.00 |
| Footed Ice Tea | $22.00 |
| Footed Juice | $20.00 |

### CREST, Cutting 843, Blank 6061

| | |
|---|---|
| Goblet | $22.00 |
| Sherbet | $20.00 |
| Cocktail/Wine/Seafood | $22.00 |
| Cordial | $25.00 |
| Footed Ice Tea | $22.00 |
| Footed Juice | $20.00 |

### PATRICIAN, Blank 6064

| | |
|---|---|
| Goblet | $28.00 |
| Champagne | $25.00 |
| Low Sherbet | $22.00 |
| Cocktail | $20.00 |
| Claret | $30.00 |
| Wine | $28.00 |
| Cordial | $34.00 |
| Seafood Cocktail | $32.00 |
| Footed Ice Tea | $28.00 |
| Footed Juice | $18.00 |

### ELEGANCE, Blank 6064½

| | |
|---|---|
| Goblet | $34.00 |
| Champagne | $30.00 |
| Low Sherbet | $22.00 |
| Cocktail | $25.00 |
| Claret | $36.00 |
| Wine | $34.00 |
| Cordial | $37.00 |
| Seafood Cocktail | $38.00 |

| | |
|---|---|
| Footed Ice Tea | $34.00 |
| Footed Juice | $20.00 |

### ROSETTE, Crystal Print 3, Blank 6064

| | |
|---|---|
| Goblet | $22.00 |
| Champagne | $20.00 |
| Low Sherbet | $16.00 |
| Cocktail | $20.00 |
| Claret | $22.00 |
| Wine | $22.00 |
| Cordial | $25.00 |
| Seafood Cocktail | $20.00 |
| Footed Ice Tea | $20.00 |
| Footed Juice | $16.00 |

### MAYTIME, Cutting 845, Blank 6064

| | |
|---|---|
| Goblet | $24.00 |
| Champagne | $20.00 |
| Low Sherbet | $18.00 |
| Cocktail | $18.00 |
| Claret | $24.00 |
| Wine | $24.00 |
| Cordial | $28.00 |
| Seafood Cocktail | $20.00 |
| Footed Ice Tea | $20.00 |
| Footed Juice | $14.00 |

### SKYLARK, Cutting 846, Blank 6064

| | |
|---|---|
| Goblet | $22.00 |
| Champagne | $20.00 |
| Low Sherbet | $18.00 |
| Cocktail | $18.00 |
| Claret | $22.00 |
| Wine | $22.00 |
| Cordial | $25.00 |
| Seafood Cocktail | $20.00 |
| Footed Ice Tea | $20.00 |
| Footed Juice | $14.00 |

### CASCADE, Decoration 636, Blank 6064½

| | |
|---|---|
| Goblet | $26.00 |
| Champagne | $22.00 |
| Low Sherbet | $20.00 |
| Cocktail | $20.00 |
| Claret | $26.00 |
| Wine | $26.00 |
| Cordial | $32.00 |
| Seafood Cocktail | $35.00 |
| Footed Ice Tea | $26.00 |
| Footed Juice | $20.00 |

### SYMPHONY, Blank 6065

| | |
|---|---|
| Goblet | $35.00 |
| Sherbet | $32.00 |
| Cocktail/Wine/Seafood | $35.00 |
| Cordial | $40.00 |

| | |
|---|---|
| Footed Ice Tea | $35.00 |
| Footed Juice | $30.00 |

### LYNWOOD, Crystal Print 4, Blank 6065

| | |
|---|---|
| Goblet | $35.00 |
| Sherbet | $32.00 |
| Cocktail/Wine/Seafood | $35.00 |
| Cordial | $42.00 |
| Footed Ice Tea | $35.00 |
| Footed Juice | $32.00 |

### LIVING ROSE, Crystal Print 5, Blank 6065

| | |
|---|---|
| Goblet | $35.00 |
| Sherbet | $32.00 |
| Cocktail/Wine/Seafood | $35.00 |
| Cordial | $45.00 |
| Footed Ice Tea | $35.00 |
| Footed Juice | $32.00 |

### BARONET, Cutting 847, Blank 6065

| | |
|---|---|
| Goblet | $35.00 |
| Sherbet | $32.00 |
| Cocktail/Wine/Seafood | $35.00 |
| Cordial | $42.00 |
| Footed Ice Tea | $35.00 |
| Footed Juice | $30.00 |

### SWIRL, Cutting 848, Blank 6065

| | |
|---|---|
| Goblet | $35.00 |
| Sherbet | $32.00 |
| Cocktail/Wine/Seafood | $35.00 |
| Cordial | $40.00 |
| Footed Ice Tea | $35.00 |
| Footed Juice | $30.00 |

### HERITAGE, Cutting 849, Blank 6065

| | |
|---|---|
| Goblet | $35.00 |
| Sherbet | $32.00 |
| Cocktail/Wine/Seafood | $35.00 |
| Cordial | $40.00 |
| Footed Ice Tea | $35.00 |
| Footed Juice | $30.00 |

### LEGACY, Decoration 635, Blank 6065

| | |
|---|---|
| Goblet | $37.00 |
| Sherbet | $34.00 |
| Cocktail/Wine/Seafood | $35.00 |
| Cordial | $44.00 |
| Footed Ice Tea | $37.00 |
| Footed Juice | $32.00 |

### AMBASSADOR, Decoration 637, Blank 6065

| | |
|---|---|
| Goblet | $37.00 |
| Sherbet | $34.00 |
| Cocktail/Wine/Seafood | $35.00 |
| Cordial | $44.00 |

Footed Ice Tea .............................. $37.00
Footed Juice ................................. $32.00

### PURITAN, Blank 6068
Goblet ........................................ $16.00
Sherbet ...................................... $14.00
Cocktail/Wine/Seafood ................. $16.00
Cordial ....................................... $20.00
Footed Ice Tea ............................ $16.00
Footed Juice ............................... $12.00

### VICTORIA, Blank 6068½
Goblet ........................................ $20.00
Sherbet ...................................... $18.00
Cocktail/Wine/Seafood ................. $20.00
Cordial ....................................... $30.00
Footed Ice Tea ............................ $20.00
Footed Juice ............................... $16.00

### AUTUMN, Cutting 850, Blank 6068
Goblet ........................................ $18.00
Sherbet ...................................... $16.00
Cocktail/Wine/Seafood ................. $18.00
Cordial ....................................... $30.00
Footed Ice Tea ............................ $18.00
Footed Juice ............................... $14.00

### STARDUST, Cutting 851, Blank 6068
Goblet ........................................ $18.00
Sherbet ...................................... $16.00
Cocktail/Wine/Seafood ................. $18.00
Cordial ....................................... $30.00
Footed Ice Tea ............................ $18.00
Footed Juice ............................... $14.00

### GOSSAMER, Cutting 852, Blank 6068
Goblet ........................................ $18.00
Sherbet ...................................... $16.00
Cocktail/Wine/Seafood ................. $18.00
Cordial ....................................... $30.00
Footed Ice Tea ............................ $18.00
Footed Juice ............................... $14.00

### DUCHESS, Cutting 853, Blank 6068
Goblet ........................................ $18.00
Sherbet ...................................... $16.00
Cocktail/Wine/Seafood ................. $18.00
Cordial ....................................... $30.00
Footed Ice Tea ............................ $18.00
Footed Juice ............................... $14.00

### APRIL LOVE, Cutting 866, Blank 6068
Goblet ........................................ $18.00
Sherbet ...................................... $16.00

Cocktail/Wine/Seafood ................. $18.00
Cordial ....................................... $30.00
Footed Ice Tea ............................ $18.00
Footed Juice ............................... $14.00

### RAINBOW, Decoration 638, Blank 6068½
Goblet ........................................ $25.00
Sherbet ...................................... $22.00
Cocktail/Wine/Seafood ................. $25.00
Cordial ....................................... $38.00
Footed Ice Tea ............................ $25.00
Footed Juice ............................... $20.00

### PRELUDE, Blank 6071
Goblet ........................................ $20.00
Sherbet ...................................... $18.00
Cocktail/Wine/Seafood ................. $22.00
Cordial ....................................... $26.00
Footed Ice Tea ............................ $20.00
Footed Juice ............................... $18.00

### WILDWOOD, Cutting 854, Blank 6071
Goblet ........................................ $20.00
Sherbet ...................................... $18.00
Cocktail/Wine/Seafood ................. $22.00
Cordial ....................................... $28.00
Footed Ice Tea ............................ $20.00
Footed Juice ............................... $18.00

### KIMBERLY, Cutting 855, Blank 6071
Goblet ........................................ $22.00
Sherbet ...................................... $20.00
Cocktail/Wine/Seafood ................. $25.00
Cordial ....................................... $35.00
Footed Ice Tea ............................ $22.00
Footed Juice ............................... $18.00

### CELESTE, Blank 6072
Goblet ........................................ $27.00
Sherbet ...................................... $22.00
Cocktail/Wine/Seafood ................. $25.00
Cordial ....................................... $34.00
Footed Ice Tea ............................ $27.00
Footed Juice ............................... $22.00

### MOONBEAM, Cutting 856, Blank 6072
Goblet ........................................ $28.00
Sherbet ...................................... $25.00
Cocktail/Wine/Seafood ................. $22.00
Cordial ....................................... $34.00
Footed Ice Tea ............................ $28.00
Footed Juice ............................... $20.00

### SERENITY, Cutting 868, Blank 6072
Goblet ........................................ $28.00
Sherbet ...................................... $22.00
Cocktail/Wine/Seafood ................. $25.00
Cordial ....................................... $34.00
Footed Ice Tea ............................ $28.00
Footed Juice ............................... $20.00

### MELODY, Cutting 881, Blank 6072
Goblet ........................................ $28.00
Sherbet ...................................... $22.00
Cocktail/Wine/Seafood ................. $25.00
Cordial ....................................... $34.00
Footed Ice Tea ............................ $28.00
Footed Juice ............................... $22.00

### BRIDAL BELLE, Decoration 639, Blank 6072
Goblet ........................................ $32.00
Sherbet ...................................... $28.00
Cocktail/Wine/Seafood ................. $32.00
Cordial ....................................... $40.00
Footed Ice Tea ............................ $32.00
Footed Juice ............................... $25.00

### ENCHANTMENT, Blank 6074
Goblet ........................................ $20.00
Sherbet ...................................... $18.00
Cocktail/Wine/Seafood ................. $20.00
Cordial ....................................... $22.00
Footed Ice Tea ............................ $20.00
Footed Juice ............................... $14.00

### SWEETBRIAR, Cutting 857, Blank 6074
Goblet ........................................ $22.00
Sherbet ...................................... $20.00
Cocktail/Wine/Seafood ................. $25.00
Cordial ....................................... $28.00
Footed Ice Tea ............................ $22.00
Footed Juice ............................... $16.00

### GOLDEN LOVE, Decoration 640, Blank 6074
Goblet ........................................ $25.00
Sherbet ...................................... $22.00
Cocktail/Wine/Seafood ................. $25.00
Cordial ....................................... $30.00
Footed Ice Tea ............................ $25.00
Footed Juice ............................... $16.00

### NORDIC, Blank 6077
Goblet ........................................ $18.00
Sherbet ...................................... $16.00

Cocktail/Wine ............................ $18.00
Cordial ..................................... $20.00
Footed Ice Tea ........................... $18.00
Footed Juice .............................. $12.00

### AMERICAN BEAUTY, Cutting 858, Blank 6077

Goblet ...................................... $28.00
Sherbet ..................................... $25.00
Cocktail/Wine/Seafood ............... $28.00
Cordial ..................................... $38.00
Footed Ice Tea ........................... $28.00
Footed Juice .............................. $24.00

### GARLAND, Cutting 859, Blank 6077

Goblet ...................................... $20.00
Sherbet ..................................... $18.00
Cocktail/Wine ............................ $20.00
Cordial ..................................... $22.00
Footed Ice Tea ........................... $20.00
Footed Juice .............................. $16.00

### ENCORE, Cutting 860, Blank 6077

Goblet ...................................... $20.00
Sherbet ..................................... $18.00
Cocktail/Wine ............................ $20.00
Cordial ..................................... $22.00
Footed Ice Tea ........................... $20.00
Footed Juice .............................. $16.00

### KENT, Blank 6079

Goblet ...................................... $18.00
Sherbet ..................................... $16.00
Cocktail .................................... $16.00
Claret-Wine ............................... $18.00
Cordial ..................................... $20.00
Footed Ice Tea ........................... $18.00
Footed Juice .............................. $14.00

### EMPRESS, Cutting 861, Blank 6079

Goblet ...................................... $20.00
Sherbet ..................................... $18.00
Cocktail .................................... $18.00
Claret-Wine ............................... $22.00
Cordial ..................................... $25.00
Footed Ice Tea ........................... $20.00
Footed Juice .............................. $15.00

### WILLIAMSBURG, Cutting 874, Blank 6079

Goblet ...................................... $20.00
Sherbet ..................................... $18.00
Cocktail .................................... $18.00
Claret-Wine ............................... $22.00
Cordial ..................................... $25.00
Footed Ice Tea ........................... $20.00
Footed Juice .............................. $16.00

### FASCINATION, Blank 6080

#### Crystal

Goblet ...................................... $18.00
Sherbet ..................................... $16.00
Cocktail .................................... $16.00
Claret-Wine ............................... $20.00
Cordial ..................................... $20.00
Footed Ice Tea ........................... $18.00
Footed Juice .............................. $14.00
Large Claret, 8 oz. ...................... $26.00
Large Claret, 6 oz. ...................... $22.00

#### Lilac

Goblet ...................................... $35.00
Sherbet ..................................... $30.00
Cocktail .................................... $30.00
Claret-Wine ............................... $40.00
Cordial ..................................... $47.00
Footed Ice Tea ........................... $35.00
Footed Juice .............................. $32.00
Large Claret, 8 oz. ...................... $45.00
Large Claret, 6 oz. ...................... $45.00

#### Ruby

Goblet ...................................... $47.00
Sherbet ..................................... $42.00
Cocktail .................................... $40.00
Claret-Wine ............................... $55.00
Cordial ..................................... $58.00
Footed Ice Tea ........................... $45.00
Footed Juice .............................. $34.00

### TRUE LOVE, Cutting 862, Blank 6080

Goblet ...................................... $20.00
Sherbet ..................................... $18.00
Cocktail .................................... $18.00
Claret-Wine ............................... $22.00
Cordial ..................................... $27.00
Footed Ice Tea ........................... $20.00
Footed Juice .............................. $16.00

### CAROUSEL, Cutting 863, Blank 6080

Goblet ...................................... $20.00
Sherbet ..................................... $18.00
Cocktail .................................... $18.00
Claret-Wine ............................... $25.00
Cordial ..................................... $30.00
Footed Ice Tea ........................... $18.00
Footed Juice .............................. $18.00
Large Claret, 8 oz. ...................... $25.00
Large Claret, 6 oz. ...................... $25.00

### CLASSIC GOLD, Decoration 641, Blank 6080

Goblet ...................................... $20.00
Sherbet ..................................... $18.00

Cocktail .................................... $18.00
Claret-Wine ............................... $22.00
Cordial ..................................... $27.00
Footed Ice Tea ........................... $18.00
Footed Juice .............................. $16.00
Claret, 8 oz. .............................. $24.00
Claret, 6 oz. .............................. $24.00

### TROUSSEAU, Decoration 642, Blank 6080

Goblet ...................................... $25.00
Sherbet ..................................... $23.00
Cocktail .................................... $22.00
Claret-Wine ............................... $28.00
Cordial ..................................... $32.00
Footed Ice Tea ........................... $25.00
Footed Juice .............................. $22.00
Large Claret, 8 oz. ...................... $35.00
Large Claret, 6 oz. ...................... $35.00

### FIRELIGHT, Decoration 657, Blank 6080½

Goblet ...................................... $30.00
Sherbet ..................................... $25.00
Cocktail .................................... $25.00
Claret-Wine ............................... $35.00
Cordial ..................................... $38.00
Footed Ice Tea ........................... $30.00
Footed Juice .............................. $24.00

### EMBASSY, Blank 6083

Goblet ...................................... $20.00
Sherbet ..................................... $18.00
Wine/Cocktail ............................ $20.00
Cordial ..................................... $22.00
Footed Ice Tea ........................... $18.00
Footed Juice .............................. $14.00

### WESTMINISTER, Cutting 872, Blank 6083

Goblet ...................................... $24.00
Sherbet ..................................... $20.00
Wine/Cocktail ............................ $26.00
Cordial ..................................... $30.00
Footed Ice Tea ........................... $24.00
Footed Juice .............................. $18.00

### ST. REGIS, Cutting 873, Blank 6083

Goblet ...................................... $22.00
Sherbet ..................................... $20.00
Wine/Cocktail ............................ $25.00
Cordial ..................................... $27.00
Footed Ice Tea ........................... $22.00
Footed Juice .............................. $14.00

### GOLDEN GRAIL, Decoration 644, Blank 6083

Goblet ...................................... $45.00

| | |
|---|---|
| Sherbet | $40.00 |
| Wine/Cocktail | $48.00 |
| Cordial | $57.00 |
| Footed Ice Tea | $45.00 |
| Footed Juice | $36.00 |

### PETITE, Blank 6085

| | |
|---|---|
| Goblet | $20.00 |
| Sherbet | $18.00 |
| Wine/Cocktail | $22.00 |
| Cordial | $25.00 |
| Footed Ice Tea | $18.00 |
| Footed Juice | $14.00 |

### JULIET, Cutting 865, Blank 6085

| | |
|---|---|
| Goblet | $22.00 |
| Sherbet | $20.00 |
| Wine/Cocktail | $24.00 |
| Cordial | $28.00 |
| Footed Ice Tea | $20.00 |
| Footed Juice | $16.00 |

### GOLDEN LACE, Decoration 645, Blank 6085

| | |
|---|---|
| Goblet | $36.00 |
| Sherbet | $34.00 |
| Wine/Cocktail | $40.00 |
| Cordial | $45.00 |
| Footed Ice Tea | $36.00 |
| Footed Juice | $34.00 |

### MOONGLOW, Decoration 649, Blank 6085

| | |
|---|---|
| Goblet | $24.00 |
| Sherbet | $22.00 |
| Wine/Cocktail | $25.00 |
| Cordial | $30.00 |
| Footed Ice Tea | $24.00 |
| Footed Juice | $18.00 |

### SUNGLOW, Decoration 650, Blank 6085

| | |
|---|---|
| Goblet | $24.00 |
| Sherbet | $22.00 |
| Wine/Cocktail | $25.00 |
| Cordial | $30.00 |
| Footed Ice Tea | $24.00 |
| Footed Juice | $18.00 |

### VESPER, Blank 6086

| | |
|---|---|
| Goblet | $20.00 |
| Sherbet | $18.00 |
| Wine/Cocktail | $22.00 |
| Cordial | $25.00 |
| Footed Ice Tea | $18.00 |
| Footed Juice | $14.00 |

### FANTASY, Crystal Print 17, Blank 6086

| | |
|---|---|
| Goblet | $22.00 |
| Sherbet | $20.00 |
| Wine/Cocktail | $22.00 |
| Cordial | $25.00 |
| Footed Ice Tea | $20.00 |
| Footed Juice | $14.00 |

### SERENADE, Cutting 864, Blank 6086

| | |
|---|---|
| Goblet | $22.00 |
| Sherbet | $20.00 |
| Wine/Cocktail | $24.00 |
| Cordial | $26.00 |
| Footed Ice Tea | $22.00 |
| Footed Juice | $16.00 |

### OVERTURE, Cutting 867, Blank 6086

| | |
|---|---|
| Goblet | $22.00 |
| Sherbet | $20.00 |
| Wine/Cocktail | $25.00 |
| Cordial | $26.00 |
| Footed Ice Tea | $22.00 |
| Footed Juice | $16.00 |

### STAR SONG, Cutting 871, Blank 6086

| | |
|---|---|
| Goblet | $22.00 |
| Sherbet | $20.00 |
| Wine/Cocktail | $24.00 |
| Cordial | $26.00 |
| Footed Ice Tea | $20.00 |
| Footed Juice | $16.00 |

### CHATEAU, Blank 6087

| | |
|---|---|
| Goblet | $22.00 |
| Sherbet | $20.00 |
| Wine/Cocktail | $25.00 |
| Cordial | $27.00 |
| Footed Ice Tea | $22.00 |
| Footed Juice | $16.00 |

### EVENING STAR, Cutting 869, Blank 6087

| | |
|---|---|
| Goblet | $22.00 |
| Sherbet | $20.00 |
| Wine/Cocktail | $25.00 |
| Cordial | $27.00 |
| Footed Ice Tea | $22.00 |
| Footed Juice | $16.00 |

### GOLDEN FLAIR, Decoration 643, Blank 6087

| | |
|---|---|
| Goblet | $22.00 |
| Sherbet | $20.00 |
| Wine/Cocktail | $25.00 |

| | |
|---|---|
| Cordial | $27.00 |
| Footed Ice Tea | $22.00 |
| Footed Juice | $16.00 |

### ORLEANS, Blank 6089

| | |
|---|---|
| Goblet | $20.00 |
| Sherbet | $18.00 |
| Wine/Cocktail | $20.00 |
| Brandy | $20.00 |
| Footed Ice Tea | $20.00 |
| Footed Juice | $14.00 |

### WHISPER, Cutting 875, Blank 6089

| | |
|---|---|
| Goblet | $22.00 |
| Sherbet | $20.00 |
| Wine/Cocktail | $22.00 |
| Brandy | $22.00 |
| Footed Ice Tea | $22.00 |
| Footed Juice | $14.00 |

### DEVON, Cutting 876, Blank 6089

| | |
|---|---|
| Goblet | $22.00 |
| Sherbet | $20.00 |
| Wine/Cocktail | $22.00 |
| Brandy | $22.00 |
| Footed Ice Tea | $22.00 |
| Footed Juice | $16.00 |

### BRIDAL CROWN, Cutting 882, Blank 6089

| | |
|---|---|
| Goblet | $22.00 |
| Sherbet | $20.00 |
| Wine/Cocktail | $22.00 |
| Brandy | $22.00 |
| Footed Ice Tea | $22.00 |
| Footed Juice | $16.00 |

### BELOVED, Decoration 647, Blank 6089

| | |
|---|---|
| Goblet | $25.00 |
| Sherbet | $22.00 |
| Wine/Cocktail | $30.00 |
| Brandy | $34.00 |
| Footed Ice Tea | $25.00 |
| Footed Juice | $22.00 |

### PRISCILLA, Blank 6092

| | |
|---|---|
| Goblet | $20.00 |
| Sherbet | $18.00 |
| Wine/Cocktail | $20.00 |
| Cordial | $22.00 |
| Footed Ice Tea | $20.00 |
| Footed Juice | $14.00 |

**SWEETHEART ROSE, Cutting 877,**
**Blank 6092**

| | |
|---|---|
| Goblet | $24.00 |
| Sherbet | $22.00 |
| Wine/Cocktail | $27.00 |
| Cordial | $30.00 |
| Footed Ice Tea | $24.00 |
| Footed Juice | $16.00 |

**BURGUNDY, Cutting 879,**
**Blank 6092**

| | |
|---|---|
| Goblet | $24.00 |
| Sherbet | $22.00 |
| Wine/Cocktail | $27.00 |
| Cordial | $30.00 |
| Footed Ice Tea | $24.00 |
| Footed Juice | $18.00 |

**TWILIGHT, Cutting 883,**
**Blank 6092**

| | |
|---|---|
| Goblet | $22.00 |
| Sherbet | $20.00 |
| Wine/Cocktail | $22.00 |
| Cordial | $25.00 |
| Footed Ice Tea | $22.00 |
| Footed Juice | $26.00 |

**SPRING SONG, Cutting 884,**
**Blank 6092**

| | |
|---|---|
| Goblet | $22.00 |
| Sherbet | $20.00 |
| Wine/Cocktail | $22.00 |
| Cordial | $25.00 |
| Footed Ice Tea | $22.00 |
| Footed Juice | $16.00 |

**ENGAGEMENT, Decoration 648,**
**Blank 6092**

| | |
|---|---|
| Goblet | $30.00 |
| Sherbet | $27.00 |
| Wine/Cocktail | $35.00 |
| Cordial | $36.00 |
| Footed Ice Tea | $30.00 |
| Footed Juice | $26.00 |

**AURORA, Decoration 651,**
**Blank 6092**

| | |
|---|---|
| Goblet | $26.00 |
| Sherbet | $24.00 |
| Wine/Cocktail | $26.00 |
| Cordial | $32.00 |
| Footed Ice Tea | $26.00 |
| Footed Juice | $22.00 |

**REGAL, Decoration 693,**
**Blank 6092**

| | |
|---|---|
| Goblet | $22.00 |
| Sherbet | $20.00 |
| Wine/Cocktail | $22.00 |
| Footed Ice Tea | $22.00 |

**STOCKHOLM, Blank 6093**

| | |
|---|---|
| Goblet | $22.00 |
| Sherbet | $20.00 |
| Wine | $25.00 |
| Cocktail | $20.00 |
| Cordial | $32.00 |
| Footed Ice Tea | $22.00 |
| Footed Juice | $20.00 |

**BRISTOL, Cutting 880, Blank 6093**

| | |
|---|---|
| Goblet | $30.00 |
| Sherbet | $25.00 |
| Wine | $35.00 |
| Cocktail | $25.00 |
| Cordial | $38.00 |
| Footed Ice Tea | $30.00 |
| Footed Juice | $24.00 |

**SHERATON, Blank 6097**

| | |
|---|---|
| Goblet | $20.00 |
| Sherbet | $18.00 |
| Claret | $22.00 |
| Wine/Cocktail | $20.00 |
| Cordial | $22.00 |
| Footed Ice Tea | $20.00 |
| Footed Juice | $18.00 |

**HARVEST, Blank HA01, 6097**

| | |
|---|---|
| Goblet | $22.00 |
| Sherbet | $20.00 |
| Claret | $22.00 |
| Magnum | $28.00 |
| Footed Ice Tea | $22.00 |

**SENTIMENTAL, Crystal Print 25,**
**Blank 6097**

| | |
|---|---|
| Goblet | $22.00 |
| Sherbet | $20.00 |
| Claret | $25.00 |
| Footed Ice Tea | $22.00 |

**GEORGIAN, Cutting 885,**
**Blank 6097**

| | |
|---|---|
| Goblet | $22.00 |
| Sherbet | $20.00 |
| Claret | $24.00 |
| Wine/Cocktail | $22.00 |
| Cordial | $28.00 |
| Footed Ice Tea | $22.00 |
| Footed Juice | $16.00 |

**MONTICELLO, Cutting 886,**
**Blank 6097**

| | |
|---|---|
| Goblet | $22.00 |
| Sherbet | $20.00 |
| Wine/Cocktail | $25.00 |

| | |
|---|---|
| Cordial | $28.00 |
| Footed Ice Tea | $22.00 |
| Footed Juice | $18.00 |

**GLOUCESTER, Cutting 898,**
**Blank 6097**

| | |
|---|---|
| Goblet | $22.00 |
| Sherbet | $20.00 |
| Wine/Cocktail | $25.00 |
| Cordial | $28.00 |
| Footed Ice Tea | $22.00 |
| Footed Juice | $16.00 |

**SHEFFIELD, Decoration 653,**
**Blank 6097**

| | |
|---|---|
| Goblet | $30.00 |
| Sherbet | $27.00 |
| Claret | $36.00 |
| Wine/Cocktail | $32.00 |
| Cordial | $38.00 |
| Footed Ice Tea | $30.00 |
| Footed Juice | $25.00 |
| Magnum | $45.00 |

**RICHMOND, Decoration 654,**
**Blank 6097**

| | |
|---|---|
| Goblet | $30.00 |
| Sherbet | $27.00 |
| Claret | $36.00 |
| Wine/Cocktail | $32.00 |
| Cordial | $38.00 |
| Footed Ice Tea | $30.00 |
| Footed Juice | $25.00 |
| Magnum | $45.00 |

**ANDOVER, Decoration 665,**
**Blank 6097**

| | |
|---|---|
| Goblet | $38.00 |
| Sherbet | $34.00 |
| Claret | $42.00 |
| Wine/Cocktail | $40.00 |
| Cordial | $45.00 |
| Footed Ice Tea | $38.00 |
| Footed Juice | $34.00 |

**VOGUE, Blank 6099**
Crystal

| | |
|---|---|
| Goblet | $20.00 |
| Sherbet | $18.00 |
| Wine/Cocktail | $22.00 |
| Cordial | $22.00 |
| Footed Ice Tea | $20.00 |
| Footed Juice | $16.00 |

Gold Tint

| | |
|---|---|
| Goblet | $28.00 |
| Sherbet | $26.00 |
| Wine/Cocktail | $30.00 |

Cordial ........................................ $35.00
Footed Ice Tea ............................ $28.00
Footed Juice ................................ $24.00

### EMBRACE, Cutting 887, Blank 6099

Goblet ........................................ $22.00
Sherbet ...................................... $20.00
Wine/Cocktail ............................ $22.00
Cordial ...................................... $24.00
Footed Ice Tea ............................ $22.00
Footed Juice ................................ $18.00

### CHAPEL BELLS, Cutting 888, Blank 6099

Goblet ........................................ $24.00
Sherbet ...................................... $20.00
Wine/Cocktail ............................ $28.00
Cordial ...................................... $30.00
Footed Ice Tea ............................ $24.00
Footed Juice ................................ $18.00

### CANDLELIGHT, Decoration 652, Blank 6099

Goblet ........................................ $22.00
Sherbet ...................................... $20.00
Wine/Cocktail ............................ $22.00
Cordial ...................................... $25.00
Footed Ice Tea ............................ $22.00
Footed Juice ................................ $16.00

### LOVE SONG, Decoration 655, Blank 6099

Goblet ........................................ $24.00
Sherbet ...................................... $22.00
Wine/Cocktail ............................ $28.00
Cordial ...................................... $35.00
Footed Ice Tea ............................ $24.00
Footed Juice ................................ $20.00

### GOLDEN SONG, Decoration 662, Blank 6099

Goblet ........................................ $24.00
Sherbet ...................................... $22.00
Wine/Cocktail ............................ $28.00
Cordial ...................................... $32.00
Footed Ice Tea ............................ $24.00
Footed Juice ................................ $18.00

### DEBUTANTE, Blank 6100

Goblet ........................................ $20.00
Sherbet ...................................... $20.00
Claret ........................................ $20.00
Tulip Wine .................................. $20.00
Brandy ....................................... $20.00
Footed Ice Tea ............................ $20.00

### EVENING BREEZE, Cutting 891, Blank 6100

Goblet ........................................ $22.00
Sherbet ...................................... $22.00
Claret ........................................ $22.00
Tulip Wine .................................. $22.00
Brandy ....................................... $22.00
Footed Ice Tea ............................ $22.00

### COTILLION, Cutting 892, Blank 6100

Goblet ........................................ $24.00
Sherbet ...................................... $24.00
Claret ........................................ $24.00
Tulip Wine .................................. $24.00
Brandy ....................................... $24.00
Footed Ice Tea ............................ $24.00

### PRINCESS ANN, Cutting 893, Blank 6100

Goblet ........................................ $24.00
Sherbet ...................................... $24.00
Claret ........................................ $24.00
Tulip Wine .................................. $24.00
Brandy ....................................... $24.00
Footed Ice Tea ............................ $24.00

### BRIDESMAID, Decoration 658, Blank 6100

Goblet ........................................ $26.00
Sherbet ...................................... $26.00
Claret ........................................ $26.00
Tulip Wine .................................. $26.00
Brandy ....................................... $26.00
Footed Ice Tea ............................ $26.00

### FLOWER GIRL, Decoration 659, Blank 6100

Goblet ........................................ $26.00
Sherbet ...................................... $26.00
Claret ........................................ $26.00
Tulip Wine .................................. $26.00
Brandy ....................................... $26.00
Footed Ice Tea ............................ $26.00

### CRYSTAL TWIST, Blank 6101

Goblet ........................................ $25.00
Sherbet ...................................... $25.00
Wine/Cocktail ............................ $25.00
Cordial ...................................... $25.00
Footed Ice Tea ............................ $25.00
Footed Juice ................................ $25.00

### FLOWER SONG, Cutting 894, Blank 6101

Goblet ........................................ $26.00
Sherbet ...................................... $26.00
Wine/Cocktail ............................ $26.00

Cordial ........................................ $26.00
Footed Ice Tea ............................ $26.00
Footed Juice ................................ $26.00

### CORONET, Decoration 656, Blank 6101

Goblet ........................................ $28.00
Sherbet ...................................... $28.00
Wine/Cocktail ............................ $28.00
Cordial ...................................... $28.00
Footed Ice Tea ............................ $28.00
Footed Juice ................................ $28.00

### SILHOUETTE, Blank 6102

Crystal

Goblet, 10 oz. ............................. $22.00
Goblet, 11 oz. ............................. $25.00
Sherbet ...................................... $22.00
Claret ........................................ $22.00
Tulip Wine .................................. $22.00
Brandy ....................................... $22.00
Footed Ice Tea ............................ $22.00
Sherry ........................................ $25.00
Flute Champagne ......................... $25.00
Large Claret, 10 oz. ..................... $25.00

Pink

Goblet, 10 oz. ............................. $35.00
Sherbet ...................................... $32.00
Claret ........................................ $40.00
Tulip Wine .................................. $40.00
Brandy ....................................... $35.00
Footed Ice Tea ............................ $35.00

### SILHOUETTE CLASSICS, Blue/Ebony

Goblet, 11 oz. ............................. $35.00
Sherry ........................................ $35.00
Flute Champagne ......................... $38.00
Large Claret, 10 oz. ..................... $40.00
Subtract 20% for Ebony

### ROSALIE, Crystal Print 19, Blank 6102

Goblet ........................................ $30.00
Sherbet ...................................... $25.00
Claret ........................................ $30.00
Tulip Wine .................................. $30.00
Brandy ....................................... $30.00
Footed Ice Tea ............................ $30.00

### BIANCA, Crystal Print 22, Blank 6102

Goblet ........................................ $25.00
Sherbet ...................................... $25.00
Claret ........................................ $25.00
Tulip Wine .................................. $25.00
Brandy ....................................... $25.00
Footed Ice Tea ............................ $25.00

### FLEURETTE, Crystal Print 26, Blank 6102
Goblet ........................................ $25.00
Sherbet ...................................... $25.00
Tulip Wine ................................. $25.00
Footed Ice Tea ............................ $25.00

### MILADY, Cutting 895, Blank 6102
Goblet ........................................ $25.00
Sherbet ...................................... $25.00
Claret ........................................ $25.00
Tulip Wine ................................. $25.00
Brandy ....................................... $25.00
Footed Ice Tea ............................ $25.00

### VENUS, Cutting 896, Blank 6102
Goblet ........................................ $25.00
Sherbet ...................................... $25.00
Claret ........................................ $25.00
Tulip Wine ................................. $25.00
Brandy ....................................... $25.00
Footed Ice Tea ............................ $25.00

### BRIDAL SHOWER, Cutting 897, Blank 6102
Goblet ........................................ $25.00
Sherbet ...................................... $25.00
Claret ........................................ $25.00
Tulip Wine ................................. $25.00
Brandy ....................................... $25.00
Footed Ice Tea ............................ $25.00

### LINEAL, Cutting 899, Blank 6102
Goblet ........................................ $24.00
Sherbet ...................................... $24.00
Claret ........................................ $24.00
Tulip Wine ................................. $24.00
Brandy ....................................... $24.00
Footed Ice Tea ............................ $24.00

### WEDDING FLOWER, Cutting 920, Blank 6102
Goblet ........................................ $40.00
Sherbet ...................................... $35.00
Claret ........................................ $45.00
Tulip Wine ................................. $45.00
Brandy ....................................... $35.00
Footed Ice Tea ............................ $40.00

### INVITATION, Decoration 660, Blank 6102
Goblet ........................................ $32.00
Sherbet ...................................... $26.00
Claret ........................................ $32.00
Tulip Wine ................................. $32.00
Brandy ....................................... $26.00
Footed Ice Tea ............................ $32.00

### VERMEIL, Decoration 661, Blank 6102
Goblet ........................................ $26.00

---

Sherbet ...................................... $26.00
Claret ........................................ $26.00
Tulip Wine ................................. $26.00
Brandy ....................................... $26.00
Footed Ice Tea ............................ $26.00

### PLATINA ROSE, Decoration 663, Blank 6102
Goblet ........................................ $35.00
Sherbet ...................................... $30.00
Claret ........................................ $35.00
Tulip Wine ................................. $35.00
Brandy ....................................... $30.00
Footed Ice Tea ............................ $35.00

### GOLDEN GARLAND, Decoration 664, Blank 6102
Goblet ........................................ $30.00
Sherbet ...................................... $30.00
Claret ........................................ $30.00
Tulip Wine ................................. $30.00
Brandy ....................................... $30.00
Footed Ice Tea ............................ $30.00

### GLAMOUR, Blank 6103
Crystal/Green/Onyx
Goblet ........................................ $20.00
Sherbet ...................................... $20.00
Claret ........................................ $20.00
Tulip Wine ................................. $20.00
Brandy ....................................... $20.00
Footed Ice Tea ............................ $20.00

Gray Mist/Blue
Goblet ........................................ $22.00
Sherbet ...................................... $22.00
Claret ........................................ $22.00
Tulip Wine ................................. $22.00
Brandy ....................................... $22.00
Footed Ice Tea ............................ $22.00

### NUPTIAL, Crystal Print 21, Blank 6103
Goblet ........................................ $22.00
Sherbet ...................................... $22.00
Claret ........................................ $22.00
Tulip Wine ................................. $22.00
Brandy ....................................... $22.00
Footed Ice Tea ............................ $22.00

### BARCELONA, Crystal Print 27, Blank 6103
Goblet ........................................ $22.00
Sherbet ...................................... $22.00
Tulip Wine ................................. $22.00
Footed Ice Tea ............................ $22.00

### BALLERINA, Cutting 900, Blank 6103
Goblet ........................................ $22.00

---

Sherbet ...................................... $22.00
Claret ........................................ $22.00
Tulip Wine ................................. $22.00
Brandy ....................................... $22.00
Footed Ice Tea ............................ $22.00

### FOUNTAIN, Cutting 901, Blank 6103
Goblet ........................................ $22.00
Sherbet ...................................... $22.00
Claret ........................................ $22.00
Tulip Wine ................................. $22.00
Brandy ....................................... $22.00
Footed Ice Tea ............................ $22.00

### FOREVER, Cutting 904, Blank 6103
Goblet ........................................ $22.00
Sherbet ...................................... $22.00
Claret ........................................ $22.00
Tulip Wine ................................. $22.00
Brandy ....................................... $22.00
Footed Ice Tea ............................ $22.00

### ANNOUNCEMENT, Decoration 666, Blank 6103
Goblet ........................................ $22.00
Sherbet ...................................... $22.00
Claret ........................................ $22.00
Tulip Wine ................................. $22.00
Brandy ....................................... $22.00
Footed Ice Tea ............................ $22.00

### REHEARSAL, Decoration 667, Blank 6103
Goblet ........................................ $22.00
Sherbet ...................................... $22.00
Claret ........................................ $22.00
Tulip Wine ................................. $22.00
Brandy ....................................... $22.00
Footed Ice Tea ............................ $22.00

### CHERISH, Decoration 681, Blank 6103
Goblet ........................................ $22.00
Sherbet ...................................... $22.00
Claret ........................................ $22.00
Tulip Wine ................................. $22.00
Brandy ....................................... $22.00
Footed Ice Tea ............................ $22.00

### SOMETHING BLUE, Decoration 685, Blank 6103
Goblet ........................................ $25.00
Sherbet ...................................... $24.00
Claret ........................................ $28.00
Tulip Wine ................................. $28.00
Brandy ....................................... $25.00
Footed Ice Tea ............................ $25.00

### JEFFERSON, Blank 6104
| | |
|---|---|
| Goblet | $22.00 |
| Sherbet | $22.00 |
| Claret | $22.00 |
| Wine | $22.00 |
| Cordial | $22.00 |
| Footed Ice Tea | $22.00 |

### SAVANNAH, Cutting 902, Blank 6104
| | |
|---|---|
| Goblet | $25.00 |
| Sherbet | $25.00 |
| Claret | $25.00 |
| Wine | $25.00 |
| Cordial | $30.00 |
| Footed Ice Tea | $25.00 |

### TIARA, Cutting 903, Blank 6104
| | |
|---|---|
| Goblet | $25.00 |
| Sherbet | $25.00 |
| Claret | $25.00 |
| Wine | $25.00 |
| Cordial | $30.00 |
| Footed Ice Tea | $25.00 |

### QUEEN ANNE, Cutting 905, Blank 6104
| | |
|---|---|
| Goblet | $25.00 |
| Sherbet | $25.00 |
| Claret | $25.00 |
| Wine | $25.00 |
| Cordial | $30.00 |
| Footed Ice Tea | $25.00 |

### MONTE CARLO, Cutting 912, Blank 6104
| | |
|---|---|
| Goblet | $25.00 |
| Sherbet | $25.00 |
| Claret | $25.00 |
| Wine | $25.00 |
| Cordial | $30.00 |
| Footed Ice Tea | $25.00 |

### CARILLON, Cutting 915, Blank 6104
| | |
|---|---|
| Goblet | $25.00 |
| Sherbet | $25.00 |
| Claret | $25.00 |
| Wine | $25.00 |
| Cordial | $30.00 |
| Footed Ice Tea | $25.00 |

### BEACON HILL, Cutting 917, Blank 6104½
| | |
|---|---|
| Goblet | $25.00 |
| Sherbet | $25.00 |
| Claret | $25.00 |
| Wine | $25.00 |
| Cordial | $30.00 |
| Footed Ice Tea | $25.00 |

### BERKSHIRE, Blank 6105
| | |
|---|---|
| Goblet | $22.00 |
| Sherbet | $22.00 |
| Claret | $22.00 |
| Wine | $22.00 |
| Cordial | $27.00 |
| Footed Ice Tea | $22.00 |

### GEORGETOWN, Cutting 906, Blank 6105
| | |
|---|---|
| Goblet | $25.00 |
| Sherbet | $25.00 |
| Claret | $25.00 |
| Wine | $25.00 |
| Cordial | $30.00 |
| Footed Ice Tea | $25.00 |

### CANTATA, Cutting 907, Blank 6105
| | |
|---|---|
| Goblet | $25.00 |
| Sherbet | $25.00 |
| Claret | $25.00 |
| Wine | $25.00 |
| Cordial | $30.00 |
| Footed Ice Tea | $25.00 |

### STRATFORD, Cutting 914, Blank 6105
| | |
|---|---|
| Goblet | $25.00 |
| Sherbet | $25.00 |
| Claret | $25.00 |
| Wine | $25.00 |
| Cordial | $30.00 |
| Footed Ice Tea | $25.00 |

### CELEBRITY, Blank 6106
| | |
|---|---|
| Goblet | $22.00 |
| Sherbet | $22.00 |
| Claret | $22.00 |
| Tulip Wine | $22.00 |
| Liqueur | $27.00 |
| Footed Ice Tea | $22.00 |

### EMPIRE, Cutting 908, Blank 6106
| | |
|---|---|
| Goblet | $23.00 |
| Sherbet | $23.00 |
| Claret | $23.00 |
| Tulip Wine | $23.00 |
| Liqueur | $28.00 |
| Footed Ice Tea | $23.00 |

### BERKELEY, Cutting 909, Blank 6106
| | |
|---|---|
| Goblet | $25.00 |
| Sherbet | $25.00 |
| Claret | $25.00 |
| Tulip Wine | $25.00 |
| Liqueur | $30.00 |
| Footed Ice Tea | $25.00 |

### BROCADE, Decoration 674, Blank 6106
| | |
|---|---|
| Goblet | $25.00 |
| Sherbet | $25.00 |
| Claret | $25.00 |
| Tulip Wine | $25.00 |
| Liqueur | $30.00 |
| Footed Ice Tea | $25.00 |

### MANTILLA, Decoration 675, Blank 6106
| | |
|---|---|
| Goblet | $25.00 |
| Sherbet | $25.00 |
| Claret | $25.00 |
| Tulip Wine | $25.00 |
| Liqueur | $30.00 |
| Footed Ice Tea | $25.00 |

### INSPIRATION, Blank 6107
| | |
|---|---|
| Goblet | $22.00 |
| Sherbet | $22.00 |
| Claret | $22.00 |
| Tulip Wine | $22.00 |
| Liqueur | $27.00 |
| Footed Ice Tea | $22.00 |

### MATRIMONY, Cutting 910, Blank 6107
| | |
|---|---|
| Goblet | $25.00 |
| Sherbet | $25.00 |
| Claret | $25.00 |
| Tulip Wine | $25.00 |
| Liqueur | $30.00 |
| Footed Ice Tea | $25.00 |

### ORANGE BLOSSOM, Cutting 911, Blank 6107
| | |
|---|---|
| Goblet | $25.00 |
| Sherbet | $25.00 |
| Claret | $25.00 |
| Tulip Wine | $25.00 |
| Liqueur | $30.00 |
| Footed Ice Tea | $25.00 |

### REMEMBRANCE, Decoration 670, Blank 6107
| | |
|---|---|
| Goblet | $23.00 |
| Sherbet | $23.00 |
| Claret | $23.00 |
| Tulip Wine | $23.00 |
| Liqueur | $28.00 |
| Footed Ice Tea | $23.00 |

### LOVELIGHT, Decoration 671, Blank 6107
| | |
|---|---|
| Goblet | $23.00 |
| Sherbet | $23.00 |
| Claret | $23.00 |
| Tulip Wine | $23.00 |

Liqueur .............................. $28.00
Footed Ice Tea ...................... $23.00

### ALLEGRO, Decoration 672, Blank 6107
Goblet .............................. $25.00
Sherbet ............................. $25.00
Claret .............................. $25.00
Tulip Wine .......................... $25.00
Liqueur ............................. $30.00
Footed Ice Tea ...................... $25.00

### BETROTHAL, Decoration 673, Blank 6107
Goblet .............................. $25.00
Sherbet ............................. $25.00
Claret .............................. $25.00
Tulip Wine .......................... $25.00
Liqueur ............................. $30.00
Footed Ice Tea ...................... $25.00

### PRECEDENCE, Blank 6108
#### Crystal
Goblet .............................. $35.00
Champagne ........................... $32.00
Claret .............................. $38.00
Tulip Wine .......................... $38.00
Liqueur ............................. $47.00
Footed Ice Tea ...................... $35.00

#### Colors
Goblet .............................. $45.00
Champagne ........................... $42.00
Claret .............................. $50.00
Tulip Wine .......................... $50.00
Liqueur ............................. $58.00
Footed Ice Tea ...................... $45.00

### EXETER, Blank 6109
#### Crystal
Goblet .............................. $35.00
Sherbet ............................. $32.00
Wine ................................ $32.00
Sherry/Liqueur ...................... $40.00
Footed Ice Tea ...................... $35.00

#### Amethyst
Goblet .............................. $75.00
Sherbet ............................. $68.00
Wine ................................ $78.00
Sherry/Liqueur ...................... $85.00
Footed Ice Tea ...................... $75.00

### PROMISE, Blank 6110
Goblet .............................. $28.00

Sherbet ............................. $25.00
Wine ................................ $32.00
Liqueur ............................. $35.00
Footed Ice Tea ...................... $28.00

### GREENFIELD, Cutting 916, Blank 6110
Goblet .............................. $30.00
Sherbet ............................. $28.00
Wine ................................ $34.00
Liqueur ............................. $38.00
Footed Ice Tea ...................... $30.00

### GLENDALE, Cutting 919, Blank 6110
Goblet .............................. $30.00
Sherbet ............................. $28.00
Wine ................................ $34.00
Liqueur ............................. $38.00
Footed Ice Tea ...................... $30.00

### RECEPTION, Decoration 676, Blank 6110
Goblet .............................. $30.00
Sherbet ............................. $28.00
Wine ................................ $34.00
Liqueur ............................. $36.00
Footed Ice Tea ...................... $30.00

### GOLDEN BELLE, Decoration 677, Blank 6110
Goblet .............................. $30.00
Sherbet ............................. $28.00
Wine ................................ $34.00
Liqueur ............................. $36.00
Footed Ice Tea ...................... $30.00

### ILLUSION, Blank 6111
Goblet .............................. $25.00
Sherbet ............................. $25.00
Claret .............................. $25.00
Wine ................................ $25.00
Cordial ............................. $25.00
Footed Ice Tea ...................... $25.00

### FIRST LOVE, Cutting 918, Blank 6111
Goblet .............................. $28.00
Sherbet ............................. $28.00
Claret .............................. $28.00
Wine ................................ $28.00
Cordial ............................. $28.00
Footed Ice Tea ...................... $28.00

### RENAISSANCE GOLD, Decoration 678, Blank 6111
Goblet .............................. $45.00
Sherbet ............................. $40.00

Claret .............................. $50.00
Wine ................................ $50.00
Cordial ............................. $65.00
Footed Ice Tea ...................... $45.00

### OLYMPIC PLATINUM, Decoration 679, Blank 6111
Goblet .............................. $30.00
Sherbet ............................. $30.00
Claret .............................. $30.00
Wine ................................ $30.00
Cordial ............................. $30.00
Footed Ice Tea ...................... $30.00

### OLYMPIC GOLD, Decoration 680, Blank 6111
Goblet .............................. $30.00
Sherbet ............................. $30.00
Claret .............................. $30.00
Wine ................................ $30.00
Cordial ............................. $30.00
Footed Ice Tea ...................... $30.00

### RENAISSANCE PLATINUM, Decoration 682, Blank 6111
Goblet .............................. $45.00
Sherbet ............................. $40.00
Claret .............................. $50.00
Wine ................................ $50.00
Cordial ............................. $65.00
Footed Ice Tea ...................... $45.00

### GOLD TRIUMPH, Blank 6112
### SILVER TRIUMPH, Blank 6112
Goblet .............................. $20.00
Sherbet ............................. $20.00
Tulip Wine .......................... $20.00
Footed Ice Tea ...................... $20.00

### VERSAILLES, Blank 6113
Goblet .............................. $50.00
Sherbet ............................. $45.00
Claret .............................. $54.00
Wine ................................ $54.00
Brandy .............................. $54.00
Footed Ice Tea ...................... $50.00

### MOON MIST, Blank 6113
Goblet .............................. $45.00
Sherbet ............................. $40.00
Claret .............................. $52.00
Wine ................................ $50.00
Brandy .............................. $50.00
Footed Ice Tea ...................... $45.00

### VENTURE, Blank 6114
Goblet ........................................ $20.00
Sherbet ...................................... $20.00
Wine .......................................... $20.00
Brandy ....................................... $22.00

### SOMMELIER COLLECTION, Blanks 6115 – 6119
Continental, 6115 ...................... $22.00
Grande, 6116 ............................. $22.00
Vin Blanc, 6117 ......................... $18.00
Sherry, 6118 .............................. $18.00
Tulip Wine, 6119 ....................... $18.00

### ELOQUENCE, Blank 6120
Crystal/Onyx Base
Goblet ........................................ $35.00
Sherbet ...................................... $35.00
Claret ........................................ $35.00
Liqueur ...................................... $60.00
Footed Ice Tea ........................... $35.00
Add 10% for Onyx Base

### CONTRAST, Blank 6120
Goblet ........................................ $55.00
Sherbet ...................................... $55.00
Claret ........................................ $55.00
Liqueur ...................................... $80.00
Footed Ice Tea ........................... $55.00

### ELOQUENCE GOLD, Decoration 686, Blank 6120
Goblet ........................................ $35.00
Sherbet ...................................... $35.00
Claret ........................................ $35.00
Liqueur ...................................... $50.00
Footed Ice Tea ........................... $35.00

### ELOQUENCE PLATINUM, Decoration 687, Blank 6120
Goblet ........................................ $35.00
Sherbet ...................................... $35.00
Claret ........................................ $35.00
Liqueur ...................................... $50.00
Footed Ice Tea ........................... $35.00

### VENISE, Decoration 688, Blank 6120
Goblet ........................................ $45.00
Sherbet ...................................... $45.00
Claret ........................................ $45.00
Liqueur ...................................... $60.00
Footed Ice Tea ........................... $45.00

### SPHERE, Blank 6121
Goblet ........................................ $15.00
Sherbet ...................................... $15.00
Wine .......................................... $15.00
Footed Ice Tea ........................... $15.00

### BISCAYNE, Blank 6122
Blue/Nutmeg/Gold
Goblet ........................................ $20.00
Sherbet ...................................... $20.00
Wine .......................................... $20.00
Footed Ice Tea ........................... $20.00
Highball ..................................... $20.00
On the Rocks ............................. $20.00

Snow/Onyx
Goblet ........................................ $22.00
Sherbet ...................................... $22.00
Wine .......................................... $22.00
Footed Ice Tea ........................... $22.00
Highball ..................................... $22.00
On the Rocks ............................. $22.00

### HALO, Decoration 689, Blank 6122
Goblet ........................................ $22.00
Sherbet ...................................... $22.00
Wine .......................................... $22.00
Footed Ice Tea ........................... $22.00

### PRINCESS, Blank 6123
Goblet ........................................ $20.00
Champagne ................................. $20.00
Wine .......................................... $20.00
Footed Ice Tea ........................... $20.00

### CAMEO, Crystal Print 28, Blank 6123
Goblet ........................................ $22.00
Sherbet ...................................... $22.00
Wine .......................................... $22.00
Footed Ice Tea ........................... $22.00

### INTIMATE, Crystal Print 31, Blank 6123
Goblet ........................................ $22.00
Sherbet ...................................... $22.00
Wine .......................................... $22.00
Footed Ice Tea ........................... $22.00

### POETRY, Crystal Print 32, Blank 6123
Goblet ........................................ $22.00
Sherbet ...................................... $22.00
Wine .......................................... $22.00
Footed Ice Tea ........................... $22.00

### PETIT FLEUR, Cutting 922, Blank 6123
Goblet ........................................ $22.00
Sherbet ...................................... $22.00
Wine .......................................... $22.00
Footed Ice Tea ........................... $22.00

### PRINCESS PLATINUM, Decoration 690, Blank 6123
Goblet ........................................ $22.00
Sherbet ...................................... $22.00
Wine .......................................... $22.00
Footed Ice Tea ........................... $22.00

### TENDERNESS, Decoration 691, Blank 6123
Goblet ........................................ $22.00
Sherbet ...................................... $22.00
Wine .......................................... $22.00
Footed Ice Tea ........................... $22.00

### MARQUIS, Decoration 692, Blank 6123
Goblet ........................................ $22.00
Sherbet ...................................... $22.00
Wine .......................................... $22.00
Footed Ice Tea ........................... $22.00

### SPLENDOR, Blank 6124
Goblet ........................................ $30.00
Sherbet ...................................... $30.00
Wine .......................................... $30.00
Footed Ice Tea ........................... $30.00

### BROCADE, Crystal Print 30, Blank 6124
Goblet ........................................ $30.00
Sherbet ...................................... $30.00
Wine .......................................... $30.00
Footed Ice Tea ........................... $30.00

### GRANADA, Cutting 923, Blank 6124
Goblet ........................................ $30.00
Sherbet ...................................... $30.00
Wine .......................................... $30.00
Footed Ice Tea ........................... $30.00

### DISTINCTION, Blank 6125
Crystal/Blue
Goblet ........................................ $30.00
Champagne ................................. $28.00
Wine .......................................... $32.00
Footed Ice Tea ........................... $30.00

Plum
Goblet ........................................ $35.00

Champagne ................................ $32.00
Wine ........................................... $38.00
Footed Ice Tea .......................... $35.00

### Ruby
Goblet ........................................ $48.00
Champagne ................................ $45.00
Wine ........................................... $50.00
Footed Ice Tea .......................... $48.00

### Cobalt
Goblet ........................................ $45.00
Champagne ................................ $42.00
Wine ........................................... $50.00
Footed Ice Tea .......................... $45.00

### WIMBLEDON, *Blank 6126*
Goblet ........................................ $20.00
Champagne ................................ $20.00
Wine ........................................... $20.00
Footed Ice Tea .......................... $20.00

### CORSAGE PLUM, *Blank 6126*
Goblet ........................................ $32.00
Champagne ................................ $30.00
Wine ........................................... $34.00
Footed Ice Tea .......................... $32.00

### GAZEBO, *Blank 6126*
Goblet ........................................ $20.00
Champagne ................................ $20.00
Wine ........................................... $20.00
Footed Ice Tea .......................... $20.00

### GAZEBO RUST, *Blank 6126*
Goblet ........................................ $20.00
Champagne ................................ $20.00
Wine ........................................... $20.00
Footed Ice Tea .......................... $20.00

### TARA, *Etching 34, Blank 6126*
Goblet ........................................ $25.00
Champagne ................................ $25.00
Wine ........................................... $25.00
Footed Ice Tea .......................... $25.00

### FESTIVE, *Blank 6127*
Goblet ........................................ $30.00
Champagne ................................ $28.00
Wine ........................................... $32.00
Footed Ice Tea .......................... $30.00

### SERENITY, *Etching 35, Blank 6127*
Goblet ........................................ $35.00
Champagne ................................ $35.00

---

Wine ........................................... $35.00
Footed Ice Tea .......................... $35.00

### REGENCY, *Blank 6128*
Goblet ........................................ $20.00
Champagne ................................ $20.00
Wine ........................................... $20.00
Footed Ice Tea .......................... $20.00

### HEIRLOOM, *Etching 36, Blank 6128*
Goblet ........................................ $25.00
Champagne ................................ $25.00
Wine ........................................... $25.00
Footed Ice Tea .......................... $25.00

### NOVA, *Cutting 934, Blank 6128*
Goblet ........................................ $20.00
Champagne ................................ $20.00
Wine ........................................... $20.00
Footed Ice Tea .......................... $20.00

### MISTY, *Blank 6129*
Goblet ........................................ $20.00
Champagne ................................ $20.00
Claret ......................................... $20.00
Magnum ..................................... $20.00
Footed Ice Tea .......................... $20.00

### MISTY PLATINUM, *Decoration 695, Blank 6129*
Goblet ........................................ $22.00
Champagne ................................ $22.00
Claret ......................................... $22.00
Magnum ..................................... $22.00
Footed Ice Tea .......................... $22.00

### SPLENDOR, *Blank 6131*
Goblet ........................................ $20.00
Champagne ................................ $20.00
Claret ......................................... $20.00
Footed Ice Tea .......................... $20.00

### PAVILION, *Blank 6143*
#### Crystal
Goblet ........................................ $25.00
Champagne ................................ $25.00

---

Wine ........................................... $25.00
Footed Ice Tea .......................... $25.00

#### Gray
Goblet ........................................ $32.00
Champagne ................................ $32.00
Wine ........................................... $32.00
Footed Ice Tea .......................... $32.00

### NOUVEAU, *Etching 42, Blank 6143*
#### Crystal
Goblet ........................................ $32.00
Champagne ................................ $32.00
Wine ........................................... $32.00
Footed Ice Tea .......................... $32.00

#### Gray
Goblet ........................................ $35.00
Champagne ................................ $35.00
Wine ........................................... $35.00
Footed Ice Tea .......................... $35.00

### LOTUS, *Blank 6144*
#### Crystal Mist
Goblet ........................................ $35.00
Champagne ................................ $35.00
Large Claret .............................. $35.00
Footed Ice Tea .......................... $35.00
Flute Champagne ...................... $38.00

#### Colors
Goblet ........................................ $40.00
Champagne ................................ $40.00
Large Claret .............................. $40.00
Footed Ice Tea .......................... $40.00
Flute Champagne ...................... $45.00

### GALA, *Blank 6147*
Goblet ........................................ $18.00
Champagne ................................ $18.00
Wine ........................................... $18.00
Footed Ice Tea .......................... $18.00

### FESTIVAL, *Etching 45, Blank 6147*
Goblet ........................................ $26.00
Champagne ................................ $26.00
Wine ........................................... $26.00
Footed Ice Tea .......................... $26.00

### ICICLE, *Carving 59, Blank 6147*
Goblet ........................................ $24.00
Champagne ................................ $24.00
Wine ........................................... $24.00
Footed Ice Tea .......................... $24.00

### CELEBRATION, Decoration 698, Blank 6147

| | |
|---|---|
| Goblet | $21.00 |
| Champagne | $21.00 |
| Wine | $21.00 |
| Footed Ice Tea | $21.00 |

### JUBILEE, Decoration 699, Blank 6147

| | |
|---|---|
| Goblet | $21.00 |
| Champagne | $21.00 |
| Wine | $21.00 |
| Footed Ice Tea | $21.00 |

### MAYPOLE, Blank 6149

| | |
|---|---|
| Goblet | $40.00 |
| Champagne | $40.00 |
| Wine | $40.00 |
| Footed Ice Tea | $40.00 |

### THE PRESIDENT'S HOUSE, Blank 7780

| | |
|---|---|
| Goblet | $20.00 |

| | |
|---|---|
| Saucer Champagne | $20.00 |
| Sherbet | $18.00 |
| Tulip Champagne | $20.00 |
| Burgundy Wine | $22.00 |
| Wine, 8 oz. | $22.00 |
| Wine, 5 oz. | $22.00 |
| Whiskey Sour/Parfait | $22.00 |
| Footed Ice Tea | $20.00 |
| Highball | $12.00 |
| Juice | $12.00 |
| Old Fashioned | $12.00 |

# Indices

PICTURE INDEX

ALPHABETICAL INDEX

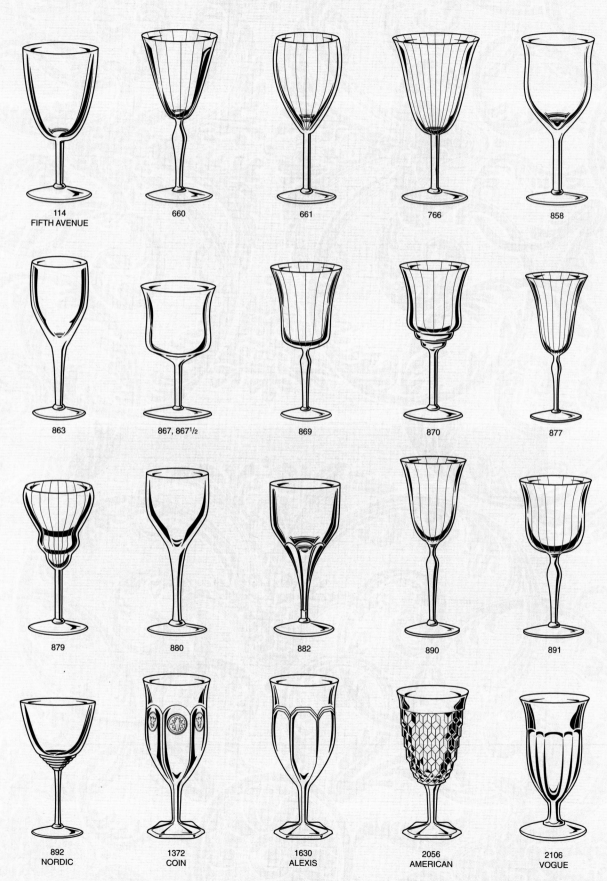

114
FIFTH AVENUE

660

661

766

858

863

867, 867½

869

870

877

879

880

882

890

891

892
NORDIC

1372
COIN

1630
ALEXIS

2056
AMERICAN

2106
VOGUE

2222
COLONIAL

2321
PRISCILLA

2412
COLONY

2449
HERMITAGE

2496
BAROQUE

2510
SUNRAY, GLACIER

2620
WISTAR, BETSY ROSS

2630
CENTURY

2700
RADIANCE

2713
VINTAGE

2718
FAIRMONT

2719
JAMESTOWN

2770
ARGUS

2806
PEBBLE BEACH

2832
SORRENTO

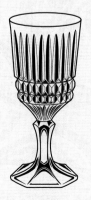
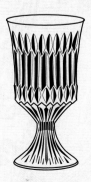

2860 PANELLED
DIAMOND POINT

2882
MOONSTONE

2885 (ST04)
STRATTON

2887 (HE03)
HERITAGE

2903 (MO11)
MONARCH

2916 (FA03)
FAIRLANE

2921
WOODLAND

2936
TRANSITION

2977
VIRGINIA

2990
KIMBERLY

3008
VISION

3113
RADIANCE

4020

4024
VICTORIAN

4186
MESA

5001

5056
AMERICAN LADY

5061

5070

5082

5083

5093

5097

5098

5099

254

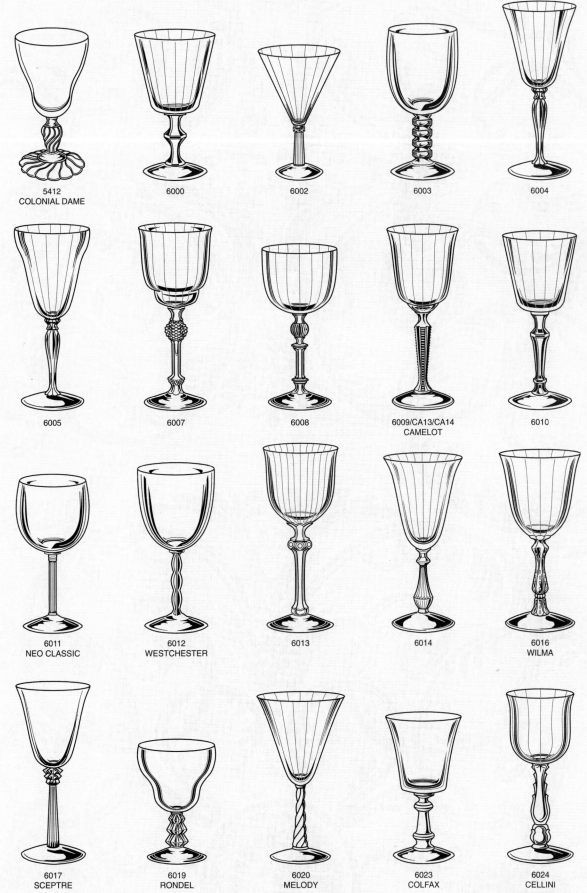

| 5412 COLONIAL DAME | 6000 | 6002 | 6003 | 6004 |

| 6005 | 6007 | 6008 | 6009/CA13/CA14 CAMELOT | 6010 |

| 6011 NEO CLASSIC | 6012 WESTCHESTER | 6013 | 6014 | 6016 WILMA |

| 6017 SCEPTRE | 6019 RONDEL | 6020 MELODY | 6023 COLFAX | 6024 CELLINI |

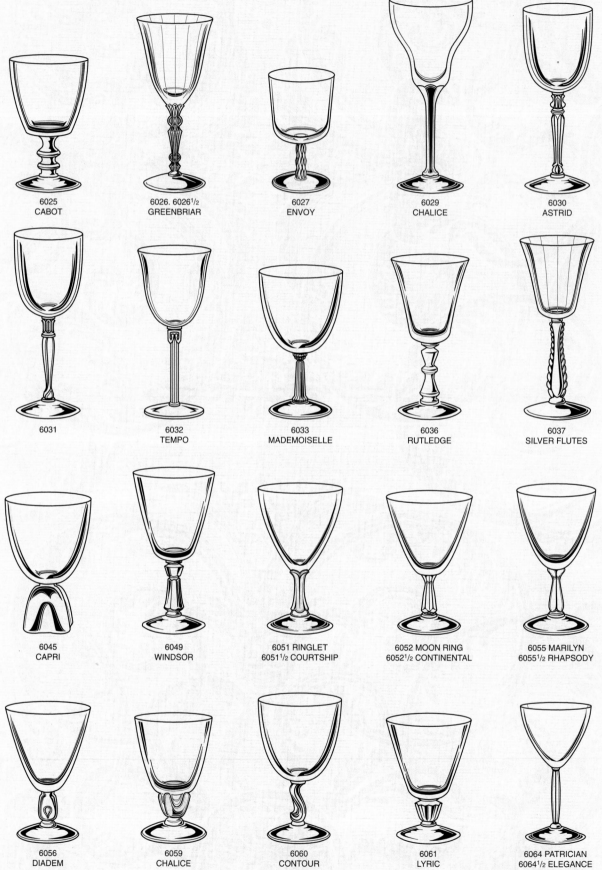

| 6025 CABOT | 6026. 6026¹/₂ GREENBRIAR | 6027 ENVOY | 6029 CHALICE | 6030 ASTRID |

| 6031 | 6032 TEMPO | 6033 MADEMOISELLE | 6036 RUTLEDGE | 6037 SILVER FLUTES |

| 6045 CAPRI | 6049 WINDSOR | 6051 RINGLET 6051¹/₂ COURTSHIP | 6052 MOON RING 6052¹/₂ CONTINENTAL | 6055 MARILYN 6055¹/₂ RHAPSODY |

| 6056 DIADEM | 6059 CHALICE | 6060 CONTOUR | 6061 LYRIC | 6064 PATRICIAN 6064¹/₂ ELEGANCE |

6065
SYMPHONY

6068 PURITAN
6068¹/₂ VICTORIA

6071
PRELUDE

6072
CELESTE

6074
ENCHANTMENT

6077
NORDIC

6079
KENT

6080
FASCINATION

6083
EMBASSY

6085
PETITE

6086
VESPER

6087
CHATEAU

6089
ORLEANS

6092
PRISCILLA

6093
STOCKHOLM

6097 SHERATON
HA 01 HARVEST

6099
VOGUE

6100
DEBUTANTE

6101
CRYSTAL TWIST

6102
SILHOUETTE

257

| 6103 | 6104 | 6105 | 6106 | 6107 |
|------|------|------|------|------|
| GLAMOUR | JEFFERSON | BERKSHIRE | CELEBRITY | INSPIRATION |

| 6108 | 6109 | 6110 | 6111 | 6112 |
|------|------|------|------|------|
| PRECEDENCE | EXETER | PROMISE | ILLUSION | GOLD TRIUMPH SILVER TRIUMPH |

| 6113 | 6114 | 6115 | 6116 | 6117 |
|------|------|------|------|------|
| VERSAILLES | VENTURE | SOMMELIER, Continental | SOMMELIER, Grande | SOMMELIER, Vin Blanc |

| 6118 | 6119 | 6120 | 6121 | 6122 |
|------|------|------|------|------|
| SOMMELIER, Sherry | SOMMELIER, Tulip | ELOQUENCE | SPHERE | BISCAYNE |

6123
PRINCESS

6124
SPLENDOR

6125
DISTINCTION

6126
WIMBLEDON

6127
FESTIVE

6128
REGENCY

6129
MISTY

6131
SPLENDOR

6143
PAVILION

6144
LOTUS

6147
GALA

6149
MAYPOLE

7780 THE
PRESIDENT'S HOUSE

# About the Authors

Mother and daughter, Milbra Long and Emily Seate have combined skills and experience, Milbra's love of glass and Emily's love of words, to create the five-book series *Fostoria, the Crystal for America*. Recognized as authorities on the Fostoria Glass Company, they have given seminars from West Virginia to Oregon, and from Tiffin, Ohio, to Tulsa, Oklahoma, to Houston, San Antonio, and the Dallas/Fort Worth Metroplex. Their business, Milbra's Crystal, is known to collectors all across the nation (www.fostoriacrystal.com). Milbra and Emily have articles in many publications, including *Glass Collector's*

*Digest, Antique Trader's Collector Magazine and Price Guide* (Krause), and *All about Glass, the Voice of the Glass Collecting Community*, a publication of the West Virginia Museum of American Glass.

Emily is a writer of fiction and poetry. She has completd the first two novels of a four-book series called *HeartMind* (www.emilyseate.com) and one poetry book, *Foolish Wisdom*.

Milbra and Emily are currently invested in creating a national glass museum in the Dallas/Fort Worth Metroplex (www.mogmia.com).

Together they are mother and daughter, partners, and lifelong friends.

# The Fostoria Value Guide

This is the ultimate value guide, the first of its kind on the market, the first complete price listing of Fostoria glass. This user-friendly guide to all stemware, tableware, and ornamental glass is designed for both beginning and advanced collectors and dealers. Organized alphabetically, making a quick reference for finding any pattern or shape, the book includes production dates, colors made, and all known decorations for each pattern, in addition to helpful illustrations. The authors have also provided informative text discussing the ever-volatile pricing trends in the glassware trade. 2003 values.

*Milbra Long & Emily Seate*

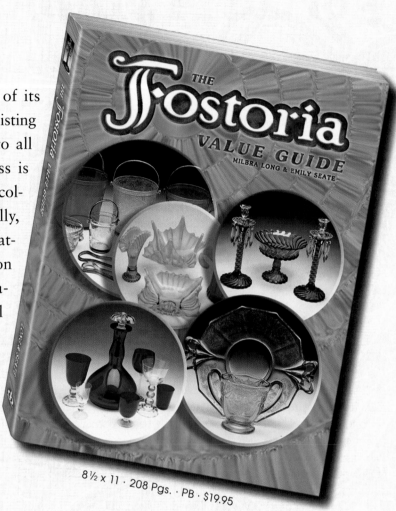

8½ x 11 · 208 Pgs. · PB · $19.95

## COLLECTOR BOOKS
P. O. BOX 3009
PADUCAH, KY 42002-3009

WWW.COLLECTORBOOKS.COM

1-800-626-5420

# more greatTITLES from collector books

## DOLLS

| | | |
|---|---|---|
| 6315 | American Character Dolls, Izen | $24.95 |
| 7346 | Barbie Doll Around the World, 1964 – 2007, Augustyniak | $29.95 |
| 2079 | Barbie Doll Fashion, Volume I, Eames | $24.95 |
| 6319 | Barbie Doll Fashion, Volume III, Eames | $29.95 |
| 7621 | Collectible African American Dolls, Ellis | $29.95 |
| 6546 | Collector's Ency. of Barbie Doll Exclusives & More, 3rd Ed., Augustyniak | $29.95 |
| 6920 | Collector's Encyclopedia of American Composition Dolls, Volume I, Mertz | $29.95 |
| 6451 | Collector's Encyclopedia of American Composition Dolls, Volume II, Mertz | $29.95 |
| 6636 | Collector's Encyclopedia of Madame Alexander Dolls, Crowsey | $24.95 |
| 6456 | Collector's Guide to Dolls of the 1960s and 1970s, Volume II, Sabulis | $24.95 |
| 6944 | The Complete Guide to Shirley Temple Dolls and Collectibles, Bervaldi-Camaratta | $29.95 |
| 7028 | Doll Values, Antique to Modern, 9th Edition, Edward | $14.95 |
| 7634 | Madame Alexander 2008 Collector's Dolls Price Guide #33, Crowsey | $14.95 |
| 6467 | Paper Dolls of the 1960s, 1970s, and 1980s, Nichols | $24.95 |
| 6642 | 20th Century Paper Dolls, Young | $19.95 |

## TOYS

| | | |
|---|---|---|
| 6938 | Everett Grist's Big Book of Marbles, 3rd Edition | $24.95 |
| 7523 | Breyer Animal Collector's Gde., 5th Ed., Browell/Korber-Weimer/Kesicki | $24.95 |
| 7527 | Collecting Disneyana, Longest | $29.95 |
| 7356 | Collector's Guide to Housekeeping Toys, Wright | $16.95 |
| 7528 | Collector's Toy Yearbook, 100 Years of Great Toys, Longest | $29.95 |
| 7355 | Hot Wheels, The Ultimate Redline Guide Companion, Clark/Wicker | $29.95 |
| 7635 | Matchbox Toys, 1947 to 2007, 5th Edition, Johnson | $24.95 |
| 7539 | Schroeder's Collectible Toys, Antique to Modern Price Guide, 11th Ed. | $19.95 |
| 6650 | Toy Car Collector's Guide, 2nd Edition, Johnson | $24.95 |

## JEWELRY, WATCHES & PURSES

| | | |
|---|---|---|
| 4704 | Antique & Collectible Buttons, Wisniewski | $19.95 |
| 4850 | Collectible Costume Jewelry, Simonds | $24.95 |
| 5675 | Collectible Silver Jewelry, Rezazadeh | $24.95 |
| 6468 | Collector's Ency. of Pocket & Pendant Watches, 1500 – 1950, Bell | $24.95 |
| 6554 | Coro Jewelry, Brown | $29.95 |
| 7529 | Costume Jewelry 101, 2nd Edition, Carroll | $24.95 |
| 7025 | Costume Jewelry 202, Carroll | $24.95 |
| 4940 | Costume Jewelry, A Practical Handbook & Value Guide, Rezazadeh | $24.95 |
| 5812 | Fifty Years of Collectible Fashion Jewelry, 1925 – 1975, Baker | $24.95 |
| 6833 | Handkerchiefs: A Collector's Guide, Volume II, Guarnaccia/Guggenheim | $24.95 |
| 6464 | Inside the Jewelry Box, Pitman | $24.95 |
| 7358 | Inside the Jewelry Box, Volume 2, Pitman | $24.95 |
| 5695 | Ladies' Vintage Accessories, Johnson | $24.95 |
| 1181 | 100 Years of Collectible Jewelry, 1850 – 1950, Baker | $9.95 |
| 6645 | 100 Years of Purses, 1880s to 1980s, Aikins | $24.95 |
| 7626 | Pictorial Guide to Costume Jewelry, Bloom | $29.95 |
| 6942 | Rhinestone Jewelry: Figurals, Animals, and Whimsicals, Brown | $24.95 |

| | | |
|---|---|---|
| 6039 | Signed Beauties of Costume Jewelry, Brown | $24.95 |
| 6341 | Signed Beauties of Costume Jewelry, Volume II, Brown | $24.95 |
| 7625 | 20th Century Costume Jewelry, 2nd Edition, Aikins | $24.95 |
| 5620 | Unsigned Beauties of Costume Jewelry, Brown | $24.95 |

## ARTIFACTS, GUNS, KNIVES, & TOOLS

| | | |
|---|---|---|
| 1868 | Antique Tools, Our American Heritage, McNerney | $9.95 |
| 6822 | Antler, Bone & Shell Artifacts, Hothem | $24.95 |
| 1426 | Arrowheads & Projectile Points, Hothem | $7.95 |
| 6231 | Indian Artifacts of the Midwest, Book V, Hothem | $24.95 |
| 7037 | Modern Guns, Identification & Values, 16th Ed., Quertermous | $16.95 |
| 7034 | Ornamental Indian Artifacts, Hothem | $34.95 |
| 6567 | Paleo-Indian Artifacts, Hothem | $29.95 |
| 6569 | Remington Knives, Past & Present, Stewart/Ritchie | $16.95 |
| 7366 | Standard Guide to Razors, 3rd Edition, Stewart/Ritchie | $12.95 |
| 7035 | Standard Knife Collector's Guide, 5th Edition, Ritchie/Stewart | $16.95 |

## PAPER COLLECTIBLES & BOOKS

| | | |
|---|---|---|
| 6623 | Collecting American Paintings, James | $29.95 |
| 7039 | Collecting Playing Cards, Pickvet | $24.95 |
| 6826 | Collecting Vintage Children's Greeting Cards, McPherson | $24.95 |
| 6553 | Collector's Guide to Cookbooks, Daniels | $24.95 |
| 1441 | Collector's Guide to Post Cards, Wood | $9.95 |
| 7622 | Encyclopedia of Collectible Children's Books, Jones | $29.95 |
| 7636 | The Golden Age of Postcards, Early 1900s, Penniston | $24.95 |
| 6936 | Leather Bound Books, Boutiette | $24.95 |
| 7036 | Old Magazine Advertisements, 1890 – 1950, Clear | $24.95 |
| 6940 | Old Magazines, 2nd Edition, Clear | $19.95 |
| 3973 | Sheet Music Reference & Price Guide, 2nd Ed., Pafik/Guiheen | $19.95 |
| 6837 | Vintage Postcards for the Holidays, 2nd Edition, Reed | $24.95 |

## GLASSWARE

| | | |
|---|---|---|
| 7362 | American Pattern Glass Table Sets, Florence/Cornelius/Jones | $24.95 |
| 6930 | Anchor Hocking's Fire-King & More, 3rd Ed., Florence | $24.95 |
| 7524 | Coll. Glassware from the 40s, 50s & 60s, 9th Edition, Florence | $19.95 |
| 6921 | Collector's Encyclopedia of American Art Glass, 2nd Edition, Shuman | $29.95 |
| 7526 | Collector's Encyclopedia of Depression Glass, 18th Ed., Florence | $19.95 |
| 3905 | Collector's Encyclopedia of Milk Glass, Newbound | $24.95 |
| 7026 | Colors in Cambridge Glass II, Natl. Cambridge Collectors, Inc. | $29.95 |
| 7029 | Elegant Glassware of the Depression Era, 12th Edition, Florence | $24.95 |
| 6334 | Encyclopedia of Paden City Glass, Domitz | $29.95 |
| 3981 | Evers' Standard Cut Glass Value Guide | $12.95 |
| 6126 | Fenton Art Glass, 1907 – 1939, 2nd Ed., Whitmyer | $29.95 |
| 6628 | Fenton Glass Made for Other Companies, Domitz | $29.95 |
| 7030 | Fenton Glass Made for Other Companies, Volume II, Domitz | $29.95 |
| 6462 | Florences' Glass Kitchen Shakers, 1930 – 1950s | $19.95 |

5042 Florences' Glassware Pattern Identification Guide, Vol. I ......................$18.95
5615 Florences' Glassware Pattern Identification Guide, Vol. II .....................$19.95
6643 Florences' Glassware Pattern Identification Guide, Vol. IV ...................$19.95
6641 Florences' Ovenware from the 1920s to the Present ...........................$24.95
7630 Fostoria Stemware, The Crystal for America, 2nd Edition, Long/Seate ... $29.95
6226 Fostoria Value Guide, Long/Seate .....................................................$19.95
6127 The Glass Candlestick Book, Volume 1, Akro Agate to Fenton, Felt/Stoer ..$24.95
6228 The Glass Candlestick Book, Volume 2, Fostoria to Jefferson, Felt/Stoer ..$24.95
6461 The Glass Candlestick Book, Volume 3, Kanawha to Wright, Felt/Stoer .. $29.95
6648 Glass Toothpick Holders, 2nd Edition, Bredehoft/Sanford .....................$29.95
5827 Kitchen Glassware of the Depression Years, 6th Edition, Florence ...........$24.95
7534 Lancaster Glass Company, 1908 –1937, Zastowney ...........................$29.95
7359 L.E. Smith Glass Company, Felt ......................................................$29.95
6133 Mt. Washington Art Glass, Sisk ......................................................$49.95
7027 Pocket Guide to Depression Glass & More, 15th Edition, Florence ..........$12.95
7623 Standard Encyclopedia of Carnival Glass, 11th Ed., Carwile ...............$29.95
7624 Standard Carnival Glass Price Guide, 16th Ed., Carwile ......................$9.95
6566 Standard Encyclopedia of Opalescent Glass, 5th Ed., Edwards/Carwile ...$29.95
7364 Standard Encyclopedia of Pressed Glass, 5th Ed., Edwards/Carwile........$29.95
6476 Westmoreland Glass, The Popular Years, 1940 – 1985, Kovar.............$29.95

## POTTERY

6922 American Art Pottery, 2nd Edition, Sigafoose ...................................$24.95
6326 Collectible Cups & Saucers, Book III, Harran ....................................$24.95
6331 Collecting Head Vases, Barron .......................................................$24.95
6943 Collecting Royal Copley, Devine .....................................................$19.95
6621 Collector's Encyclopedia of American Dinnerware, 2nd Ed., Cunningham....$29.95
5034 Collector's Encyclopedia of California Pottery, 2nd Ed., Chipman ...........$24.95
6629 Collector's Encyclopedia of Fiesta, 10th Ed., Huxford .........................$24.95
1276 Collector's Encyclopedia of Hull Pottery, Roberts ..............................$19.95
5609 Collector's Encyclopedia of Limoges Porcelain, 3rd Ed., Gaston .............$29.95
6637 Collector's Encyclopedia of Made in Japan Ceramics, First Ed., White.......$24.95
5841 Collector's Encyclopedia of Roseville Pottery, Vol. 1, Huxford/Nickel ..... $24.95
5842 Collector's Encyclopedia of Roseville Pottery, Vol. 2, Huxford/Nickel...... $24.95
6646 Collector's Ency. of Stangl Artware, Lamps, and Birds, 2nd Ed., Runge ...$29.95
6634 Collector's Ultimate Ency. of Hull Pottery, Volume 1, Roberts ...............$29.95
6829 The Complete Guide to Corning Ware & Visions Cookware, Coroneos...$19.95
7530 Decorative Plates, Harran..............................................................$29.95
7638 Encyclopedia of Universal Potteries, Chorey ....................................$29.95
7628 English China Patterns & Pieces, Gaston .........................................$29.95
5918 Florences' Big Book of Salt & Pepper Shakers ...................................$24.95
6320 Gaston's Blue Willow, 3rd Edition ...................................................$19.95
6630 Gaston's Flow Blue China, The Comprehensive Guide .........................$29.95
7021 Hansons' American Art Pottery Collection..........................................$29.95

7032 Head Vases, 2nd Edition, Cole........................................................$24.95
2379 Lehner's Ency. of U.S. Marks on Pottery, Porcelain & China, no values ...$24.95
4722 McCoy Pottery Collector's Reference & Value Guide, Hanson/Nissen ......$19.95
5913 McCoy Pottery, Volume III, Hanson/Nissen .....................................$24.95
6835 Meissen Porcelain, Harran.............................................................$29.95
7536 The Official Precious Moments® Collector's Guide to Figurines, 3rd Ed., Bomm...$19.95
6335 Pictorial Guide to Pottery & Porcelain Marks, Lage, No values .............$29.95
1440 Red Wing Stoneware, DePasquale/Peck/Peterson .............................$9.95
6838 R.S. Prussia & More, McCaslin .......................................................$29.95
7637 RumRill Pottery, The Ohio Years, 1938 –1942, Fisher ........................$29.95
6945 TV Lamps to Light the World, Shuman .............................................$29.95
7043 Uhl Pottery, 2nd Edition, Feldmeyer/Holtzman .................................$16.95
6828 The Ultimate Collector's Encyclopedia of Cookie Jars, Roerig ...............$29.95
6640 Van Patten's ABC's of Collecting Nippon Porcelain ............................$29.95

## OTHER COLLECTIBLES

7627 Antique and Collectible Dictionary, Reed, No values............................$24.95
6446 Antique & Contemporary Advertising Memorabilia, 2nd Edition, Summers ..$29.95
6935 Antique Golf Collectibles, Georgiady ...............................................$29.95
1880 Antique Iron, McNerney ...............................................................$9.95
7024 B.J. Summers' Guide to Coca-Cola, 6th Edition ................................$29.95
1128 Bottle Pricing Guide, 3rd Ed., Cleveland .........................................$7.95
7532 Bud Hastin's Avon Collector's Encyclopedia, 18th Edition.....................$29.95
6924 Captain John's Fishing Tackle Price Guide, 2nd Edition, Kolbeck ...........$24.95
6342 Collectible Soda Pop Memorabilia, Summers ...................................$24.95
6625 Collector's Encyclopedia of Bookends, Kuritzky/De Costa....................$29.95
7365 Collector's Guide to Antique Radios, 7th Edition, Slusser/Radio Daze.....$24.95
7023 The Complete Guide to Vintage Children's Records, Muldavin ...............$24.95
6928 Early American Furniture, Obbard...................................................$19.95
7042 The Ency. of Early American & Antique Sewing Machines, 3rd Ed., Bays ..$29.95
7031 Fishing Lure Collectibles, An Ency. of the Early Years, Murphy/Edmisten ...$29.95
7629 Flea Market Trader, 17th Edition ....................................................$15.95
6458 Fountain Pens, Past & Present, 2nd Edition, Erano ............................$24.95
7631 Garage Sale & Flea Market Annual, 16th Edition ...............................$19.95
3906 Heywood-Wakefield Modern Furniture, Rouland ...............................$18.95
7033 Hot Kitchen & Home Collectibles of the 30s, 40s, and 50s, Zweig .........$24.95
7038 The Marketplace Guide to Oak Furniture, 2nd Edition, Blundell.............$29.95
6939 Modern Collectible Tins, 2nd Edition, McPherson .............................$24.95
6564 Modern Fishing Lure Collectibles, Volume 3, Lewis ...........................$24.95
6832 Modern Fishing Lure Collectibles, Volume 4, Lewis ...........................$24.95
7349 Modern Fishing Lure Collectibles, Volume 5, Lewis ...........................$29.95
6322 Pictorial Guide to Christmas Ornaments & Collectibles, Johnson ...........$29.95
6842 Raycrafts' Americana Price Guide & DVD .........................................$19.95
6923 Raycrafts' Auction Field Guide, Volume One, Price Guide & DVD...........$19.95

News for Collectors

Request a Catalog

Meet the Authors

Find Newest Releases

Calendar of Events

Special Sale Items

www.collectorbooks.com

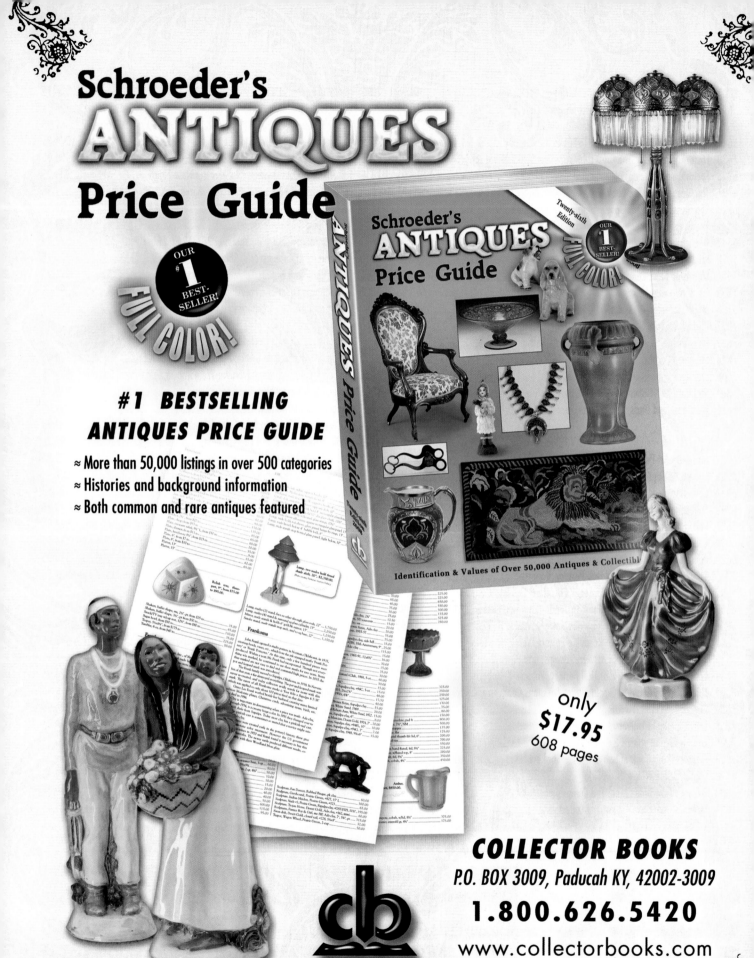